Flower Child

Other books by the author:

HERBS OF GRACE:
Becoming Independently Healthy

CREATIVE MENOPAUSE:
Illuminating Women's Health and Spirituality

IRIDOLOGY:
A Complete Guide

IRIDOLOGY COLORING BOOK

A DICTIONARY OF IRIDOLOGY

Flower Child

Farida Sharan

Wisdome Press
A Division of School of Natural Medicine
Boulder, Colorado

WISDOME PRESS
School of Natural Medicine
Post Office Box 7369
Boulder, Colorado 80306-7369, U.S.A.

Tel: 888-229-3558
Email: farida@flowerchildlove.com
Website: www.flowerchildlove.com

©2000 by Farida Jeannine Sharan. All rights reserved

Registered WPG West

Original Artwork "Hawaiian Goddess"
©1996 by Mara Friedman. All rights reserved.

No portion of this book may be reproduced or used in any form or by
any means, electronic or mechanical, including photocopying,
recording, or by any information storage and retrieval system, without
prior written permission of the publisher and author.

10 9 8 7 6 5 4 3 2 1

Sharan, Farida
    Flower Child / Farida Sharan
    p. cm.
    ISBN 1-57093-013-9
    1. Memoir 2. Spirituality 3. Women's Spirituality
    4. Popular Culture 5. Sixties

Printed and bound on acid-free paper
in Boulder, Colorado, United States of America.

Dedication

THE SANDDUNES

I dedicate this book to my three beloved children
who came into this world bearing the gift of love.
Thank you for sharing this life journey with me.

Author's Note

While this is a true story of my inner life during the tumultuous sixties era, I have changed the names and characters of everyone with the exception of those where I use both their first and last names. All the other characters are fictional composites and do not resemble anyone living or dead. Any similarity is purely coincidental and non-intentional. I have given my family members fictional names to protect their privacy.

Some exterior events also have been fictionalized to some degree to enhance the storytelling and to expand the archetypal nature of Flower Child.

Only those who have experienced the darkness
can appreciate the light.

Acknowledgements

Flower Child was a family project. My eldest daughter has been generously supportive every step of the way, offering editing, discussions, research and loving encouragement. We shared many special times when we read the manuscript out loud during the last month of her pregnancy. My youngest daughter contributed her invaluable screenwriting expertise, structural advice and editing skills, and my son read through the manuscript and offered a thorough edit and many enjoyable in-depth discussions. *Flower Child* marks a milestone of healing and open communication in our family history. Every year we open to deeper levels of understanding, loving and supporting each other. Thanks also to my two sons-in-law for their patient encouragement and generous hospitality during the incubation of this book, and to my youngest sister who offered many excellent suggestions.

A special thank you to Dan Millman for encouraging me and connecting me with his editor and copy editor.

Deep appreciation to my editor, 'Seeing Eye' Doug Childers who inspired and guided me so that *Flower Child* could reach its full potential. Many thanks to Robert Alexander who helped polish a diamond in the rough and to David Joel for inspiration in the early stages.

The cover design began with my dear friend Carolyn Oakley, was seasoned with Megan Miller's ideas and skill, and was brought to completion by the fine, responsive expertise of Jeff Fuller in Boulder, Colorado. Jeff also worked hand in hand with me on the layout of the inner pages from start to finish.

Many dear friends read *Flower Child* during its evolution and encouraged and supported me with warmth and enthusiasm: Thanks to Marie Michelle Bailey, Anthea Becker, Sandra Patterson-Slaydon, Anna Chitty, Shady Sirotkin, Robert Stevens, Merrin Stein, Tyke O'Brian, Charise Diamond, Diane Fairechild, Amy Spadafora, Christine Devenney and Michelle Ambler. A special thanks to Patricia and Joseph Hanwright who offered me their Kauai "Hana Honu" beach home for a writing retreat.

Contents

"Were You a Sixties Flower Child?"

I looked at the sad young faces around me. After Jerry Garcia, the visionary leader of the Grateful Dead, died in August '95, spontaneous communal grief birthed a full-on sixties flashback on the Pearl Street Mall in Boulder, Colorado.

Thousands of Deadheads streamed down the Mall and merged into the dense cacophony of mourning in front of the courthouse between 13th and 14th Streets where candles, pictures, albums, and flowers decorated the stone fountain on the lawn. Fresh college kids, tattooed modern primitives, and baggy-jeaned skateboarders hung out in whispering, weeping clusters Silver-haired hippies and sixties old-timers mingled with the grief-stricken youngsters, trying their best to comfort them. The cries of Garcia's mourners mingled with dozens of boomboxes screeching Dead sets and merged into one unearthly wail that soared toward the heavens. As I wandered among the crowds, tears flowed down my cheeks.

My daughter, a sixties Love-In cherub grown into a beautiful young woman, looked at me with understanding.

"I knew you had to see this, Mom," she said with a wise-woman smile.

These nineties hipsters were hungry. They were searching. They were looking for love. I'd been passing them for years on the Boulder Mall. Although I always smiled at them, tonight was different. Tonight, the distance of years had dissolved. I was one of them again. The sixties and the nineties had merged with a power that had shaken everyone out of their local mindset.

"Were you a sixties flower child?" a young voice called.

The question thrilled through me, my grasshopper mind jumping instantly back to that magic time. Turning, I looked into the softly yearning eyes of a young girl, her lovely face framed by long black wavy hair. Innocent, vulnerable, and wearing a flower-print dress, she was the mirror of myself in the mystical, magical, psychedelic sixties.

"Yes, I was a flower child," I answered with a surge of poignant pride. "And I think I still am," I added with a laugh.

"Tell us about the sixties," her dreadlocked boyfriend asked, his glance wavering between respectful curiosity and a distant cool disdain.

"There was an intense energy, like everyone shared the same dream," I said. "We recognized each other. We wanted out of our families, out of our culture. We wanted love. The rock stars sang our dreams and their music brought us together. Creativity burst free in wild, colorful Be-Ins and Love-Ins. It was a happening," I bubbled excitedly, the energy of the past returning in the present. Remembering the shadow side I'd been so afraid of in the sixties, I also added, "And then there were the police, the establishment, the media, and the politicians who made sure the dream didn't happen."

Slowly a group of young people gathered around us. We sat in a circle on the damp night grass – a still center in a hurricane of sorrow.

"What about the Summer of Love?" a leather-clad girl challenged as she slouched on the grass. Flaunting a snake tattoo that ran around her neck and up her shaved head, and multiple nose and ear rings, she asked, "Was that for real?"

I sighed, "The Summer of Love was real, all right. It changed my life forever."

The longing that had carried me out of my fearful youth to the flowering richness of my present life surfaced once more in my heart. In the sixties, I was a seed longing for the sun, a flower seeking her garden of love.

"What did it feel like to be a flower child?" a street savvy youth asked, his pierced street-warrior guise a far cry from the bells and flowers of my time.

"Empty. Lonely. Hungry. The world was cold, hard, and harsh. What people called love didn't feel like love. I was always looking, searching. I was always hungry for love."

He nodded, as if to say we were the same.

Hundreds of candles flamed softly in the misting darkness. Rivers of melting wax flowed down the base of the courthouse fountain. Jerry Garcia may have passed on, but his spirit was profoundly present.

The more I talked, the more the sixties feelings flowed, and the more I remembered. When I returned home late that night, I knew the time had come to share my story.

Five years later, in the millennium year of 2000, I offer *Flower Child* to the flower children of the past, present, and future in whatever costume they choose to adorn themselves.

If you feel moved when you read *Flower Child*, pass it on with the true spirit of the flower children. Pass it on with love and a blessing, or perhaps a flower or a song.

Pass it on.

BOOK ONE

Flower Power

Free Love

I am going to find love if it's the last thing I ever do.

A surge of confidence pulsed through me as I sped east on the freeway. Cool, windy, fog-bound Santa Monica turned into a rear-view mirror blur as the skyscrapers of Los Angeles loomed ahead. Then the city disappeared like a mirage into the smog as I headed toward the desert. The engine hummed. My foot pressed hard on the accelerator. I didn't know where I was going, but I knew what I was leaving behind.

For a moment I looked at my infant daughter, Love, asleep on the seat beside me. Adoring the beauty of her sweet-sleeping face, I sighed before turning my eyes back to the freeway.

A passing car displayed a bumper sticker that shouted in psychedelic neon, "I am a human being. Do not fold, spindle or mutilate." At that synchronicity, I laughed my first laugh in a very long time.

Good people out there were sending messages to help me along. I wanted more, so I tuned the dial to the hottest flower power station on the radio waves and sang along with the Cyrkle.

"...got my life to live..."

I just didn't know what that was yet.

"...don't need you at all..."

Damn right!

"...bought my ticket with my tears..."

Sure did.

"...and that's all I'm gonna spend..."

Hope I learned my lesson this time.

It was 1966. Everyone out there was saying you could make your dreams come true. This had to be my year. That thought started my hands shaking on the wheel and soon my whole body was trembling. As the fury that had made it possible for me to leave dissipated, shock set in. Fear returned, filling me with the familiar presence that had choked my voice and held me prisoner for years. A couple of hours earlier, anger had burned through me, pure and clear. I had yelled and screamed. And then I had left. God, I can't believe I did that, and now what was I going to do? Where was I going to go? I didn't know the answer. Heading east would have to be good enough for now.

As images of what had happened flashed through my mind, I smiled with a pleasure I wanted to hide from myself even as I was feeling it. I had always thought anger was some horrible thing a nice person never felt. No matter how bad things were, I denied the problem, pleased others, and endured anything and everything. No matter what was happening, I would always act nice and sweet and kind, but today I had gotten so mad I did something I never thought was possible.

I had come upstairs to the sculpture studio and walked right into a scene. My husband, Taz; his assistant, a wild Aussie dude named Chanter; and their latest Sunset Strip pick-up chick were coming down off an acid trip. Taz and Chanter were mocking the young girl, pushing

4

her onto the bed, trying to tempt her into a sexual threesome.

She was pleading, "No," and trying to push them away, but they weren't listening.

When they saw me, Taz smirked guiltily and turned away, but Chanter challenged me openly, lifting one eyebrow, slouching as he stood on one leg, his insolent "Yes?" pressuring me to explain why I was there.

I didn't say anything. Shock, jealousy, and fear wove a painful path through my heart and mind. I saw what I'd always feared. I couldn't deny it any more.

A flame of intense rage surged through me and I picked up the closest thing to me, a portable sewing machine. Without hesitation, I threw it at Taz, just missing him as he jumped out of the way.

"What? Are you crazy?" Taz shouted, his usual cool utterly disrupted.

Frightened by my unexpected passion and strength, I still could not summon words. The flame of anger and the force of my action had burned through the veil of enchantment that had always clouded my perception of him. For once his handsome face did not charm me or weaken my resolve. At that moment, I saw through his charisma. I'd always made excuses for him, fueling the pretense that he loved me even though he was not kind or loving. Now I saw him as he was.

My brain was on overload, firing this way and that, trying to make sense of my new perspective on reality.

Poised like a jaguar in his black tights and turtleneck, Taz waited to see what I would do next.

Frozen by the shock of my action, I returned Chanter's stare with cool fire, refusing to be distracted by the wild blond Afro frizzing around his head, seeing the man submerged beneath the multitude of chains and power symbols clanking and glittering on his naked torso. The contempt I usually tried to hide was showing on my face, but I didn't care. Hiding behind Taz, feigning indifference but obviously excited by my anger, he scratched his belly under his tight Hawaiian shorts. Swaying sensuously, he smiled a mock invitation. He was ridiculing me, but I wasn't going for it.

Questions I'd never dared ask myself wailed around inside me. Taz, why is he your friend? Why did you bring him here? Don't you see who he is? Or, worse, if you know who he is, why do you want him here? I couldn't summon the power to give voice to my questions. I was not only afraid to ask them, I was afraid to hear the answers.

About three months before, Taz had met Chanter on a night-tripping cruise of the Sunset Strip clubs and invited him to a party, and Chanter had never left. Crudely arrogant, he dominated Taz's sculpture studio. With worshipful servitude, he cleaned the studio, cooked the meals, did the laundry, ran the errands, and waited on Taz.

"I'm a true apprentice," he boasted to me, with the added put-down, "*I'm* here to help Taz," insinuating that I wasn't.

On the surface, Chanter did seem to be the perfect apprentice, but the subtle power trips he was spinning around Taz suggested darker motives. Even though the studio was clean, it had degenerated into a pleasure dome. Taz wasn't making art anymore. He was burning himself out on drugs, alcohol, parties, and women. After hanging out at the cool night spots like Cantor's or Shelley's Manne Hole, cruising the Strip, or making the in-party scenes, they brought young girls home and turned them on under the strobes and black lights, tripping on the psychedelic sculpture, deep into their highs. Night after night, I heard the footsteps and plugged my ears against the blatant rock music and loud voices, but I never went upstairs. When I saw them during the day, I never asked what they were up to at night. I was afraid to find out.

The pause was suddenly broken as the pig-tailed, freckled young girl, shyly covered in oversized patchwork jeans and layers of torn, tie-dyed T-shirts, got up, whisper-crying and sniffling, and headed for the door.

Pleased that I'd rescued her, I smiled with a rare sense of satisfaction. As soon as the door slammed behind her, I was raging mad again.

"You're animals. You disgust me," I screamed, wanting to wake them from their dark selfishness.

"You're angry. That's news," Taz joked, trying to break the tension. "I finally did something that blew your cool," he boasted, slapping Chanter on the shoulder, as if they were both in on some macho conspiracy.

"She's angry," Chanter crooned, making fun of me.

Another flame of rage burst free, burning me clean.

"I don't want to be near either of you. I want out," I yelled, waving my arms, my voice cracking. "You're both sick."

"You want out?" Taz snarled. "Go right ahead. I could dig you being independent, then I could be free to do whatever I want without you hanging around."

"Free? You mean free to destroy yourself. You can have your freedom. I'm going to do my own trip."

"Your own trip?" he said scathingly. "And what might that be? File clerk? Bank teller? Waitress? Babysitter? And what happens to your children when you go to work? What kind of life is that?"

"Better than this," I shouted, letting off the surface steam, but still holding back a volcano that wanted to hit and hurt and do anything to break apart their indulgent cool.

"Go then! Go! But you're not taking Choo!" Taz yelled, his eyes narrowing belligerently.

He was getting mean, so I shut up and split. My solar plexus churning, tears burning, I ran downstairs, seeking the shelter of my room. I paced back and forth, trying to calm the raw, powerful energy that was running through me. Now that I knew what was going on upstairs, I had to leave, but what would I do, where would I go? I felt I could do anything, but what?

Holding back tears, holding back laughter, I talked to myself.

A sewing machine! I can't believe I did that. Calm down. Look, there's your son, Choo, sleeping in his bed, and there's your newborn daughter. They're what matters. Breathe deeply. Think. You have to go now, today, but where? How?

Trembling, I approached my daughter and lay gently next to her, adoring her soft, relaxed arms open above her face, and the long black lashes brushing against her tender cheeks.

It was hard to imagine Taz as a vulnerable, soft baby. Because I knew what his parents had done to him, I'd always made excuses for him, believing that I'd find the way to make him open to love. I stifled a sob and promised myself that I'd never get hard and mean like Taz. I'd rather die first.

I took my daughter's tiny hand in mine and whispered, "I have to leave for you. I have to be strong for you."

Slowly, as the trembling subsided, I thought about Love's birth. When she outgrew my womb, she had to pass through the pain and pressure of the birth canal to come into the world. She didn't know where she was going, what she would find, or even if she would make it, but the forces around her were making her go. She must have pushed with her little feet so that her head would press against my cervix, helping it to thin and open and release her. She must have felt trapped as she endured both the struggle and the surrender, just as I did. Death of the womb released her to life in the world. For the first time, I realized Love's birth wasn't just about me birthing her. She had birthed herself too.

It was time for me to birth myself out of Taz's scene. Living with him was like being imprisoned in an underworld. The world outside ceased to exist. I never saw friends. I never went anywhere. I even forgot there was a beach a couple of miles away and a park down the street. I felt like I was living the Greek myth about the young girl who got dragged into the underworld. Yeah, I too was a prisoner in a shadow-land that was the opposite of everything I loved.

I was scared to leave, but when you can't stay, you have no choice. You have to go, but where could I go? What could I do? I had my own dreams, but how could I make them come true? Don't think about that, I reasoned. Just leave. It doesn't matter if you don't know where you're going. The important thing is to leave.

"Love, we're getting out of here," I said as I pulled my suitcase out of the closet.

When I turned around, Taz was hovering in the doorway, watching me pack, nervously uncertain before my fury. He'd never seen me angry before. I was raised to be sweet and kind and to wash the dishes and say nice things, but it didn't work. Maybe anger was the way to find myself again, even if it was against my nature. Maybe I should tell that to my mother.

"You're really going? It's not easy out there, you know. If you go, I won't take you back," Taz wheedled, trying to scare me into changing my mind.

Ignoring him, I folded Love's clothes into my suitcase.

"Look. Why freak out over free love? It's the happening thing," he coaxed with a sly look that made me feel as if he were temptation itself.

"It's not free love when you're hurting someone," I protested, amazed that I was telling him my true feelings. "Sure, I want love, real love, not just free sex, and sex isn't free anyway."

"It's how people get to know each other. No hangups. It's cool," he urged with seductive cool.

"Well it's not how I want to get to know someone," I stated with a force that still carried the clear, clean power of anger.

9

"Yeah! You want someone all to yourself. Selfish. Possessive. Boring," he ridiculed, hitting the door with his fist. "That's old-fashioned."

"That's love. That's commitment. That's marriage," I asserted stubbornly as I closed my suitcase, "and we don't have a marriage. In fact, we haven't had a marriage for a long time. It's over. I'm leaving."

Just then, our three-year-old son, Choo, woke up whimpering. I picked him up and snuggled him close to my heart.

Taz stopped raving and changed tactics.

"You gonna tell your son you're leaving him?" he challenged.

That was just like Taz, first telling me I couldn't take Choo and then trying to make me feel bad because I was leaving him. I wanted to cry like I usually did when he pressured me with his will, but there was a new energy swirling inside me. Rage had taken me to a new place. I wasn't stuck in fear anymore. I was willing to take a chance. Nothing could be worse than staying with Taz.

Beautiful Choo clung to me, his sleep-dampened golden curls brushing softly against my face. Love started crying, so I picked her up too and sat down on the bed. Holding an angel child in each arm, I wondered why, with such beautiful children, I had to have Taz for a husband and they had to have him for a father.

"Choo, Love and I have to go away for a while," I said.

Choo rubbed his eyes sleepily and asked, "Why?"

I have to find my own place to live," I whispered, my voice catching in my throat.

"Why?" he said again, looking like he was going to cry.

Mutually inarticulate, my son and I mirrored confused despair. I couldn't explain what was happening. Even if I found the words, he couldn't understand them. The only thing I could do was to say something that would make him feel better.

"We'll come back soon," I promised Choo before I surrendered him to his father. I didn't have it in me to fight Taz for our son. That would have to wait.

Fighting back tears, I picked up Love in one arm, lifted the suitcase with the other, and headed downstairs to my car. As I turned on the ignition, I cursed the sensitivity that made me feel everything so intensely. Maybe it would be easier to turn off and be like him, but I didn't want to be like him. I wanted to be myself. I had a world inside me and I wanted to find a way to make that world happen for me and for my children.

"I'll find good, loving people if it's the last thing I ever do," I promised myself out loud, "and if I don't find them, I'd rather be alone."

I took one last look in the rear view mirror as I peeled out of the parking lot. Taz and Choo were crazy-waving from the rooftop, like I was going away on a holiday. God, that guy knew just what to do to make me mad. As I revved the gas, I let out a yell that sounded like one of the war whoops I screamed when I was a child. Yeah, I'm a warrior. That's me. I've fought myself free.

"Free, Love. We made it. We're free. We're on our way," I sang to my daughter as we sped away.

Shifting gears and memories, I wondered who'd been doing the driving while I'd been head-tripping on my escape from Taz. The city was far behind. Lush, spring-green hills and snow-white blossoming orange groves spread out on either side of the freeway. Captivated by a beauty that was in such intense contrast to the scene I'd left behind, I pulled over to the side of the road and rolled down the window. The scent of orange blossoms wafted through the air, tantalizingly, intoxicatingly beautiful.

"Oh Love, you have to see this," I said, turning to my daughter.

Her eyes opened as I lifted her up to the window. She immediately breathed several, excited gasps, and waved her arms and legs.

"You like orange blossoms, do you? Well, sweetheart, let's go closer."

Feeling as though I was entering a sacred shrine, I carried Love into the orange grove and sank to my knees on a soft carpet of grass. I closed my eyes for a moment, then lifted them to the sun and the deep blue sky beyond the breezing leaves. Orange blossoms danced above us, bursting fragrance into the warm, dry air as white petals drifted slowly down. My relief, grief, and gratitude for the gift of the beauty of the grove overflowed into tears.

Crying made me feel soft and sweet again. Anger may have given me the power to break free, but it was a relief to return to my more natural self.

I watched Love stare at the canopy of flowers above her with newborn eyes, her little arms waving excitedly as she breathed quickly. Instinctively wanting to see nature as if I were looking through Love's eyes, I narrowed my eyelids, looked off-center and discovered swirls of pure light, soft, diffused colors, and an undefined radiance glowing around the trees. That must be how it looks to her, I thought, more like undefined energy.

I wished beauty could be more than an ephemeral high, but I knew that this spring blossoming was only one part of the life cycle of the orange trees. Soon, the perfumed petals would blow away or disappear into the golden grasses. Then the oranges would ripen through the hot summer. In the autumn, the leaves would fall, and the retreat into winter would leave only the skeleton of this perfumed spring beauty.

I felt as if I'd been submerged in a long, harsh winter and it was my time to burst into spring. It had to happen. I couldn't hold back anymore. I had to find out who I was. Just as I thought that, a beautiful memory came back to me of my beloved grandmother taking me into her garden when I was a little girl. She showed me the crocuses, violets and daffodils peeking out of the snow and told me that the early spring flowers were very special because they had to be very brave to flower so early in the season and cheer people after the long, dark winter. If only my grandmother hadn't died when I was a child, I wouldn't have been so lonely. She would have taught me what I needed to know. She would have cared about me. She would have wanted to know what I was thinking and feeling and doing. She would have asked me to tell her what had happened to me at school.

I once asked my mother why she never paid me any attention, and she looked surprised for a moment before she said, "Why, you always do fine. You don't need my attention." I guess she never understood that a relationship wasn't necessarily about need, although that obviously comes into it. For me, parenting was more about opening to the opportunity of knowing another person and being there for them. Perhaps if my mother had been able to do that, she wouldn't have been so unhappy.

"Oh, Love, I called you into my life and here you are, my friend," I said, giving thanks in my heart for my beloved daughter. At last, I had the opportunity to give and receive love in the way I had always longed for. Taz had taken away Choo, but he wasn't going to take away Love.

I lifted Love's tender body toward the pure white blossoms.

"Flower child of a flower child, we will find our garden of love," I promised gently. "Hmmm. That sounds nice. I think I'll call myself Flower Child from now on."

Then, holding my infant in my arms, I closed my eyes and savored the living fragrance surrounding us.

"Free, Love. We're free at last, free to be, you and me."

Oceano Genesis

In May of the previous year, spring had felt like winter in my heart. I was living in the back of our La Cienega art gallery, an exile from my own family, while Taz and Choo lived up the coast in Oceano, near Pismo Beach. All Taz ever talked about was freedom – to create art, to take lovers, to do what he wanted to do, whenever he wanted to do it. He gave me the same freedom, but I didn't want it. I wanted him. I loved him; I could not imagine loving another.

Unable to overcome my loneliness and my jealousy, I focused my mind on the one goal I believed would ease my pain. Against all reason, I would ask my husband for another child. Even though it didn't make sense, considering the state of our marriage, he had to be the father. In the early dawn, my longing erupted, melting my inarticulate fear. Desperately nervous and excited, I paced around the gallery, my courage increasing with the morning sun. Outside, the streets were quiet and empty, like a beach at low tide.

Unable to hold myself back, I jumped in my station wagon and headed north on PCH, the Pacific Coast Highway. Action eased my tension as I sped through the early dawn. Whizzing past Santa Barbara and the spring-green California hills, I sang along with the Stones.

15

"I try and I try and I try and I try,
...I can't get no...satisfaction..."

Three hours later, I pulled off the freeway at the Pismo Beach exit and headed toward the Oceano Airport. Glad to slow down, I opened the car windows and breathed in the fresh sea air, trying to ease the fear and excitement churning in my stomach. I turned into the airport, drove through the gate and along the runway to Taz's corrugated-metal, aircraft-hangar studio. Taz's car was gone. The studio and the trailer were locked. Only the beach buggy and the Cessna were parked in the drive.

I sighed with relief. I never knew who would be there, what Taz would be like, or what he would do. I got out, stretched, then sat on the hood of my station wagon. A few minutes later, I lay back, arms wide behind my head, listening to the boom of the distant surf. The sun's warmth gradually eased the tension in my belly.

As a child, I had been fearless, full of enthusiastic chatter and energetic joy. Somewhere along the line I'd lost the strength to resist Taz's will. Afraid to stand up to him, I had become silent and submissive, enduring a life that was nothing like I wanted it to be, in the hope that one day he would make my dreams come true. Worse than that, I felt that if I lost him I would lose everything. I had to do something. Having another child seemed to be the only answer. Gradually, I let my thoughts whirl away into the cloud dancing sky. The sound of the rhythmic booming surf and the caresses of the gentle, warm sea breezes lulled me into a drifting, dreaming sleep.

An hour or so later, a horn blared. Startled from my slumber, I slid off the hood to stand uncertainly on the ground. Taz swooped up in his yellow Lincoln convertible, the top down, Choo standing proudly beside his father on the front seat. Taz's assistants, Yoni and Day Glo, huddled windblown in the back, shopping bags piled high around them.

My son jumped out of the car and threw himself into my arms with wild joy. I drank in the love from his merry smile and soft brown eyes and ran my fingers through his golden curls, rejoicing in his sweet, affectionate clinging. Just as quickly, he wriggled out of my arms and ran away, giggling, teasing me to chase him, but I wasn't ready to play games.

"Later, Choo. Let me talk to your dad first," I called.

As I turned toward Taz, I encountered Yoni's desperate blue eyes peering out of a mass of straw-blonde hair, blown wild by the wind. She turned away immediately. Obviously unable to handle my unexpected arrival, she muttered angrily, "Bummer, bummer," as she lifted a couple of grocery bags out of the Lincoln. Refusing to look at me, she stomped over to the Airstream.

Jealousy flamed between us more articulately than words.

Day Glo offered a shaded, drugged nod, and I answered with a wave. Hidden behind mirrored sunglasses and an unruly, unwashed mop of tobacco-colored dreadlocks, he presented a dusty, wrinkled, and shabby appearance. Except for the accidental, sporadic collection of fluorescent paint spills on his ragged sneakers, he was about as far away from looking like Day Glo as you could get. Hippies usually gave themselves new names to create new personalities, but he had never made Day Glo happen. I figured he should call himself Wishful Thinking instead. Even though he'd been in Taz's scene for nearly two years, I had no idea who he really was. I'd never even seen his eyes.

A hard edge to his voice, Taz asked, "Can't stay away, eh? What's up?"

I took refuge in my son's mischievous laughter as he threw himself once more into my arms. A humming sigh escaped my heart as I realized he was the only one of us who was not afraid to love.

"Nothing. I had to get out of L.A.," I lied.

"Any sales?"

"Yeah, one, and another coming through next week."

"Cool. Just in time for the rent," he said approvingly.

Yoni passed by, head down, ignoring us as she carried the last two bags of groceries to the trailer.

Day Glo shambled between the studio and the car, unloading supplies in his downbeat, shuffling style.

My stomach eased. Taz was mellow.

Suddenly, sooner than I'd planned, I blurted out, "I want another child."

Immediately furious, Taz yelled, "You must be crazy!"

"No. I'm not crazy. You took Choo away from me," I said, pain surging as my helpless longing welled into tears. "I don't have anyone to love. I want a daughter, a friend. I want somebody to love."

"Get a cat or a boyfriend," he jeered.

"Please," I pleaded, "be serious. I want a daughter."

"Why do you need me to get pregnant? There are a million guys out there waiting to get laid," Taz dared, struggling against the forces that imprisoned his love.

I plunged into my truth.

"I'm not like you. I can't be with anyone else. You have to be the father," I stated simply, touching his hand, resisting a desire to kneel at his feet and beg him to give me what I wanted.

Taz took his hand away and lit a cigarette.

"We already have our own lives," I continued. "I can't bear being away from Choo. If I had a daughter, I'd be okay. I am a person who has to love. I want to bring love into the world. I want to love."

As my sense of desperation increased, conflict played over his face, hardening his beauty and narrowing his eyes. Locked under his skin were his rage at his parents and his fear of love.

"All this – you, the marriage, Choo, it stops me from concentrating. I want to be free to focus on my work," he said impatiently, clearly bugged at my unexpected insistence.

"I'm not stopping you from focusing on your work," I defended.

"Hah! You're trouble. Nothing but trouble," he complained.

"You forget how much I've helped you," I said, my heart hurting again.

"I want to forget. I just want to work," he stated angrily.

"Work isn't everything. We need to love and be loved. We need family," I pleaded, searching for a way to melt him down.

"I don't want a family," Taz protested stubbornly as he took a drag. "A family is nothing but pain."

"Maybe your parents' family was nothing but pain, but you could have your own loving family. You're the one who's creating the pain by pushing us away. Why?"

"Damn right I push you away. I want my scene, my way," he said, crossing his arms as if to protect himself.

Even though I was discouraged, I refused to give up. "Why does it have to be this way? Why can't we share love?" I cried passionately.

"I don't want to share love. Love doesn't feel good. Love hurts," he spat out. As if the truth of those words were something he had to run away from, Taz stalked into the aircraft hangar.

I followed into the dark, cold building. The wind that had been so fresh outside rattled the tin roof like an enemy and blasted through the jagged cracks in the metal walls and broken windowpanes. I shivered and rubbed my arms with my hands. Trembling, I waited, breathing deeply as I listened to the boom of the distant breakers. For a moment I retreated, then my courage resurfaced.

"I want a daughter," I repeated with stubborn determination.

Taz turned away from me, absently picking up a screwdriver and a wrench, then putting them down again. Moving like an ebony panther through his forest of incandescent bronze sculptures and translucent psychedelic plastic fountains, his voice pulsed out of his incessant pacing.

"I want you to have your own trip. I don't want you to hang around, waiting on my every move, being dependent. I want you to do your own thing."

"How am I dependent?" I argued. "I run the gallery. I've always earned my own way. Taz, I need someone to love."

"If we had another child, you'd want me to take care of her," he protested.

"No, I wouldn't," I insisted, intense desire surging through me.

At that moment I tuned into another level of what was happening with Taz. Instinctively, I knew he was going to say yes. Certainty added to my power and I felt my will penetrate his defenses. He relaxed, stopped pacing, lit another cigarette, and turned toward me.

"Okay. Have your own way if it'll keep you away from me."

He laughed when I jumped all over him, hugging and kissing him. I didn't even care that he thought another child would keep me away from him.

"Okay. Okay. Cool it," he said, trying not to smile as he pushed me away. Let me get used to the idea. Hang out. Play with Choo. I need to work."

A couple of days later, a perfect June morning shone California clear. Excited and impatient, I walked up the circular staircase to Taz's tower room in the ramshackle Victorian house he called home. Once a grand mansion surrounded by farms, it stood like a lonely artifact in a sea of trailers and motor homes.

Brilliant sunshine poured through arched windows onto a cocoon of wrinkled white sheets. Glimpsing his tousled black hair among the tangled bedding, I jumped on the bed and shook him awake with unaccustomed courage.

"Taz. It's a beautiful day, Taz."

He stirred and rolled over, groaning and shading his eyes against the light.

"Come on. It's time to make a baby," I said.

A smile dawned when he realized what I was saying.

"You mean I'm going to get my piece of tail today?" he said with a lazy smile, lifting the sheets, inviting me into his drowsy sexuality.

I shook my head, insisting, "I want to do it in the dunes."

"God, give you one thing and you want it all your way," he complained, but the idea must have captured his imagination, because he leapt out of bed, stepping out of his world and coming into mine.

A short while later, after leaving Choo with Yoni, we revved up the beach buggy and roared toward the Oceano pier. The wind and the waves were all-powerful here. Driving down the beach, the vista opened to sand, sea, and sky. Twenty miles of seashore contained thousands of acres of tawny sand dunes that looked like they belonged in the Sahara. Coming out onto the beach, our eyes were drawn to a scarlet line edging the foaming shore. Hearing a tumultuous sound, we lifted our heads to the sky. Thousands of seagulls screeched and hovered above the breakers. The only human observers of this cosmic phenomenon, we climbed out of the dune buggy to take a closer look.

"They're ladybugs!" Taz whispered incredulously.

We dipped our hands into the fluttering red and black ladybug stream. They crawled over our fingers and flew onto our clothes. We knelt on the sand, looking down the scarlet line curving south along miles of beach. Where had they come from? Where were they going? Had anyone seen a giant red cloud?

"Ladybugs, billions of them. It's a miracle!" Taz said, shaking his head in wonder.

I looked from the ladybugs to the seagull sky.

"It's a miracle of wings," I whispered, trembling with awe.

Unable to penetrate the mystery, stunned and altered by the vast play of nature around us, we hiked into the dunes. Descending into a sand valley, we sheltered ourselves under windswept bushes. I spread my brilliant Guatemalan blanket over us – magenta, yellow, and green striping our presence upon the golden sand. Shaking, I clung to Taz, uncertain and shy.

Unaware of any change in me, he pulled a folded paper out of his shirt pocket and announced, "I brought acid for us," before placing one white tab on his tongue and offering the other to me.

Fear struck like a pain. I didn't want to follow him into an acid trip. I wanted my daughter's conception to be on my terms. Desire burned in his eyes as he waited. My resistance melted as I reluctantly accepted his unspoken condition that if I were to have my way, he must also have his. I nodded in acquiescence and he placed the tab on my tongue.

Saliva welled in my mouth as the tab dissolved. The familiar chemical dance surged in me as I relaxed into an unbounded interior space. My body yearned for touch, for comfort. Huddling under the blanket, we slipped out of our clothes. I sighed with relief and pleasure as my body touched his. Holding back was hard. Living love was good.

Cuddling shifted to desire as we shared gentle kisses, touches, licking, and tender caresses. A thought surfaced like a balloon in my mind – what was love for me was sex for him – but then I let even that thought fly into the sky. All that mattered was that it was love for me. Pulsing, blood-muscular-hardness entered yearning, blood-muscular-moistness, undulations returning undulations. Vibrational ripples blessed us with oneness as desire's rhythms throbbed an elemental wave resonance with the sand, sea, sun, and sky. Coupled, our fluid molecules merged into a juicy stream while sand traced a microscopic geometry of rainbow crystals upon our naked bodies. Separation awakened realization.

"She hasn't come," I said, seeking the love in his eyes.

"Let's try again," he replied, opening his love into mine.

"Yes, let's go to my favorite dune valley," I said, shading my eyes against the increasing sun.

"Sure," he agreed, in that moment being all I had ever wanted.

At ease with each other, we brushed the sand off our skin and dressed. The acid was coming on strong. Shift: microscopic vision glimpsed infinitely small consciousness contraction while telescopic vision grasped infinitely vast expansion. Enchanted, I observed with total focus how the movement of one grain of sand shifted the construction of a dune and thus, the entire universe. Everything was important in this vast oceanic expanse of energetic creation.

Like explorers in a raw, untouched land, we strode over the crest of the sand dunes into a merging, misting blue of sea and sky that offered great white breakers roaring an Odyssian cry of surrender to the shore. Ladybugs fluttered like fire above the bubbling sea foam. A hovering winged cloud, the gulls shrieked and darted through shining mandalas dancing in the vast sky of wind. Whistling, groaning waves disappeared into a grinding, foaming cascade of bleached wood, seaweed, shells, coral, pebbles and sand at our feet.

We climbed into the dune buggy and Taz started the engine. Ridiculously rigid, the buggy growled like a monster of steel and grime, resisting the living energy surging around us. The roar of the engine drowned the roar of the sea as, gasping for breath, we hurtled through living rhythms that pulsed wind waves into oceanic waves into sand waves, Godward, into waves of golden love on the field of creation.

A stream that flowed from the dunes signaled the threshold to my sanctuary. We jumped down from the buggy and pressed our way upward through the rustling, golden grasses clinging to the sand hills. Descending from the crest of the highest dune, sheltered from the winds, we removed our shoes and padded over softer, sifting, powdered grains into my favorite dune valley.

Tearing off my clothes, I tumbled onto the warm sand and shouted to the vibration web weaving the world, "I want to make love to the universe!"

God was all around me, dissolving me, becoming me. Spirit molecules merging with cellular molecules, I opened my petal self to the sun, the wind, and my husband. Taz, naked, perched like a panther ready to spring.

"Don't hold on. Come," I cried.

He slid down the dune and fell on his knees, trying to hold onto the sand.

"Come to me," I called as if he were a child.

Opening to him, I felt vast and infinitely powerful.

"Come into me," I commanded like a goddess.

Compassion rolled out of me in billowing clouds.

Taz crawled into me, sensuous-hardness entering yearning-softness, pulsing-searching against undulating-responding. Celebrating joy spiraling into infinity, rainbow bubbles foamed on my spiritual seashore. My essence surged upward in light-love expansion as my spirit merged with my soul daughter. Taz seemed far way, immersed, lost in his thrusting undulations. Suddenly, pulled by Taz's urgent coming, my tenderness descended, welcoming his sperm flash into my interior womb juices. Laughing tears, my body savored his offering.

"She's here. I feel her inside me," I marveled, aware of the new energy of my daughter's soul that was now a part of me. My womb felt warm and glowing as if the light that had beamed her into me was still radiating the heat of creation.

When I took his hand and placed it on my belly, conflict distorted his face, wonderment warring with resistance. As I glimpsed the fear that held him back from love and captured him in conflict, a living fog seemed to swirl around him, dulling and imprisoning his potential. In that moment, he was both the perfect husband and father of my dreams and a vulnerable, imperfect, wounded man.

Momentarily at peace with the painful paradox of our marriage, we played within the vibrational hallucinations surrounding us. Explorers in a visionary world of glowing geometric patterns, we discovered an enchanted world of infinitesimal insects, watching their shifting, intricate movements until the burning midday sun reminded us to put our clothes back on.

Hiking back, we inhaled the buffeting wind, leaning against it as we pressed down the sand dunes toward the shifting shore. How I longed to dissolve into this vast dance of cosmic energy, but it was not the time for release. It was the time for life.

What was empty was now full. I carried love within me. I would birth love into the world and make it mine. Millions of ecstatic cells opened into millions of eyes. I had become a transparent woman, awake with living love and my new soul-daughter. I had become my Self!

Roaring down the beach at high speed, happy, hungry, and thirsty, burned by the sun and wind, we returned to Taz's sharp, hard metal hangar submerged in the swaying, wind-breathing grasses beside the Oceano Airport runway. Wandering through Taz's junkyard of materials and circling his sculptures, I paid homage to his burnt symbols wrestled from tortured mind and torched metal. From piles of plastic, shining sheets of stainless steel, and welding rods, his creativity had forged opalescent, petal fountains; ravaged iron skeletons stretching toward an unobtainable heaven; bronze sunbursts; lacquered metal landscapes containing opaque, plastic jewels; and delicate wire sconces. Usually entranced by their visionary beauty, I found myself shrinking from their metallic hardness. Luminous and open, I hugged my abdomen containing my treasure, my daughter. The intensity of Taz's mind-visions invaded my vulnerable reality. I longed for safety and escape.

Yoni approached, cautiously curious, sensing our primal energy. Even though I knew she was sleeping with my husband and that she wanted everything that was rightfully mine – my husband, my child, my home – I felt only love for her in that moment. What had been hurtful didn't seem to matter. Like the sun, I couldn't stop myself from shining love. I gazed openly at my shadow sister, who defied all grooming, absorbing her reality instead of reacting against it. I observed her muddy sneakers and torn jeans, the man's shirt knotted above her bare midriff, and her ragged hair. I saw her hunger and accepted it. Openly indulgent with her desire for smoking, eating, talking, chewing gum, and sex, her lips licked at everything; her mouth was her main groove. I knew I was tripping on her, but I wanted to understand her voracious oral appetites. The only thing I could think of giving her was my news.

"We took an acid trip in the dunes. We're going to have a daughter," I rejoiced, fully expecting her to share my joy.

Yoni's face grimaced in shocked surprise, then hardened to hold back the anger, jealousy and fear that sprang to the surface.

She grunted, "Can't believe you guys," and lit a cigarette.

Her huge, watery blue eyes flickered uncertainly between Taz and me, waiting to see if Taz would say anything, but he was lost in contemplation of his latest sculpture and ignored her. Shaking, she inhaled deeply, licked her lips, and flicked non-existent ashes off the end of her cigarette. Abruptly, she dropped it and ground it under her heel. Out of sync with our ecstasy, unable to look at me, she turned and left. For a year she'd stood her ground, outlasting our fights, my jealousy, and Taz's domination, determined to remain a part of our scene. Pain tore through me. Why must love for one create pain for another?

Shifting my attention, I worshipped Taz, panther-pacing among his creations. Looking intensely at one sculpture, then another, his lean, muscular body moved like a dancer in his tight black pants and turtleneck sweater. My eyes caressed his aristocratic features and savored his olive-skinned charisma that evoked images of the leafy crowns and togas of ancient times. As thought patterns recreated my mind prison, the power that had awakened in the dunes flowed out of me and into him, my love once again imprisoned by a bond that took away my reason, my freedom, and my strength. Even though I allowed him to dominate my heart, my brain, and my womb, I was caught in conflict. Unable to say no or to let go, I believed my love would rescue him, not understanding that blind loyalty, slavish devotion, and illusory projection were not love. I had not yet realized I needed to rescue myself.

Our marriage was not a merging of worlds, a melting of waves on a mutual shore. My every effort to create love was rebuffed and my every advance caused him to retreat. I lived in a quicksand of fear. Never knowing what Taz would be like from moment to moment and lost in my need for him, I didn't know I deserved anything better. I tried to please him, but nothing I did was ever enough.

He pushed me away, just like the lyrics in Dylan's song:

"...it ain't me babe, it ain't me you're looking for..."

But whenever I tried to leave, he pulled me back.

I looked at my hands. The lines on them undulated like waves. What did these lines mean? What was I going to do with these hands?

Choo ran into the studio and threw himself into my arms, offering a squiggling, giggling, energetic embrace.

"Oh, dear Choo, you're going to have a sister," I whispered.

Laughing, he invited me to play. We walked hand in hand in the lush grasses and among the bushes bursting with radiant flowers. The powerful rush of acid over, dissolving ecstasy floated like sweet sadness among magenta-leaf mandalas and visually vibrating bird song. Messages of love burst like day-stars all around me. Light, color, sweetness, and beauty drifted over me, covering me, blessing me.

My son's mischievously joyful laughter sparkled like rainbow snowflakes in the luminous landscape. Enjoying the feeling of the warm, moist dirt on my bare feet, I followed Choo down the path beside the brook, through a tunnel of flowering bushes, to the back of the dunes. After climbing a coarse sand hill, we lay down and peered over the top. Foaming breakers rolled thunderously out of advancing fog banks that eclipsed the sun. Cold wind tore at us as the ghostly mist crept threateningly toward us. Suddenly tired and irritable, Choo demanded to go home. I carried him down the dune and past the flowering bushes whipping madly in the increasing winds. At home, playing in his bath, his good spirits returned, and I marveled at his boundless resilience.

For the next couple of days, I drifted down from the acid trip, my soul daughter blossoming like a great light of joy within. Taz hovered near, seemingly moved by the conception and our shared ecstasy. Then, he pulled back abruptly, breaking the warm connection. Openly taking up with Yoni, he told me to split.

Acid could take you up, but it couldn't keep you there. It could give you glimpses of what you longed for, but it couldn't make them real and it couldn't make them last. What was the point of reaching for heaven if you slid right back into hell? Everyone around me was dropping acid and dropping out. I wanted to drop out from dropping out. I wanted to drop in, but where was that? I didn't fit anywhere.

A kernel of knowing whispered that the only way out was in and that I had to make my own scene. I listened and I dreamed.

Living Love

It was time to let the memories go. Taking one last breath of the divine orange blossom perfume from the orchards, I settled Love in the car and continued east. Excited and scared at the same time, my mind expanded like the desert sky opening before me. I sifted through a galaxy of possibilities. One question repeated with the rhythm of the tires:

What am I going to do? What am I going to do? What am I...?

I'd been letting things slide, dreaming of leaving but always putting it off, so it was good that Taz and Chanter's stupid scene pushed me over the edge, good that I got mad, and definitely good that I was on the road, heading away from them.

I sped through Beaumont and Banning, up over the wind-blasted pass, and down into the Coachella Valley. Relieved at shedding the L.A. scene, I slowed down and opened to the new landscape, feeling tender and brand new. The shock of my departure had opened some new sensibility in me that received impressions in a more direct way. I absorbed the effect of the sun's fire on the land around me, noticing the parched sand that waited for the blessing of rain. Rose-petal clouds drifted purple shadows over the circle of sage-and-chaparral-covered hills rising in the southwest

31

toward San Jacinto Mountain above Palm Springs. Immediately, there was a sense of connection. The arid, barren desert reflected the empty space I had created in my life. Aware that it was welcoming me, I slowed down and breathed in the burning air. A thrill shivered through me.

As I entered Palm Springs, nature receded. The sun blazed mercilessly over quiet, deserted streets. The only sign of life was an occasional luxury car sailing slowly along a palm-lined drive or a rare retiree, dressed in tennis whites, sauntering between their car and an air-conditioned shop or cafe. Seeking relief from the heat, I pulled into a motel shadowed from the scorching late-afternoon sun by the mountain. As dusk deepened into shadow, I stretched out on a lawn chair, nursing Love as I watched night purples and indigos awaken brilliant stars. Gusts of hot, dry air carried hints of delicate aromas that were soon overshadowed by the dominating pungent chaparral.

Later, snuggled next to my daughter on the bed, I became aware of feelings I had ignored or denied for a long time. Beyond my fatigue, I sensed a deeper tension that represented the part of me that never felt safe, the part that was always fighting for my life. I was too tired to fight any more, so I sank willingly into the tension, thinking there had to be a beginning to the fear that had wound itself around my life like a wild vine and strangled my essential joy. Falling deeper, I entered a place of deep exhaustion where a weight of utter hopelessness bound me fast, rendering me unable to move or think. Aching, utterly spent, I was overcome by despair. Hovering between sleep and dreams, my mind agonized over painful memories and fearful thoughts.

Hours later, when my daughter's cry stirred me out of my depths to offer her my breast, a raw sensitivity remained. Outer sounds were intensely magnified: air conditioning, traffic, the rasping and rustling of palm fronds outside my room; even Love's breathing irritated me. Finally I closed my eyes, but not to sleep. Seeking understanding, my mind explored, remembered, questioned, but found only confusion, fear, and uncertainty. I could not make sense of my life. In the end, there was only one question. How could I bring light into my darkness? Where was the dawn inside of me?

Awake at first light, seeking relief from my soul searching, I stepped barefoot onto the lawn outside my room. Welcoming the touch of cool, moist grass on the soles of my feet, I looked at the rugged mountain illuminated by the morning light and felt grateful for the beauty around me. Even though I was tired, I felt excited, on the brink of adventure. Shedding the shadow lands of the night with a toss of my head, I made a promise to myself that calmed my frightened heart.

"I will follow what I love and find my life," I said out loud, feeling surprisingly certain I would find my way.

In any journey, the first steps are important, I decided; so I followed a tantalizing aroma wafting through the air and discovered flowering jasmine. After breathing in the fragrance of the white star-shaped blossoms, I lifted my arms to the sky, let out a soft sigh and opened to the promise of the day.

Eager to soak in the hot-spring pools, I carried my daughter to the Canyon Spa at Tahquitz Canyon Way and Indian Canyon. We were the only guests in the turquoise-tiled pools so I played freely with Love in the sparkling warm water. As the hot spring soothed me, my worries faded. It didn't matter that I'd shed one life but had not yet found another. Slowly, the tension eased and I relaxed. While Love napped on a deck chair in the shade, I swam and dived in the pools, recovering the memory of how I loved to swim when I was a child.

In the dressing room, I stared at my naked body in the mirror. My face looked so young, vulnerable, and untouched by the tumult of feelings and questions within me. Why was the inside so different from the outside? No wonder Taz's face fooled me. I could never figure out what was going on inside him. How had I turned from a fearless tomboy into a shy, scared young woman? How did I come to be alone in the world with nowhere to go? When I loved so much, why did no one love me? My image reflected no answers. Why had this happened to me? What could I do? I wanted to see inside myself, but how could I do that? How could I find out who I really was? Where would I have to look from to see myself?

My mind screamed questions inside my head but there was no one to give me any answers, so I hummed some tunes. As I brushed out my long black hair I looked at my old blue jeans and T-shirt and promised myself I'd wear beautiful clothes in my new life. My heart brightened as I started to imagine the outfits I would make. Maybe that was an answer. Turn my mind to creativity and stop thinking about what I don't know.

Feeling soft and fresh from my swim in the hot springs, I walked down Palm Canyon Drive carrying Love close to my heart. I wanted to do something great with this feeling, but what?

After breakfast in a cute fifties-style coffee shop, I saw a sign that advertised tram rides up the mountain and went for it. That was my kind of high, my kind of cool.

The cable car lifted us slowly up San Jacinto Mountain, far above the baked desert floor that surrounded the emerald gardens and turquoise pools of Palm Springs. The expanding view exposed the shimmering ribbon of freeway that crossed the arid valley.

The air cooled with the increase in altitude, offering welcome relief from the blazing sun. We passed over a lush natural spring, camouflaged by a tumble of vines and overgrown palms. The cable car lifted us up the steeply inclined valley over a rugged rock-and-pine landscape. At the summit, I stepped out onto the landing and saw the world spread out below in miniature. I wished I could see my own life from a higher perspective. Maybe that would help me make sense of what was happening. When my heart and mind were so immersed in what was going on, I couldn't see a clear path to follow.

High above the desert, I carried Love along crackling pine-needled trails. With every step, a powerful pine aroma burst into the crisp, clean air. Slowly, my mind cleared and a fresh, new feeling of lightness, openness, and freedom sparkled in my mind. Enlivened, I left the path and walked toward an outcropping of rocks, where I discovered a grassy meadow surrounded by tall evergreens. There, resting on a lichen-cushioned rock, I nursed Love in a blissful communion of soft, tender suckling. When I looked at my daughter's innocent, radiant beauty, a fierce love flared in my heart. I had called her into my life and here she was – living Love. She was completely open, soft, trusting and malleable, yet she already was showing amazing strength, perseverance and energy for growth, physical development and exploration. She was divine raw material. She had the potential to become anything, speak any language, develop any skill, yet I knew her destiny would be determined by the opportunities that unfolded before her day by day. Love and responsibility mingled with sadness. How was I going to be able to give her all she deserved?

What was it about Love that captured and opened my heart? Why was she so irresistible? I knew my love for my children filled my heart because I did not have to divide my love between my children and my husband, but it was more than that. When I looked into my daughter's eyes, love shone out of her into me. I must have been like her when I was a baby but I had lost it. How was I going to find the way to love again?

My attempt to use logic to penetrate the mystery of my life hurt my head, so I let my thoughts go and surrendered to the warmth of the shafts of sunlight streaming through the trees like searchlights on the grassy meadow. When the sunlight fell on me, I felt as though I had been blessed. Transfixed in the light, I wished I could stay there forever. Forever? What a thought! I was always running away, going somewhere, trying to find out what was missing. I was always looking for a place where I felt at home. Even when I had a home I still felt homeless, as though my real home was somewhere else. When I was a child, I had been so convinced that I had been adopted that I asked my parents where my real mother and father were. I wanted to find them and live with them.

Sadness swept over me. I longed to be with someone I could talk to, someone who loved and understood me. I felt so alone. Just as I was starting to feel sorry for myself, humor bubbled up from my heart and I laughed. What would God think if he looked down on me right now? I'm sure He'd think I was pretty dumb and that I definitely needed help. I'd never laughed at myself before. Looking at my life, you'd think I preferred tragedy. That thought made me laugh even more. I could sure use a fairy godmother, I thought, enjoying the feeling bubbling up from my solar plexus.

The laughter felt so good that I closed my eyes and let myself feel the pine forest sheltering me in its fragrant embrace, imagining what I would do if I were my own fairy godmother. I could wave my wand and weave my life into what I loved. Images played through my mind; a family sharing gentle, human touch; love flowing from eyes and smiles; a husband and wife creating beautiful things together; a simple, natural home and garden; happy, playful children who were well loved; an ocean of spirit filled with an infinity of love.

I'd never been around a family that knew how to love each other, but that's what I'd always wanted – living love that flowed into everything I did every moment of every day. Living love must be possible or I wouldn't want it, I reasoned.

The answer dropped like a feather through still air as I realized I *could* be my own fairy godmother. Struck by the simplicity of the idea, I closed my eyes and a vision of a flower appeared in my mind.

First, I glimpsed my soul seed, a dormant yet powerful energy contracted against its impulse to bloom. Then I felt the promise of my inevitable flowering. When I heard a presence whisper, *it's just a matter of time*, I was so happy I laughed out loud, startling Love.

Returning to my reverie, I imagined the life cycle of the plants around me. Beginning as seeds hidden in the dark moist earth, they longed for the sun. As they searched upward, their roots grew strong as they absorbed moisture and minerals from the soil. Just as plants need the correct combination of warmth, shade, moisture and soil to flourish, I needed to find a place where I could grow and blossom. I'd only lived in places that felt harsh and alien. It was time to find somewhere to live that was nourishing, safe, and comfortable.

Carefully holding a blissed-out, sleeping Love, I walked on. At the far end of the meadow, a giant tree lay on its side. Torn from the earth, dirt clinging to its exposed roots, it looked like a giant who had outreached its roots and caused its own fall. I walked cautiously over and leaned against the tree, feeling the power that had held it straight and tall for so many years, realizing that only because it had sent its roots deep into the earth had it been able to grow so far into the sky. I imagined that a great storm must have set it free from the earth it had clung to for so long.

Unlike this tree, I had never had roots in this world. I had never had a sense of belonging anywhere. Like a leaf in the wind, I'd never found a place I wanted to be. The thought occurred to me that perhaps I needed to sink my roots inside myself. Even though my inner world was uncomfortable, it was the only place that felt real to me.

As soon as my attention shifted to my inner world, I got a sense that the nature around me was a mirror that was helping me to discover who I was. Nature seemed to be speaking to me, helping me to understand the cycles of creation. Even though I felt comforted by this communion, I was also scared. I was on my own for the first time in my life. There was no one to help me, but there was also no one to stop me from doing things my way. I felt an immediate responsibility as I realized that every choice I made was important. One wrong decision could ruin everything, so I had to be sure to make the choices that would take me toward the life I wanted to live.

I looked at my daughter's sweetly sleeping face and knew I couldn't leave her. I'd have to find a way to work from home, and I'd have to live in L.A. so I could be near my son. I knew it was risky being near my husband, but I didn't have a choice. I'd helped Taz make sculptures and run our art galleries, so why not make my own designs? If I could sell his art, I could sell my own. Suddenly everything clicked into place. I knew what I had to do. I needed a studio and a place to live.

At that moment, the last rays of light illuminated the tips of the golden grasses and the meadow glowed with an incandescent brilliance. For an instant, I stood in a pool of luminous radiance before the sun disappeared behind the hill. As I looked up at the darkening sky, pine needles trembled black against the glowing evening clouds. It was time to go.

Swinging down the mountain, my whole being celebrated as a glorious rose-violet sunset lit up the sky. Rainbows arched between sky and land. Somber shafts of rain angled toward the hazy, purple hills beyond Desert Hot Springs. While nature played out its magnificent farewell to a magical day, I returned to the desert floor with fresh purpose.

"I know where I'm going,
and I know who is going with me..."

"Yeah, Love, we're on our way. We're going to live love every day."

Roots of Pain, Shame & Blame

The second night in Palm Springs, I was filled with energy, turned on; my brain was alight and alive with visions of my own studio and what my new life might bring. The fire that had set me free burned like lava, energizing my creativity and filling me with the power to shape my new life.

I looked at my daughter and wondered if she felt what was happening to me. Did she know I'd broken free? Another, even wilder thought occurred like a flash: maybe she was making this happen. A moment later the image of my mother emerged in my mind, awakening the stream of sadness that flowed deep within me. I felt a profound connection of generations open in my consciousness as I sensed my grandmothers flowing into me at the same time as future granddaughters flowed out of me. As I realized how important it was for me to break free for the sake of my children and my children's children, I thought spontaneously, "Oh, mother, if only I could take you with me." As I explored that impulse, another thought came: if I freed myself, maybe she would feel it too. One thing for sure, though, I wasn't going back to my mother's home again.

I'd gone home before Love was born, soon after pot-blasted Chanter joined Taz's scene. Desperate to break free of their night-tripping party scene, I grasped at an idea I thought Taz might go for. Seven months pregnant, holding my belly, I climbed slowly up the stairs to Taz's studio and hung around for a while, listening to music, building up courage until I saw my opening.

"Taz, I want to visit my mom. I'll take Choo, give you some space," I said casually.

Taz lit a cigarette and looked over, trying to figure out what was going on in my head.

"It's time my mom saw Choo," I explained, then added a sudden inspiration, "and if I give birth in Canada we'd save a lot of money." Until that moment, I hadn't thought of staying that long, but I would have said anything to convince Taz to let me go.

That made an impression, but Taz still held back.

Chanter's eyes lit up at the thought of Taz's pregnant wife and kid being out of their scene.

"Taz, that's a great idea. She deserves a break," Chanter said with a sly smile.

"Yeah, you can go," Taz agreed reluctantly, giving in.

Like refugees from the battleground for Taz's soul, Choo and I flew to Vancouver, British Columbia.

For a few hours, high in the sky, Choo and I shared a brief freedom. Excited by our adventure, Choo charmed the stewardesses and talked to everyone around us, telling them it was his first plane trip and that he was going to visit his grandmother. Later, when he curled up on the seat beside me and fell asleep, I gazed at his exquisite face, his golden curls, and strong, perfect body, vowing to do everything I could to protect and preserve his happy, enthusiastic nature.

Choo thought it was his first plane trip, but he'd been to Vancouver before. He didn't remember, but I sure did. Taz and I were separated at the time. He was making the cool early-sixties San Francisco scene and had a bevy of young girls hanging around his studio while I was running a small gallery in Carmel and taking care of Choo.

Aside from the push-pull torture of Taz's coming and going and the inevitable loneliness of being on my own, I was madly in love with my son. Whenever Taz came around, he resented my close bond with Choo, and acted jealous whenever I was nursing. Naïve as I was, I never imagined what he was cooking in his head.

In November of '64, when Choo was a year old, Taz insisted on taking Choo to visit his parents in Vancouver. I didn't know how to resist his will, so I let him go. I'll never forget the radiant, trusting smile Choo gave me as I hugged him and put him in the car with his father. I suffered for three days, counting the hours, suffering the discomfort of withdrawing from breastfeeding and longing for my son.

When Taz returned, Choo was not with him. He had left our son with his parents.

"Cool, huh? They wanted to take care of him and give you a break," he said in an offhand way, his eyes narrowing against my shock.

The pain of the separation howled through my body, throbbing in my breasts and womb.

I begged Taz to bring him back, but he muttered impatiently, "You're too hung up on Choo. Why can't you groove?"

That night I screamed into my pillow, unable to dissolve the image of my infant son and my need to hold him safely in my arms. Whether I focused on my own pain or the image of Choo calling out for me, I felt helpless. I never thought of getting on a plane to bring him home. A couple of months later, Taz's parents brought him back, but Taz wouldn't let me take care of him any more.

"From now on, I'm going to raise him," Taz ruled ruthlessly. "I'll never let you do to Choo what my mother did to me."

"Then why did you leave him with your mother?" I asked desperately, but he would not answer.

I argued, "It wasn't just your mother. Your father hurt you too," but he refused to change his mind. When I promised, "I would never do to Choo what your mother did to you," he would not listen.

From then on, Taz was in control. He moved Choo into the studio and took over. He fed him, dressed him, and put him to sleep. I had to beg to be allowed to be with my own son.

"Wake up, Choo. Look, there's Vancouver," I whispered, gently rocking my son awake.

He got up and peered out the window, "It's all dark and rainy," he said as he rubbed his eyes.

"Yes, it is," I said. "That's where mommy was born."

It had been several years since I had been home. In my heart I wished I could be a child and put my head in my mother's lap and feel her arms around me. I wanted to cry and be comforted, but I knew she would not take me in her arms.

As we drove through the city, the atmosphere of my youth penetrated me, making me shiver in dread. More than the cold, the dark and the damp of the British Columbia rainforest climate, the memory of my isolation, my longing, and my fearful inhibitions swept over me, returning me to the roots of my pain and shame. Turning my attention to the warmth of Choo's sleeping body snuggling close to me, I felt grateful for the presence of my son in my life and the child in my womb. I would birth love into this world, I determined, and make love mine.

The views of the city and harbor expanded as the taxi climbed up Grouse Mountain, offering a spectacular light show softened by rain and cloud. By the time we reached my parents' house, we were immersed in clouds, unable to see anything through the misted windows but blurred lights and the rain pelting down in the darkness.

As we reached the top of Lonsdale and turned onto Prospect Road, I was deep in memories of the year Taz and I lived there when we were first married. I had been pregnant; not only with Choo, but also with hopes and dreams of the life we would create together. Taz was hot to move to California, because American tourists bought his sculptures. He wanted to make the big time art scene in the States. We sold the house to my parents and moved just after Choo was born.

The taxi slowed and stopped in front of a charming old cottage surrounded by evergreens and shrubs. I opened the door and stepped out into the rain. The driver carried my suitcase as I led Choo carefully down the path. A pitched roof porch sheltered the carved wooden door bordered by green, crimson, and gold stained-glass windows that glowed from the light within the house. Even though the door looked like the threshold to a land of enchantment, I knew I would not be stepping into any fairy tale. I knew only too well what sorrow this house contained.

When I rang the bell, Blackie, my sister's dog, barked in immediate response. When the door opened a moment later, I glimpsed my mother's face, noticing immediately how she withheld her welcome. Blackie more than made up for her lack of affection as he pushed past her and threw himself at me, licking and sniffing as he pranced around us, his coal-black eyes alive with joy. Choo hid behind me to escape the first onslaught of Blackie's welcome, then gained the courage to pet him, laughing all the while.

"Don't stand out there. You're letting in the cold. Come in, for heaven's sake," my mother said impatiently."

Choo, this is your grandmother," I said.

Suddenly shy, he peeked out behind my coat, giggled, then hid again.

"You can stay upstairs. I cleared it out the best I could," my mother said drearily.

Once inside the house, I saw even more clearly the changes the years had etched upon my mother. Her bitter, internal world had seeped out and eroded her physical beauty. She had cut, permed and dyed her long, lustrous, blue-black hair. Puckered lids drooped over her eyes and wrinkles distorted her once voluptuous mouth. I looked at the polyester pants, nylon blouse, and cheap vinyl shoes she was wearing with disbelief. She had always worn beautiful fabrics, even if she had to wear the same clothes every day, no matter how long Father was out of work or how many times she had to serve us rice and milk when she was waiting for paychecks.

Distractedly distant, her attention had always been focused on some invisible horizon, circling hawk-like over dark secrets and inarticulate longing. Even though she lived in a permanent depression, she read books on yoga, spirituality, mysticism, philosophy, and healing. When I was a child, she took me to philosophical lectures, all manner of churches, spiritualist and mediumistic seances, and yoga classes. After years of searching, she announced one day that she wasn't going to any more meetings.

"They're all fakes," she said with rancor.

Instead, she started taking long walks and bought a TV. During my childhood, she'd refused to have one in the house, complaining that TV ruined your mind and weakened your moral fiber just like white bread. She still hated TV, but she watched it every night, endlessly raging against events and people as she criticized the quality of the programs. Restless and impatient, she picked at cuts or burns until they became permanent sores. Consumed by her negativity, my mother's dark currents dominated our home, dissolving any possibility of joy. The invisible had become visible.

Increasingly ashamed of my mother during my teenage years, I began to avoid her. Separating myself from my family, I invented my own world to protect myself. A stranger to love and affection, I cloaked myself in shyness and escaped into books and movies. If I was attracted to a young man, I didn't move toward him with confident curiosity. Fearing rejection, I drew away. Even though I longed for loving intimacy, I feared it at the same time, because I didn't know what to say or what to do when I tried to make friends. Yet, I dreamed and longed for someone to make me come alive, for something to set me free.

A free-spirited tomboy who evolved into a natural beatnik, I wore black dance tights under my skirts rather than freeze like the other bobby-soxers in the cold British Columbia winters. Later, when I saw newspaper articles about wild beatnik women who wore black stockings, I discovered I was part of a much larger beat scene that was digging its way into the culture. My friends and I hung out in Vancouver's jazz cellars and coffee shops, played chess on Robson Street with European immigrants, made the rounds of artists' studios, ate Chinese meals late at night in Chinatown, read and argued about existential philosophy, and wrote poetry. We acknowledged each other's poetic howling and comforted each other with rebellion. For the first time, I belonged.

In July 1962, the Vancouver summer days had been hot and humid. After I got home from my summer office job, I changed into jeans and a T-shirt, then set off up Dunbar to meet my friends at our local hangout, the Black Spot Beatnik Coffee Shop. As I walked along, I went over chess moves in my head, looking forward to an evening of winning another game or two and listening to jazz. As I neared the Black Spot, I looked up and glimpsed a man standing out front. Even though I'd devoured literary classics and adventure and romance novels since I was a child, nothing fully prepared me for meeting Taz. As all the romance books had promised, my heart started beating like crazy.

I'd never seen anyone like him. Dressed in a tight, black turtleneck and perfectly cut black silk trousers, muscled arms folded across his chest, he stood poised like an elegant acrobat waiting to do something extraordinary. My steps slowed. I don't know whether it was to savor the approach or put off the meeting as long as possible.

When Ian smiled at me and said, "Hi," the man turned.

When I saw his face, I was lost. I could only stare at the most beautiful man I had ever seen.

"Taz," the stranger said with a slow seductive smile, as he scanned my face and body. Turning to Ian, he said, "Where have you been hiding *her*?"

My face flushed red and I fled inside, my feelings flipping from excitement to relief to shame. When I joined my friends, dissociation took hold of me. Even though my body was sitting on the chair, my attention was completely focused on the stranger outside. A few minutes later, as if I had called him to me, he slid onto the bench beside me and pressed his thigh against mine. I flushed again, but I did not want to escape this time.

"Want to play a game of chess?" he whispered as he blew his warm breath against my ear, sending shivers up my spine.

I nodded and he led me to another table where he sat opposite me. Annoyingly cocksure, confident of his conquest, he gazed lazily at me as a complex of emotions gyrated inside me – shyness mingled with pleasure turned into embarrassment, which melted into helpless bewilderment. Unable to concentrate, I lost the game. Then I sat helplessly staring at him, wordlessly. I was totally, stupidly captured. He didn't seem to mind. He lounged back, staring, devouring me with his eyes, smiling, even laughing. From time to time he asked questions about me which I answered like a child.

And then he said, "Let's go," and I followed him. When he opened the door of his Morris Minor convertible, I slid in, terrified, excited, lost to myself.

"I've got a portable record player. We'll go to the beach and dance under the stars," he announced. I nodded again, eyes wild wide with thrilling fear.

Windblown from the drive, I shivered as I got out of the car. The night was cooler now and the stars were bright above the shimmering waves lapping Kitsalino Beach. I followed Taz down the path. He spread a plaid blanket on the sand. I waited, unsure and shy as I watched him set up his stereo and put on a record. He pulled me into his arms and soon we were dancing barefoot on the sand to the rhythms of the cha-cha and the tango. When he led me to the blanket and pulled me down beside him, I was already his, and he knew it.

For the rest of the summer I rushed home from work and waited for him on the steps of my parents' house, impatient for him to pick me up and make me come alive. A naïve innocent, hungry for touch, affection, and love, I fell into his world. As Taz pursued and dominated me, I thought passionate submission was love. By the time I realized I had exchanged one hell for another, it was too late. I was already married.

Taz insisted on total submission. He took me away from all that I loved, and demanded I live only for him, but it wasn't long before he became impatient with my total dependence on him. Increasingly angry, he started going out at night, leaving me home alone. Even when I cried and begged him not to go, he went out anyway. When he returned late at night, he refused to tell me where he had been.

Denied all that I loved, separated from my music, books, and dance, my imagination obsessed on torturous fears and imaginings of where he was going and what he might be doing. Pregnant with Choo, my only solace was my kitty, named Motor Boat because of his incredibly loud purr, and a Great Dane puppy, Goldie. When Taz was out, I snuggled with them in front of the fireplace. Goldie licked my face and hands and Motor Boat purred while I cried.

It had been three years since my son's birth and my departure from Vancouver, three years since I had been in the Prospect Avenue house. I took off my coat and looked around the living room. A fire crackled in the fireplace that Taz had trimmed with burnished copper. The sofa, chairs, and carved wooden coffee table – all the things we'd owned before we left for California – remained in their original places. The carpets Taz had traded for sculptures still covered the floor and his paintings hung on the walls we had covered with burlap before we had painted them white.

I never saw it then, but his paintings were all variations on the same theme: two brooding, impending ellipses, no doubt representing Taz and I, falling into each other, unable to escape our inevitable merging.

I looked out the large picture window into the dark night, just making out the bare branches of the apple and cherry trees in the orchard garden below. I remembered the orchard's spring-bursting blossoming, its rampant riot of fragrance and joyful color followed by luscious summer greening, then the autumn gathering of ripe fruit. Bears loved the garden. More than once, I'd looked up to see a brown bear peeking out of the evergreens, waiting for a turn at the fruits of the garden.

The tropical fish tank bubbled behind me.

"Look, at all the fish, Choo. See the pretty colors," I enthused.

Leaving Choo to enjoy the aquarium, I sat in front of the fire, glad for the warmth and the rest. Blackie crouched at my feet, looking up at me with love and devotion.

I whispered to him, "Oh, Blackie, thank you for loving me, thank you for remembering me."

Sadness welled up in me. Tears were near. Stop, I warned myself. You just got here. This is no time to cry.

"We don't have vegetarian food, you know. You'll have to eat what we eat," my mother said, standing over me.

"No, problem, Mom. Vegetables are fine. I'll go shopping tomorrow," I replied.

Here come the rules, I thought, feeling like I'd never left home.

My mom walked into the kitchen to make tea and toast, reciting her regulations as she waited for the kettle to boil.

"Don't ask me to baby sit," she called out.

"I'm not going anywhere, Mom."

"You have to put Choo to bed right after supper. Your Dad watches TV and he won't want to be disturbed."

I heard what she said, but I knew what she really meant was that she didn't want to be disturbed.

"Where did you get that silly name? Choo, indeed," she complained scornfully.

"It's a fun nickname," I said. "You know, Chugga Chugga Choo Choo. He loves that sound and it makes him happy. Its fun."

"Fun! Hah! Children need rules. They need regularity; then they know what is expected of them."

"Yes, Mom. He'll be good," I said as I lifted Choo onto my lap and held him close.

"We're saving for retirement. We can't spend extra on food," she shouted suddenly, her voice nervous and shrill.

"It's okay, Mom. I have money," I reassured her.

The kettle whistled and a few minutes later when she brought in the tea tray, the scent of jasmine briefly lightened the atmosphere. Choo caught sight of his cocoa and the toast and cookies and slipped off my lap to sit on the floor beside Blackie. For a moment, sipping tea in the darkening dusk and the warmth of the firelight, I felt something unwinding within me that gave me a sense that I could open to my mother, but she turned on the TV and the opportunity was lost. I had escaped to my mother's house but I had not escaped from pain.

After tea, I took Choo upstairs for a nap and fell asleep. I did not hear my father return that evening, but he woke me in the morning in the same way he had wakened me all the days of my childhood. Even though it was still dark outside, I knew it was six in the morning because he was filling the house with the sizzle of bacon, the fragrance of freshly brewed coffee, and the sweetness of toast mingled with cigarette smoke.

Excited, I put on my robe and went downstairs. Face bright, he rose like a gentleman, kissed me on the cheek, then returned to his newspaper and his cigarette. I helped myself to coffee and sat opposite him, waiting, hoping he would talk to me, but he was the same ritualistically punctual, cheerily disconnected father I had always known. Quietly, I sipped my coffee. He peered over the edge of the paper now and then, his bright blue eyes resting on me for a moment, but it was clear he wasn't going to stop his morning routine even for me, and I was afraid to initiate change.

After Dad left, Mother punctuated her tasks with sighs and mournful looks out the window. Relieved when she went out to visit a neighbor, I turned on the radio, searching for a flower power station. Oh, good, I sighed when the Beatles came on the radio. They knew what was happening.

"...all the lonely people, where do they all come from?"

Absent in my family constellation was all that I longed for: touch, tenderness, sharing, and affection.

My younger sister, Bella, crept up. Even though she'd been in the house when I arrived last night, she'd hidden away. You could not go to her. You had to wait for her to come to you. Now sixteen, she still seemed like a strange child. Shy, inarticulate, and depressed, she

refused to go to school. No one could make her go. Her will could not be broken. If mother, the truant officer, or the school psychiatrist threatened her or tried to bribe her, she screamed, locked herself in her room, or ran away. No one understood her fear, her rebellious self-imprisonment, or her love-hate relationship with mother.

Reading her book in a corner of the living room, she pretended as though Choo and I were not there. Once in a while, I caught a rare flash of her brilliant blue eyes burning desperately beneath unkempt copper curls. She peeked cautiously at Choo, but if he tried to move toward her in playful fun, she turned her back on him. Confused, Choo looked at me, so I distracted him with stories. The day passed in a logjam of communal loneliness while the radio station played out our sorrows and our dreams.

Father returned at seven, happily drunk, the evening newspaper nattily tucked under his arm, his tweed jacket musty with Player's Please cigarette smoke. Eyes glazed, reeking of rum, he rambled about what was happening in his office, a card game he had played with the fellows after work, or what he had read in the newspaper as he rode home on the bus. He never inquired about how we felt or what we'd been doing. After dinner my mother washed the dishes and my father snoozed in front of the television. I put Choo to bed and Bella disappeared into her room. When my mother joined my dad in front of the television, they sat silently side by side, the black and white screen flickering while she picked the scabs off her sores and he sipped his drinks. Sometimes I sat with them for a while before I slipped away to snuggle with Choo and fall asleep. Every night the same question loomed in my mind. Why don't people do the wonderful things that would make them happy? Why don't people know how to love each other?

On the weekends my father worked in the garden, played cards, or fixed things around the house, making regular trips to the damp earthy basement where he guzzled his smuggled booze. By the end of the day, he was soused. On Sundays he turned his attention to the dinner roast, basting it slowly all day, looking forward to the supreme moment of his week, when he carved the meat and served it to us. I could hardly bear the look on his face when I refused my portion.

"Dad, you know I'm vegetarian, and so is Choo. Thanks, we'll just have the vegetables and the salad; Anyway, you know you like to take roast beef sandwiches to work," I explained as gently as I could, hoping he would forgive me.

He let it go but I saw my mother tense and heard her snort her derision. I would have to be careful. I didn't want to make her angry.

The days that followed were endlessly slow and relentlessly similar. Avoiding my mother and sister as much as I could, I rested, played with Choo and Blackie, read books, and took short walks in the rain. About two weeks later, the sky opened into brilliant sunlight and the view cleared over the Vancouver harbor. My belly full with child, I walked slowly down Lonsdale into North Vancouver, Choo chattering excitedly beside me.

Then the sun went behind clouds and the air turned bitterly cold. Gusts of sleeting wind forewarned an approaching storm. I wanted to take shelter in a restaurant, but discovered I had forgotten my purse. Without money for bus fares, I carried my son slowly back up the hill, my desolation so deep I didn't even think to ask for help.

At home I collapsed in front of the fire, exhausted, shaking, cramps hardening my belly in regular spasms. Later in the evening my water broke and my father took me to the hospital. Only seven and one half months pregnant, I was glad my child was not born that night.

The cramps subsided, but the water still flowed. The doctors insisted I stay in the hospital to reduce the danger of infection and postpone the birth as long as possible. They put me in the women's birthing ward, assigning me a corner bed by a south-facing window that caught every rare ray of sunlight that filtered through the leaden winter clouds. Even though my separation from Choo tugged at my heart, I would not let myself think about what it must be like for him to be alone with my mother and sister. Never having known such rest or peace, I dreamed and drowsed the days away. Sometimes I read or knitted brilliant magenta and persimmon wool into a dress. Without anyone to put me down or suppress me with sadness or rage, I could simply be myself. Supported and nourished by the comforting structure of the maternity ward, I immersed myself in dreams, visions, and radiant communions with the child I carried in my womb.

Surrounded by the excitement and confusion of birthing, nursing mothers, and the efficient and friendly hospital staff, I discovered that I had a gift for helping women.

When I listened to their stories, I understood their suffering and their fear and wanted to help them. Braver for them than for myself, I spoke to the nurses and doctors when women felt too shy to ask for help. The happiness that came from these simple encounters startled me.

During my daydreams, I imagined what the world might be like if women were honored and protected in beautiful buildings during their pregnancies and when they were birthing. I drew architectural plans for columnar temples reminiscent of Egypt and Greece. There, women would rest in circular rooms bathed in soft rainbow mists that pulsed to angelic music, or recline in waterfall gardens where the fragrance and colors of beautiful flowers lifted their spirits. As I visited these temples in my mind, bliss swelled in waves that burst like stars being born in my heart. Everything made me happy, whether it was a ray of sun, a flower, a meal, a nap, or a smile. My inner world became more real than the world outside me. Not even the tedium of the hospital procedures or regulations diminished my joy.

At the height of these ecstatic visions, Taz telephoned. He'd thrown Chanter out and was coming to bring us home. Hope flared once again in my heart. Embracing my ripe abdomen, I lay on my side, remembering the acid trip in the dunes when my daughter had been conceived.

Spiraling into visions, I glimpsed immense dragon energies coupled as light and dark, night and day, heaven and earth, swirling in a universe of stars. Male and female emerged out of these cosmic currents, drawn like magnets to exchange and balance. I saw my own microcosmic union with my husband. What did our struggle mean? Why was our marriage so full of suffering? What was the purpose of pain? Why did love hold me prisoner?

Without language for, or understanding of, my internal experience, what I saw inside myself didn't match my outer reality. I felt confused. Enduring the weight of carrying light in darkness, submerged, cast down, I felt stripped of all but my longing for something I had lost. My soul waited like a coal, glowing with secret strength, containing the power of fire, biding its time.

Truths and images surfaced as poetic rhythms pulsed from the source of my being. My mind, usually full of fear and pain, drowned all mystic realizations before they could emerge out of my iceberg being. I didn't realize I was experiencing a descent into the shadow lands of my unconscious. I only sensed that my life was woven of myths, and that divine themes were playing out in the journey of my soul. Even as I experienced myself as the feminine goddess of nature speaking to the masculine god of spirit, I was also myself, speaking to Taz in my heart.

I have made you my world.
You are my ground of being.
I long to cover you with flowers
But you will not relinquish winter.

I offer myself to the seasons of your moods,
But in your bitter heart spring never flows,
Absent summer denies the fullness of love,
And frozen land refuses the golden harvest.

I put paper and pencil aside. I couldn't live without the hope of love. Poetry exposed the truth as bare as a winter tree. No matter where I turned, everything was imperfect, everything held suffering at its core.

Taz stood beside my hospital bed, shyly offering a bouquet of daisies. The moment I saw my husband's handsome face and heard his voice, I forgot myself. I believed again that if I did everything his way, we'd become a real family.

Downstairs, I embraced my son. He clung to me and my heart broke open. Tears of sadness flowed for our separation; tears of joy celebrated our reunion. As we drove away, Taz raved about his latest sculptures, his eyes afire. Didn't he see our tears or did they just not matter to him? Why didn't he just stop the car so we could hold each other for a while? I felt like I was going crazy. How could I make my love big enough to absorb our madness?

When I noticed that Taz was driving to his parents' Granville Street mansion, my tears stopped immediately. Dread quickly replaced grief, but I knew better than to say I did not want to visit them.

We stood at his parents' door: a mad psychedelic artist, a pregnant flower child, and a golden son. My rising fear made the child within me kick her heels. For an instant, I caught a glimpse of what it must be like for my unborn daughter. She must be feeling the pull of gravity and the need to get out of her confinement, but she must also be scared. Until the cervix opens, it must seem like there is no way out.

Taz rang the bell. His mother, an aging bleached blonde with false eyelashes laden with mascara, opened the door. We upset her cool for a moment, but she hid it well.

Touching her garish red lips to my cheek, she said, "Well, what a surprise. You should have let us known you were in town."

I did not remind her that I had telephoned them when I first got into town, but they had made excuses, telling me to call again before I left. Maybe they didn't want to see me, but how could they not want to see their grandson?

His father, dark, wiry, and tense as a coiled spring, kept his hands in his pocket as he grunted a reluctant hello, followed by, "You should have called first. We were watching our favorite TV show."

"My, what a big boy you are," Taz's mother whined at Choo in a loud, surreal voice, as if she were talking to a stuffed animal.

Taz's mother led us into their formal parlor, where we perched on the edge of fragile antique furniture. The TV still blared in the family room down the hall. Taz's father sat by the door, his ear still tuned to the program, making it obvious he hoped we'd leave as soon as possible.

Holding Choo on his knee, Taz brought out pictures of his latest sculptures and passed them to his father, who looked at them without comment and passed them on to his wife.

Unable to watch the replay of the same tense, defensive standoff that had been going on for years, I closed my eyes, trying to escape the feeling that the screams Taz had made when he was a child still echoed through the halls. I knew they reverberated in his heart.

They had burned him with matches when he would not submit to their will. They had thrown him out in the snow, barefoot, clad only in his pajamas, until he fainted from cold. They had starved him and taken away his toys and his pets. Worst of all, his mother would regularly wake him up in the middle of the night, screaming and beating at him. When he was older, they drove him miles from home and left him to find his way back alone in the dark. Each step of the way, he took defiance to another level, daring them to hurt or kill him.

Portraits of Taz in fine silver and inlaid wood frames hung on striped wallpapered walls and covered spindly antique tables. The photos chronicled his childhood and the same sullen expression marked them all.

Taz had told me that they had never bathed him or given him clean clothes except when friends and family visited. Then they would spruce him up and show him off in a fancy velvet outfit. If he misbehaved while their friends were there, he was beaten. When Taz realized that the only time he had power over them was when they had company, he devised infinitely outrageous ways of embarrassing his parents. That strategy drove his mother and father to even more severe punishments.

Taz left home in his teens, creating a rebellious, bohemian lifestyle that devalued everything his parents strove for. All of the pretensions they'd spent a lifetime building up, Taz ridiculed and destroyed. Yet, from time to time, he returned to his family, just as I did. Perhaps he still hoped for love. Perhaps he just needed to return to the source of his pain so that he could leave again.

Holding my own son closely, I wondered how it was that parents could hurt their own children. Vulnerable and weak from my month in the hospital, I could not bear the dark emotions surging between Taz and his parents. I closed my eyes and returned to my hospital dreams, imagining a place beyond the masks of anger, greed and blame, a place where human kindness reigned. Renewed, I opened my eyes and smiled at his mother. Startled, she received the rays of love that sprang spontaneously from my heart and stopped talking mid-sentence. During that brief exchange, I glimpsed that love could be a source of power. If only love could shine like the sun into every situation, I thought with a leap of hope, it could change everything. As this realization dawned, a shaft of sunlight beamed through dark clouds and for a moment the living room was bathed in light. Then the clouds closed over again. The next thing I knew, Taz was arguing with his father.

"I don't know why I bother coming here," Taz yelled. "You don't care about me."

"Come on. Let's get out of here," he ordered, picking up a startled Choo and stomping toward the door.

"Why are we going, Daddy?" Choo asked, but Taz did not answer him.

I followed more slowly, trying to avoid the spiteful words, the daggering eyes, and the faces grimacing like masks of hatred and anger. The moment the three of us stood on the porch, the door slammed.

"Why were they mad at us, Mommy?" Choo asked in confusion.

"Well, they just had a fight, you know, like when you fight with your friends," I said, trying to make him feel better about what had happened.

The cold winter afternoon darkened as we drove through Stanley Park and over the Lion's Gate Bridge toward my parents' home. Taz was fuming. He hit the steering wheel with his fist and when he looked at me, his eyes shot fire and pain.

"Damn them. That's it. That's the last time I'm visiting them. I'm never going there again," he vowed.

I held Choo and whispered into his ear, trying to explain why Taz was fighting with his parents. Then I sang a song, rocking him until his body relaxed.

Once more the drive up the mountain, once more the vision of the enchanted cottage, once more the carved wooden door of my family's home opened. Only this time, my father offered a drink to Taz, my mother complained about how hard it had been to take care of Choo, and my sister Bella watched us from her distant, silent sorrow. For the first time since she was a young child, I felt a surge of love flow out to her. I wanted to know her. I wanted to help her.

"Come with us to Los Angeles," I invited spontaneously. Surprised, she nodded her immediate, silent assent.

Back at the motel, Taz was turned on.

He raved, "What a great idea. She's beautiful. How old is she?"

"Sixteen."

"She must be ready for a lover. We could have a Mormon scene, like with two wives. That'd keep me off the streets. How about that?"

Horrified, I stuttered, "You can't do that. She's my sister."

Taz laughed wildly, sending chills down my spine. Dependent on him, I was afraid to say more.

What had seemed like a beautiful idea had already become another one of Taz's depraved trips. Burdened by anxiety for my sister and the discomfort of my pregnant belly, I couldn't sleep. I had returned to Taz's underworld.

In the morning I tried to talk my sister out of coming with us, but she was already packed. My hopes of a new beginning already crushed, ashamed to tell her the truth of Taz's intentions, I vowed to protect her.

Back in the City of Angels, Taz showed off his turquoise and coral penthouse studio and swept my sister away. Turned on by her adoring enthusiasm, he showed her how to cut metal and weld simple sculptures. Leaving the Sunset Strip cruising and the night trips behind, he stayed home, dancing to his music tapes, grooving with my sister in his black light, psychedelic visionary world.

One night he went too far. He laced Bella's strawberry shortcake with acid. Freaked out by his free-love mind game and the hallucinations, she ran downstairs and threw herself into my arms. She screamed and cried all night long, but she wouldn't tell me what was happening to her.

In the morning, she yelled at me, "How can you stay with him? Why don't you leave?"

Without giving me time to answer, she announced angrily, "I'm going home today."

Gone was the shy, strange, inarticulate wild child, and in her place was a strong young woman who had found the courage to refuse Taz. In finding her voice, she had found herself.

Stunned by her fury, I took her to the airport. After I got her ticket, I tried to hug her, but she pushed me away. She didn't even say goodbye.

 Taz raged, impatient for the birth of our child.

Ignoring all that had happened with Bella, he demanded, "You've got to have this baby. Now! Today! Do something or I'll take you for a ride on my motorcycle. That'll shake your baby out of you."

Scared of what Taz might do, I drank a bottle of castor oil mixed with Seven Up. Soon labor started and by the end of the day the cramps surged in regular cycles. Taz dropped me off at the Rose Hospital in Culver City and split. I was glad to see him go.

The nurses welcomed me and soon I was deep in labor. The doctor, a kind elderly European woman with tissue-soft hands and a gentle, wrinkled face, stayed with me throughout the night, massaging me and covering me with warm blankets until Love was born, soft and fresh from my womb, rosy cheeked, dimpled and plump.

"Love," I whispered. "Welcome, my little Love."

As she slept in my arms, I inhaled her sweetness, feeling the joy of giving and receiving love without fear. This was one child Taz was not going to take away from me.

The next afternoon, Taz and Choo arrived to bring us home. Fragile with fatigue, delicate with joy, I trembled, fearful of returning to his studio. Choo enclosed Love's tiny hand in his own, awed at the wonder of his baby sister, but Taz seemed hard and distant. I hoped he would be kind, but when we reached the studio, Taz announced that a runaway chick was staying upstairs. Never imagining he'd be with another woman when I brought our daughter home, a lightning pain cut through my heart.

"Here? Now?" I stammered in disbelief.

"No hang-ups, that's what I dig," he said with a snide laugh before he stomped upstairs.

Shaking with shock and weakness, I entered my room and lay down on the bed with Love.

"Come on, Choo," I said, and he climbed up and snuggled down beside me.

"Mommy's so tired. She can't put you to bed, so let's cover up and go to sleep."

I stroked his head as he drifted off, the music playing upstairs as tears flowed down my cheeks.

Taz's neglect made an indelible mark upon my spirit, erasing all hope. After that night I dreamed only of escape.

Every day, I repeated my determination, "As soon as I am strong, we'll leave and never come back."

As the days went by, I shut out Taz and his pick-up chicks and turned my attention to my children. Their bright eyes and smiles, glowing with love, kept me going.

Choo took great delight in his baby sister. He loved to watch me bathe her and change her diapers, all the while asking questions about when he was a baby. He also loved to cuddle close when I nursed her. Our eyes mirroring love, we shared tender embraces, sweet snuggling naps, and skin softness. I was fully in love with my children.

When I held Love near my breast, she turned her head toward it, waaed, and rooted around until her rosy mouth fastened onto my nipple. Her strong, sucking pull drew my milk and contracted my womb.

"Oh, Love," I whispered one night, "You're going to be strong and true to yourself. You'll never give yourself to a man like your father."

Clara

When Love and I took off from Palm Springs to return to Los Angeles, a buoyant energy took hold of me. Cruising along, I thought about what I wanted and tried to imagine where I could live. Smiling at my daughter cooing in her basket beside me, I chanted a song, asking questions and giving answers with a rhythmic certainty that amazed me.

What do I need?

A home and a studio.

What do I want?

Bright, sunny rooms, a garden, and nice neighbors.

Where?

West Hollywood – yeah!

I had lived there when we had our art gallery on La Cienega. It was close to the action, the happening boutiques, and Beverly Hills.

When?

I want it right now, today.

Questions with answers. That was a switch. I'd been waiting for answers for a very long time.

Putting off my reunion with Choo, I curved off the freeway onto quiet, empty Sunday streets. Following my inclinations, I drove north along La Cienega, scouting the stores for "For Rent" signs. A few minutes after turning west onto Santa Monica Boulevard, I glimpsed a sign on the street behind Doug Weston's folk-singing hangout, the Troubadour, and pulled over in front of a tiny shop on Nemo Street.

Tucking a bright-eyed, smiling Love securely into my arms, I peered into the tiny storefront and then through expansive windows into two rooms that overlooked a cobbled courtyard driveway. Beyond the courtyard, a small cottage nestled behind thick flowering shrubs. Behind the sheltering avocado tree at the back of the property, I glimpsed a woodworking studio. It was perfect, just what I'd imagined.

Feeling a bit like Alice in Wonderland, I went in the direction indicated by the arrow on the "For Rent" sign. Brushing by bushes and bending under overhanging branches, I tiptoed carefully on carved stepping stones. Beyond the flourishing fragrant herbs, a profusion of spring flowers, a birdbath, and an elf sculpture, I discovered a cottage door. Offering a silent prayer that someone would be home, I knocked.

After a moment, an elderly, white-bearded gentleman appeared and smiled kindly at me.

"Well, hello young lady, or should I say young *ladies*?" he questioned, looking at Love.

"This is Love, and yes, she's a girl," I said, too excited to introduce myself. "Is the studio still for rent?"

"Why, yes it is. We just put up the sign yesterday."

"Well, I want it; I mean, I think I want it. How much is it?" I asked nervously, my fingers crossed behind my back.

"Seventy-five dollars a month."

"Oh, good, I can manage that. Can I live there, I mean, can we live there?"

"I'm sure you can," he laughed, "but don't you want to see it first?"

"Yes, oh yes," I said, stepping aside so he could lead me back along the path. A quick walk through the rooms confirmed my decision. It was perfect.

"I want to rent it right away, like today," I said.

"Well," he laughed, "that might be possible, but I'm not the landlord. I'm Winston, an old friend of the Bellmans. I take care of the place for them. If you'll just wait a minute, I'll give them a call."

I waited impatiently in the courtyard, walking back and forth, praying the studio would be mine. When Winston came out of his cottage, his wide smile told me I was on.

"They're at home. They said to come on up and meet them," he said. "I told them you'd be a nice neighbor."

As I thanked Winston, a marvelous feeling thrilled through me. I had asked for what I wanted and received it. That was new for me. During my years with Taz, my desires had been honed toward turning him into an ideal husband and father, but he always made sure that never came true. I had to let go of him before I could have what I really wanted or needed. It sounded simple now that it was happening, but what were all those years of suffering about? Unable to understand, let alone answer that question, I turned off my mind, turned on the radio, and drove up Beverly Glen.

Full of anticipation, feeling as if I was on the edge of a miracle, I turned down a long gravel drive edged with pampas grass and wildflowers. Feeling as though I'd entered a California dream, I stepped slowly out of the car and looked around. A fountain sparkled in the bricked courtyard entry of a spacious adobe hacienda. Pots of geraniums and nasturtiums edged the patios and sheltered walkways that opened onto lush gardens and orchards. It was the most magnificent property I'd ever seen, but it was also natural, as though the owner's creativity had enhanced nature, rather than diminishing it.

I got an immediate sense of the owners' commitment to the land and their home, followed quickly by a flash of fear and a strong sense of my own unworthiness.

What was I doing here? I must be crazy. Why would people who owned a place like this want to rent their studio to someone like me? Aware of my fatigue, I looked down at my travel-worn clothes: tired jeans, wrinkled white shirt, and cheap flip-flop sandals. I wanted to run away. I was about to follow that impulse when the door opened and an elderly white-haired couple came out to greet us.

When the man held out his hand, I shyly offered mine to his firm grasp and received the welcome of his sparkling, friendly eyes and sweet smile.

"I'm Arnie, and this is my wonderful wife, Clara," he said in a most gentlemanly manner as he looked lovingly at his wife.

"Oh, shush," she giggled as she took my arm with gracious formality and led me toward the house. "I'm so happy to meet you," she said, a faint accent enriching her refined voice. "Please come in."

As I walked through the arched doorway into the living room, my sense of unworthiness increased. I hesitated at the threshold, afraid to place my worn sandals on the rich oriental carpet that graced the polished wood floor.

"Come, my dear," she invited, gently pulling me along.

I followed her in a trance, taking in glorious paintings hanging on pale golden walls, vases of fresh flowers, and views of the garden through arched windows. Clara settled us onto a brightly-pillowed sofa. After making a fuss over Love, Arnie returned to the garden.

"Now, dear, you want to rent the studio. Tell me about yourself," she said, giving me her full attention.

At that moment, the enthusiasm that had carried me this far dissolved like chalk paintings in the rain. As fear overtook me again, I cried within myself, oh, no, not even courage is real, not even enthusiasm lasts. Intimidated by their wealth and the beauty of the home and gardens, I looked down at my hands. Trembling, on the verge of tears,

I could not speak. A moment later, she touched me gently on the shoulder.

"What is it, dear?" she asked, her voice like silk.

I was so afraid she would say no, I couldn't say anything.

"It's all right, my dear. You can tell me," she offered softly.

Reassured, I looked at her again. Feeling the goodness emanating from her, I took a deep breath and plunged in.

"I just left my husband. I need a home and a studio, a place to live and work," I explained, sorrow awakening with the telling of the truth.

"What will you do in the studio, dear?" she asked, her eyes bright with interest.

"Jewelry. Sculpture. I've worked in my husband's studio and I ran our art galleries," I said, gaining courage.

"You're an artist. Oh, how wonderful," she enthused.

I cheered up. Maybe she'd rent the studio to me after all.

"I know I can make a go of it," I assured her.

"Of course you can. We'll be glad to have you there."

Relief surged. The studio was mine.

"Arnie, we have a new tenant," she called through the open patio doors.

"Wonderful. That's wonderful," he called back.

"He's always in his garden," she smiled. "He says he's closer to God in a garden than anywhere else, although I think he's made our home every bit as beautiful as a garden," she said charmingly, surveying her rooms with satisfaction.

Switching to a more conspiratorial tone, she continued, "Good; now that's settled, I'd like to show you something."

Clara rose gracefully and took down an antique inlaid box from a shelf above the fireplace.

"I'm a jewelry designer, too," she said as she carefully took several silver brooches out of the box and set them onto the glass coffee table. Each brooch was a delightfully unique, art nouveau shape with playful spirals.

"I made them in Paris," she said wistfully, "many years ago, at the turn of the century, when I was a young woman like you."

I looked from the jewelry back to Clara, suddenly opening to her full-bodied beauty. An older woman, perhaps in her eighties, Clara's wisdom shone from a face that was exquisitely alive. Her green eyes sparkled with child-like joy. Soft silver curls and wisps of stray hair radiated around her head like an aura, and her glowing skin suggested both vigorous health and contentment. Her pewter-gray, raw silk tunic was gathered at the waist by an intricately woven amethyst woolen cord and graced at the shoulder by a unique antique silver brooch. Large black pearl drops hung from her ears, the perfect complement to the shimmering silver of her attire. I was mystified. Naturally elegant, she was without a doubt the most magical older woman I'd ever seen and yet, lost in my own fear and shyness when I arrived, I had hardly noticed how extraordinary she was. Now I couldn't take my eyes off her.

"This one; I want you to have this one," she said as she held up one of the brooches.

"Me? I couldn't. It's too valuable," I refused, feeling embarrassed and undeserving.

"Nonsense. I want it to be worn by someone like you."

Surprised, I could only repeat her words, "Someone like me?"

"Yes, someone just like you," she said with loving humor as she leaned over and pinned it onto my white shirt.

"Come," she invited, pulling me to my feet and leading me over to a large framed mirror. "Look at how beautiful you are."

When I looked in the mirror, Clara was smiling behind me and the silver pin was shining over my heart, an image so wonderful I vowed to remember it forever.

"Now, let's have tea. Come into my kitchen," she said warmly.

I followed her into a saffron colored room that made me feel as if I was walking into a fairytale. French doors opened to an abundant kitchen garden growing wild around a bubbling fountain. Glowing beams of sunlight shone through arched stained glass windows, illuminating polished wood counters and floors with living color. A fragrance woven of flowers, herbs, fruit, and spices filled the room. I gasped involuntarily, breathing the happiness of this beautiful home into my being and making it a part of me forever.

Clara bounced lightly, almost dancing, as she placed a copper kettle on the golden-yellow enameled stove and lit the gas. As eagerly impressionable as my infant daughter, I watched her choose unique, delicate cups from a cupboard overflowing with a rich assortment of crockery, count out tiny silver spoons from a drawer, and, humming quietly to herself, collect honey and cream from the pantry. She placed everything she had gathered on a silver tray and added white linen napkins, a vase of wildflowers, and homemade chocolate chip cookies.

This was real living love. I could see it. I could feel it. Awed by the beauty and love that flowed into everything she touched, I gave thanks for the opportunity to be in the company of someone so naturally happy. At the same time, I tried to imagine what it might be like to have been raised in a home like this.

"Why don't you take this tray outside, dear, and set the table," she suggested, startling me out of my daydream. "I'd love to hold your daughter for a moment."

Happy to help out and remembering her example, I carried the tray outside, carefully setting it down before I laid the table, all the while imagining that love was pouring out of me into everything I touched. Clara watched me through the door as she bounced Love in her arms, an approving, motherly smile lighting up her face.

Oh, if only I'd had a mother like Clara, I thought, aware of a new kind of pain in my heart. The longing that had filled me for years merged with joy as I realized that someday, I too could have a home like this. I touched the silver pin, hoping her magic would rub off on me.

When I came back into the kitchen, she motioned for me to sit in a wicker chair and then she returned Love to my arms.

Suddenly, as though she had just made up her mind about something, she pulled another chair over and placed it in front of me. Sitting down, she looked at me for a moment with her startlingly clear, sea-green eyes.

"I wasn't always as fortunate as this, you know. I was just like you, an innocent young woman who trusted the wrong man. I went through some very hard times."

Touched that she had confided in me, and curious to hear what had happened to her, I leaned forward, waiting for her to continue.

"What happened?" I said, unable to wait a moment longer.

"I was born in Iceland, and I never thought I'd leave the Pure Land, but when a handsome young Frenchman came to Reykjavik and proposed to me, I said yes because I didn't know how to say no. He took me to Paris. I hardly spoke French, and the charming man who courted me was not a kind or friendly husband. It was very difficult. I left him and went out on my own after my daughter was born," she said wistfully, and then added with a hint of pride, "and that wasn't easy to do at the turn of the century."

"What did you do?"

"I sold my jewelry to pay the rent for a year on a small room for my daughter and me. Then I took my wedding silver and the traditional golden belt that my grandmother had given me and had them melted down and worked into thin sheets. It may sound romantic now, but at the time it was pretty scary. With simple cutters and files, I fashioned silver and gold brooches and took them first to outdoor markets and then to small shops." She laughed, "Eventually, I got the courage to take them to the design houses and managed to make a comfortable living."

"Then I met Arnie. I was playing with my daughter in the park near the Louvre. He came over and watched us for a while. Soon we were all playing together."

She sighed, closing her eyes for a moment as she whispered, "He was so handsome and charming and kind."

Then her amazing sea-green eyes were shining on me again and she was laughing like a young girl as she said, "He was a set designer on holiday in Paris after making a movie. The next thing I knew, he proposed and I said yes, and we were married here in Hollywood. I came to this house as his bride and I have been here ever since."

She looked around with pleasure at her beautiful home before she sighed again, "We've had a very good life."

"Did you and Arnie have children?"

"Yes, a son and another daughter. All three are grown and married now, and we have five grandchildren. Life has been very good to me since I left my first husband. His cruelty to me was one thing, but I couldn't let him hurt my daughter."

"I know what you mean. I feel like I have to be strong for her," I said, looking at Love.

"You're very strong, dear," she said before she turned off the whistling kettle and poured the boiling water into a hand painted floral teapot.

"Now, let's call Arnie and have our tea."

As we sat on the patio surrounded by the abundant kitchen garden, the fountain chuckling at our feet, Arnie chatted about his beloved garden and Clara told stories about their life together.

"I love it here," I murmured, contentedly sipping herbal tea and munching cookies. "It's so beautiful, a world all its own."

"Well, you must come again," Arnie invited warmly, beaming his welcome.

"Arnie was always very good at making sets," she teased her husband lovingly, rumpling his curly white hair.

"Well, I must go," I said, picking up Love. "Thank you so much for renting the studio to me. I promise I'll be a good tenant."

Clara and Arnie walked me to my car.

"Bless. Bless." Clara said, holding both my hands in her tissue soft hands. "That's how they say goodbye and hello in Iceland, so you never really say goodbye."

Driving away, I felt I had been blessed by a fairy godmother. I'd finally met a woman I admired. Even more, I felt inspired by her story. If she'd found her way to happiness, so could I, and that was a gift even greater than the silver brooch.

Silver Dreams

I couldn't believe it. Within hours of leaving Palm Springs, I had a home and a studio. In three days my life had turned around, all because I'd finally got mad at my husband. Why did I put up with him for so long? I should have thrown a sewing machine at him a long time ago. Remembering his shocked expression, I laughed out loud. I'd finally done something that surprised him.

As I neared Sunset Boulevard, I wondered what to do. I wanted to see Choo. Should I turn right and head toward Taz's Santa Monica studio, or turn left and go to a motel for the night? Although I had the key to my new home, all of my things were at Taz's. If I went there to get my stuff, it would be too late to make it back to Nemo Street and settle in for the night. With new expenses on the horizon, staying in a motel seemed like a waste of money. There was only one reasonable option, spending one last night at Taz's, but the idea scared me. My longing to see my son finally tempered my fear, and I turned toward Santa Monica. Strange, even though we'd been married for years, I never thought of his studio as my home.

Lights blazed on Taz's rooftop, but the first floor was dark. I parked my car around the corner so he wouldn't know I was there. My heart pounding, I walked toward the front door, then tiptoed up the stairs. Thankfully, Taz's door was shut and I was able to creep into my room without him hearing me. Even as I settled myself into bed with Love, I couldn't turn off my mind. I kept thinking about my son upstairs and how much I wanted to see him.

Trembling, I reasoned with myself. Go to sleep. Taz doesn't know you're here. You can get all your things together in the morning and leave, and you won't ever have to stay here again. You have your own studio now. You have your own home.

Searching for relief, I forced my mind to remember the orange grove. Yearning for love, my spirit flew free and danced with the falling blossoms until I fell asleep.

The next morning, still cocooned in early morning nursing dreams, I heard Taz's footsteps approaching my room.

"You back already?" he mocked with sarcastic laughter.

When I opened my eyes, I didn't see the noble Taz who looked as if he should be wearing a Roman toga and a wreath on his head. I didn't see the handsome Taz whose fine features hinted at seductive arrogance. I didn't see the Taz whose charisma had enchanted me for so long, but instead some ravaged, night-tripping, drugged-out stranger. For sure, this Taz had been around for a while, but I'd kept my fantasy version of him intact, refusing to see how his indulgent life had coarsened and drained him. Two days away had cleared my vision. I noticed black circles under his red eyes and a sickly yellow undertone to his smooth olive complexion that enhanced his sad fatigue, making him look much older than his thirty-three years.

For a moment, I wondered if my departure had made him suffer and felt the impulse to comfort him, but I pulled myself back. This was not the time to fool myself into imagining I was the cause of his suffering.

"I knew you wouldn't be gone long," he smirked.

Bob Dylan's lyric played through my mind.

*"How many times can a man look away
and pretend that he just doesn't see...?"*

I couldn't look at his face. I turned away.

*"...and how many years must some people exist
before they're allowed to be free...?"*

"I found my own studio. I'm moving in today," I said as I picked up Love and turned my back on him.

A moment of silence seemed to go on forever.

"Then split," he shouted, "and don't come back!" he added before he stomped upstairs.

Shaking, I hugged my daughter fiercely.

A few minutes later, Choo ran in and threw his arms around me. I could hardly bear the chasm between how things were and how I knew they could be. Painfully aware of his confusion, I tried to explain what was happening.

"Choo, sweetheart. You have two homes now; one with your Dad and one with us and you can visit us anytime you want. We won't be far away."

My son struggled with tears as he climbed on the bed and snuggled with his baby sister. I lay down beside him, holding him, reassuring him that somehow everything was going to be okay.

"...the answer, my friend, is blowin' in the wind..."

Later, I went upstairs to get some of my things. When I looked at the chaos in Taz's studio, another surge of rage overwhelmed me. Without hesitation, I pulled off my wedding ring, turned on the acetylene torch and melted it into a golden ball.

Taz was soaking in the hot tub on the deck. I walked outside and threw the metal ball at him.

The golden missile hit him in the chest and dropped into the water. "What was that?" he asked, confused.

"That was my wedding ring."

"Jeez, what did you do that for? I made that for you."

"Well, I just unmade it. Our marriage is over, finished. I never want you to think for a moment we'll ever be together again."

Downstairs again, I hugged my son, trying to give him all my love in one embrace. Tickling him, I called him by his nickname, trying to cheer him up.

"Choo, Choo, Chugga Choo, Choo, fast train chugging on the track, you'll come chugging to see me and we'll do fun things," I promised.

Unable to stop his giggles, he asked questions about where our new home was, what it was like, and where we would sleep. Finally he was satisfied and he did his best to help me pack.

When it was time for me to leave, he took my hand in a solemn, courtly manner and walked me to my car. An hour later, after making slow progress through rush hour traffic, I pulled into the driveway on Nemo Street.

"Love, we made it. We're home."

Bursting with happiness, I opened the door and breathed in the promise of the empty rooms that made me feel like the first day of school when fresh new notebooks made me want to do everything perfectly.

I unpacked a few things before settling on the mattress to nurse Love. The swish of cars passing by pulsed like ocean waves. Leafy light filtered through the windows and birds sang as they fluttered through the trees. Love's suckling sounds and our soft synchronized breathing lulled me into a dreamland where petals fell with velvet caresses.

Some time later, I was startled out of my reverie by my new neighbor, Winston, calling through the open window.

"Hi. Came by to see if you needed anything."

"Guess I fell asleep. It's been a long day," I yawned sleepily.

"Come on over for a sandwich and a hot cup of cocoa. A young mother like you needs to eat something."

Picking up Love, I followed him across the drive and into a cozy kitchen filled with hanging plants and piles of books. A retired English teacher, he spent most of his time gardening and reading. Winston beamed good will while I munched a toasted cheese sandwich and sipped cocoa. He could see I was too tired to talk, so he shooed me back across the courtyard as soon as I was finished. Appreciative of my friendly neighbor, I thanked him and said good night.

The next morning, I celebrated my new life with a pancake breakfast at Denny's Restaurant on La Cienega. When I returned to the studio, I didn't know where to start or how I was going to decorate my studio, so I lay down on the mattress to nurse Love and slipped easily into a new dream where blossoms fell in silvery moonlight. Suddenly I came out of my trance. Silver? I looked at Clara's pin.

"Silver! That's it. Come on, lovely Love. Let's go buy silver paint."

Lining up dozens of spray paint cans on the store counter, I wondered if anyone had ever bought this much silver paint at one time. The salesman offered a discount and easy returns. I laughed, thinking I would probably need more, and I did. I made two more trips to the paint store before the job was done.

After setting up Love's bassinet in Winston's garden, I sprayed silver paint all day, covering the ceiling, the walls, and the floor. I sprayed till my thumbs ached. I didn't have much, but the silver made everything look beautiful.

That night, the silver carried me deeper into a magic place where moonlight shimmered on sheltering pines and petals fell gently through the air. The blossoming orange groves had merged with the pine trees on San Jacinto. A new landscape had birthed within me.

The next day I went on a shopping spree, buying decorative bricks and wooden doors at a lumberyard, then tools and equipment at hardware stores.

After spraying all the bricks a brilliant turquoise, I stacked them into four towers and laid two silver-sprayed doors down on top of them, creating instant worktables that overlooked the garden. Then I put a row of metal shelves against the wall opposite the tables. After spraying the shelves silver, I set out all the materials and equipment I'd bought for my studio – drills, hammers, cutters, paints, plastics, scissors, heat gun, welding rods, and an acetylene torch. In a corner of one of the worktables, I formed a sandbox for casting plastic shapes.

Over the next couple of days, I concentrated on my living space. Silver and blue paint transformed a garage sale cabinet into a kitchen counter for a hot plate and blender, shelves for dishes and cups, and storage for food supplies in the drawers below. Hand woven natural-cotton curtains closed off the bedroom and living areas from the store and the studio. Bricks and doors provided a foundation for my mattress, and when covered with striped Guatemalan blankets and velvet pillows, my bed doubled as a sofa during the day. I placed a crib, another garage sale find, in front of the window so Love could enjoy the sunlight and the garden during the day.

Winston watched all the goings-on with amazement. He helped out whenever I needed assistance and offered the use of his garden sink for Love's daily bath. My other neighbors, Holly and Brit, were a sophisticated couple who owned the woodworking shop in the barn. They swooshed in early in the morning or late at night in their matching Mustang convertibles to check on their employees and supervise the finished products.

Sometimes they offered a brief wave as they flashed by, but they never stopped to talk.

By the end of the week, I was adding the finishing touches to my new home. Placing Clara's silver pin and my favorite photos of the children carefully against a vase of flowers on the shelf above my bed, I created a simple altar that represented my aspirations. One evening I strung crystal beads from necklaces gathered at garage sales and wove them into a mobile to hang over Love's crib. After making a few decorative pillows for my bed, I couldn't think of anything else to do, so I slowed down and savored the results of my creative whirlwind.

At last, I was myself, living love.

My first visitor was Clara. Dressed in a gray chiffon tea dress and wearing a sweeping straw hat that barely contained her silvery wisps of hair, she stepped lightly over the threshold into my studio. Surprised and delighted, I felt as though a fairy godmother had entered my silver world.

"Look what you have done! How wonderful," she complimented.

"You like it?" I asked shyly. "See how the silver reflects all the colors?"

"Oh, yes, who would have thought of silver paint, but yes, this is very nice."

She walked into the studio and looked around.

"So organized, so quickly. You are very fast."

"Once I thought of the silver, everything just came together," I explained happily, pleased that she approved.

Clara took Love in her arms and sat down on my bed.

"You couldn't imagine this when you wanted to leave, could you?" she said with a smile.

"No," I answered. "If I'd known I could do this, I would have left a long time ago."

"Such a good thing you have done, and look at your daughter. See how sweetly she smiles. She's happy here."

"We're both happy here. Thanks for renting me the studio."

Clara stayed a while. I showed her some of the jewelry I'd made for myself when I was with Taz. When she admired a pair of bronze earrings, I gave them to her.

As she waved goodbye, I thought, if she can create a beautiful life, so can I.

On the weekend, Taz came over to drop Choo off.

Blown away by my silver studio, he hid surprise with an aggressive challenge, "So, how are you going to make a living?"

"Don't know yet," I said, snuggling Choo in my arms.

"Making something good is hard enough, but selling it is harder," he warned.

"I'll be fine," I said.

How's your money holding out?" he asked with a hint of concern.

"I've got enough, more than enough, of everything," I answered. "You don't have to worry about me."

"Worry about you? Hah! You've got to be kidding. I'm enjoying not worrying about you for a change," he said defensively.

He looked around my home, hung around for a while as if he wished he could stay, then left quickly as if he were late for an appointment.

I made a promise to myself as I watched him drive away. No way would I ever get hooked up with him again. I'd make it on my own if it was the last thing I ever did. I felt that if I repeated these words, they would have to come true.

Paper Clothes

When I went to Taz's studio to pick up the rest of my things, my sewing machine was still lying on its side, looking sadly bent and broken. I picked it up, wondering if it could be fixed.

"Might as well throw it away. It'll never work again," Taz proclaimed.

"Yes, it will. I'll get it repaired," I insisted, rescuing it.

The next morning, I rose with the morning glories, rejoicing that I no longer needed to sleep like some abandoned concubine underneath Taz's studio, wondering how late he'd be out, hearing footsteps and the voices in the early morning when he staggered upstairs with his latest new-found friends. I had claimed my own life.

Driving down Wilshire, looking for a sewing machine repair shop, I passed a store with a big banner draped across the window announcing the opening of the Judith Brewer Paper Boutique. Excited, I swung into a parking spot to take a closer look.

Paper clothes! Far out!

When I peeked in the open door, a tall young woman greeted me warmly. Beautifully groomed, with fashionable blonde hair brushed sleekly back from a dramatic model's face, she glowed with creative vitality.

"Hi. I'm Judith. Come on in. We're still setting up. but you can take a look around. We'll be open in a few days," she chattered, gesturing with her manicured fingers.

I wandered around for a few minutes, listening to Judith direct her helpers as I checked out the scene. With an air of confidence and command, Judith was obviously someone who knew how to make things happen. She didn't have any trouble telling people what she wanted them to do.

Simply styled paper dresses hung on circular racks and in closets on either side of a central display table displaying bikinis and underwear. A few far-out paper and plastic outfits were featured, but as cool as they were, most women wouldn't wear them. Wild fashion blow-ups hanging at erratic angles completed the décor.

"Paper clothes are the latest thing. I came up with the idea when I was getting my degree in UCLA. Think about it. How would you like never to have to wash clothes again? Think of all the time you'd save," Judith raved, clearly passionate about her revolutionary fashion ideas.

After looking at the price tags, I quickly decided disposable clothes were out of my price range, even though I admired the way Judith looked in her paper dress.

"That's a great idea," I enthused, touching the panties and bras, thinking a nursing mother would have to throw away a lot of clothes. The paper was amazingly soft and flexible.

"Aren't these bikinis cute, and they don't fall apart when you swim," she laughed. "You want to be noticed when you wear paper clothes, but not to that extent."

I stopped looking at the clothes and watched her show off her creations. Here was one woman who was making her dreams come true. Just as I was wishing I were more like her, an idea burst in my mind.

"I don't see any jewelry," I said, looking around. "I make jewelry. See these earrings?"

Trembling, I brushed my long black hair aside. It was hard for me to assert myself, but flower power was moving me along.

"Interesting. They might work," she said as she touched them, her designer's mind clearly considering the possibilities.

Turned on by her passionate approach to salesmanship, I decided to tempt her with my jewelry.

"They're completely unique designs. I'm using new materials that no one has ever seen before. That's what you need to show off your paper clothes," I enthused, aware of a strong feeling like a survival instinct with a creative edge that was building up inside me.

"They are different. Fresh and new – just the look we want for paper clothes. When can you bring some by?"

"Tomorrow afternoon," I promised, wondering how I dared say such a thing.

"Good. We need big bold earrings, lots of them, and bracelets, the bigger the better. We'll feature your work, so make as many pieces as you can."

My silver studio was ready for its virgin voyage. The shelves were full of earring fixtures, links of chain, fasteners, plastics, and paints waiting for creative inspiration. I didn't have time to think or plan, so I jumped right in. Working instinctively, I cut thin clear plastic into strips. Next, holding several layers of the strips together, I fused them with the heat gun, shaping them into bracelets and earrings. Then I burned irregular shapes through the layers. After spraying several layers of different iridescent colors on the bracelets, I rubbed the surface and luminous violet, emerald, indigo and turquoise blends appeared. Two weeks after a flash of anger had set me free, I was making what I called "thermoplastic spontaneous jewelry" for a boutique in

Beverly Hills. The broken sewing machine had led me to this opportunity. Far out!

Later that night, I fell asleep dreaming of iridescent waves, happiness bubbling like a fountain of light. As soon as I awoke, I couldn't wait to see what I'd made. Were they as good in the light of day? Yes! They were great!

"Love, this is our lucky day," I sang as I bathed and dressed her.

Shower. Dress. Pack the jewelry. Blend a quick breakfast with milk, bananas, and protein powder.

"Let's go!"

Eager and scared, I crossed the threshold into Judith's store, carrying Love in one arm and my jewelry in the other. The room was packed with photographers and a TV crew. A stunning six-foot model wearing a paper dress looked like she had stepped out of a James Bond movie. When I opened my bag and showered the jewelry on the table, everyone crowded around.

"Far out."

"Cool."

"Beautiful."

The model chose the longest earrings she could find, and slid several bracelets up each arm.

"Yes! Yes!" Judith exclaimed enthusiastically.

My first pieces of jewelry were photographed for the Los Angeles Times, Women's Wear Daily, Vogue, and Harper's Bazaar, and featured on TV.

"We need more for our Friday opening," Judith said, "Can you do it? Can I count on you?"

I nodded my head. I didn't know how I was going to do it, but I wasn't going to say no.

"Make sure you're here before six. Get a baby-sitter. Dress up," she commanded before she turned back to the models and photographers.

The next day, I drove into central L.A. to buy jewelry fixings, paint, and plastics. The materials themselves were so beautiful and malleable, they almost told me what to do with them. Night after night, I played with the materials, fusing layers, burning holes, shaping bracelets and earrings, and blending colors. The more I played, the freer and wilder the designs got. Shimmering like iridescent glass, they looked like artifacts from some ancient underwater civilization. I was on to something.

Late Friday afternoon, I turned off the flow of creativity and packed up the jewelry. I dressed up in one of my own creations – blue velvet capri pants and a matching silk-lined jacket that had been inspired by Gainsborough's Blue Boy painting that hung in my parents' house. Leaving Love with Winston for a couple of hours, I felt ready to take on the world.

Judith's store was a hive of frenzied activity and chic chatter. I stood in the doorway for a few moments, not knowing what to do. Judith caught sight of me and pulled me into the action. Swept up in her whirlwind, I dressed Judith, her staff, and the models with the jewelry and displayed the rest in the jewelry cases.

Once my job was done, I stood in the back, watching the TV cameramen and musicians set up their equipment. Models and staff scurried around. Guests poured in. Waiters served champagne. Soon the store was so packed you couldn't see the clothes. As the shrill voices of glamorous fashion icons competed with raucous rock music, I reached sensory overload. My breasts swelled with milk. It was time to go home.

The next time Clara came by, I showed her the iridescent, thermoplastic jewelry I'd made to go with the paper clothes.

"This is very beautiful," she said.

After putting on her reading glasses so she could take a closer look at the bracelet in her hand, she examined it carefully.

While she looked at my work, I admired her fine, embroidered silk caftan that she had folded and pinned with a yellow-gold and amber brooch.

"How did you think of this, my dear?" she asked, startling me.

"I don't know. It just happened. One thing led to another. Everything's happening so fast. It's like being on a roller coaster," I gushed, still on overload.

"So, your life is opening up now that you're living your dreams."

"Yes, yes, it is, and it's wonderful," I enthused.

"This is good. God is taking good care of you," she mused approvingly.

I couldn't figure out what it was about Clara that made me feel so good. She used simple words and phrases, but the way she spoke her words affected me deeply. Something rare and wonderful emanated from her, a radiance that made me feel as if I had been bathed in love. I always felt she saw the real me, and like the sun, she encouraged my blossoming.

Jump Suits
& Silver Boots

Eager to experiment with designer fabric remnants I'd picked up in downtown Los Angeles, I set up a cutting table in the little shop in the front of my studio. Paper fashions were a fun idea, but I wanted soft comfortable clothes that let me move in a natural way when I was working and nursing. Stretch fabrics were the latest fad, but the designers weren't fulfilling the potential of the fabric. Ideas perking in my brain, I went to see Genie the Tailor. I'd seen her ad in the Free Press and figured she'd be the one to help me out.

"Hey, whatcha want? I'm busy," she spat out impatiently when she opened her apartment door.

Sandy hair pulled back from her sallow face, with wrinkled conservative clothes hanging on her pale, skinny body, Genie was no advertisement for the exotic rock star clothes hanging around her messy apartment.

Shaken by this outburst from this hard Hollywood chick, I could only say, "I want a jump suit."

"Come on in then, but make it fast. Put that baby over there," she ordered, "I don't have time to waste."

While I was laying Love carefully on the sofa, Genie picked up the length of lime-green stretch fabric I'd brought with me.

"I want to stretch the fabric, pull it around the body like this, all in one piece, with only one seam down the middle," I said, taking the fabric from her and draping it around me.

"Okay, okay, I've got it," she said, grabbing the fabric back and pulling it roughly around me.

"I can't believe I'm doing this when I'm working non-stop for the Iron Butterfly," she complained, shushing me when I tried to open my mouth.

"You need a seamstress, not a designer. You already know what you want. Tell you what, I'll make you one jump suit. I like your idea of stretching the fabric around the leg and waist. Hmmm, only one seam. That'll look stunning with a zipper down the front."

As she took my measurements, Genie pushed me this way and that, pinching me as she turned me around.

"Eric'll want a jump suit for the Iron Butterfly performances. He'll dig a fresh new look. Hmmm, great bracelet." She paused for a moment as she took one of my iridescent bangles in her hand and turned it around.

"I make them for the Paper Clothes store in Beverly Hills," I managed to say.

"Cool. Leave the fabric with me and I'll call you when it's ready," she said, barely giving me time to pick up Love and the rest of the fabric before she pushed me out the door. "I have a deadline with the Byrds. Your outfit is small fry, little lady."

Relieved to be out of Genie's weird scene, refusing to let her cynical put-downs spoil my excitement, I walked to my car, remembering the games I'd played as a child. In the early mornings, eyes closed, dozing in bed, I'd imagine myself standing inside a golden light. When I thought of rainbows, sunsets, or flowers, a dress woven of their colors would form around me. It was time to make my dreams real, so I headed down Melrose to Carlos's Dress Shop. Maria, his wife, had made the blue velvet pantsuit to my design. I felt sure I could talk her into making a few new outfits I could use for samples.

The shop was empty, but I found Maria hunched over her sewing machine in the workroom in the back. She was only a few years older than I was, but her unkempt bleached hair and missing teeth made her appear middle-aged. Her husband, Carlos, kept her busy night and day, seven days a week, sewing custom clothes for rich women. Toiling in submissive fear while Carlos preened around town gathering clients, Maria was afraid to stand up to him because he threatened to send her back to Brazil.

Her face lit up when she saw Love.

"A daughter. How beautiful! Oh, look at her beautiful little fingers and her beautiful little feet," she sighed. "I want a baby, but Carlos says no, babies take too much time. Oh, look at her dimples. How sweet she is."

Maria held Love while I draped my fabrics and explained my ideas. I told her I wanted to display samples in my shop so clients could order them in the fabric of their choice.

Maria's face lit up.

"We be partners, you and me, silent partners. Ssssh. We never want Carlos find out. Okay?"

We agreed that I'd take the measurements and cut the fabric. Maria promised to make the samples and sew the outfits to order. Caught up in creativity, her face shining with joy, Maria almost looked young again.

"These better than Carlos. We have our own business. I sew for you and one day we have our own store and I leave Carlos."

Her eyes gleamed as she imagined outwitting him.

"I sew. He take everything. I have no money for teeth, no money for hair, no money to leave. We make our own money, eh?"

On the way home, I pulled into the little park where Melrose triangles into Santa Monica.

"What a day. Wow, Love. We're on our way."

I held her in my lap on the playground swing.

"I'm going to design the most beautiful, comfortable, far out clothes, and I'm going to make the prettiest little dresses for you," I promised my daughter, happiness flowing through me like a river of joy.

Just then a longhaired freak wearing black jeans and a black bomber jacket bounded into the park and right up to us.

"Hi. I was at a party at your Berkeley Street studio. Frank Zappa, Mothers of Invention," he said with humorous warmth.

I looked into his wild piercing eyes hooded by bushy black brows, thinking he looked familiar, and said, "Hi" shyly, not knowing what else to say to this wild guy.

"Wowie zowie. That was some party! Acid punch for the in-crowd of the far-out. Outta sight black light. A happening! I remember seeing you sleeping with your children on that airplane wing sofa."

Zappa punched his lines out, making excessively expressive faces to demonstrate his comments. His merry face peered out of a black beard, a mustache drooping under his gargantuan nose. He was a living antidote to our culture. A drop of him changed everything.

At ease now, I laughed at his witty, pop culture cool.

"Hey. I've heard your latest album, 'Freak Out'. It's really happening!"

"That's where it's at, baby. You got it. Hotcha!"

I watched him play on the swings and the slides. Like a kid, he had a light, fun-filled touch, but a serious message.

As he was walking out of the park, he suddenly jumped up on the wall and screamed, "Good vibes! Dig it, Flower Child!"

"Zappa Happy!" I yelled back at him.

After he left, I lay on the grass with Love, basking in the sunshine.

"Oh, Love," I said, "I am a flower child. Look at me, I'm dreaming my dreams like all the rest of them, making costumes, wanting to be someone new."

I'd heard about Zappa. I knew he'd managed to find a way to live in both worlds. A Harvard grad, he looked like the wildest hippie going, even though he was a true-blue family man who loved good fun. He never took drugs or drank alcohol. Brilliantly creative, he saw through the culture but he didn't sell his soul. If only Taz had Zappa's morality and discipline, we could have had a wonderful life together. There was no telling what Taz could have accomplished, but Taz destroyed as much he created.

I got up off the grass and left my thoughts of Taz behind as I carried Love to the car. Happiness filled my heart as I headed back to my studio and my own life.

A few days later, I drove over to Genie's to try on the jump suit.

After zipping up the front and feeling the lime-green stretch fabric curve softly around my body, I slipped on silver knee-high leather boots. Iridescent earrings gleamed like stars in my long black hair. I stared at myself. A blue velvet suit for parties was one thing, but the idea of running around dressed like this blew my mind.

Genie talked at high speed.

"Far out. Faaarrr out. You are where it's at! You can sell these jump suits and make separates too, stretch-fitted tops and bell-bottoms. Everyone will want them."

"But how can I sell them? Only a few people see my shop."

"Put an ad in the Free Press. Design catchy artwork. I'll bring Eric over to help you get started, but it's not a favor. He'll thank me for turning him on to a fresh look. Once he's got a jump suit, the rest of the Butterfly will want them, then their fans."

"Thanks, thanks a lot," I said and hugged her impulsively.

Genie pushed me away, embarrassed, talking fast.

"Okay. Okay. I dig seeing happening people in cool clothes, and the Butterfly like to be first. They pay me for that. Now get that baby out of here."

Stunned, I couldn't respond.

"I hate babies. Don't bring your kid next time," she ordered, making sure I got the message loud and clear.

There won't be a next time," I said.

Out on the street, I was glad my mirrored sunglasses protected me from eyes that seemed to be looking at me from all directions. Free from the resistance of jeans, the jump suit made me want to dance.

"Who's tripping down the streets of the city,
smiling at everybody she sees...?"

Plump, bald Carlos walked in when I was showing Maria the jump suit. Sporting a dapper pinstriped suit, twisting his mustache, he stepped back, whistled and twirled his cane.

"Wow. Where'd you get that outfit?"

"Designed it myself," I boasted, openly proud.

"Very good. Very good," He said as he walked slowly around me, checking it out. "I can sell these for you. Come and work for me."

"No, thanks. I'm going to open my own boutique," I announced proudly.

Having said it out loud, I felt like I'd have to make my boast come true.

After Carlos left, Maria showed me the jump suits and dresses she had finished.

"Wow. You're fast," I complimented her.

"Fast. That's me. We're going to make clothes and sell them and we're going to make a lot of money. Yes?"

"Yes," I agreed, matching her enthusiasm. "Yes, we are."

It was time to make the little shop in the front of my studio into a happening store. I hung the outfits Maria had made on silver hangers suspended on clear fishing line from hooks on the ceiling. Then I clipped earrings, necklaces and bracelets onto the hangers. After pinning the rest of the jewelry on the silver-sprayed pin-boards I had screwed onto the walls, the effect, especially at night, was startlingly beautiful. The slightest breeze would make the delicate leaves of the sparkling mylar earrings and necklaces twinkle as the clothes turned slowly on their silver hangers.

I played around with ideas for a Free Press ad. Remembering how cool Frank Zappa was, I penned a catch line, "Clothes for a World of Be-Ins, Love-Ins, Freak-Outs, and Freedom". Laughing with delight, one idea leading to another, I made a little drawing composed of an eye containing a yin-yang symbol in the pupil. Then I wove decorative vines and flowers around my name, address, and phone number.

The day the ad came out, the telephone started ringing. Customers started visiting my shop and placing orders. I was in business.

A couple of weeks after I picked up the jump suit, Genie dropped by my Nemo Street studio with Eric, the guitarist from the Iron Butterfly.

Princely handsome, his smooth brown hair waving over his shoulders, Eric raved, "Dig this place. Far out."

Eric wanted to see my jump suit in action, so I demonstrated the freedom of movement the stretch fabric offered. I sat cross-legged. I bent over. I danced around, and then I let him feel how soft and flexible the stretch fabric was.

"Wow. You're right, Genie. A stretch fabric jump suit would be cool," he said, enthusiastically.

"What color do you want?" I asked.

Eric knew exactly what he wanted.

"Blue, I want it bright blue. Make it hug the body in the legs and hips, but I want it looser around the waist, so I can move freely. No fabric sleeves, just straps over the shoulder. I'll wear it over a white cotton peasant shirt, you know, the ones without a collar."

"Cool. I can make it so you don't have to have a zipper," I suggested, finding it hard to believe Genie was taking a back seat in our negotiations.

"Yeah, I can pull it on," he agreed. "Groovy."

After taking Eric's measurements, I told him to come back in a week, but he didn't seem ready to leave. He pranced around my studio, picking up things and looking at them, humming songs, and asking me questions about my work.

He invited me to come with them to Malibu, but when I got to the car and saw his stoned friends lolling around wasted in the back of the Rolls, I waved goodbye to them instead. I didn't understand why the stars of psychedelic rock scene thought that the ultimate cool was to indulge in as much acid, pot, drugs, alcohol, and sex as they could, and blow their way out of the square universe.

My jump suits would soon be jumping at the rock shows. That was good enough for me.

Clara's next visit was perfectly timed. It was fun to watch her expression when she saw me wearing the stretch jump suit and silver boots.

"Every time I visit, you're a new person," she laughed as she walked around me. "How many persons are inside of you?" she said, poking my chest in fun.

I laughed with happiness. Clara always made me feel good about myself.

"You're the most interesting person in the universe," she continued. "Never forget that. I never forget I am the most interesting person, to me. What do you think about that?"

Surprised by a new thought form that reshaped my view of the world in an instant, I said, "How could I be the most interesting person? I always think everyone else is more interesting."

"Only because you have only just begun to discover the treasures inside you," she interjected with a smile.

"You're more interesting to me," I continued. "Look at all your beautiful clothes. You have many people inside of you, too. You always look like a queen of some distant magical land," I said, admiring her blue-green shot-silk tunic with a matching shawl that draped casually over her shoulder.

"Queen of Arnie's magical land, you mean," she laughed with gentle pleasure. "You see, I lived in Paris, where fashion creativity is a way of life. It's my play. I love the beautiful fabrics and the colors," she murmured, with a far-away look. "It gives me something fun to do."

"How can I think I'm the most interesting person in the universe," I asked, "when everyone does so much better than me."

"Well, my dear, it's time to change that attitude. You do very well, better than you think," she declared strongly. "Look at what's inside of you. You'll never find out who you are if you don't bring yourself out of yourself. See, even your bad husband was a friend. You wouldn't be doing this if he didn't make you leave him. God is a mystery, no?"

"God is a mystery, yes!" I agreed, and we laughed together.

The first time Taz saw me wearing the stretch jump suit and silver boots, his eyes popped wide open, and I had to turn away and fuss with Love to keep from laughing. Now that I was in my own scene, I saw Taz as he was, human, imperfect, and a most undesirable husband and father. I found it hard to believe I had infused him with God-like charisma and power and made myself a slave to his will. I couldn't help wondering why I preferred longing for something to having something real. If I wanted to have a loving family, why didn't I have the good sense to find a good husband and father? Whenever I tried to see beyond the confusion I was met with an impenetrable wall of darkness.

Our relationship took a new turn as his put-downs switched to surprised approval. Every time he visited, he examined my latest creations, sometimes offering technical advice. He always asked me what was happening in my life, but I never asked about his.

One Saturday night, as the Troubadour crowds were filling up the parking spaces on Nemo Street, two older white-haired men peered in the shop window. I watched them talking and pointing at the dress and jewelry samples twirling on the clear fishing line. After a few minutes, they peered in the open door and asked if they could come in. Even though they were dressed in immaculately tailored shirts and khaki pants, they exuded an air of creative elegance that lifted them out of the conformist mindset.

"Hello, I'm Jason," the taller man said with a mild touch of arrogance. His sensitive face was crowned by a graying Picasso haircut. When he offered a light handshake,

I noticed graceful, long, tapering fingers that revealed an artistic nature. A flash of camaraderie from clear, blue, intelligent eyes hinted at carefully edited friendliness.

"We've just been admiring your little shop," he said.

Then his friend stepped toward me and took both my hands in his. When I glanced into his intense face, my shy gaze met dazzling white teeth and merry green eyes, topped by a thicket of silver curls.

"And I'm Byron," he said, looking at me for an instant before his eyes shifted quickly from item to item, professionally focusing with razor-sharp attention on each of my designs.

"We love your shop. So space age hip," Jason smiled. "So fun," Byron complimented. "We're from the new TV show, *Star Trek*."

Oh, yes. I watched your show a couple of times. It's fun," I said nervously, overwhelmed by their presence in my studio.

"You have just the look we want for our next show," Byron said, pointing to the stretch fabric fashions and jewelry.

"Come on over to the set tomorrow. We'd like you to make a necklace for our monster," Jason said. "We're looking for something bold and geometrical, something that suggests that the monster's necklace might have hidden powers."

"We like the freeform plastic materials you use," Byron added quickly, his high-speed enthusiasm a delightful counterpoint to Jason's suave elegance, "but we need something ordered and structural."

"It should look like a symbol of power, something only a leader of a highly intelligent outer space civilization would wear," Jason said.

Byron scribbled a note on a business card and told me to present it to the guard at the studio gate at 2 p.m. the next day. Then they took off to catch the show at the Troubadour.

The next day I visited the *Star Trek* set, watched the crew film a scene, and met the stars. I marveled at how the simple set constructions looked like sophisticated spaceships on the television screen.

Later, in wardrobe, the designers showed me a green, wrinkly, rubber head with huge lips. I was surprised. This monster didn't look like he came from a highly intelligent outer space civilization. He looked like he had just emerged, dripping, from a dark lagoon.

As Jason and Byron explained their instructions, I was too shy to say that I didn't think that ghoulish creature would wear what they were suggesting. Instead, I supported their ideas by saying that the plastic would give a unique touch to their designs, and suggested fluorescent colors to make the necklace glow under black light. They went for it. I had a week to make it happen.

That night, I paced around the studio, uncertain and afraid. I didn't know how to construct the complicated geometric design they'd asked for. After three unproductive nights, I called Taz and asked him for help. He came over, rejected their instructions and created a flowing plastic collar with a central medallion that harmonized with the wrinkles of the monster's rubber head. When it was finished, I tried on the head and collar and looked in the mirror. Horrified by my reflection, I tore it off. When Taz tried it on, I freaked out even more.

"Take it off," I shrieked, and ran into the garden. Turned on by my fear, he chased after me. Scared, I hid behind a tree until he took the monster head off.

The next morning, I painted the necklace and medallion in brilliant day-glo fluorescent colors and took it to the *Star Trek* set.

The stars and staff loved it. The actor who was supposed to wear it put on his head and paraded around the set, scaring everyone. But when Jason and Byron saw it, they acted cool, and examined it from every angle for several minutes. The cast and crew rolled their eyes at me or winked, trying to make me feel better while the two costume designers took their time looking at my necklace.

"This isn't what we asked for," Byron complained.

"You should have followed our instructions," Jason said haughtily.

"This is great! It's exactly what a monster that looks like this would wear," the actor said, defending me.

He put the mask and the necklace on, and it did look just right. The crew clapped and Jason and Byron had to accept the decision. They paid me, but I knew they wouldn't ask me to do anything for them again.

After that episode, I resolved never to try to make anyone else's ideas. I had enough ideas of my own.

Every week, I watched *Star Trek* at Winston's, waiting for the monster to appear. Sure enough, a few weeks later, there he was, wearing the plastic collar on the show. *Star Trek* was wonderful fun, but the creator of the show was wrong about one thing. Space was not the final frontier. I believed the final frontier was inside of me, and that was where I wanted to go.

Maria was ecstatic. She'd taken on an assistant who sewed the outfits at home and delivered them to Maria.

"I boss now," she crowed happily. "I have employee. I have bank account. I have my own money."

Every now and then, she'd switch to the downtrodden, fearful Maria and look furtively at the door to make sure Carlos wasn't coming in. When she saw the coast was clear, she started her singsong chanting again.

"Carlos doesn't know what we're doing. Soon I free. I have money. I have bank account."

One sprinkly spring day when intermittent showers freshened the air between outbursts of hopeful sun, a perfectly groomed and obviously wealthy woman walked into my studio. Wearing a "Make Love, Not War" button on her fashionable straw hat, she was a walking advertisement for the privileged upper class. Exquisitely blonde-beautiful, she looked like someone who had everything. I was staring at her just as hard as she was staring at me when I realized she looked familiar.

"You're from the Mediterranean restaurant in Beverly Hills," I said impetuously.

"You've been there? My husband and I opened it together, for a lark. He wanted to do something creative," she said, laughing harshly, releasing a wave of pain that wafted through the air like cigarette smoke.

"Then he started hanging out on Sunset Strip. He met new friends, all the wild young things. Next thing I knew, he was smoking pot and dropping acid. Then he was gone," she said, a sob catching in her throat. "Now he's a religion. He wears white biblical robes and young women worship him. Can you believe that? His followers run a salad, shake, and smoothie bar on the beach, wear robes and headdresses, and eat sprouts and pray."

Surprised at how this seemingly perfect woman had exposed these profoundly unhappy, personal revelations within a minute of her arrival, I dropped into the connection.

"I know how you feel. I lost my husband to free love. He sleeps with every flower child he can pick up. That's why I left him, why I'm doing my own thing."

"And look at what you're doing, making beautiful clothes and jewelry," she complimented. "You have your own shop. I'd love to do something, anything."

"Everyone wants to dress up and live their fantasy. See this jump suit? I feel completely different when I'm wearing it.

I can't stand to wear jeans anymore. They make me feel like I'm in prison."

"I know what you mean. My clothes just scream Beverly Hills rich. I'd like to look different, but how? What?"

"Mmm, let me think," I mused, admiring her smooth, shoulder-length, pale blonde hair that crowned her classic American Beauty face, and perfect body.

"I know – a Grecian tunic, white with gold borders, a golden belt and sandals, and a circlet of flowers in your hair," I said a moment later.

She laughed briefly, then turned away. "My husband would just think I was trying to join his sect. He turned from a Beverly Hills playboy into a cult leader so fast I hardly knew what happened. I wait for change, but nothing happens. I wake up each morning and I am the same dull, perfectly brought up rich girl. I put on the same dreary, boring, safe, expensive clothes and see the same boring friends."

Her voice took on a desperate tone. "And they all try to pretend my husband hasn't left me for a wild, long-haired hippie girl, but I know it. I feel like I'm locked in a perfect, size ten Saks Fifth Avenue straight jacket, and I can't get out. I'd love to be wild and free like her, but all I know is how to walk gracefully, dress beautifully, and say all the right things, like someone else is writing the script. Where is my own script? That's what I want to know."

The only thing I could think of to say was, "Becoming yourself seems to be the hardest thing to do."

"I think I know why all these people are taking drugs," she said, looking around and whispering, "They're tired of being locked inside themselves."

Then, as if afraid of what she'd just said, she moved abruptly over to Love's crib.

"Oh, what a sweet, dear baby. They way she lies there, she's completely, naturally herself. Look how open and soft she is. I'd love to hold her in my arms. I didn't want babies because I was having too much fun; now, I'll never have them," she said sadly, her back to me, trying to hide how close she was to tears.

"You're still young," I consoled her, "you can still have babies."

"But not with him," she whimpered, her voice taking on the quality of the mistress of a Southern manor in a costumed civil war movie. "I'll never have a baby with him."

Seeing how deeply she was into her grief, and wanting to cheer her up, I changed the subject.

"Last week I was at a peace march. There were thousands of hippies, freaks, flower children, and activists, dressed in every possible style. They marched down the Avenue of the Stars to the Century City Hotel where President Johnson was staying. Everyone was chanting 'Make Love, Not War' and 'Hell No, We Won't Go'. Then the cops got uptight. When their eyes turned cold and hard, I ran away as fast as I could. About five minutes later it turned into a riot. Police struck out indiscriminately with their clubs, attacking everyone, even women with children. Even then the demonstrators screamed, 'Love Builds, War Destroys'. What were the police afraid of? No one had any weapons. We weren't doing any harm. I thought this was a free country."

"Governments don't want happy, free people demanding their rights," she said bitterly. "Even though my family has the best this country has to offer, I've been imprisoned by it all my life. I know that's why my husband left. He wanted freedom. Can you believe that? He wanted freedom from the freedom that wealth gave him."

"I want to be happy and free, too," I bubbled, still trying to ease her pain, "The jump suit, silver boots, and all this wild jewelry help me feel that way. Wonder Woman was my favorite comic strip when I was a kid and now I dress like her. Where's it all coming from?"

"From you, dear," she said, suddenly soft and tender. "You're like a little lotus blossom in the mud of the City of Angels."

Then, switching to a brighter mode, she snapped open her purse and pulled out a roll of cash. "I want to buy these earrings and this bracelet," she said, pointing to her choices, laughing with pleasure. "I can't wait to show my friends what I've found in your sweet little shop, and I know they'll come to see you too."

Shortly after she left, Love woke up. I carried her into the courtyard and sat on the bench under the avocado tree. Nuzzle-nestled into nursing, I absorbed the sun's warmth that filtered through the swaying leaves and danced light patterns over my eyelids. Beyond our courtyard arbor, traffic swished like sighing breakers, easing away the frantic Los Angeles rhythms.

Thinking about the woman who had just visited me, I realized happiness wasn't about having things. It was about not having the things that stopped you from being happy. She had everything the world could offer, but she couldn't stop her husband from wanting more.

Looking into my daughter's eyes, feeling her tongue pulling on my breast, I murmured, "Don't need much to make me happy, do I, Love? Happiness is already here."

Rainbow

The jewelry and fashions were taking off. Hardly able to keep up with the demand, I worked far into the night to fill orders, humming along to the radio and watching over Love. A few times I found myself wishing I had someone to help me. A few days later, help materialized in a most unexpected way.

One stormy night around ten o'clock, Taz appeared with a shivering, scared teenager named Rainbow. He'd seen her on Sunset Strip and stopped to talk to her. Realizing she wasn't up to his scene and thinking I might need help with Love, he offered to bring her to me.

Surprised at how my wish had suddenly manifested in front of me, and amazed at Taz's unusual thoughtfulness, I welcomed her into my home.

After Taz split, I wrapped Rainbow in one of my brightly striped Mexican blankets, sat her in front of the electric heater, and turned on the flower power station. Shaking, she huddled shyly in the brilliant yellow, pink, and orange blanket, her blue eyes glancing furtively here and there, checking everything out, making sure she was safe. A wild head of teased, curly red hair surrounded her freckled face, and she was dressed in blue jeans, a T-shirt and worn white sneakers. She didn't even have a sweater.

No wonder she was cold. She looked so young, my heart went out to her.

"What's your baby's name?" she asked, still shivering.

"Love," I said.

"Cool," she approved with a tiny smile.

"Did you run away from home?" I inquired gently.

"Yeah, I can't stay there anymore," she replied without explanation.

As I heated milk for cocoa, sympathy rose in my heart. I knew what it was like to want to leave your family. I knew what it was like to be alone in the world.

"Is he your husband?" she asked carefully, eyes averted.

"*Was* my husband," I responded, wondering if he had come on to her. "I've been on my own for nearly a year."

Wishful longing glimmered on her expressive face for a moment before she whispered wistfully, almost to herself, "I'd love to be able to make it on my own. I'd like to live in the country, have a garden, and weave and make pots and have babies and cook, and have a wonderful husband, and good friends who stopped in to see me."

"I'd love to have that too," I shared. "I had a hard time with Taz. It took me years to break free. You're lucky you know what you want."

"I know what I want but how do I get it?" she asked passionately.

"Questions, questions, questions. I have a lot of those too," I said, feeling like a wise woman for the first time in my life. "Even when you don't know the answers, it's important to keep asking the questions."

"It feels good to talk to you. I could never talk to my parents," she shared with the first hint of a smile.

Sipping cocoa, warming her hands on the cup, Rainbow shared her story.

"Couldn't stay at home any more. My parents wouldn't let me be myself or have any fun. Work, work, work! That's all they thought about. Study, study, study! That's all they wanted from me. I used to love to go to school. I was a top student, but the way they pushed me, I started to hate it."

She trembled and drew the blanket around her. I waited silently, not wanting to interrupt.

A few moments later, she continued.

"They were yelling at me. I turned around and walked out of the living room. They thought I was going to the bathroom, but I kept on going down the hall and out the front door, just like this, wearing my blue jeans and my favorite peace symbol T-shirt. I didn't care about anything except getting away. I didn't have any money. I wasn't even afraid. I hitchhiked and slept in bus stations. I wanted to find the flower children on Sunset Strip."

"By the time I got dropped off on the Strip, I was already hungry and cold. I was sure I'd find young kids like myself, but there were only tourists, night clubbers, flashy groupies, and burned-out druggies. No one was interested in talking to me or helping me find a safe place to crash. I thought I was going to have to turn myself into the police and go home. I sat down on the sidewalk near the Whiskey-A-Go-Go and put my arms over my head and cried. That's when your old man appeared. When I told him my story, he offered to bring me here. I knew I was taking a chance getting into his car, but I'm glad now. Can I stay? Please?"

"Yes, you can," I laughed. "I've been wishing for someone like you, and here you are."

The next day I bought her a toothbrush and a piece of foam for a bed and gave her one of my sweaters. In the daytime, we put the foam under the welding table and at night the studio was her bedroom. Rainbow was glad to come and live with me, but she never told me her real name or where she came from.

As Rainbow eased into our studio scene, she brought magic and youthful laughter to our lives. She was my sister, apprentice, baby-sitter, friend, daughter, and helper all mixed into one. She looked up to me, and I sheltered her with an open heart. She admired what I was doing and wanted to learn, so I slipped easily into the role of a teacher.

Choo took to Rainbow the moment she lifted him up and swung him around, making him shriek with delight. Whenever she wanted to take him anywhere, he offered his hand to her without hesitation. He quickly realized that going somewhere with Rainbow meant having a good time. When she joined him on the slides and swings and bars, their laughter filled the park. Even though Rainbow loved to play games and tease and act like a child herself, she was also a natural mother who was thoughtful and considerate of my children's safety and comfort. After a time, I knew I could trust her to watch over them.

Gradually she settled in, but if she saw a police car she went into a paranoid panic and hid under the welding table, sure they were coming to get her and take her back to her parents. At night, when Love was asleep, she begged me to show her how to make jewelry. Soon she was assembling earrings while she sang along with the radio. Rainbow hung on every word of the DJs' raves. She not only knew the words to every song, she believed them. Her eyes glistened with excitement when she told me what was happening in the world of hippies and flower children.

The next time Clara came around, I introduced Rainbow.

"So, you're populating your world. Very good," Clara said approvingly.

Populating my world? What an interesting concept, I thought to myself as I took a new look at my studio. Yes, this was my world, and now it had its first new citizen. Groovy.

Turning off my head-tripping, I tuned back into Clara

in time to hear her say, "You are friends and helpers to each other. This is the way it is supposed to be."

Rainbow warmed instantly to Clara. It made me happy to see Clara's wise, silver head bent closely to Rainbow's wild, red one as Clara looked over the jewelry Rainbow was putting together.

I told Clara how I had wished for a helper just before Rainbow arrived, and she smiled mysteriously.

"If you are getting what you wish for, then you really are in tune," she said, and then she was gone.

In tune with what? I made a mental note to ask her more about that the next time I saw her.

February storms blew through, bringing torrential downpours that were followed by fresh, breezy, sunshiny, smog-free days. A ten-month toddler, Love stood sturdily on her little legs, holding on to things and pulling herself around the studio. We had to watch her carefully because she wanted to explore and touch and taste everything around her.

"She's a little trucker," Rainbow laughed every time she saw Love scooting about, and soon Rainbow's nickname for Love became Little Trucker. My nickname for Love came to me spontaneously in play, as had Choo's. Every time I'd throw her up in the air, I'd call out, "Chickadee, flying in the sky like a bird. Chickadee."

With Rainbow there to take care of Love, I was able to run errands, go shopping in downtown Los Angeles, and sell jewelry to boutiques without taking her with me. On the weekends, Rainbow and I took the kids to the beach or hung out at fairs or markets, selling the jewelry. It was the first time a friend was coming along on my trip and sharing my way of doing things. Becoming the mother-teacher-sister of a sixteen-year-old flower child increased my happiness and supported my creativity. I was glad of the second chance to have a sister.

I'd never been around someone so easy and happy and good-natured. There was no resistance between us as we talked and shared and helped each other out. Sometimes I felt Rainbow was idolizing me, so I'd tell her about some of my hard times. Most evenings we curled up on the sofa and listened to the latest songs on the radio while we dreamed away, sharing stories and playing with Love and Choo, whenever he was with us. The happiness that came from our friendship made me realize I'd never had a real friend before.

One night, Rainbow looked up shyly, like she'd been thinking about something for a long time, and it was finally time to do something about it.

She said, "Thanks for letting me help you with the jewelry. I always wanted to be an artist, but my parents made me study science."

"Did you like science?" I asked.

"Yeah, science is interesting, but they way they teach it, God, what a bummer. I was good at it, but it never captured my heart the way art did. My parents said they wouldn't put me through art school, so I did what they wanted."

"Then I made a new friend. Her name was Hummer, short for hummingbird, because she always hummed when she was a child. She was everything I wanted to be. Her parents were so cool. They wanted her to do what she loved, and they all enjoyed being around each other and doing things together. I started going to her place after school, but I never told my parents. They would have freaked out. It was Hummer who named me Rainbow. She said I wouldn't have to look for the pot of gold because it would always be within me. She was always saying cool things like that. She was pure magic."

"For a few months, I got away with it. Hummer frizzed my hair and gave me a pair of her old bell-bottom embroidered jeans. I bought a few groovy T-shirts with my allowance. After school, we'd hang out at her place and listen to the flower power stations. I started making friends at school. I was on a high. Soon I was humming all the songs. My parents knew something was up, but my grades were good, so they figured it was just teenage stuff. They thought I was still coming home after school to study by myself till they got back from work. This one day, my mom got sick and came home early, and I wasn't home. When I came in, my mom went wild. When my dad came home, they both started in on me, like I was evil or something. I felt like they hated me, the way they were yelling at me and putting me down."

"What did they say?"

"They threatened me. They told me they were going to throw away all my new clothes, cut my hair, and get a baby sitter to meet me after school. God, it was like they were the Gestapo or something. But I was so cool. I pretended I was Hummer. I sat there, real quiet, listening to them, humming quietly to myself. Then, I saw it all, clear as day. My own parents didn't know me at all. They didn't care who I was. They weren't even interested in what I wanted to do," she said with nervous excitement.

A minute later, she added, "That's when I got up and walked out. By the time they figured out that I was gone, I'd already hitchhiked my first ride. I'm never going back."

"Wow, it's amazing you did that. I never ran away from my parents, even though I wanted to. When I finally left home, I went straight into marriage with Taz, and then it took me years to leave him. This is the first time I've been out in the world on my own."

"But you did it. That's what counts," Rainbow said.

"By the time I left, I had no choice. You've got courage. You walked into the night and took your chances," I said, impressed with her spunk.

"Yeah, I did, didn't I? And I ended up with you, so I must have done something right," she agreed cheerfully.

117

"Don't you think they're worried about you?" I asked.

"Sure, they're worried all right, but I know if I went back it'd just be the same scene all over again. I can't live like that anymore."

"What about school?"

"Oh, I'm real good at that. I'll catch up later. Right now, I want to be with you and Love, and Choo. I love learning how to make the jewelry. Please don't send me home. Let me stay with you. Promise?"

"I promise. You're part of our family now," I said.

After that conversation, Rainbow relaxed. The days and weeks flew by as we worked on orders and shared our daily lives. At times I'd catch my breath and marvel at the joyous, creative energy of our home and studio. A surge of gratitude would sweep through and my heart would ache with happiness. I was nearly twenty-six, and this was the first time since I was a child that I had felt so much happiness.

On the hunt for jewelry materials in downtown Los Angeles, I discovered new plastic materials: thin, flexible sheets of silver and gold mylar, and brilliant, transparent colors. After buying a dozen sheets of every color, I drove back to the studio.

"Rainbow! Look. New materials! We're going to make the greatest jewelry," I proclaimed as I threw the mylar on the worktable and reached for the scissors.

"See, we'll cut leaves, stars, flowers, and geometric shapes and gather them in bunches with these silver rings. Then we'll mix and blend the transparent colors over the silver and gold."

Rainbow dove into the action with me. We stayed up all night, singing along to the radio as we perfected the new designs. We didn't stop until we had a dozen samples for a new line of jewelry.

"I'll take them to Judith's Paper Clothes Shop and to all the cool boutiques in Hollywood and Beverly Hills. Let's call the Women's Wear Daily editor. We can sell these to department stores, too."

Judith ordered a supply for her store and also decided to use the mylar jewelry to accessorize her paper clothes on the Gypsy Rose Lee TV show in San Francisco. When Gypsy saw the jewelry she invited me to appear on her show a few weeks later.

Work was play. Play was work. High on creativity, we watched our ideas manifest in everyday reality. Flower Power energized our world.

One warm, sunny afternoon, Clara appeared in the studio doorway, surprising us with her exquisite presence. She was dressed in a pure white-on-white embroidered cotton dress, with shoulder pleats stitched down the side. One of her silver pins held a transparent white gauze scarf that floated over her shoulders. A lacy rattan hat shaded her face.

Stunned by her beauty, I managed to say, "It's so good to see you. Please come in."

Rainbow clapped her hands, "Come and see what we've been doing."

"You are happy together. This is good, very good," she complimented, laughing her joy.

Rainbow and I laughed with her, and put our arms around each other.

"When you said NO to your husband, you didn't know you were saying YES to all this, did you?" Clara asked.

As always, Clara offered a shift in perception.

"One day you realize there is no YES and there is no NO, and that only one thing is possible – YES! Even when you don't know what you're saying YES to yet, and think you're saying NO – it's still YES, yes?"

"Yes!" we shouted. "Yes, yes, yes!"
Laughter filled the studio and my heart.

Women's Wear Daily featured an article on my jewelry. Editors and journalists from Vogue, Cosmo and Harper's came to the Nemo Street studio and bought jewelry samples for photo shoots. My business expanded as orders poured in from boutiques and department stores. Passers-by who saw the window display on Nemo Street came in and ordered custom clothes.

One day Judith called me and asked me to come over to her shop. When I arrived at the Paper Clothes Store, Baroness Fiona Thyssen was trying on my jewelry. Glorious auburn hair waved over her shoulders, crowning her perfect glowing body. One of the most beautiful women in the world, she was also divinely charming. She spoke to us kindly with an exquisite melodious voice. After placing an order for her boutique in the Grand Hotel in Switzerland, she walked out wearing my jewelry.

Soon, Rainbow was making all the jewelry and I was concentrating on designing the clothes. After nursing Love, I would race away for a couple of hours to see Maria, buy materials, and run errands, glad that Rainbow was there to take care of Love. Feeling like I was bursting out of my studio, I dreamed of a store of my own.

One afternoon, when we were making jewelry and grooving to the latest tunes, Rainbow laughed, held up her arm and clenched her fist.

"Flower Power!" she shouted.

I lifted both my arms heavenward and mirrored her with my own fierce cry.

"Flower Power!" I yelled triumphantly to the sky.

BOOK TWO
Psychedelia

Psychedelic Conspiracy

A primo store came up for rent on Sunset Strip. I wanted Maria to go in on it with me, but she was afraid to leave Carlos and I didn't have enough money or confidence to go it alone. I tried to think of a way to make it happen, but the only possibility seemed to be Taz. I talked myself into believing it would help both of us, convincing myself that being in business together would be different than being married.

I drove over to Taz's studio; it was the first time I'd been there since I'd moved. Surprised to see me, he showed off his latest sculptures. He knew something was up, but he played it cool. I hung out for a while, listening to his latest music tapes, then I dropped the idea. He went for it immediately, like he'd already thought about it. Turned on by the creative possibilities, we shared ideas, merged resources, and shook hands. The next day we signed the lease.

The location was perfect. The store had a highly visible front window on the south side of the Strip, just east of Whiskey-A-Go-Go, which meant everyone that cruised the Strip would see our store. We decided to call it The Psychedelic Conspiracy, to acknowledge the power and greed forces manipulating the sixties dream. Psyche meant "soul" or "mind" and delic meant "to show" or "reveal". Everyone who was hip knew that psychedelics were turning the world inside out.

We created a walk-in psychedelic environment that featured silver walls, a mylar ceiling, stainless steel floors, and transparent lucite display counters and benches. Tracks of black lights and strobes illuminated and intensified the colors, making the lucite glow like rainbow prisms. Using the thermoplastic technique I had discovered when making my jewelry, Taz shaped three free-flowing plastic dressing rooms with entrances that spelled the three letters of LSD. Then we sprayed the rooms with brilliant fluorescent colors. The combination of silver, mirror mylar and stainless steel reflected the pulsing psychedelic visuals, creating a disorientation that shifted consciousness and altered perception. My far-out fashions twirled on plastic tubes or hung on shiny metal racks and the jewelry glittered on the silver walls and inside the glowing display cases.

On opening night, we uncovered the front window and released our vision onto Sunset Strip. The light show in the window created a sensation. Cruisers screeched to a halt and came in. On weekends, the line of people waiting to get in stretched a block long. Movie and rock stars, groupies, musicians, hippies, flower children, peaceniks, beatniks, freaks, and hordes of gawking tourists paraded through our store night after night, walking around wide-eyed, buying everything in sight.

One night the brothers of the spiritual Fountain of the World commune in Box Canyon graced the store with a biblical happening. Wearing their long white robes, beaming beatifically, they smiled and whispered among themselves as they examined the sculptures and fashions. Making themselves at home, they sat on the lucite benches and watched the happening scene before bowing their way out of the store. After they left, I wished that I had asked them what they thought about the Conspiracy. I felt a tug on my heart that surprised me, an urge to follow them and find out how they lived. I vowed to find out more about them if they came into the store again.

Psychedelic Conspiracy

The New York Times wrote a feature article on the store: "...the most impressive and genuinely psychedelic of all the shops in Los Angeles was the Psychedelic Conspiracy at 8802 Sunset. The basic, dazzling effect of the store was achieved by a silver ceiling that reflected light from a complicated deployment of colored lamps above, below, and inside some large, translucent plastic sculptures made by the owner. A new arrival in the shop could spend several moments looking around, adjusting his eyes to the lights, his lungs and sinuses to the thick haze of incense, and his ears to the super decibel rock. Plastic was the medium for his particular message, which was futuristic, Utopian, and obscure. His sculptures were strictly indescribable, but there was something scientific about them – as though they had been magnified representations of totally new and alarming phenomena recently observed under a microscope."

During the week, I drove downtown and picked up accessories, psychedelia, jewelry fixings, and materials. Rainbow worked late into the night making jewelry. Maria hired another seamstress. National magazine photographers shot their models in the LSD doorways. The Psychedelic Conspiracy was the in-place for the in-crowd.

The California Stylist reported: "A new breed of store is sprouting in L.A. It's a PSYCHEDELIQUE...a boutique with a mind-bending futuristic twist. It offers freaky fashions, out-of-sight accessories, and psychedelic toys...all standard fare for the flower-power, under-25 generation. We decided to leg it over to the most mind-bending psychedelique going: The Psychedelic Conspiracy. This store has a psychedelic fluorescent light show in the window, there's plastic sculpture to absorb you into the store's environment, and the walls and ceiling are lined in aluminum foil. It's a mind blowing scene."

In the midst of our whirlwind of success, I missed Love, so I started bringing her to the store. A year-old toddler now, she ran around, laughing and talking baby talk to the customers. She was in a teasing phase where she loved to crawl or run away from me, only to look back to see if I was watching or following her. Then she'd run again, hiding, laughing, and peeking out at everyone. Wearing dresses I'd made from the remnants of the most beautiful fabrics in my studio, with bright ribbon bows tied in her hair, Love's happy presence added enchantment to my days at the Conspiracy.

Taz brought Choo over on the weekends so he could play with his sister. Choo loved to show off his drawing and reading skills to his sister, so they'd camp out in the back or take over one of the benches. Even though the store was busy, the children grooved in the action.

Vogue photographed Cher in the 'S' dressing room and the magazine featured the photo with the caption, "There's one place Cher loves to visit on the strip. It's called 'The Psychedelic Conspiracy'. The decor is wildly extraordinary, imaginative, all blown free shapes of plastic."

Questions, propositions, compliments, requests and complaints came at me from hundreds of customers and sightseers, while I struggled to keep my balance on the success merry-go-round. There was no way to stop the flow. The needs of the store took over our lives. Living on the run, I missed my quiet Nemo Street life, but I adjusted to the new pace and started to groove in the fast lane.

The Psychedelic Conspiracy and my studio hummed with success. Rainbow and I stayed up night after night turning out jewelry. Every day, I cut out new outfits and delivered them to Maria. She and her assistant sewed them up and delivered them to the store the next morning. I drove downtown a couple of times a week to buy jewelry fixings and search for designer remnants in the garment district. When the rich and famous discovered our store, custom orders from rock and film stars and a host of hip characters who wanted unique costumes challenged my skills.

Jim & Pam

One morning, Pam Courson breezed into the Conspiracy. Restless and thin, with a mane of shiny, coppery-brown hair, she wore a beaded top with tight bell-bottom pants that showed off her slender body. Pam raced around the shop, quickly choosing one dress after the other to hold up in front of the mirror.

"I'm looking for something special. I'm Pam, Jim Morrison's woman," she announced speedily, as if she were Alice in Wonderland's white rabbit and had only a moment to spare.

"Cool," I responded slowly, watching her tense, impatient search through the racks. "I've been wanting to meet you."

Spinning off, she danced through the store like a nervous colt, calling over her shoulder, "I need a special dress, something really wild."

"You can wear wild, but let me show you elegant," I said even more slowly, wishing I were a magnet that could make her stop her clockwork spinning.

Despite her hyper cool, she seemed vulnerable, even child-like. I wanted to enhance that quality rather than hide it with flashy, sexy styles, so I took her into my cutting room and showed her the dress I'd just made for Peter Fonda's movie, *The Trip*.

"It's an original. I made the pattern myself," I said, handing her the silver dress.

"See, this neckline scarf drapes in the front or in the back, or over your head like a hood. It's three styles in one. The movie won't be out for months. You can be the first to show it off."

As she slipped it over her head, she was transformed. Her tender little girl's face peered seductively out of the silver hood and the dress enhanced her slender body, revealing soft curves.

"This is primo, absolutely wild. Jim'll love this."

As she preened in front of the mirror, I showed her my line of stretch pants, tops, and jump suits. Grooving now, she tried them all on, seeing herself in a new light, watching her beauty come alive.

"I'd love to have a store and do what you're doing," she enthused. "It's so creative. You're designing fantasies, making dreams come true. That's what I want to do. We need to hang out. I want you to make all my clothes."

After Pam left, I laughed with pleasure. I loved turning people on, helping them see themselves in another way, creating costumes for their dreams. I took Love's dimpled hands and swung her around, lifting her into the air as she squealed with delight. Catching her, I hugged her fragrant, sweet softness, breathing in love.

A few days later, Pam invited me over to her Laurel Canyon house. When I admired her California garden bungalow, she made a face.

"I hate this place. We're never left alone. I want to move," she complained bitterly.

I poured my jewelry on the table.

"Look! These will be great with the silver dress," I enthused, trying to swing her off her bad trip.

Jim & Pam

The door opened and Jim Morrison lounged on the threshold, a black leather shadow against the light from the garden. He sauntered in, holding a brown paper bag in one hand. Silent and moody, his handsome face was hidden behind unshaven stubble and altered by half-closed eyes. With an indulgent grin that shifted easily into a seductive sneer, he threw himself down in a chair and lifted his lizard skin boots onto the coffee table. Taking a bottle of Scotch out of the bag, he twisted it open and guzzled a long drink.

Pam walked over and took the bottle out of his hands.

"It's early Jim, please be cool," she pleaded.

Jim winked at me and turned on the television, losing himself in an old black and white movie.

Pam took me into her bedroom. After she closed the door, she said, "I need you to make something special for me. I have a secret even Jim doesn't know about." Coming closer, she whispered in my ear, "I dance at a topless club in Westwood during the lunch hour. I make good money and it's mine to spend on clothes and makeup and jewelry, and I get to dance. I always imagine Jim might walk in and see me. It turns me on."

"Look," she said as she pulled a G-string out of a stuffed animal.

"This is what I've been wearing, but it's boring. I want something fluffier, sexier, more suggestive. Can you do it?"

I nodded incredulously while she put on the G-string.

"I almost got caught once, and was that a turn-on, but I tore it off, acting all hot to make love and distracted him," she giggled, admiring her reflection in the mirror. Then moving to her own tune, breasts rolling, reddish-brown hair flying, she beat a rhythmic undulation with her hips.

"It's the way I get even for all his running around," she added, a fierce look taking over her beautiful face.

Trying to stay cool, I took measurements. Pam took off the G-string and dressed, and we talked about fashions for a while. When I passed through the living room when it was time to go home, Jim didn't look up. He was glued to the television, slugging down liquor, lost in his river of pain.

The next time Pam dropped into the Conspiracy, she asked me to come over for lunch the next day. When I walked down the path to the house, the door was open and I walked in on a raging fight. Tears pouring down her face, Pam was pounding on Jim's chest, screaming about some woman who'd called to tell Pam she'd slept with Jim.

I stood still for a moment, not knowing whether to leave or wait.

"I told her it didn't mean anything. I asked her if you'd bought her a Porsche. That shut her up. I told her you'd sleep with anyone, but I'm the one you come home to, if you can call this a home. I want a stereo. I can't even listen to your music. The other guys in the Doors have homes and children and stereos. We have nothing."

Jim didn't answer or defend himself or make her any promises. He held her close, humming and crooning in her ear as he softly embraced her. The next minute they were kissing passionately.

I slipped by them and went outside. As I wandered in the garden, I picked a bouquet of flowers, thinking it might cheer them up.

A few minutes later, when I was sure the fight was over, I walked back in and offered them the flowers.

Jim's face lit up, and gesturing majestically, he cried like a street seller, "Flowers for the gods. Dionysius rejoices!"

Pam laughed like a delighted little girl as Jim crowned her burnished hair with delicate ferns. In loving response, she playfully tucked blossoms behind his ears. Glad to see them happy again, I bowed my head as they both wove leaves and posies through my long black hair.

Continuing the game with a lightheartedness that eclipsed his self-destructive side, Jim raised his right hand high and chanted, "A Love-In feast celebrating the sacrifice of the Lizard King..."

Eyes widening in fear, Pamela interrupted him and begged, "Don't say that. You don't have to sacrifice yourself."

They looked like they were about to start arguing, so I jumped in. "Hey, Jim, I love your song, *Light My Fire*. Your music usually scares me, but that song turns me on," I said.

His interest piqued, he turned to me with his full attention. "My music scares you, huh? Why?"

"I'm afraid of darkness. I see darkness all around and I don't want to lose myself in it. I want to go toward the light."

"How are you gonna to do that without breaking free?" he asked, laughing at me like I was being childish.

"I don't know. I don't think about breaking free. I see everyone trying to break free all around me, but I don't like the way they're doing it. The only thing I know for sure is that I have a feeling that tells me to go toward the light. I don't want to be part of this dark world."

"What other world is there?" he said as he rose from his chair.

"The world inside me. I want to make it real. I know I'm searching for something, a path, and a teacher to show me the way. I'm searching for love. I may have to leave my body behind in this world, but I feel there is another world, a finer world, a world of spirit...."

Gesturing wildly as he paced the room, Jim interrupted me. "The City of Angels is the City of Night. You're an L.A. woman. You're out there on the Strip, night after night, with all the happening people coming into your store, offering a million temptations. I accept everything that comes. I want it all and hate it all. I take it all so I can go beyond it. What's your trip?"

"My trip? Well that's simple. I don't take drugs. I don't drink and I don't sleep around. Those things don't make me feel good. I'd rather be high on something that makes me feel good, like my children. Their love lets me know there's something greater. I never found love with a man, so I give my love to my children and my work."

Jim and Pam looked at me as if I was crazy.

"How can babies make you high? They're crying and needing all your time and attention," Pam said in disbelief. "I don't want babies. I wouldn't be able to do anything."

Jim grumbled, "Love's a lie. Love's selfish. We only love people when they give us what we want. Love is pain. Everyone leaves. You have to do what you can to lessen the pain."

Pam looked like she was going to cry.

I searched for words to dispel his dark vision.

"All the stuff that turns you on, turns me off," was the only thing I could think of saying.

"No wonder I never see you out there," Jim said, grinning like a madman. "You're into enterprise."

I wanted to leave but when Jim shifted to a music mode, I was enchanted again. He picked up his guitar, and slouched back in a chair, strumming and reciting Rimbaud's poetry, raving about Dionysius and the Greek myths, singing and explaining his songs.

I figured Rimbaud, the wild young French poet, had a lot to do with Jim's "killer on the road" complex. I remembered a line from one of Rimbaud's poems, "a long, boundless and systematic disordering of the senses." It seemed Jim was trying on that line for size.

For sure, Jim had a unique brand of courage. He plumbed the shadow lands like a snake exploring the depths of darkness. Maybe he had eyes that could see in the dark, but I didn't. I was afraid of indulgence, afraid to let all the rules go, afraid to sink into alcohol, drugs, and sex. Not only was I afraid, but I couldn't see what people got out of it. Seeing Jim on the verge of disintegration reminded me of Taz. There was no way I wanted to be like either of them. Instead, I bore the pain of my loneliness and my despair, paring down my desires until there was only the desire for love.

Jim Morrison was a rock star pushing the edges of life. I loved his music and so did the millions of fans that idolized him, but would any of them want to live his life if they knew how much he was suffering?

A few weeks later, Pam called in the middle of the night and asked for help. She was disoriented, almost incoherent. High on drugs and alcohol, she alternated between outbursts of rage and desperate tears.

"Some creep just called me. Jim's gone over the edge. He vomited and passed out. They want me to pick him up in Hollywood," she cried hysterically. "Please, please. I need someone to help me, someone I can trust."

A short while later, she screeched her Porsche to a halt outside my studio. When I went outside to get in the car, Pam was a wild woman. Yelling, swearing, crying, praying, tears running down her face, she sped wildly to a grimy West Hollywood motel. Slamming on the brakes in the parking lot, Pam leaned on the horn, angry as hell.

"I'm not going in there with his groupies and his phony friends," she spat out furiously. "They can bring him out."

A doped, longhaired freak stumbled out of a motel room and leaned over the balcony.

"Bring Jim out!" she screamed at him.

A few minutes later, two stoned deadbeats dragged an unconscious Jim Morrison down the stairs. I moved to the back seat of the Porsche as they folded Jim into the passenger seat, filling the car with the bittersweet smell of vomit.

Gagging, I held my hand to my nose and opened the window. Jim was dead drunk. Pam was hysterical. I kept talking, trying to calm her down. I wanted to help. I just didn't know what to do.

"You fuckers, you're killing him," she screamed at them as she peeled out.

"Pam, slow down. Cool it. Take it easy," I said. "It's going to be okay. We'll get him home and put him in a bath and bring him around."

It was tough dragging him into the house. He was dead-weight heavy. Finally, he lay on the living room floor, totally out, virtually comatose.

"Do you think we should call a doctor?" I asked.

"No, no. Jim can't take any more bad publicity. They'll be swarming all over him. We have to bring him around," she sobbed.

"I'll make some coffee," I said and went into the kitchen.

I heard Pam pleading with him, "Wake up, Jim. Please, wake up."

As Pam slapped Jim's face and poured water over his head, he started coming out of it, mumbling, "My friend, the end," while he was groaning, and thrashing about on the floor. After I'd made the coffee, I pulled off his boots while Pamela removed his shirt. Together, one of us on each leg, we pulled off his lizard skin pants. We dragged him into the bathroom. Sputtering, spitting, making faces, he resisted the coffee we held to his lips. Lifting him, dragging him, begging him, we finally managed to get him, naked as a babe, into the tub.

Pam was crying her heart out like a lost little girl. Her love, her hero, was receding from her in ever-ebbing waves. She knelt on the floor beside the tub.

"Jim, please come to your senses," she begged.

Suddenly Jim opened his eyes, looked at us, and spoke slowly and calmly, "I am in my senses. That's why I'm trying to get out of them."

Then his head fell and he was gone again.

Stunned, I realized he was doing all this on purpose. This was his way of checking out of his mind.

We pulled him out of the bath and dragged him into bed. Pam curled up beside him, her arms around him, whimpering, and whispering his name. After turning out the light, I slipped out the door.

High Times

Vivid dreams of ancient Egypt took over my dream life. Every night, I saw visions of noble men and women wearing headdresses and circular jeweled collars over transparent linen robes. They walked gracefully through magnificent gardens, reclined in temples of brilliant light, and glided down the Nile in gilded canopied rafts. Inspired by these dreams, I immersed myself into the creation of a mylar dress.

"Rainbow, I want to make a dress of small silver rectangles linked together, with a matching headdress. I can see it now, a hip Cleopatra, shining and sparkling in a dress of light."

"Wow! What a great idea!" she replied.

We cut hundreds of iridescent mylar rectangles. Linking them with silver rings, we curved a collar to fit smoothly over the shoulders, then hung rows of the mylar rectangles to knee-length. Linked sideways, they formed a tunic. An opening in the back allowed the wearer to move the dress aside and sit down. Using the same technique, we linked a headdress to fit over my Cleopatra haircut. After carefully placing the mylar dress over black leotards and tights, I slipped on my knee-high silver boots and took a long look at myself in the full-length mirror. Groovy. Ancient Egypt had been resurrected on the Sunset Strip.

Book Two: Psychedelia

I hung the mylar on a transparent plastic cord in the Conspiracy window, and as it spun around, it was a light-show all its own.

Clara's face lit up the next time she dropped in to the Conspiracy. As soon as she saw the mylar dress, she walked over to it, twirled the dress on its cord, and examined carefully how it was made. After whistling twice, she sat down, waved her slim purse like a fan, and looked at me intensely. I looked back, waiting impatiently for her to speak.

"Whatever were you thinking when you made this dress?" she asked.

"Well, it came from a dream of Egypt. I saw these beautiful, shining, mirror tunics in my dream, and I had to make this dress," I explained.

"But how did you work out the details?"

"Step by step. Rainbow and I shaped and cut and linked the mylar, and it just worked out somehow," I said.

"Just worked out?" she said. "This is so beautiful. This could be in Paris. This is high fashion. This is how good you are. Never forget this. You had a vision and you made it real. Not everyone can do this, you know."

"Wow. Thank you. It seemed to happen naturally and easily, but it is pretty wild, isn't it? I love wearing it, too," I said, with shy pleasure.

"This dress is beautiful, like the inside of you that you are so afraid to let out. Other people will never know who you are until you are brave enough to be yourself."

With that, she hugged me and said goodbye.

I marveled at the way creativity transformed my deepest longings and fears into material form. More than a far-out costume, the mylar dress was both mirrored armor to deflect an unloving world and a suit of light to protect me from the darkness. It was the dress of my soul.

Taz flipped over the mylar dress.

"Far out! Let's make the scene Friday on the Venice Pier."

Amazed that he had invited me to go somewhere with him, I said okay. Usually I didn't go to the rock concerts, but the Iron Butterfly would be playing. Maybe Eric would be wearing the blue jump suit I had made for him.

When Taz came to pick me up on Friday night, he had added a sunburst buckle on his silver belt, silver boots, and a plastic jewel necklace to his usual black pant-and-sweater combo. He had dressed to match the mylar dress.

When we got to the Venice Pier, we were the most far-out of the far-out. Crowds gathered and followed us along the pier to the pavilion. Strobe lights turned my dress into a sparkling dazzle as we danced to the Iron Butterfly. Photographers and TV cameramen followed our every move as they tried to capture the light show dress.

The crowds rocked out around us; so many different trips, everyone full-on into their personal costume creations. Eric was up there playing and dancing in the jump suit I'd designed for him. The Butterfly were singing "Inna Gadda Da Vida", but I kept hearing the real words, "In the Garden of Eden". I wanted the real Garden of Eden, the Garden of Love. Suddenly, the loud music and the crowd made me tired. The excitement was over. The mylar dress felt prickly and strange.

When I told Taz I wanted to go home, he raged, "You always want to go home early. That's why I never take you anywhere."

It was okay for him to want to stay, but it was not okay for me to want to go. That was Taz. What would have wounded me desperately only a few months ago hardly touched me now.

Jerry Garcia and Pigpen were hanging out on the pier when we left. Tuned to the heart and soul of our time, the

Dead wove our dreams into their songs. They were playing in town and had dropped into the Conspiracy earlier that week. They walked on either side of me, escorting me down the pier. They wanted to know about the light-show mylar dress. When I told them about my visions of ancient Egypt and how I needed the mirror dress to protect me in this harsh world, Jerry's eyes lit up with understanding. To me, those two were like light-knights in a world of darkness. They knew how to dissolve the material world and bring everyone together in loving ecstasy.

Timothy Leary, the prophet of the psychedelic revolution, was the rage in the City of Angels. The catch phrase for all the hippies, flower children and culture escapees, was his mantra, "Turn on, tune in, drop out." LSD was not just an acronym for lysergic acid diethylamide. It also stood for Leary's League of Spiritual Discovery.

The "Illumination of the Buddha" lecture in January 1967 at the Santa Monica Civic Auditorium was one big contact high. Surrounded by flowers, Dr. Tim was dressed in white linen. The star of his own vision show, he also wore a crucifix and held prayer beads in his hands. Freaks, hippies, housewives, flower children, secretaries, groupies, professors, and college kids grooved to the musical light show.

"This time around, you can be anyone!" Leary raved, his seductive voice leading us down his LSD vision path.

"Drift within on a thread of sound, focus on the center, down vibration's thread. You are light. Sit in the diamond peacock eye of God."

I heard his words and they sounded great, but my personal experience had been different. As far as I was concerned, an acid high was still a mind trip. Sure, your mind expanded and you dissolved into the pulsing web of creation, but when the acid wore off, you came back. I wanted everyday living to be my best trip. I didn't want my life to be something I wanted to escape from.

Leary believed the government should make people happy. His advice was, "Don't vote, don't protest, don't picket, don't politic, don't let them take your mind."

Not being politically inclined, I couldn't understand how non-participation could change anything for the better. In fact, I was sure that participating from a loving place and offering whatever good you could to the world would be the only way to change things, if there was a point to changing things. The world and life seemed too big to change. I could only imagine doing my best to change myself. Because I believed it was up to each individual to seek their version of happiness, Leary's version didn't sit right with me.

With everyone screaming, "Cool; groovy; yeah, man; right on!" all around me, I didn't understand where my attitude was coming from. It was just the way I felt. I couldn't go along with Leary's scene.

"The name of the game is to feel good" sounded great, but something in me knew there was more to life than feeling good. During my childhood, I'd read my mother's spiritual books. Buddhists, yogis, and mystics all agreed that suffering was part of the path to enlightenment. Now Leary was saying that wasn't true.

I resonated more deeply with Leary's phrase, "the pulse of creation, the breath of life, expansion and contraction, in and out in an oscillating rhythm in an alternating galaxy; we live in a world of duality."

The word duality perked me up. That was the clue I'd been looking for. Duality stood for everything I didn't want; yet our world was made up of opposites. If duality still reigned in the Sandoz acid world, highs couldn't take us to a place where you didn't measure how much you gave and how much you got. I'd never met an acidhead who lived from that place. I wanted to find a teacher who had. Each teacher shared a piece of the truth. I wanted a teacher who knew the whole picture.

Even though I respected Leary's search and his experience, I couldn't believe the only way to get high was to take LSD. He made getting high sound wonderful, mentioning all the words we longed to experience: union, revelation, wonder, bliss, and joy. Sure, you hit on those places on a trip, but I'd been to some scary places, too.

Although my few mind-expanding, ego-dissolving LSD trips had helped me on my life journey, they hadn't given me the answer I was looking for. I didn't want more illusion. I wanted to go beyond illusion. Mind expansion dropped me off where I started. Maybe what I was after was mind contraction. Wow! What a thought!

I was beginning to understand that hate, anger, greed, and desire weren't only in the world. They were within each one of us. I wasn't an activist dying to fight against the war in Vietnam or ride the freedom buses in the South. Even though I cared deeply about these things, it wasn't my nature to fight outwardly. I was an internal person, determined to win the war inside myself. I believed if people changed themselves, they could change the world.

My favorite button said, "Let peace begin with me."

While the flower children were expanding their love scene, the police were hassling everyone on the street, swooping down, busting the kids, and treating them harshly. Judges and juries treated playful young hippies and flower children like hardened criminals. Some were sent to prison for years for smoking a joint.

One day an idea blossomed in my mind. If I could find something legal that gave a really cool high, the cops wouldn't be able to bust people for smoking. I bought a few herbs at the health food store and rolled them in different blends until I hit on an herbal mix that produced a mild euphoria. I packaged dozens of boxes and started talking it up to everyone that came in the store. The word spread like wildfire. Excited hippies and flower children came in to buy their boxes of instant legal high and roll their own. When the police pulled the heads over and tested their roaches, were they surprised! No pot! They had to let the kids go free.

The next thing I knew, some guy hanging out in a coffee house up the Strip took the game a step further with the Mellow Yellow trip on banana peels. Donovan created a song and carried the fun to the radio waves. The Free Press picked up the story on the Banana Conspiracy. "Burn Banana Burn" became the latest war cry of the flower children. With everyone smoking up a legal storm, they had to give up busting all the kids smoking on the street. There weren't enough policemen to go around.

High times!

Gypsy

When the producers of the Gypsy Rose Lee Show sent me plane tickets for San Francisco, I called Yoni and told her to tune in, thinking it might cheer her up to watch me on TV. Surprised to hear about the changes in my life, she offered to pick me up and show me the Haight Ashbury and Berkeley scenes.

When Love and I arrived at the airport, we were met by a uniformed chauffeur holding a sign spelling out my name. He drove us to the TV station in downtown San Francisco in a sleek black limousine and introduced us to a hostess who took us to the lunchroom for refreshments. Once Love was settled in childcare, I changed into my jump suit and silver boots, and put on an assortment of my thermoplastic spontaneous plastic bracelets and mylar jewelry. After the makeup artist worked on me, she took me into the TV studio. While the crew buzzed around preparing the show, Gypsy was relaxing on the sofa. When she saw me, she waved at me to come over and sit opposite her on a comfortable upholstered armchair. Even though we were on a TV set, Gypsy made me feel that I was back in her living room in Beverly Hills.

Gypsy was a rare woman. When she interviewed me in Los Angeles, I had to bring Love with me. Instead of being bugged, she held out her arms and took Love into her lap.

She wanted to know all about me, and then she told me about some of the hard times she'd been through. Life had dealt her some pretty rough hands, as she put it, but she felt sure she was on a winning streak with her new show.

Then we were on! Once we started talking, I forgot the lights, the cameras, and the crew. During the first half of the program, I demonstrated how I made thermoplastic spontaneous jewelry with my heat gun, and for fun, I demonstrated how I used the heat gun to dry my hair. Before the commercial, Gypsy announced I was going to change into something special. A few minutes later, in my mylar dress and headdress, I whirled around, shining and sparkling, a light-show all my own. When the show was over, the crew crowded round, clapping their congratulations.

Gypsy gave me a warm hug and said, "Thank you, my dear, and whenever you make anything new and exciting, I'll give you a spot. You've got it girl, so go for it!"

When I picked up Love from the studio assistant and returned to the station lobby, Yoni was waiting with her family. Ragged and drab, wearing downbeat browns, she clung to her newborn baby daughter, Sunshine. Yoni's face was heavy with despair. Out of place in this hip media scene, her large blue eyes blazed with desperation. Tensely stepping backward, she introduced her frowning, bearded old man, H, and her pale, painfully shy, four-year-old son, Teddy, who hid behind his mother's skirt. I pulled on the brilliant orange-magenta mohair dress I'd knitted in the hospital in Vancouver and followed them into the foggy night. A bright L.A. flower child out of place in a damp, gray landscape, I shivered with apprehension and cold as I headed into Yoni's world.

H threw my suitcase into the back of his covered pickup truck and gestured roughly for me to get in with Teddy. We hardly had time to climb in and settle safely on a lumpy, damp old mattress before he took off, tires squealing and sped onto the freeway. Love, Teddy, and I huddled together for warmth, shivering under grimy blankets. Strings of bells and shells tinkled above the dark undercurrents.

Teddy had told H he needed to pee before we took off, but H wouldn't stop. Caught between the fear of wetting his pants and the pain of holding his pee, Teddy whimpered all the way home. After H dropped us off at Yoni's ramshackle house in the Berkeley slums and split, Teddy peed his pants on the sidewalk. Yoni tried to comfort her son by calling him "Teddy Bear, Teddy Bear," but he pushed her away. Sobbing, yet proudly stubborn, he sat on the cold stairs in his wet pants with his head in his hands and refused to come in the house.

Yoni rolled her eyes. "H is burned out. He works around the clock with his anti-war and civil rights groups," she explained, blaming his meanness on his up-tight anarchist activities.

"Save the world and hurt a kid," I grumbled.

Yoni defended H, "When you're in pain yourself, you can't help taking it out on someone else."

She was making excuses. I knew what that was like.

"Yoni, nothing is going to change until we stop hurting one other," I insisted.

She turned away, fussing with Sunshine and I knew that was one truth she couldn't face right now.

"Yoni, what kind of name is H, anyway?" I asked, figuring it might offer clues to his nasty nature.

"H? Why, it's short for H-bomb, Hiroshima, Horror, Horrible, Hell," she said with a laugh that sounded like a gunshot. "H was born on the day they bombed Hiroshima. He says he feels the H-bomb inside him. He believes he was killed by it and reincarnated here to fight the system," Yoni said casually, dragging deeply on a cigarette like she was smoking a joint.

Just then, Teddy came inside. Still trembling from his ordeal, he wouldn't look at his mom. Instead, he turned to me, and sniffling, asked me for a cookie. I gave him a handful of cookies, and he went in his room and shut the door.

"What's happening with you, Yoni?" I asked, deciding it was best to change the subject.

"I'm on probation and that's a drag. I have to go in every week to take a drug test so my probation officer can be sure I don't take any smack. They've got me on methadone and that's just as bad as heroin, but as long as they control my drug intake, it has their stamp of approval. You know the scene – welfare, social workers, and psychiatrists, and you know what? None of them knows me, and none of them cares. I didn't need heavy drugs when I was working for Taz. H does what he can for me, but I'm trapped. I can't go anywhere. I'm a prisoner in my own house." She looked around for a moment and then asked brightly, "Hey, how do you like my place?"

I looked around, appreciating the homey garage sale eclectics.

"It's cute," I said.

Yoni made tea and sandwiches while I told her about Nemo Street and Rainbow and the Conspiracy. When Yoni tried to take Teddy his supper, he wouldn't let her in his room, so I took it in and sat with him while he nibbled at his food. He was still sniffling, so I rocked him gently and sang softly to him until he fell asleep.

After Teddy was settled, Yoni and I lay down on either end of the sofa, facing each other. Love nestled closely in my arms, and Yoni nursed her daughter, while the radio played the latest flower power songs.

I looked at Yoni, feeling her pain.

"Yoni, you'll break free one day. Your life won't be like this forever," I burst out passionately.

"Where can I go? What can I do? You hated me for wanting Taz, but he was my chance for a new life. I wanted to be part of his trip because mine was going nowhere. You're different. You're like Taz. You make your dreams come true. You're on TV. Look at your clothes. You're going somewhere. I'm not going anywhere. And now I have two kids. I had my chance and blew it."

"Does H hurt you?" I asked cautiously.

"He doesn't beat me, if that's what you mean. He stays. That's something. He knows what I need, and he gets it for me when I need it. It's the most I could hope for."

"Would you go back to Taz if you could?" I asked.

"Sure. He made me feel alive. He filled my head with dreams. For the first time, I didn't need heavy drugs. When I came back to San Fran to see my kid, I couldn't take my mom's yelling and my son hardly knowing me. It blew my mind. I took smack and got picked up. Now, I'm caught in their net like a dead fish," she said with a grimace. Then she added, "Would you go back to Taz?"

"No, I'm never going back. I'm happy with my own life," I said with a surge of pride that I could say those words and mean them.

"You've got the real thing, your own trip. Hah! All I've got are drug trips," she murmured, her lips quivering.

"Is Sunshine H's baby?" I asked gently.

"I guess; I mean, it's probably his. He was with me, so he thinks she's his, that's what counts. He's not into babies; I don't think he's even picked her up, but he might get interested later, when she's older and cuter. H named her Sunshine, you know, for orange sunshine acid."

We talked far into the night, our babies sleeping, the music weaving a spell around us, the songs giving voice to our hopes and dreams while I told Yoni about my studio and the store. Even after she went to bed, she left her bedroom door open and the radio played into the night. Unable to sleep, I asked her why she left it on.

"It comforts me. I never really sleep," she murmured sleepily. "I can't let go. Too many worries. Too many problems."

H came in after midnight. Morose, complaining, he crawled into bed.

"When's she splitting? I want my space back," he grumbled.

"Hang loose, H, Flower Child and I shared deep time. You know they're leaving tomorrow."

H moved on top of Yoni and a minute later grunted to a climax.

How could she stand this slavery to drugs, the social services, and H? Only drug dreams kept her going. Reality was too tough to take.

"H, I need something to tide me over. I feel down. What can I take that won't show up on the test?" Yoni asked.

"I could get you some uppers. Maybe then you'd clean the house," he said.

"That'd help, baby," she crooned.

They talked on and the radio played far into the night. Holding the pillow over my head, I dreamed about the studio, the store, and my life with Rainbow and Love.

In the morning, I looked out the kitchen window and saw a charming cottage surrounded by a rose garden.

"Yoni, that's such a beautiful little house."

"Yeah, it's cute all right, but it's been empty for months. The owner won't take deadbeats or drug heads, like me, and in this neighborhood that's all you get."

"It's so pretty. I wish I could find one like that in L.A."

On the way to the airport, H took me to Haight Ashbury to show me the scene. The same wildly costumed, long-haired hippies, groupies, druggies, and flower children were hanging out, but the San Francisco vibe was mysterious, the palette somber. The coffeehouse crowds exuded a whispering, secretive, intensely political energy as activist hippies plotted to bring down the culture with psychedelics, hip games, free love, cool words, and neon day-glo paint.

Walking down Haight Street, we passed the street actors who called themselves the Diggers. They were having a great time play-acting their anarchistic version of reality. Pulling passers-by into dramas, they turned the audience into participants, thus dissolving the boundaries of cultural restriction. The spontaneous skill of the players charmed us, but also awakened us to a deeper note of truth.

As interesting as the Haight was, I knew I belonged in the City of Angels, where the scene was light, bright, and colorful. My vivid green jump suit and magenta mohair sweater were too brilliant for this foggy, rainy land. Walking in the park where the famous Love-Ins had taken place, I picked up on the subtle drug and sex signals coming off the hippies, but they didn't feel like good vibes to me.

After a bell-tinkling wild freeway ride, Yoni walked me into the airport terminal.

"You must break free. You must," I begged Yoni, appalled at her resignation.

Surprised by my concern, she tried to explain.

"It's too late for me. I'm caught, lost; I can't ever get out, so I let my appetites comfort me. Taz was a way out. I'm sorry my being there was so hard for you."

I looked deeply into Yoni's hungry blue eyes. Seeing her as she was, accepting her suffering and feeling her pain, my heart opened and my arms encircled her. Love flowed between us, forgiveness dissolving the painful past. After enclosing our daughters in a long and tender embrace, we separated slowly.

"I love you. You'll always be my sister," I whispered.

Yoni's face was softer now. Tears gathered in her eyes, trembling, ready to fall. She rubbed them away as she said, "Sisters, huh? Sounds good. Always wanted a sister."

Then her quivering voice took on a determined edge as she turned and waved, "Have to go. 'Bye."

As I watched her disappear into the airport crowd, I couldn't help praying that Teddy didn't have to pee on the way home.

My heart swelled with thankfulness as the plane rose in the sky. Lights twinkled beneath me like downward stars. I'd had hard times too, but seeing Yoni put everything in perspective. I cherished the longing that had woven itself around my dreams, knowing that somehow, somewhere I'd find my garden of love. Like a seed in the dark, cold winter of earth, I didn't know what force pulled me toward my flowering, but I felt the pull just the same.

When I started my car in the parking lot of the Los Angeles airport, the radio spun out a song,

"...nowhere to run, nowhere to hide..."

That was Yoni's song. There was a song for everyone.

L.A. welcomed me into its smoggy embrace, pulling me into its pulsing energy and its freeway rhythms. All was quiet and dark in my fragrant, flowering, leafy courtyard. It felt good to be home in my garden of love.

154

The Renaissance Faire

It was the spring of the Summer of Love. When I awoke on May Day, the sun was shining. The birds were chirping in the avocado tree and Love was cooing sweet sounds in her crib. All was well with the world, but I was burned out and dead tired. Magic was in the air, but I was curled up in bed, wishing I could get beyond the aching fatigue that had taken over my body and my mind. I'd been working too hard, too late, too much.

The Conspiracy was a success. It took all my time to keep the store stocked, let alone to do what was needed to run it and keep accounts. I was thinking about the price I was paying for success, when I heard Rainbow moving around in the studio. A few minutes later, she pulled aside the curtain and peeked into my room.

"The Renaissance Pleasure Faire is starting today. Can we go?" she pleaded, her eyes shining like stars in her chubby freckled face.

"Yes, let's go," I said, cheering up at the thought of taking the day off. My thirteen-month-old daughter smiled at me from her crib and held up her dimpled arms, so I picked her up and swung her around till she squealed with delight. It was May Day. It was time to play.

After breakfast, we searched through the latest dress samples, draping different outfits over us in front of the mirror. Posing dramatically, Rainbow showed off each dress she held in front of her. Finally she slipped on a brilliant tie-dyed smock and wrapped a matching scarf around her frizzy red hair. Meanwhile, my fingers searched through piles of soft, colorful silk until they came to rest on an elegant, full-length, floral print. After pulling the coral and turquoise dress over my head, I buttoned the fitted Empire bodice and threw the matching shawl across my shoulders. Yes, that was what I wanted to look like today.

Love watched our every move with the complete attention of a baby lion. As soon as we were dressed, she ran over to her basket of clothes and lifted up her favorite outfit, crying, "Aah. Aah," the sound she made whenever she wanted something.

Love stood proud on her chubby legs while we pulled on her patterned magenta-and-yellow shift and matching bloomers, and tied ribbons in her golden, cherubic curls. When we looked in the mirror, three California flower children smiled back. If only Choo was here, it would be perfect, I thought. But Choo was with Taz this weekend, and there wasn't anything I could do about it.

After we gathered what we needed for the day into our embroidered backpacks, we took off in my old yellow Ford station wagon. Singing along with the Beatles and Jefferson Airplane, we curved through Laurel Canyon, over the hill, and into the Valley. Then we headed north on the freeway until we saw signs directing us toward Paramount Ranch in Thousand Oaks. As soon as we pulled into the crowded, dusty parking lot, we were captured by the spirit of the day. Rainbow slung our packs over her shoulder as I lifted Love into my arms, and we joined the costumed crowds streaming toward the Faire.

Holding hands, we crossed a wooden bridge and walked down a shady lane into a magic world of green meadows, grassy hills, shaded ravines, and giant oak trees.

Caught up in light-hearted play, we skipped like children along one of the pathways, passing charming craft and food booths displaying colorful banners and flags. Women sashayed along the footpaths, showing off their luscious, jewel-red, sapphire-blue, royal-purple, and emerald-green velvet Renaissance dresses and robes, while the men cavorted in colorful silk and satin tunics, tights, high leather boots, and feather-plumed hats. Free to express creative joy, costumed children skipped, played, teased, and laughed as they raced around the Faire. Enchanted by the laughing faces, the brilliant outfits, and the medieval music, we merged into the revelry. Flutes soared over drum rhythms, calling us toward a wooden stage in the center of a village green where white-faced mimes silently acted out their captivating stories. As the morning progressed, the fantasy atmosphere deepened. Transformed by the powerful energy, we left the green and explored the craft lanes, dancing and playing along the way.

As the sun reached its fiery apex, Love fell asleep in my arms. Too tired to carry her, I headed toward a grove of grand oak trees. There, sheltered under their shade, we curled up on the grass while primitive drums and melodic flutes carried us into dreamland.

Later, we stirred from our slumber when the music took on a new urgency. Costumed dancers were prancing around us, beckoning us to play with them, so we leapt up and joined their circle. Love sat in the center of our ring, laughing and rubbing her eyes, clearly wondering if she was still in a dream. We danced like fairies in a magical realm. As pure joy expanded from within us, we merged with the music and the laughter. Each dancer's play became an invitation to create an even more ecstatic response until, dizzy from leaping and spinning, I fell on the soft grass. When I closed my eyes to the magic outside, I discovered magic within. My body felt transparent. The connectedness was as great as an acid trip, but the communion was deep and true, not strange like a drug high.

Repeating, "God is love," to myself, I cuddled close to my daughter and fell into a dream. Eyes closed, submerged in the music as the merry-making and laughter whirled around us, I felt lifted into a golden light. Later, when the music mellowed, I opened my eyes to the late afternoon sun glowing through the trees. Renewed, free of the fatigue that had weighed so heavily on me in the early morning, I felt filled with love. The air seemed to shine with the love that flowed all around us.

Rainbow's dear, happily smiling face appeared above mine, the sunlight illuminating her curls into a crimson halo.

"Come on. Let's get some food," she pleaded, picking up our bag. "I'm starved."

I lifted Love, holding her soft, fragrant body close to me as we walked up the ravine to the path. Fearlessly, I met the eyes of the merrymakers passing by, flashing love, joy and recognition in the free love currency of the day. When we reached the path, I put Love down, and Rainbow and I swung her between us as we skipped along. The radiant joy that was in Love was at last in me.

When we reached the food booths, Love and I stayed on the green with our bags while Rainbow went off to purchase food and drinks. As soon as I sat on the grass, an ecstatic Love leapt on me, laughing, hugging, and kissing me with the spirit of the day. Receiving her direct transmission of wild joy, I responded by lifting her off the ground and swinging her around in circles.

At that moment a calm Red Sea voice parted the waves of revelry.

"You are so beautiful," a man's melodious voice called to me.

I turned toward a silhouette shadowed against the reddening, lowering sun.

"Who are you?" he asked.

I lifted my hand to my eyes so that I could see more clearly, but the sun was so bright I only saw an aura of golden hair and eyes of love that shone like sapphire stars.

At that moment Rainbow called, "Come and get it!"

I turned for an instant toward her, and when I looked back, the man had disappeared into the crowd. For a moment, a sense of loss eclipsed my joy. He had asked the question that played like a theme in my mind. What was the answer to "Who are you?" I was just about to go off into one of my internal explorations, but Rainbow pulled at me and we tucked into our snacks.

"There's the Byrds," Rainbow whispered excitedly, pointing to a group of hip young men hanging out together. You know they sang the Turn, Turn, Turn song.

"To everything, turn, turn, turn,
there is a season, turn, turn, turn..."

Reluctant to leave, we wandered slowly through the dusk toward the parking lot. Soon, only the artisans and theatrical players would remain to camp out for the night. We would have loved to stay and sleep under the stars, but we were unprepared for such an adventure, and the cooling air urged our departure. Sun-kissed, love-kissed, dream-kissed, we floated home, listening to the Byrds singing the magic of the Renaissance Faire.

"...maybe I'm dreaming,
music everywhere...
a kaleidoscope of colors,
crystalline laughter,
flowers in their hair,
recalling lands I've never been to..."

The next morning, Sunday, the dawn chorus vibrated like a cry of love heralding the sun. My body tingled as though my cells were woven of vibrating light. The Renaissance Faire was calling me.

"...let the morning time drop all its petals on me,
life, I love you, all is groovy."

Eager to choose a dress for another day of magic play, I jumped out of bed. I tried to wake Rainbow, but she was flaked out, and Love was tired and grumpy. I wanted to go to the Faire, so I called one of my customers, Angie, a Whiskey-A-Go-Go dancer, and talked her into coming with me. Impatient to return to the magic, I slipped on one of my favorite dresses, a silvery sage and violet silken shift with a border of flowering wreaths that ran from the left shoulder and circled the hem. Looking in the mirror, I shook my long hair free, added silver-leaf earrings and several iridescent bracelets. After kissing my two beloved sleepyheads, I took off for the Faire.

Angie lived in an apartment above the garage of a rundown Hollywood estate. I walked up crumbling stairs into a jungle of plants enclosing a white sheepskin lair and found Angie lounging on a black leather sofa. Angie tapped her red patent slings to Trini Lopez's latest hit and ran her fingers through her gleaming black mane of hair as she nodded her welcome. She had squeezed her long legs into white pedal pushers and painted her lips and nails a luscious candy-apple red to match her tight red and white striped T-shirt. Seductive cool was her thing.

What a combo! A petite biblical maiden and a tall red-hot groupie roared off in Angie's purple Jaguar toward the magic of the Faire.

At first, Angie was reluctant to join the wildly costumed throng, but I took her hand and pulled her over the bridge and onto the green. Slowly tuning in to the enchantment, she joined the playful fairies, elves, and jesters prancing through the crowds while I clapped and laughed at her spontaneous joy. Her Renaissance Faire dance was a far cry from her near-naked, voluptuous nightly grinds on the Whiskey-A-Go-Go dance platform. By noon, she was carrying a high-heeled shoe in each hand. Flashing a happy, open connection to everyone she passed, the Go-Go girl had been transformed into a barefoot Venus.

Later in the afternoon, as we were about to walk over a wooden bridge, I noticed a man and four women lounging on the grassy bank on the other side. Grouped in a biblical tableau, dressed in robes and long dresses, they stared openly at me. As soon as I caught the look from the man's piercing sapphire eyes, I knew he was the man who had spoken to me the night before. Everything else passed out of focus. I was irresistibly pulled toward him. Held by the power of the love stream radiating from his eyes, I walked over the bridge and, knees shaking, sank onto the grass a few feet away from him while he waited, leaning on his hand, gazing fully into me. Eyes wide open, I became the shore that received his waves of love.

Confused at my behavior, Angie whispered anxiously, "What's going on? Let's go."

Lost in the flowering of love, I heard her but could not answer.

Angie pulled at me impatiently. "For God's sake, I have to get home. I have to get ready for work."

Startled, I got up, but couldn't leave without saying something.

"Who are you?" I asked shyly, lost in his eyes as I repeated the question he had asked me the night before.

"I'm Bodhi, and these are my friends, Magda, Lola, Starry, and Deva," he said with a mysterious smile that tore at my heartstrings.

"Come on," Angie demanded petulantly, used to getting her own way.

"I have to go," I explained. "My friend wants to leave."

He nodded, then said, "We saw you with your daughter yesterday."

"I know," I said shyly.

"Are you coming next weekend?" he asked.

"Yes," I replied, trembling before his gaze.

"Good. Let's meet here at noon on Saturday," he suggested warmly.

"Yes," I agreed. Seeking relief, I looked at the grass for a moment, but felt immediate loss. I had to look once more into the brilliant, luminous blue eyes that pierced my heart and soul.

"I wish I could stay," I said, reluctant to take my leave.

Angie called out impatiently, "Let's go. Come on."

"We'll meet you here next week," he promised.

Awed by the potency of the encounter, overcoming my resistance to leave, I forced myself to walk away.

On the freeway, the radio played the song of my heart.

"...love that flows within the heart of me..."

Songs were singing my world into creation.

"...becomes a part of me..."

After I left Angie off, I couldn't wait to get home. Pulling into the driveway, I opened the door and hugged a delighted Rainbow, then took Love in my arms.

"Rainbow, I'm in love. I've fallen in love."

"You're going to be mine...I know it..."

High on anticipation, I no longer needed to sing, "Come on Baby, Light my Fire." I was the fire. Sparkling thrills ran through me every time I thought about seeing Bodhi again. The week flashed by on a high, but when I got home on Friday, Rainbow's face told me something was wrong.

"They've canceled the Faire. They just announced it on the radio," she said gloomily. "What a bummer."

Shock erased my inner landscape of loving creativity. My intense longing to see Bodhi became charged with the pain of loss. Surging dark emotions overtook my heart. First I was angry with Angie for forcing me to leave. Then I was filled with regret. I cursed the shyness that had held me back. Negative thoughts etched repetitive grooves in my mind stream. Feelings raged through me, destroying my happiness, capturing my energy, and diminishing my joy. I'd thought I had a happy life until I looked in his eyes and saw the promise of his love.

"Bodhi, where are you?" I called in my heart.

I needed his love. I had to find him.

True love had spun into my life like cotton candy. Now it was dissolving before I had a chance to taste it. The intensity of my feelings compelled me to action. Early Saturday morning, I drove to the Faire grounds and sat by the bridge, but he didn't come. I drove around the Valley, looking for him in the streets, in the mall, and in coffee shops. I knew I was acting like a madwoman, but I didn't care.

"I saw you...come back to me..."

As the bottom dropped out of my life, the memory of his eyes burned within me. I thought I'd found my garden of love on Nemo Street, but Bodhi promised a new love that made my humble scene pale by comparison. I needed his love. I had to find him. I was consumed by a hunger that could only be quenched by him. The image of his face, his eyes, had taken over my mind.

"I saw you...come back to me..."

Before I met him, I was blossoming with flower power. I could not bear this return to the mud of fear and longing. Even though I tried to return to the way it was before I met Bodhi, I couldn't stop thinking about him. Obsessed by the love in his eyes and all that it promised, I believed I couldn't live without him. The great hunger had returned.

"...if you feel that you can't go on,
because all of your love is gone..."

Taz picked up on my downward spiral and started giving me a hard time. Immersed in internal longing, I didn't have the joy to spin him away or the energy to resist the pressure of his will, so I succumbed to his insults in silence.

"...your life is filled with much confusion..."

Captured by desire, my love for Bodhi replaced all others. I longed to be different, but I didn't know how to free my love from his image, from the memory of his eyes. Like a moth, I could not resist the flame. I was helpless before the desire that was destroying my life.

Prophet

"*Happiness is just an illusion...*"
Drowning in passion, unable to sleep, my nights turned into an endless tunnel of searching. One night I woke from a feverish dream, the face of an aged, bearded man burning in my mind, a vision of an even greater love. Rising from my bed, I began to weld a bronze sculpture of this dream image.

> "*...reach out for me...I'll be there,*
> *with a love that will shelter you...*"

The vision of this elderly man with a gaunt, noble face and piercing eyes represented someone I longed to find from some memory I couldn't define. He held a staff and leaned into a strong wind, his shawl blowing behind him. I stood for hours at my welding table, cutting, shaping, and torching until the bronze figure evoked a powerful spiritual intent. The face, even more difficult to fashion, finally satisfied me when it embodied a hint of the nobility, truth, and mystical power that the dream had revealed. Finally "Prophet" was as perfect as it ever was going to be. Satisfied, I curled up beside Love, and fell into a deep, nourishing sleep.

The birth of "Prophet" released me from my obsession with Bodhi and eased my heart and mind. The act of creation restored balance to my life and clarified my desire for a spiritual teacher. My hunger for the love that Bodhi promised blended into the deep stream of longing that had always flowed within the depths of my being.

When I displayed "Prophet" in my shop window, Holly, the artisan tenant in the barn, came in and told me she wanted to buy it. I'd never had much to do with Holly. Always on the run, with a self-important air, she dressed like a prim, turn-of-the century old maid in high-collared white shirts and pleated black skirts. Whenever we bumped into each other, she displayed an arched eyebrow and a disapproving air, as though I wasn't good enough for her to talk to.

I wasn't ready to let go of "Prophet", but she persuaded me to sell it for two hundred dollars and let her take it home to show her dinner guests. Even though she promised to bring the payment in the morning, I reluctantly placed the sculpture in her hands. The memory of the night when it was forged from spirit into metal was still singing inside me. I found it hard to exchange the creative result of a transcendental experience for mere money.

The next day passed, then two more. Holly didn't return with the check. On the fourth day, I saw her getting out of her car and went outside to talk to her.

"Hi, Holly. How'd your guests like the sculpture?"

With an impatient shrug, she snapped, "They liked it fine."

Then, cold and hurried, she turned her back on me.

I forced myself to call after her, "You said you'd pay me the next day. It's already been four days."

I wasn't prepared when she swung around angrily, her face a mask of contempt, and spat out, "We don't need to pay you anything. You owe us for the utilities."

"What? Owe you? What do you mean? I pay my share of the bill every month," I defended, shocked to the core.

Holly's eyes glittered and her face took on a terrible look as she hissed, "Your share? Hah! The three of you live illegally in that shack, and you use more electricity."

"You've never said anything about that before. You promised to pay for the sculpture. That's dishonest," I argued.

"The sculpture makes us fair and square. We owe you nothing," Holly shouted, her hands on her hips like a bawdy street fighter.

"You can't do that. It's stealing," I cried.

"You have nothing in writing. If you try anything I'll get you thrown out. I'll call the health inspector. They'll take your baby away," she threatened, then she walked into the barn and slammed the door.

From that day on, our beloved courtyard garden was permeated by Holly's betrayal. The simple beauty of sitting in the doorway under the shade of the avocado tree or bathing Love in the garden sink was spoiled. I felt the threat of her presence whenever I went outside.

"...go ahead and hate your neighbor,
go ahead and cheat your friend..."

For over a year I'd been swept along in a tide of creative, positive energy. Now that the tide had turned, I didn't know what to do. Winston was away. I felt alone. I didn't know how to ask for help.

One morning a few days later, I heard the courtyard birds shrieking and ran out to find Holly trying to knock down their nest with a broom.

"That'll teach you to shit on my car," she yelled

When she saw me, she waved her broom at me and went back inside her studio.

I looked up at the birds and said loud enough for Holly to hear me, "Don't worry, mama bird. We won't let her hurt you or your babies."

When Rainbow went outside later in the day, Holly yelled at her, "You little lesbian. People like you shouldn't be allowed to live here."

I rushed outside and yelled right back at Holly, "How dare you pick on a young girl. You're nothing but a thief and a liar."

Holly turned her back and retreated into her barn.

I sent Rainbow and Love to the park, then walked over to Holly's door and confronted her.

Surprised at my advance into her territory, she backed away at first, then rallied, spitefully spewing her hatred. "There's only one bed in there. People like you should be driven out!"

Shocked, I defended my young friend.

"Rainbow's bed is under the work table. She sleeps in the studio at night."

"Hah," she sneered. "You expect me to believe that?"

Shocked that my courtyard neighbor could be thinking thoughts like that about our happy life in our studio, I fled back inside. Holding back my tears, I closed the curtains, shut the door, and turned on the radio. Then I threw myself on my bed and cried until there were no more tears.

When Rainbow came back with Love, I told her that we must never go outside without checking to make sure Holly wasn't around. Holly must have been doing the same thing because we never saw her again.

River of Peace

A couple of days later, torrential rains let loose, as if nature was trying to clear the energy. Streets flooded. Traffic came to a standstill. No one was coming into the Conspiracy, so I locked the door and worked on new designs in the cutting room. About five o'clock, I got a call from Choo's nursery school. His teacher said that Taz hadn't arrived to pick Choo up. She'd called him, but he didn't answer. With the rain, the rush hour traffic and the distance, we figured it would take me over an hour to get there, and we were sure Taz would show up before then.

"If he doesn't," she said, "I'll take him home. Don't worry, this is the first time we've had a problem. We'll work it out."

I promised to leave as soon as the traffic started moving, and I said that in the meantime I'd make a few calls and do what I could to find Taz. First, I called the studio landlord and asked him to go upstairs and knock on Taz's door. When he called back, he said no one had answered. I asked him to see if Taz's car was there. He looked out the window and said that it was, so I asked him to knock again and yell loudly to try to wake Taz up. If that didn't work, I asked him to use his own key to go in and see what was happening.

If his car was there, Taz must be home. I figured he was probably dead drunk, doped-up, or making out with someone, but he must be home. I called a few of his friends to make sure he wasn't partying somewhere, but no one had seen him.

A short time later, the rain stopped and traffic began to move. I was leaving to pick up Choo when his teacher telephone and said Taz had just called and was on his way to pick up Choo.

Just then the landlord called and told me he had opened the door, gone in, and woken Taz up.

A few minutes later, Taz called.

"You're no mother. You wouldn't even pick up your own son," he yelled viciously, and hung up.

Hurt to the core, stunned that Taz was blaming me for his own negligence, I stood at the window, watching the rain, feeling sadness seep through me as I listened to the cars swishing through the streams of water pouring down Sunset Strip. Finally, I returned to my fabrics and patterns. A couple of hours later, Taz rushed in, his face contorted into a devil's mask.

"You really piss me off, bitch," he swore as he pinned me against the wall.

"You wouldn't even pick up your own son," he yelled in my face.

Crying, I tried to explain.

"It was raining. Traffic wasn't moving. I was just leaving to pick him up when you got there. I called your landlord..."

Lost in his rage, he twisted my arm behind my back.

"Taz, stop. You're hurting me," I sobbed, scared.

"Bitch, fucking bitch," he growled, pushing me down on a pile of plastic.

"No," I pleaded, struggling, weeping.

He hit me, held both my hands with one of his, and began to tear off my clothes.

"No, no," I sobbed hysterically, pushing him away.

He hit me again, then entered me, swearing, overpowering me with his rage

"Dirty fucking bitch!"

When he was finished with his assault, he stood above me and shouted, "That'll teach you a lesson!" Then he left, slamming the door behind him.

Violated, flushed with shame, I couldn't move. Tears burned my cheeks. My sobbing increased in tidal waves that shook my body as I realized Taz's violence had deeper roots than today's events. How could I have trusted him? When would I ever learn?

Even though I lay there naked and bruised, I couldn't summon anger. Apathy sank into my bones and numbing cold immobilized me. Finally, I struggled to my feet. Weak and shaking, I took off my torn clothes and slipped into a flower print dress.

Burdened by deep shame, I crept out of the store. The night sky was clear with stars, and the air was cool and moist. Holding onto the stair rail, I trembled as I walked down the steps to my car. As I drove home, I shook almost uncontrollably. Glad the girls were asleep, I slipped into my bed and cried myself to sleep. The rainstorm was over, but it felt like it was within me now. I could only blame myself for what had happened. There was only one problem, Taz; and only one answer, to get away, finally, and forever. My life in the Conspiracy was over.

The next morning, exhausted, the rape replaying endlessly in my mind, I couldn't get out of bed.

Rainbow looked at me with concern.

"Are you sick?"

Hiding my tear-stained, swollen face, I made excuses.

"Yeah, not feeling well. Think I'll stay home today. Why don't you take Love to the beach?"

After they left, the morning slipped by in cycles of sleep, tears, and painful remembrance. Disturbing thoughts crept through my mind like little demons, making me feel bad about myself, tearing apart my fantasy of my happy little life. I'm not strong enough to stand up to Taz, I thought. I can't even stand up to my neighbor's mean dishonesty. I am so stupid, so naïve. I can't see what's right in front of my face. No wonder my life was a mess.

Why did I sacrifice my independence with a partnership with Taz? Why didn't I stay small? Things were okay when I was on my own. Where could I go? What could I do?

As the desire to escape took over once again, a familiar phrase surfaced in my mind, the phrase I used to repeat before I finally left Taz.

"I hate this world. I don't want to be here."

In the afternoon, when the sun streamed into the courtyard, I got up, opened the top half of the Dutch door, and then crawled back into bed. My body ached with a deep, sad fatigue. My world had been washed away. Mourning, I felt abandoned like broken rubble on the seashore. What would I do? Where would I go? Would I be able to create another studio? Weeping, I fell asleep again.

Some time later, I woke to a feeling that someone was watching me. I nervously opened my eyes to the unexpected vision of an elderly, bearded man peering through the half-open door. Wise, compassionately humorous eyes glowed from a radiant face framed by a halo of silver hair and a white shawl that draped softly over his shoulders. Sitting up, I pulled the covers shyly up to my chin and opened my eyes wider, staring fully, openly at him. I couldn't get enough of the loving eye light that seemed to shine into my darkest shame and lighten the burden of my heavy heart.

"Why are you worrying about these material things?" he asked gently, pulling at his snowy beard.

"What do you mean? You mean Taz? The store?" I stuttered, surprised, assuming he knew everything about me.

"Yes," he said with such profound understanding that my pain melted away. Happiness leapt like a flame from my source and my eyes opened further into his without fear or shame, spirit meeting spirit, purely and freely.

"These things mean nothing. Concentrate on what's important," he instructed, waving his right hand gracefully in beautiful patterns.

My heart opened in response, releasing its painful constriction.

"What's important?" I asked, wanting to know the answer with all of my heart.

"What do you want?" he asked lightheartedly with a mysterious smile, as if he were playing a game with me.

"Love, only love," I said passionately, pouring all my longing into those words.

"Love will come when you are ready," he promised, smiling tenderly before he turned and left.

Awestruck, I sat still for a moment, savoring the strangely mystical visitation. My mind moved at warp speed. Who was he? His face reminded me of my "Prophet" sculpture. Whoever he was, I didn't want him to leave. I wanted to talk to him. I jumped out of bed and ran outside, but he was gone. Back in my bed, trying to remember him, something expanded within my heart and his loving eyes became a part of my inner landscape, like twin suns lighting the darkness within me. I lay down, not to mourn or sleep, but to rest blissfully in a river of peace.

Some time later I heard a car, then footsteps. Taz came in, closing the door behind him. I looked at him quietly from my river of calm, deep peace. When he unexpectedly knelt down and put his head on my breast, I couldn't summon anger. I couldn't ask him to leave. I felt only love.

"I don't know why I hurt you. I'm so sorry," he said, tears running down his face.

Wanting to share my love and my peace, I took his head in my hands and kissed him on the forehead, feeling a great wave of forgiveness flow through me.

He whimpered like a child, "The thing with my parents kicked in and I lost it. I remembered all the times they dropped me and left me."

"It's all right," I said, stroking him like he was a child, kissing his tears. "It's all over now."

He lay down beside me and held me tight. We snuggled for a while, then his hands caressed me with desire.

Although a voice whispered inside me, "How can you make love to him when he has hurt you so deeply?" I didn't listen. Somehow, nothing mattered except the great love that flowed from my source and encompassed him. I shared the blessing of my river of peace, and made tender love to him. He lay in my arms a long time before he rose to leave.

The next morning, I couldn't move or open my eyes when I woke up. At first I struggled against the sensation, then had to let go. As soon as I surrendered, an eye opened in my forehead and I saw three silver-haired, bearded men in bright white turbans and long robes staring down at me. The light was so brilliant that I couldn't see very much, but it looked as though they were in a garden of beautiful, glowing flowers. I struggled to see more, but they were silhouetted against rays of blinding light. Mysteriously, at the same time that I was seeing the men, I also saw my own body, as if I were looking through their eyes. Even though I felt immobilized by the force coming from them, I was not afraid. I felt their love.

"She's an unusual one," one of the men commented as he shone his cosmic wisdom like a searchlight through my being, looking toward something beyond my vision. Suddenly, I saw what he was seeing. A pattern like a segment of grapefruit emerged inside my forehead. Even though I saw it vividly, its meaning eluded me.

"Unique," the second agreed with a smile.

The third turbaned man sent beams of light into my heart, saying, "Ah ha," as if he had found something.

Holding me in a combined physical and mental energy field, they examined every part of my being, their eyes and hands emitting powerful rays. Without fear, I watched them explore my past, present, and future, exposing me to myself at the same time. Visions rose and fell within this interior vision. Images of past lives, strange worlds, and events both violent and ordinary wove a pattern that turned into a spiraling whirlpool sound. Then the three men faded into a blinding light that seemed to be made of a mysterious humming ringing. When I was able to open my eyes and move my body, I ran outside. Half expecting a space ship or a gathering outside my studio, I was disappointed when there was nothing there.

Who were they? I wasn't on drugs. They weren't aliens from outer space. They felt real, only different, as if they were in another reality. Whoever they were, they must have felt my pain. They must have felt my longing. Whoever they were, I knew they wanted to help me.

Immediately I felt different, empty and clear. There was only one thought in my mind. I had to leave my beloved studio. Even though I was scared, I also believed things would work out. Lifted into heaven at the Renaissance Faire, abused by Taz, and altered by mysterious encounters, I felt as though invisible cords had been cut and the universe was telling me to go.

Book Two: Psychedelia

Remembering my arrival in Nemo Street just over a year ago, I wished I was strong enough to transcend the heartache and hang on to what I'd worked so hard to create, but I felt that everything had been ruined. Even though Flower Power had helped me ride a high tide of success, I was tired of false hopes. I had to face the reality that I could not build a future with Taz. It was time for me to move on.

The only place I could think of going was the cottage in the rose garden next to Yoni's house in Berkeley. Maybe Yoni and I could share a studio and help each other out. She'd worked with Taz. She had the skills. Desperate, I convinced myself it could work.

Going to San Francisco

"**R**ainbow, we're moving to San Francisco," I announced, hoping my upbeat confidence would inspire Rainbow to come with me.

"Oh, no! I love it here. I don't want to leave," she replied immediately, reverting to the scared little-girl look she took on every time her safety was threatened.

"We don't have a choice. The signs are everywhere. Holly's ruined our life here. Taz and I had a fight. I can't go back to the store. We have to make a fresh start."

"Well, I've always wanted to go to San Francisco," she said reluctantly, slowly warming to the idea.

"That's the spirit. Come on, Rainbow. Let's pack up."

Rainbow turned on the radio, and we sang as we packed.

"If you're going to San Francisco..."

"We're taking all this stuff?" Rainbow asked incredulously.

"...be sure to wear some flowers in your hair..."

"No, silly. We'll have a garage sale and travel as light as we can," I teased, trying my best to keep the energy lighthearted.

"...you're gonna meet some gentle people there..."

We put out garage sale signs and piled all our stuff in the driveway.

"...*summer time will be a Love-In there...*"

Our Saturday garage sale was a sell-out.

"...*such a strange vibration...people in motion...*"

Early Sunday morning, I hauled a trailer over to the Conspiracy to pick up my things. As soon as I took my beautiful clothes off the hangers and the jewelry out of the cases, the store felt like an empty husk, as if the living love that had enlivened it had retreated. I took one last look at another old dream and closed the door.

After dropping the trailer off at the studio, I headed for Carlos's shop. Even on a Sunday morning, Maria was hunched over her sewing machine.

When I told her I was leaving, she started to cry, "You're so brave. I wish I could go with you."

Then she turned toward the mirror, looked at herself and sobbed, "Look at me. I'm only thirty-five but I'm already worn out. It's Sunday morning, it's the weekend, but I never get a day off. I'm working and Carlos is sleeping in. I do everything he says. I hate being here but I can't leave. I have money of my own, but I'm afraid to spend it. He might find out and get mad. He might send me back to Brazil."

I couldn't argue with fear, so I hugged Maria until she calmed down. "Don't worry, Maria. Your time will come. One day you'll be able to leave him," I promised.

Rainbow and I packed the trailer and piled the trash in the lane. I figured by the time Taz found out we were gone we'd be half way to San Francisco. After everything was packed and clean, I walked around the courtyard, gently touching the trees, the plants, everything I had grown to love.

When I stood in front of Holly's workshop, I smiled, imagining her surprise when she saw that we had gone. Unexpectedly, at that moment, a wider reality expanded through me and I glimpsed the fear and greed and anger within her that had made her steal my sculpture. Suddenly I felt sorry for her. As understanding dawned, a profound realization blossomed in my heart. If I wanted to become love, I would have to love someone even if they cheated me. As soon as my love included her, regardless of what she had done to me, I felt the living energy of "Prophet" within me, and knew I could not lose what already belonged to me. Forgiveness welled up in my heart and the pain from the loss of my sculpture disappeared as I shed a few tears.

As soon as the anger that had motivated my departure melted, my heart softened. As if waking from a dream, I looked at my empty studio and felt intense confusion. Although I was ready to leave, I didn't want to go. I couldn't help wishing we were back in the studio, safe and settled and making beautiful things; but committed to my decision, I drove away without looking back. I'd proven myself in the Nemo Street studio, so I was sure I could do it again somewhere far away from Taz.

As we headed down Sunset toward the ocean, I suddenly remembered my son. How could I live away from Choo? Stunned, wondering if the shocks, strange encounters, and visions of the past few days had caused partial amnesia, I turned toward the Berkeley Street studio and parked on a side street to hide the trailer. Fighting back tears, I steeled myself against the familiar whirlpool of doubt and fear that assaulted me every time I came near Taz's studio, before walking slowly upstairs. Love toddled beside me, laughing as she tried to walk upstairs.

Choo threw himself into my arms, teasing me with his boyish giggles and wriggly, happy cuddles. I held him fiercely for a moment, breathing in his open, loving spirit before he and Love went off to play.

Unshaven, sporting black bags under his eyes, Taz was clearly annoyed to see me. There was no trace of the gentle sorrow or humility of our last encounter, but I wasn't surprised. I'd seen the softness of his core before, usually after some blast of violence had thinned his armor.

"Why so early? What's up?" he demanded, eyeing me resentfully as he crunched spoonfuls of corn flakes and milk.

"We're going to the beach. I just wanted to say hi," I said breezily, watching Choo and Love so I wouldn't have to look at him.

"Taking the Choo with you?" he asked belligerently, as if he was looking for a fight.

"No, not today. I've got things to do," I said, looking away again.

Then he sat back, lit a cigarette and took a sip of his morning coffee laced with cream and sugar.

Uptight, afraid he was going to find out what I was up to, I made too many excuses. "Just want to visit Choo and split."

"Hear that, Choo? Your mom won't take you to the beach," he yelled.

Choo looked up at us, confusion flying across his face like a cloud, then he returned to his play with Love.

"Taz, don't," I pleaded, wondering how I was going to say goodbye to my son.

Riding our downward spiral, caught in Taz's scene before I'd even left town, I started to cry.

"Something's up," he asked suspiciously, walking out on the roof patio. "What's going on?" he yelled back at me.

"Nothing," I said, my voice shaking.

"Where's your car?" he demanded as he peered down at the street.

"It's up the street, around the corner," I sniffled.

"What are you hiding?" he shouted angrily, as if he was a Nazi interrogator.

I took a deep breath through my increasing sobs, and managed to say, "We're going to Berkeley. I'm leaving L.A. for good."

"Dumb bitch! You left your studio?" he said scathingly.

"Had to. Can't take any more scenes like the other night," I whispered, hoping Choo wasn't listening.

"Hah! You've tried that before, but you always crawl back, broke, a failure, or wanting something. We made up. It would have been okay. What about Choo? You're going to disappear out of his life, take away his sister? How's he going to feel about that?"

The pressure of his angry logic made my head ache. I couldn't explain anything to him. My feelings never had any meaning in his world. Tears stinging my cheeks, I picked up Love and headed toward the door.

"Okay, okay. Wait. Take Choo with you. I'll help you get started and send you money. It'll take a while to get a scene going in San Francisco."

Surprised at his sudden change of heart, scared that he might change his mind, I packed Choo's things quickly and left.

Rainbow's face lit up when she saw Choo.

"Now our family's complete," she said with a Cheshire cat smile.

Once everyone was settled, we headed north on the Pacific Coast Highway, driving past Santa Barbara toward San Luis Obispo. After lunch in the Oceano Beach Café, I rented a dune buggy so the children could visit the valley where Love was conceived. We bundled up and roared down the beach to the stream. After climbing the dunes to my favorite valley, I turned off the engine and silence settled around us. The quiet felt deeply profound. Gradually our ears tuned to the whispering, sifting sounds of the sands sighing around us.

Rainbow jumped off the buggy and helped Choo and Love down. Soon they were chasing each other, sliding down the sand hills, and shrieking with laughter before they climbed up to do it all over again.

Seeking rest, I lay on the sun-warmed sand. Soothed by the powerful, elemental beauty of my sanctuary, I sifted the rough, dry granules through my hands as potent memories rose to the surface of my mind.

The Bad Trip

Nearly two years before, a year before Love's conception in the dunes, I'd had one big, bad acid trip in the spring of '65.

I was feeling pretty low after I found out that Taz and Yoni were making it. For a long time, I'd refused to believe that he was running around with other women, but having a live-in lover and all-around helper taking over my mothering roles with Choo was something else. There was no way I could pretend Yoni wasn't there. Forced by Taz to live in exile in the City of Angels and unable to resolve or extricate myself from the love, desire, and pain that bound me to him, I imagined the worst possible scenarios evolving out of Taz's and Yoni's coupling and endured relentless mental and emotional suffering.

I'd take care of our La Cienega gallery until the separation became unbearable. Then I'd jump in the car and drive north, only to find my anticipation switching to fear of what might happen when I got there. Only my time with my son eased my heart, but if I came too often or stayed too long, Taz would get on my case.

"Go sell some art," he'd yell as soon as he wanted me out of his way.

If I dared mention his relationship with Yoni, he'd blast me with scathing remarks like, "God, you always have to bad-trip everything," or, "What are you afraid of? We work together. She needs sex and so do I, so we do it. Big deal," or, "Why can't you get it that you don't have to be in love with everyone you sleep with?" or, "You really think I'd do anything with her but put her to work or fuck her? You've got to be kidding."

Taz's remarks cut me to the core, so I pretended to accept his scene, even though my heart felt like it was being torn apart. Fear, rejection, desire, and jealousy whirled around inside me, keeping me in endless torment. Relating to Taz was hard enough, but relating to Yoni proved impossible. The fact that I tried at all was amazing, and that I failed, not surprising.

Yoni took over as wife, lover, and mother while I was gone. Then she had to watch me move in for a few days every couple of weeks. We gave each other space. We acted like it was cool when in truth, we hated and feared each other, and wanted each other gone. The tension went on for months. One day I couldn't take it any more. I was ready to try anything.

The buzz was all around about how acid could take you to new dimensions of spirituality, dissolve your ego, and increase love and freedom. If that was possible, I was willing to give acid one more try.

I'd tripped on acid only once before. Taz had given me a tab one cold Monterey winter night before Love was born, when my one-year-old son, Choo, was fast asleep in his crib.

"Take this," he said roughly, shoving the white pill at me.

"What is it?" I asked.

"Acid," he said.

"What's it going to do?" I questioned, fear of the unknown cramping my stomach.

"It's going to set you free, baby. Take it," he insisted as he put it on my tongue.

I'd never heard of acid. I had no idea what was happening to me when the house started to writhe and undulate, and brilliant, swirling patterns took over my vision. I started to freak out and snuggled up to Taz, wanting comfort from him, begging him to tell me what was happening.

He pushed me away, yelling, "Go on your own trip. Leave me alone."

His rejection tumbled me into deep fear. I thought I was losing my mind, so I crawled over to my son's bed to take what I thought was my last look at his sweet face, but his pure infant energy pulled me out of my horror. Even so, the hallucinations continued all though the long, lonely, early-morning hours as my deranged psychedelic attention immersed me in seemingly eternal muscular intestinal rumblings. Later, when I had learned more about LSD, I wondered why people said acid gave you glimpses of God. In my experience, it had only made everything seem worse than it already was.

The next morning, Taz made fun of me, saying things like, "God, you're square. I give you acid and you waste it freaking out and hiding in bed. No wonder I'm always looking for someone cool to hang out with. You want to know what they call a bad trip? A bummer! That's what you are, a bummer."

I'd learned a lot since that first trip, how the setting and who you tripped with influenced the kind of trip you had, and how important it was to have an experienced guide who was willing to be there for you.

When I told that to Taz, he jeered, "Still looking for excuses for your bad trip? Well, I'm not going for them."

When the threesome scene got worse than taking another risk, I was willing to drop acid again. I hoped that if Yoni and I tripped together in the dunes, we might be able to break through our resistance to sharing love and achieve a workable truce. I couldn't enter Taz's world with my concepts of morality, so I wanted to see if acid would help me attain the state of free love that everyone was talking about. I couldn't imagine anything more wonderful than being free of fear and jealousy.

On my next trip to Oceano, I brought up the idea over dinner in the local Chinese restaurant and had the momentary satisfaction of watching their mutual shock.

"And I always thought you were so square!" Yoni blurted impetuously. "What a cool idea."

Taz pushed away his plate, lit a cigarette, and looked at me through the smoke rings, clearly assessing whether he thought acid could really break me out of my square mindset, and what would happen if I did.

"You think you're ready for that?" he finally said, gruffly pleased with my suggestion.

"Yeah, I'm ready," I said firmly, proud of myself.

The next morning, after taking Choo to a local play school, the three of us set off in the dune buggy. I insisted we find a place where I felt comfortable, so we drove around until we discovered a remote little valley of dunes near the stream, about midway down Oceano Beach.

Taz turned off the roaring dune buggy and the natural sounds returned – the whisper of sand shifting; the fresh, blustery winds; and the distant roar of the waves breaking on the shore. The three of us sat uneasily on the top of a dune, not knowing how to start or what to say. Taz made the first move. He took out a folded paper and threw it at me. I caught it, unfolded the paper, and held it out for Yoni to take her tab. She took it with experienced bravado and threw it into her mouth.

Holding my tab in cupped hands in front of my heart, I made a silent prayer to find a way beyond fear and jealousy.

Then I placed it carefully on my tongue, praying that the trip would melt down our trio of control, jealousy and fear.

When Taz got back into the dune buggy, I asked him where he was going to hang out while we were tripping.

Shaming me in front of Yoni, he hooted derisively, "You want me to waste my day hanging around you two? Forget it, I've got better things to do," he said scornfully, muttering, "Idiot," under his breath.

Feeling nervous that he was backing out of being there for us, I insisted, "Trippers are supposed to have experienced guides in case they need help."

"You've got each other. That's what you wanted, wasn't it?" he sneered.

"But you promised," I said, getting uptight.

"What do you think is going to happen to you out here in the middle of nowhere?" he ridiculed. "Guess what? Nothing. You wanted a trip? Here it is. Go for it. I'll pick you up this afternoon."

With that, Taz and Yoni jumped back into the dune buggy and took off to the top of another dune a few hundred yards off. He dropped her off, then roared down the dunes and back along the beach to Oceano.

Yoni and I sat for a while on top of our dunes, looking at each other occasionally from our distance, and then as the trip surged full on, I forgot about her. Breezes blew gently under the sun. The sand was soft and warm. Laughing, I took off my white sneakers and, like a child, slid down the sand hill into the little valley. Wanting to touch the sand with all of my body, I slipped off my brown suede pants. Then I untied the belt of the matching jacket and let it drop off my shoulders onto the sand. Leaving on the bronzed medallion Taz had made for me before we were married, I lifted my black T-shirt over my head and threw it in the air, before rolling around on the sand. I couldn't get enough of the sand. I wanted to make love to it. It was beautiful, warm, and silky. I felt like it was loving me with its granular responsiveness that adjusted to every movement, while it supported me with its billions of layers of density. Delighted, I began to dance and sing like a primitive warrior, luxuriating in wild, birdlike cries.

Slowly, I became aware of the energy flowing in, out, and around the molecules of so-called solid sand reality, uniting, integrating, and melting everything into one. As I moved, my dance became a part of the surging patterning that connected separateness into one great unity of creative fluid, the essence of which was total love.

When I looked at my hands, the lines appeared like calligraphy, speaking divine messages that explained my destiny, my life. I read them with a primal mind, awestruck by my physical reality.

"What must I do with these hands?" I wailed to the sky. "Tell me what to do with my life."

Intricate geometric mandalas began to appear in my field of vision. They contained glowing, infinitesimal threads that connected everything in the living, surging cosmos. So-called empty space was actually full of constantly changing, exquisite patterning. Sound was visual. Ordinary visual impressions expanded beyond their edges and revealed their connections to invisible mandalic waves of light and sound. It was all beautiful and incredibly divine. I felt like I could look at it forever. Nature was a feast I wanted to eat with my eyes.

With a subtle shift of perception, as though I had microscopic vision, I began to see the fine mist of tiny sand granules reshaping the dunes, following the currents of air that formed themselves to the shape of the waves of the dunes. Each grain of sand was interconnected by geometric patterns that shifted quickly, altering constantly under the influence of swirling breezes, minute insect movements, and the heat of the sun.

After a time, the sensual and visual overload shifted back toward the feeling level as I immersed myself bodily, sensuously, into the mystical, waving flow. I rolled around in the sand. I couldn't get enough of it. I devoured it with all my senses. I wanted to eat it and have it pass through me and become me but when I put it in my mouth I choked and had to spit it out. Instead, laughing with delight, I rubbed it all over me, delighting in the sandpapering of the envelope of my being.

My body longed to expand, to make even more space for the vastness that was opening within me. The energies of life flowed into and all around the molecules of my being – lifting, expanding, and dissolving them. Physical reality melted into radiant light that was a fluid and alive love that was so boundless, so profound, so deep that I trembled in awe as I felt myself being drawn into and absorbed into the light fluid alive love. There was an ecstatic rapturous excitement that felt like joyous magnetism as my spirit recognized God and I screamed, "I didn't know. I didn't know everything was God. I am so sorry I forgot you were everywhere and in everything." I lay in the sand, undulating with the waves of creation, and then just as I was dissolving into this mystical, divine ocean God of love, fear struck at my heart and I held back.

"No, no. I don't want to die," I wailed as the image of my son emerged on my mind screen. "I want to raise my son. I want to take care of him," I screamed to this love that was God, that was life, that was all that I was.

Curling into the fetal position, I refused the opening into life-love-death-life, and begged God to let me live. No one had told me that acid ego death did not lead to physical death, so I fought it with every particle of my being.

An infinite time later, when I realized I was going to live, I cautiously released my contracted body and looked around at the miraculous beauty of the dune valley. Beautiful as it was, it felt unsafe. I could not see over the top of the dunes. Where was Yoni? Where was Taz? I climbed to the top and looked around. Not only was Yoni not there, but I could not remember which dune she had gone to. Taz was nowhere to be seen.

"They've left me here. They're not coming back. It's a plot. They're trying to get rid of me," I thought, watching these terrible words emerge from my fear and penetrate the flowing, light-energy field of the world around me.

Paranoia took over my mind. Filled with terror, I scrambled down the dune and pulled on my clothes. Shaking, heart pounding, I looked in every direction, expecting something horrible to come over the edge of the dune and kill me.

Fully dressed, I climbed quickly back to the top of the dune. Yoni was still nowhere to be seen. I was alone and that felt scary.

"I'll have to walk home," I said out loud, talking to God, who was also myself, an imperfect, lost, scared God. With fearful determination, I plunged down the sand waves of the dunes, pressing against fierce winds toward the raging, whistling, dragon-booming seashore.

"I'll make it if it's the last thing I ever do," I chanted fearfully, my folded arms holding me together, my eyes focused straight in front of me. "I'll make it if it's the last thing I ever do."

I turned right when I hit the seashore and strode quickly down the beach toward the Oceano pier, barely visible in the sea mist several miles away. I was determined to keep the vision of my son's face in my mind's eye. Choo was my haven, my goal, and my safety. I had to find him and hold him; then I would be okay.

"I'll make it if it's the last thing I ever do," I repeated, looking carefully in every direction, sure something awful was coming to get me.

As I waded through the creek, a huge, bearded man wearing a black hat appeared on the top of a dune and stared intensely at me. Terror froze my heart, but I kept walking. He waved at me and shouted something, but I could not hear what he said.

Determined that nothing would keep me from my son, I waved back as if everything was okay.

He moved to intersect me, clumping over the sand in heavy black motorcycle boots. A sly, expectant grin on his face, he watched me walk up to him.

As I got closer, I could see his dirty, dark gray coveralls and grimy red neckerchief. He blocked my way so I stopped two or three feet in front of him. When I looked up into his hard, coal-black, bloodshot eyes overshadowed by bushy eyebrows and greasy, shoulder-length silvering-brown hair and beard, I recognized him as the rapist-murderer of my worst nightmares.

A dark shadow hovered around him that seemed to be woven partly of the smells of rancid meat, beer, and cigarette smells, a bitter poisonous acid-perspiration rage, and cruel intent. Seeking connection, I stared into his eyes, trying my best to ignore the pocked, pimply face that emanated red and purple colors, and the ominous nose that looked as if it had been broken several times.

Just as I was feeling that I was going to be swallowed by his hard black eyes and meet a terrible death at his hands, a voice whispered within me, "If love is in every particle of sand around you, surely love must also be in this horrible man. If he's a Hell's Angel, you just have to concentrate on the angel part." This was such an amazing message, that I laughed out loud, startling him out of an intense thought form he was weaving around me.

"What'cha doing here all by yourself, little lady?" he asked with a Southern slur, looking around to see if anyone else was watching, his sly smile revealing discolored, broken teeth.

Feeling his words swirling though me, I looked at his hairy hands and was repulsed by the grimy, black fingernails. A skull and crossbones ring flashed on the first finger on his right hand. If I didn't want those hands to touch me, I had to let him know there were other people around, so I waved casually at the dunes behind me.

"My husband and a friend are over there," I said in an off-hand way, "but I wanted to walk down the beach for a while. They're coming along soon."

"I don't see anyone," he said gruffly, picking his nose, looking like he didn't believe me.

"There they are," I said, praying he had a long-distance sight problem. "Can't you see them? They're right over there," I said as I pointed in the direction of my dune sanctuary, wondering how long I was going to be able to keep up this game. "My husband has binoculars, so he's probably watching us right now."

"I don't know why your husband would let you go walking in this lonely place," he drawled, standing with his legs apart, his hands on his hips. "What's he doing out there in the dunes anyway?"

"Oh, he has a beach buggy. He loves to roar up and down the dunes, but I like it quiet. Can't stand noisy engines, I just want to listen to the sound of the wind and the waves."

"You sure sound different than your husband," he said, moving closer to me. "Do you get along with him?"

I stepped back instinctively, trying to keep my distance.

"Oh yeah, we get along fine," I answered, and then I looked back at the dunes and waved, pretending that I saw Taz. "I want to go home and see my son. I'm worried about him. We've been away from him all day."

"You want to see your son, do you? Well, I've got my car back there in the dunes. I could take you with me," he offered, clearly not able to make up his mind what to do with me.

"Wow, that's really kind," I said, knowing that if I resisted him, or ran away, he would overpower me. Where was Taz? Where was Yoni? What was I doing out here alone with this guy?

"I don't see a car," I said.

"It's just over the top of the first dune," he answered.

"Oh, yeah, that's right, the parking lot is there," I said with relief, hoping someone else might be there as I started walking up the hill.

Surprised that I was heading for his car, he followed behind me, stomping roughly on the sand.

"What's your name?" I yelled back at him, trying to keep his mind busy with questions so he wouldn't have time to think about doing anything to me.

"Name's Dag, that's short for Dagger," he laughed ominously, as, hands in his pockets, head bent forward, he took slow, massive steps to stay in sync with my more hurried progress up the sand dunes.

"You live around here?" I asked over my shoulder, yelling against the roar of the wind and the sea, afraid that any moment he would leap on me and cover me with his dark-shadowed, odorously grimy body and his evil intent.

"No, just passing through. I like to hunt," he said, sizing me up, looking around, clearly wondering what his chances were for some awful purpose he had in his mind. "I like to sneak up on rabbits and foxes, and sometimes I hunt other things," he said threateningly, sending a fresh wave of terror through me.

"My dad was a hunter," I said cheerfully, keeping up the game, "And so was my brother. I used to hunt with them when I was a child."

"You know how to use a gun?" he asked, surprised.

"Yeah, I love guns. It's fun to shoot. Taz, my husband has a gun. He's got it with him in the dune buggy. He likes to practice shooting," I said, making it up as I went along. "Do you have a gun?"

"Guns!" he snorted ominously. "I'll show you guns."

Toiling over the sand was tough. The late afternoon wind was blowing strong. I was cold, thirsty, hungry, and thoroughly scared, but also I felt a fierce will to survive, like a fire burning through me. Nothing and no one was going to stop me from finding my son.

"We live at the airport," I chatted like a tea party social climber. "My husband has a studio there and a Cessna airplane," I said, changing the subject, grasping at straws, amazed that my mind was working at all, totally aware that I was doing everything I could to save my life.

He didn't answer. He was huffing, puffing, and grunting as he hiked up the dunes. It sounded terrible, but at the same time it gave me some hope. He was clearly out of condition. I could probably outrun him, I thought, wondering what my chances would be. Just as quickly, I decided not to run unless that was my last resort.

"We can take you for a ride in our airplane," I offered, trying to give him something fun to think about. "Would you like that?"

"You'd take me for a ride?" he asked, surprised by my friendly offer.

"Yeah, it's so much fun," I said, trying to get him thinking about planes. "It's a little plane, but easy to fly. I tried it a few times myself, but of course my husband was sitting beside me. Oh, it's so much fun. We cruise along the beach, and then go up over the hills into the Valley. We land at a little airport there and have a drink before flying home again."

For a moment, his dark face lit up with child-like excitement as he said, "Wow. I always wanted to fly in one of those little planes, but," he said, his face dark again, "I bet your husband wouldn't let me come."

"Oh, yes he would," I said. "He likes to take people for rides. He's a sculptor, you know, and we have a son. That's why I set off ahead. I want to go home and play with him."

"How old is your son?" he asked, out of breath, slowing down as we reached the parking lot. There were no other cars there, only his rusty, scratched, black station wagon.

As I answered, "Two years old," he opened the back of the wagon and showed me a scattered collection of guns and knives strewn between broken bottles, cases of beer and boxes of bullets.

"Oh, look, there's Taz. He's waving at me. I'll just signal that I'm catching a ride with you and he can follow us," I said, waving my arms around, pointing at the license plate, and jerking my thumb toward Oceano.

Dag looked around, slammed the trunk, walked over to the driver's side of the car and got in. Without hesitation, I got in the passenger side.

"Let's see if we can beat him to the airport," I challenged, instinctively knowing I had to keep his simple, slow mind busy.

Dag looked at me with an incredulous look, like I was putting him on, but he was digging it.

"I bet this car goes real fast," I complimented. "Why don't you show me how fast you can go."

With a wild laugh, he peeled out of there, tearing up the road leading out of the dunes. Amazed that he seemed to be doing whatever I wanted him to do, I rolled down the window and took a few deep breaths. Holding on to the door as he sped past farm country and through green fields, I thought, well, at least I'm out of the dunes.

When we passed a field of farm workers, I was so relieved so see other people that the terror I'd been holding back flew out of me, and I screamed, "Help! Help!"

Several curious Mexican itinerant workers looked up at me hanging out of the window, screaming, but they couldn't do anything.

Meanwhile Dag was clearly getting bugged. "You're crazy," he snarled, getting nasty.

I knew I had to get out of his car real quick.

"Yes, I am," I said, looking him in the eyes, feeling like I was shooting my version of a dagger straight into his brain, "and if you don't drop me at that store over there, you have no idea what I'm going to do to you."

"What do you mean?" he said, moving from snarling nasty to scared stiff in a flash.

"I'm the dune witch and you don't want to know what I'm going to do to you," I threatened, with a weird, scary voice, like I was playing the Witch of the East in my favorite childhood book, The Wizard of Oz.

He threw the steering wheel to the left, screeched into the gas station and dropped me off right then and there. I was blowing my own mind with my power. I'd turned the tables on a bad guy with bad intentions on a bad acid trip. What a turn-on!

I staggered into the store and got hit with electric, neon, and plastic vibes that sent a shudder through me. The store was one weird conglomeration of undulating, primary-colored paper and plastic containers, neon lights, snakelike electric cords, and humming freezers and fridges. Long white hairy fibers popped and frizzed out of people's skins, and even through their clothes. Their strange, rubbery, wrinkly, cartoon faces radiated dull colors and rancid smells. Unable to bear the gross ugliness of the sensory overload, I went nuts.

I screamed at the grossly made-up, fat, reptile-wrinkled old lady behind the counter, "I don't have any money and I've lost my husband in the dunes. You have to help me. Please help me."

I saw and felt the shock of my just-coming-out-of-the-dunes-on-acid-after-outwitting-a-murderer energy hit her in a curving wave. Time slowed, and it seemed like ages before my energy swept through her and curved around like an infinity sign and returned to me.

"Take it easy. Sit down. We'll help you. How'd you get here?" she asked, visibly upset.

As she came nearer, I recoiled, drawing back against the window, shocked by what I perceived as thick, dark resistant skin that locked all the light inside her.

"I walked all the way from the dunes," I said, holding on to the wall, "and I'm dying of thirst and starving, and I've got to find my son," I wailed, desperate to be with Choo, who represented all the love and goodness that I knew.

"Calm down. Here, sit down, dear," she said as she pulled a chair over and pushed me gently into it. She padded over to the counter on legs bulging with varicose veins and took a Coke out of a monster cooler. As she limped back, she took a couple of Oreos out of an open bag and gave them to me. I took one sip of the Coke and choked, so I nibbled on a cookie.

"Water, I need water," I cried, jumping up from the chair. Even though I was aware that other customers were watching, I couldn't stop myself. "Where's my son?"

At this point, I couldn't tell whether I was meaning all this panic or if I was acting. It seemed I had to act like this to fit into the electricity and phone wires, the water pipes and the gasoline pumps of the little country store beside the greasy, oil-covered, falling-apart gas station on the edge of the dunes. Even though the ramshackle gas station and little store were sheltered from the powerful energy of the dunes by a small hill and green fields, it felt like a space station in the midst of awesome, oceanic, divine creation. Worst of all, the people seemed disconnected from the raw power so close at hand. It was as though they had switched off the major game that was playing in the universe. I couldn't take it in. My mind kept freaking out and the part of my brain that usually inhibited inappropriate social behavior was out to lunch.

I kept yelling, "I'm lost. I'm hungry. I want to go home. I want to see my son. I want to get out of here. Please help me."

Cartoon space-station people came in and out and stared at me, clearly thinking I was a nut case from another planet, and that it would be just a matter of time before the space police came to take me away. I could feel their thoughts and their fear, and that only increased my panic and my impatience to see Choo. If I could see him and hold him, I knew I would be okay.

I called, "Choo, Choo, Choo," and then laughed hysterically because I saw the old folks look at each other as if to say, she thinks she is a train.

Then the elderly white-haired gas station attendant walked in the store and the room instantly changed. His presence calmed all the electrical connections. Everything started humming in tune and I felt a lot better. His eyes glowed like clear, shining blue diamonds.

"Now, Vera, what do we have here? Is she lost," he asked the old lady.

"She must have got real scared out in the dunes because she's not making much sense. I think I should call the police," she muttered grumpily.

"No need for that, is there young lady?" he said with a smile that felt like sunshine.

He looked right at me with his diamond eyes. Instinctively, I knew that he was someone I could trust. He seemed warmer, more real, and his stringy fibers glowed like Christmas lights.

"Hi, I'm Dusty Dan, the sand dune man," he said, holding out his hand. "Now, what's happening, young lady?"

I put my hand in his and an electric current went through my nervous system, humming along, until I felt I was like one of the coolers or fridges or fluorescent lights that had calmed down the moment he walked into the store.

"I got lost in the dunes and I want to go home and be with my son," I said, more calmly, fascinated by the effect his energy had on me. Dag had put me into a fight-for-my-life survival mode, and this guy was taking me out of it.

"Why, sure you do," he agreed. "We get people coming in off the dunes all wound up. It can be pretty intense out there," he said, looking off into the distance.

"Yeah, it is, but I'm starting to feel better now."

"Well, good," he said, taking his hand out of mine. "Now tell me where you live. Who can I call to come get you?"

"My husband's still out in the dunes. We got separated out there, so I know he's not at home, but if you call the dune buggy guys on the pier and tell them Taz's wife is here, they'll probably come and get me," I replied.

Fifteen minutes later, two local dune buggy freaks, Gamble and Teton, pulled up in a chromed pick-up lifted high off the ground by massive tires. Dusty Dan went out and talked to them for a while, and they looked at me and nodded their heads. Then Dusty Dan came back and took my hand again. Wow! Did that feel nice! He put his other hand on my shoulder, and holding me in his current of calm, he led me to the truck. Before I climbed in, I searched Dusty Dan's face, wondering who he was and how his energy could be so soothing and healing.

Eventually, words surfaced and I said, "Thank you for helping me. Who are you?"

He smiled, looked up at the sky for a moment, then answered. "I used to belong to a spiritual community on the edge of the dunes, over by that tall Victorian house, a place we named Halcyon. Learned a thing or two," he smiled mysteriously, and then whispered like a conspirator, "but don't tell anyone."

"I won't," I whispered back. "Thanks again."

Teton, lanky and hungry-looking, with a shock of pitch-black hair falling over his eyes, jumped out of the passenger side and flashed a slick smile as he held the door open for me. I sidestepped him, grabbed the door handle and pulled myself up. Sliding along the cracked leather seat toward Gamble, I avoided looking at the dragon tattoos crawling down his muscled arms onto the greasy hands that gripped the steering wheel. Gamble, the ultimate redneck, wore a black cap perched backward on his head and a red plaid flannel shirt at least two sizes too small that made the buttons look like they were about to pop off his hairy chest.

Recoiling from the rank body odors steaming like swirling gray clouds from their darkly tanned skin, dirty blue jeans, sweaty plaid shirts, and scuffed cowboy boots, I could hardly breathe. Feeling assaulted by the emanations coming off them, I stiffened and scrunched as small as I could, trying not to touch them. Their mind thoughts were visual and very real to me. Their actions were exaggerated, instead of simple and true like Dusty Dan. Their smiles could not hide their sexual hunger, and they turned me off big-time. When Teton cracked a beer and offered it to me, I felt safer taking it, but it made me choke.

Gamble and Teton were supposed to be Taz's dune buggy buddies, but I'd heard them put down Taz's harem with the locals and laugh behind his back in the Oceano Coffee Shop. I couldn't imagine what went on in their minds about Taz's menagerie but their lustful scorn scared me.

"What's the matter, little lady?" Gamble drawled, his body pressing against mine as he started up the engine.

"I lost Taz, so I walked out of the dunes. Maybe we should take a plane and go and look for him," I said, pulling further away from him, wishing I could make myself smaller like Alice in Wonderland.

"Now, why should Taz be lost? He has the dune buggy, doesn't he?" he sneered, clearly thinking I was a nut case.

"Yes, but it must be broken. It's almost the end of the day, and he's not back. What if he's lost or hurt? Maybe the dune buggy turned over. You know how wild he is," I ranted, feeling the panic building up inside me again. "I don't want my son to lose his father."

"Okay. Okay. We'll look for him. Don't worry, little lady. We'll find him for you," Gamble promised, as he gunned the truck.

Gamble and Teton got into total redneck rescue mode, whooping and laughing, raving about how they were going to rescue Taz. After speeding through Oceano, they roared into the airport, tires squealing. They dropped me off and tore down the runway to their plane. A few minutes later, they were up in the sky.

The moment they were gone, everything changed. After thanking God for getting me out of the dunes, I lay on the grass and basked in the sun. Breathing in the uplifting fragrance of nature, once again enchanted by the colors and patterns of beauty pulsating all around me, I wondered what had happened to me out there in the dunes. I had thought I was dying, but I didn't want to die. I wanted to raise my son. When I contracted against dying, fear took over. Then I walked straight toward what I feared. What a trip!

Then, empty of thoughts, I listened to the birds' warbling. As I watched their calls pattern into the air and merge with the magenta auras vibrating around every green leaf and every blade of grass, it felt as though creation itself was a song. Flowers sang with color, their petal radiations extending far into the sky. The living air resounded with beautiful energy mandalas that shaped moment-to-moment all the connections between every living species. This newly visible invisibility was more interesting than regular reality. I was tripping blissfully when Taz and Yoni roared up in the dune buggy, Choo sitting between them.

After taking Choo in my arms and holding him and breathing him into me for a very long moment, I looked at Taz and Yoni.

Taz was pissed. Surprisingly, I watched his anger from an amused, distant place. He was all locked up, pretending to be what he wasn't, and that thought seemed so ultimately cool that I laughed out loud. That did not go down well. It made him even madder.

"Where'd you go? Why'd you leave? What the hell were you thinking? They're all laughing at me. Damn idiot," he ranted, pacing back and forth in front of me, making menacing faces.

When I tried to tell Taz what had happened to me in the dunes, he didn't want to know. Sure, I'd acted dumb and scared. I knew that, but he'd agreed to be there for us and then he took off. All I had needed was to see either him or Yoni and I would have been fine.

Unusually immune to his storming temper, realizing there was no point in talking to him, I smiled at Yoni who was wide open, acid-blasted. Her immense, sky-blue eyes were wild with the winds and waves of the dunes, and she smiled back with heart-yearning hunger.

"Let's go get some supper," she said as if we shared a secret, and I said, "Cool."

Ignoring Taz, we took off up the road. Choo ran after us and lifted his hands up to us, and we each took a hand as he led the way. Miraculously, now that we had left Taz behind, the energy between Yoni and me felt clear.

"God, what happened to you?" she asked.

"I got scared when I couldn't see you. I wanted to find Choo, so I split," I said, feeling unwilling to turn the magical present into a story of the past. The real story would have to wait.

The Bad Trip

When we walked into the Oceano Beach Cafe, everyone stopped talking and looked at us. It was the first time the local crowd had seen both of us together with Choo, and no doubt the story of me walking out of the dunes and the airplane search for Taz had spread through the tight little beach community like wildfire. Smiling at everyone like we were on stage, Yoni and I sat down at a table, somehow mysteriously in charge of the situation, while Choo ran around saying hi to everyone.

After ordering, I looked around the coffee shop. I'd thought the little store on the edge of the dunes had turned into a space station, but this café was from some even weirder planet. Suddenly I was staring at people I'd been shyly ignoring every time I'd been in the coffee shop for the last year. I knew they felt sorry for me, and as their thought forms washed over me, I suddenly felt ashamed and embarrassed because I was Taz's wife and had to put up with another woman living with him and taking care of my kid.

My shame reaction was quickly replaced by horror as I saw transparent fibrous hairs sprout out of the jelly flesh of the counter-stool coffee-sippers. Then I was repulsed by burgers-and-fries-eaters whose dark, hard, tight flesh held all the hairs inside. Their wrinkled faces grimaced into masks that told stories of pain, sorrow and unfulfilled desire. And the colors, God: the purple, brown, black, and red that seeped out of faces and bodies made me want to throw up. Pulsing vibrations spun out from each person's sexual center, changing shape as they commingled with others. On overload, I put my hands over my eyes.

"Take my advice. Don't look at them," Yoni, an experienced tripper, said with understanding. "Just look at Choo. That'll pull you out of it."

I took her advice and called Choo over and took him in my arms. Closing my eyes, I breathed in his living light, feeling soft, vibrant energy streaming through his skin into me. The light inside him radiated golden and soft like a beeswax candle in a church, and his love laughter sent spirals of joy all around him, lightening up the room. The people in the coffee shop fed off him. They sipped their iced cokes and watched everything he did. They couldn't take their eyes off him.

At that moment, I realized that people radiate invisible patterns into seemingly invisible space, as do birds, flowers and leaves. It frightened me to think how unhappy most people are, and how their energy would affect the world. I didn't have time to go further on this mind groove because Yoni started talking to me.

"Where did you go?" she said. "I looked for you and saw you trucking down the beach. I tried to catch up, but you were moving too fast. Then I had to sit down, the trip was coming on too strong."

"I got scared when I couldn't see you," I said.

"Yeah, we should have been closer. I shouldn't have let Taz take me so far away from you. You're pretty new at this, aren't you?" she said sympathetically.

Just as I felt myself shifting into a heart-to-heart mode with Yoni, Taz walked in. Conversation stopped. Everyone in the coffee shop, including the waitress and short-order cook, watched Taz join us and order a cup of coffee.

The scene took on another dimension at that moment. I was in myself and out of myself at the same moment, an actor on stage playing my part. Gone were all the personal thoughts, fears, imaginations, and reactions. Instead, I felt empty. There was only the moment, and that moment was just great. Words and feelings dropped in only when they were needed.

There was dear Choo, the little love ambassador, going up to everyone and turning them on with his radiant energy. There was Taz sipping his coffee and smoking his cigarette as he watched Yoni and me laughing and talking and chomping down our hash browns and toast. I felt no fear or jealousy with Yoni, only a sense of affectionate sisterhood. Understanding and affection glowed like fireflies in the air as she and I shared our experiences.

As we talked, a dark cloud began to seep out of Taz, curling around us like evening fog. Yoni and I felt it and looked at each other, eyes wide, digging the clarity with which we were sensing what was happening. The trip had made a difference to us. We'd broken through our fear, but now Taz was jealous. Clearly not wanting us to be friends, his energy shut down our happy chatter.

Instantly diminished by his control, feeling lost, I helped Choo eat his food. I could not look at Taz and Yoni as my heart contracted and swirls of pain and fear coursed through my solar plexus. Tears gathered in my eyes as I realized the door to love was closing. I knew it wouldn't be long before the walls of mistrust, possessiveness, and fear built up again.

When we walked out of the restaurant, the three of us shared an awkward moment. No one knew where to go or with whom.

Unexpectedly, I spoke up, "Yoni, let's put Choo to bed."

Yoni looked at Taz. Taz shrugged and took off in his car. We walked back down the road toward the airport, holding dear little Choo's hands.

I'd never been inside Yoni's house before. Like everything else around the edge of the Oceano dunes, it was wearing down from the onslaught of wind, sand, and salt water.

Yoni's low-rent one bedroom house was in shocking disrepair. As we walked in the back door, my vision was repelled by the grimy old linoleum tiles on the kitchen floor, the cracks running over the dirty cream plaster walls, and the moldy green wall-to-wall shag carpet. She had made no attempt at decorating or even cleaning.

Trying my best to stay cool, I followed Choo into his room. His crib stood like a little island surrounded by a scattering of play toys, blocks, and books on the worn wooden floors. Happy to be back in his room, he picked up a few blocks and busied himself constructing something. Yoni and I returned to the living room. The only furniture was Yoni's bed, a tangle of mismatched sheets and odd blankets jumbled on a mattress that she'd placed in front of the picture window facing the dunes.

"When I lie here, I look at the dunes so I don't have to look at where I live," she mocked.

Lighting a cigarette, she inhaled deeply, then blew smoke through her nostrils like a dragon while she waved the matchstick around in her hand until the flame died.

"Choo stays here only when Taz goes away," she added apologetically, aware of what I might be thinking. "But most of the time, they're over at Taz's house. They're pretty tight, you know. That's cool for a dad and son, to hang out like that. My dad was never around."

"Yeah," I couldn't help agreeing, grief filling out my words as I added, "only in Choo's case, it's his mom who's not around."

"He loves you. He knows you're his mom," she hurried to assure me. "And you see him a lot, more than I see my son," she sighed, fighting to regain control over her trembling mouth by inhaling her cigarette and blowing storms of smoke.

Ready for a heart-to-heart, we sat on the mattress, cross-legged, facing each other.

"I know what happened the night we met in San Francisco was just a one-night stand for him," she said with some embarrassment, "but I couldn't let him go. When he told me about his art studio in Oceano, he opened a door to a new life. For the first time, I saw a way out of the Berkeley drug scene, so I left my son and my stuff with my mother and hitchhiked down here.

"He wasn't real pleased to see me," she added, "but I begged him to teach me how to make sculptures. I told him I'd work for nothing if he'd pay my living expenses."

That was an offer Taz couldn't refuse. Yoni worked twelve hours a day every day of the week. She cleaned, shopped, cooked, and took care of Choo, as well as helping out in the studio. To top it off, she shared Taz's bed whenever he wanted her. Even though she took care of Choo, Taz wouldn't let her bring her own son down to live with them. He said that would be too distracting to the studio scene. On one level that was true, but on another, Taz's scene was always about Taz having what he wanted, the way he wanted it, and that made me mad.

As I listened to Yoni's story, I glimpsed how men run the world. Women make it possible by taking care of all the details of their lives. No wonder the women's movement was gaining power. It was time for change. It was time we started to take care of ourselves. I wondered what it might be like if I could find a man-wife to do all those things for me. When I shared my wild thought with Yoni, she said she'd rather be part of a man's scene. She liked helping Taz do his trip. Neither of us could figure out what we'd do if we were free to have our own scene, so the only thing left to do was laugh about it, and that felt good.

Choo came over and climbed onto my lap. He was rubbing his eyes and yawning, so I took him into the bathroom and turned on the bath water. As I slipped off his sweatshirt and cord pants, I noticed dozens of torn fashion magazine pages pasted on the walls. As I turned on the water, mixed the hot and cold to the right temperature and waited for the bath to fill, I looked at the photos of the empty, too-perfect, over-made-up mask faces and the weird clothes hanging off their skinny starving model bodies. Why was Yoni pasting all these fashion pages in her bathroom?

Answering my unspoken question, Yoni said, "They're there to remind me that I'll never have a life. I'll never be beautiful. I'll never have beautiful things. They're there to remind me to take what I can, whenever I can, because that's all I'm ever going to get."

The shock of her words went through me like a truth sword.

Before I had a chance to say anything, Yoni continued, "Look at you. You're together. You're happening. You have your own life. You have your own car. You run an art gallery and you have nice clothes. Look at me. I could never take your place, even though I wish I could. I wish I could be you."

"Mama, Mama. The bath is full," Choo called out just in time. I turned off the taps, and teasing and tickling him, I put him in the bath. Choo splashed and played with his ducks while I soaped him down.

"Don't ever wish you were me," I said, feeling Yoni's pain as if it were my own. "You can't imagine how I suffer being away from Choo, having Taz push me away, watching him be with other women. I don't have anything the way I want it."

Then, going beyond words, we looked into each other's eyes and became real with each other. We recognized each other's longing and each other's pain. We saw ourselves in each other.

"Wanna get out," Choo said, lifting up his arms for me to pick him up.

"He's so cute when he does that, don't you think?" Yoni asked, not minding he'd offered his arms to me instead of to her.

As I wrapped the towel around him and lifted him out of the bath, I admired my son's strength and beauty. His skin shone golden with health and vitality. Irresistible, positive, laughing life energy poured through him.

The Bad Trip

We dressed him in snap-up stretch pajamas with little red fire engines printed all over the soft cotton. Yoni kissed Choo, then wandered out. I tucked him into his crib and read to him until he fell asleep.

When I came back into the living room, the lights were out and the radio was on. I could tell Yoni was sitting by the window more from the sounds she was making than by my ability to see in the dark. Deep and hungry drags off a cigarette were punctuated by her furious crunching of potato chips and gurgling slugs of Coke.

The Stones groaned, "Satisfaction" on the radio, their heavy lyrics describing our lives.

"Ain't that the truth," I laughed, moving and singing to the tune.

*"Can't get no satisfaction....
And I try, and I try, and I try, and I try..."*

Yoni watched me for a moment, then she got up and we danced together. Singing, closing our eyes, we went into our own heads as we danced our inner worlds. When the song was over, a wild, raw, indulgent, hungry blonde looked clearly at a dark-haired, square, scared, hungry mom and wife, and I looked back, and we seemed the same – soul sisters.

Later, we walked outside and gazed at the moon and the stars. The wind was quieter now. The distant boom of the breakers beat a constant reminder of the powerful oceanic wave rhythms landing on the shore. The garden breathed around us, emanating a life force that felt warm, fragrant, and comforting. We stayed out there for hours, reclining on rusty, ragged deck chairs. Wrapped in old cotton blankets, we smoked, talked, and floated down from the acid trip.

I awoke in the foggy damp dawn, holding the blankets tight against the chilly morning mist. Choo was calling me.

When I passed through the living room, Yoni was snoring, her mouth wide open. As I bathed and dressed

Choo, I heard Yoni groaning awake. Sleepy, yawning, smoking her cigarette, she watched me make breakfast. We shared a hurried meal of oatmeal, coffee, and toast, while glimmers of yesterday's trip still sparkled between us.

It was time to return to Los Angeles. Feeling my solar plexus tightening as I prepared to leave my son, I gave Choo a fierce hug, followed by one with Yoni, and split. I didn't say goodbye to Taz. That would blow his mind, I chuckled to myself, as I headed south. That would leave him wondering. Even though Taz's scene hadn't changed, my heart didn't hurt any more. Yoni was just like me. We were both doing the best we could. If it wasn't for Taz, we might have been friends.

So even the bad trip had a good ending. By facing the murderer-rapist nightmare man and his weapons in the lonely dunes where he could have overpowered me physically, I discovered strength I never knew I had. I also learned that the outer world was a malleable energy field that shaped itself according to our minds. Interacting with the energy field was like a dance that showed us, sooner or later, that our thoughts and desires do become real. Questions bubbled up with every new discovery-thought. How do I prune the thoughts that create problems? How do I create the thoughts that will take me where I want to go?

As I awakened to multi-dimensional reality, the graphic pain of my locked dynamic with Taz started to melt down. I achieved a clearer sense of Taz and my part in his scene. All three of us were needy. We were all vulnerable. We were all in pain.

I decided not to take acid anymore. It was too risky, too intense. You never knew what was going to happen. There had to be a way to live love that didn't involve drugs, and I was determined to find it.

The Bad Trip

The relief lasted for awhile, and then the need for Taz and Choo started to drive me wild again. As the fear increased, my mind imagined all sorts of scenarios. Jealousy and rage flamed in my sea of despair. The next time I drove up to Oceano, our triangle had reverted back to isolated, defense-oriented, sharp paranoia points. Yoni and I could hardly look at each other, let alone talk. So much for acid dreams!

Rainbow's End

Choo and Love jumped on me, covering me with sandy kisses and giggling hugs, quickly pulling me back to the awesome reality of the Oceano sand dunes. I hugged and kissed them in return as they snuggled on my tummy. Restless again, the children jumped off me and ran away to play in the dunes. I stretched out on the warm sand and noticed Rainbow sitting on top of a dune looking toward the ocean. With her coppery-red curls blowing with the breezes, she looked like a beautiful Renaissance maiden. I wondered how long it would be before she met someone and left me, and then I sent that thought far away.

Diving into old Oceano memories had renewed my courage. Knowing I'd come so far in the two years since that bad trip with Yoni, I felt I could go further.

How I loved the dunes. The sweet, natural fragrance of shrubs and grasses lifted my spirits. The buffeting winds cleared the L.A. cobwebs from my mind. The boom of the ocean surged through my bones into a deeper pulse that connected me to the raw, all-powerful nature within and without me.

May was always a month of change for me. I was born in May and it seemed that every year, one way or another, I birthed a new self during the spring.

"Maybe one year I'll flower into the Garden of Love," I whispered into the sand-shifting breezes, and then I shivered.

Walking to the top of the dune, I looked toward the sea. The late afternoon fog bank held offshore during the heat of the day, had erased the view of the breakers. The sun dimmed, then disappeared, as damp mist crept inland in sneaking gray tendrils.

Carrying Love, I led our little parade to the dune buggy and we roared down the beach to Oceano. After eating in the Oceano Coffee Shop, we drove to Avila Hot Springs and set up our campsite. After swimming and soaking in the hot pools, we snuggled down in our tent for the night. Unable to sleep, I lay still, aware that the power of the Oceano dunes had switched my energy. Instead of grooving on my dream of living in the rose garden cottage and sharing a studio with Yoni, I felt the reality of my very vulnerable situation. With a shock, I realized I did not want to go to San Francisco.

Why had the vision of the rose garden overtaken my mind? Why had I been so certain that it was what I was supposed to do? What if Yoni didn't want to go into business? She'd worked for Taz because she was hung up on him. Doing something with someone else was a different matter. For sure, I'd have to stay clear of her bummer partner. H was scary.

I tried to force my mind to think about something positive, like the beautiful little house with the rose garden, but it circled over dark memories, dredging up the autumn of '65, when Taz moved his studio from Oceano to Santa Monica. After Love's conception, Taz went to Los Angeles to deliver a sculpture and rented the third floor of an old warehouse on Berkeley Street. Spread out over the entire top floor of a tool factory, Taz's new studio was an industrial penthouse, a huge space with windows all around and an outdoor rooftop patio on three sides. Taz wanted to close the gallery and show the art at his studio. Sharing an uneasy truce, Taz, Yoni, Day-glo and I put the new studio together. Taz settled on the top floor in his penthouse studio, and the rest of us took rooms on the second floor.

Abrupt, impatient, and slamming doors, Yoni acted out her restless helplessness with the City of Dark Angels. After work she took off into the night scene and staggered home wasted, often sleeping until noon the next day. Taz got on her case because she wasn't pulling her weight. One night I heard her crying in her room and after hesitating, I knocked and opened the door.

Before I had a chance to ask her what was the matter, she started sobbing, "I miss my son. I pretended Choo was mine but I'm just like you. I want my own son. I don't belong here. L.A. pulls me down. I'm on heavy drugs again, and I can't stop myself. I'm scared."

I held her in my arms, listening, feeling her desperate sorrow matching my own stream of suffering – soul sisters.

Yoni split for San Francisco a couple of days later, telling Taz she had to see her son. The next thing we knew, a social worker called and told us she wasn't coming back. Yoni had been busted for shooting heroin. Instead of doing time, her probation officer put her on methadone and welfare. She got her son back, but she was stuck in Berkeley.

With Yoni gone, Taz and I drew close again. Magic flowed between us when he touched my swelling belly, kindling the memory of Love's conception in the dunes. Whenever he turned his attention toward me, I couldn't restrain my hopeful dreaming for a happy family. Distracted from his art by the coming birth, he fashioned a bassinet from aircraft parts and added a wicker sunshade. But, like a high tide, his attentions didn't last. Waves of change rolled in again when Chanter joined our scene.

The thought of Chanter was enough to bring me back to the problems of the moment. With a shock, I realized Yoni didn't even know I was moving to San Francisco. I hadn't thought to call her. What if the rose-garden cottage was already rented? In my rush to escape, I had not only forgotten Choo but also Bodhi, and dear, wise, beautiful Clara. How could I have forgotten her? The rest of the long night was a torment of fearful endurance. The loss of my beloved studio felt like a wound. However much I doubted my decision and was afraid to go forward, I did not return to Nemo Street.

In the morning, even a long soak in the hot pools did not relieve my tension. Back on the road, Rainbow played with Love and Choo while we drove north. Doing my best to appear confident, I turned on the radio and sang along to the flower power songs. I didn't want Rainbow to know how scared I was.

We pulled into Berkeley after dark. By the time I found my way to Yoni's place, Rainbow and the kids were asleep in the back of the station wagon. Sure that I'd made a mistake, I walked hesitantly up the steps and rang the bell. A few moments later the porch light came on and Yoni, wrapped in an old violet chenille bathrobe, opened the door. Confused, her eyes glazed with drugs, she didn't know who I was.

"God! What are you doing here?" she exclaimed when she finally recognized me.

"We're moving to Berkeley We're all here: Love, Choo, and Rainbow, my assistant," I explained wearily.

"Wow. Far out. Why didn't you let me know?" she said impatiently, looking over my shoulder at the car and the U-Haul.

"It all happened so fast..." I started to explain.

Yoni interrupted me, "Well, come on in. I can't wait to see Choo."

She pushed by me, padded to the car in her bedroom slippers, lifted Choo into her arms, and carried him inside.

I shook Rainbow awake and picked up Love. Rainbow stumbled in after me and crashed on the sofa. Yoni and I pulled out a spare mattress and made a bed on the living-room floor. Dead tired, I snuggled next to my children while the radio played through my restless dreams.

H crashed in after midnight. Reeking of alcohol, he fell on Yoni's bed, groaning, "I don't want them here."

"It's just for a few days. I want to help them out," she whispered. "Did you bring me something to tide me over?" she whimpered like a child.

Hanging on to my rose-cottage dream, I prayed things would work out, but the scene in the morning was chaotic. Rainbow sulked. Choo and Teddy ran around screaming like twin Tarzans, wild and out of control. The babies cried. Despair was in the air.

Every few minutes, H yelled, "Shut up!" or "Damn kids," from the bedroom, but he never got up to help out.

Yoni swallowed some pills and sat at the kitchen table.

On the edge of losing my cool, I took action.

"Yoni, we need to get settled. I'm going over to talk to the landlord about renting the cottage."

"I'll go by myself. He knows me," she said strongly. "Don't let H turn you off. This is my home. You guys can stay here for a few days. It's cool."

Yoni slipped quickly out the door. Surprised she didn't want me to meet the landlord, I watched her walk across the street and knock on her neighbor's door. They talked for a couple of minutes and when she turned around, her thundercloud face told me we didn't get the cottage.

"Bastard doesn't want his rose garden wrecked. Doesn't want kids," she cussed.

Holding back tears, I wouldn't give up. "I'll go over and talk to him. We lived in a garden in West Hollywood. The kids never hurt anything."

"I told him that," Yoni fumed. "No use talking to that creep. No one's good enough for his roses. We'll get a newspaper."

Upset that she didn't want me to talk to the landlord, paranoia took over. Now, I was convinced she didn't want me around. After that disappointment, hopelessness took over. Every day, even though I dragged the kids around to look at places, I always knew we would never find anything, and we never did. No one would rent to us. Feeling like a refugee, I was desperate, uptight, and thoroughly scared. To make matters worse, my money was running out. No matter how I tried to spruce us up, we still looked like a small tribe of losers. As soon as I heard someone say they wouldn't rent to us, I turned away. I didn't have the energy to argue or insist.

Silver Bullet had it right on the radio waves.

"...searching for shelter...against the wind..."

One mean old lady said, "We don't take children," before she slammed the door in our faces.

"There's just too many of you," an elderly couple said gently after taking one look at us. "We like a quiet building."

When we answered an ad for a basement apartment in an old Victorian home, the woman looked me up and down and said, "We don't take single parents."

"Why didn't she want us to live there?" Choo asked, his dear face looking sadly up at mine as we retreated down the stairs.

"We just haven't found the right place," I said, avoiding the real question. "When we do, they'll say yes, you'll see," but I didn't believe my own words.

Each day, after checking out the new rentals in the paper, we wandered through the streets and parks of Berkeley, searching the hangouts for friendly faces, looking for connections, but we felt like strangers. Political activists dominated the coffeehouses and the street scene. Berkeley's idealistic intellectuals and fiery freedom fighters seemed the opposite of the dreamy City of Angels flower children. They were fighting for change at radical rallies, resisting police clubs and tear gas, chanting "We are the people".

"Where are the loving people?" I asked Rainbow as we looked at the peace symbols and slogans covering the sidewalks, fences, and walls. "Where are the people that live the ideals?" She just shook her head.

Difficulties increased at Yoni's house. Too many people hanging out in one little house created too much tension. Choo and Teddy Bear were either out of control or fighting over something, and Choo kept asking to go home to his dad. Love was tired and cranky like I'd never seen her before, and Rainbow was on a downer.

"Get rid of Rainbow," Yoni whispered after the children went to bed. "There's too many people in the house."

"Yoni, Rainbow is family," I said, upset at Yoni for saying such a thing. "I couldn't do without her."

Later, Rainbow whispered to me, tears welling in her eyes, "I heard what Yoni said. It'd be better if I left, wouldn't it?'

"No, it wouldn't," I insisted. "Once we get a place and start making all our groovy things, you'll see. It'll be okay."

"Yoni bad-vibes me," Rainbow said. "I want to get out of her scene."

"Then let's go back to L.A.," I offered, desperate for a solution.

"There's nothing to go back to," she mourned, as a tear slid sadly down her cheek.

"We can start again," I promised. "I know we can."

"Let's try Haight Ashbury tomorrow," she suggested, suddenly brighter. "Let's see if we can find a place to rent there."

The next morning when we set out for the city, Yoni came along to score some drugs. After we parked, she disappeared into the dingy basement of an old Victorian house while we hung out in the little park on Buena Vista. The park seemed like a zone from another planet. Wild, costumed hippies sauntered lazily down the paths, lay on the grass, tripped in playful groups, beat drums, danced, or individually contemplated the stoned universe. Vibrations spun off the characters. Gestures spoke volumes. Sex and sleeping connections happened with a glance or a suggestive smile. Free-spirited, costumed characters played out their need-and-want games within the context of the drug culture universe. Even though I was a flower child, I felt uncomfortable and out of place. Sure that dark energies had entered a once-idealistic community consciousness, I didn't want in. I wanted out. I wanted to return to my true home where I believed I would find love. Even though I didn't know where that was, finding my way back there was the only thing that made sense to me.

"We'll go back. Maybe our studio is still empty, and if not, we'll put another studio together, maybe in Venice, by the ocean," I rambled, finding it hard to believe that could happen. "That'd be fun, wouldn't it?" I asked, trying for a response.

Rainbow was sulking. I'd never seen her like that before. I kept trying to make her come out of her downer, but she ignored me. What I didn't know was that she had her own dream cooking in her head.

"I want to go to one of those Flower Power centers," she insisted, her eyes fixed straight ahead.

Fear leapt in my heart. What would I do without her?

"You don't have to do that. Stay with us. We love you," I pleaded.

She looked away. She wanted out of my scene and I understood why.

"Always wanted to go to a Flower Power center," she repeated stubbornly.

Rainbow was the last of the Nemo Street magic. I didn't want her to go. "Please stay with us," I begged.

"It's time for me to go," she stated stubbornly.

"We can have another studio," I promised.

She wouldn't listen, so I had to let her go. Crying, we fell into each other's arms. Choo and Love hugged and petted us, trying to make us feel better.

"What's the matter, Rainbow? What's the matter, Mama?" Choo asked, with a worried expression on his face.

"Rainbow's leaving," I said to Choo, pulling him into our embrace. Love pulled herself onto my lap and listened, eyes wide.

"Why?" he asked, whimpering his sad confusion.

"It's time to move on, Choo," Rainbow explained.

"But I love you," Choo said. "Don't go."

"I love you too, but I have to go," she whimpered like a little child and wiped her eyes. "I have to find my own life."

"Whass happenin'? Why're ya crying?" Yoni mumbled, stumbling up to us, stoned out of her mind.

Her slurred voice broke us apart.

"Rainbow's leaving," I said flatly, defeated.

Rainbow stood up, determined, ready to go.

"Do you know where a Flower Power center is?" she asked Yoni.

"Yeah, the Diggers are near here somewhere," Yoni said, looking around. "They'll take care of you."

Rainbow took her bag out of the car. I hadn't noticed she'd brought it with her, but she'd obviously come prepared to leave us. Holding hands with Choo, Rainbow followed Yoni down the streets of Haight Ashbury. I followed, carrying Love.

"Here's the Diggers," Yoni announced as we approached a decrepit old building painted with psychedelic art.

After a hug and kiss for each of us, Rainbow picked up her bag and ran inside. In that whirlpool instant, feeling loss and fear, I knew I'd have to pull myself out before it was too late. I'd driven blindly into Yoni's scene, ignoring all the signs. Fleeing from one bad trip, I'd landed in another. It was time to leave.

As we returned to the car, Yoni's high came on strong. She was vibing other turned-on chicks and bros with the knowing looks and signals of the turned-on elite. She felt good now – on top of the world – like she could do anything, but I knew the relief was temporary. She'd come back to the reality of her life, and then, instead of doing something about it, she'd try to escape with drugs again. That was Yoni.

Why did I always hope for the best, instead of seeing what was real? How could I have imagined that Yoni could work with me and be a friend and helper like Rainbow? Why didn't I go to Clara and tell her about Holly? I could have talked everything over with her. She cared about me. She would have helped me. She was always asking me to come and visit her, but I was too shy and afraid to accept. I wanted love with all my heart, but I was afraid of it at the same time. Fear and shame blocked the love. How could I get rid of fear? How could I be free of shame? When would I stop repeating the same old patterns?

"I'm leaving tomorrow," I told Yoni.

Yoni licked her lips, deep into her high.

"Cool. Far out," she said, but she hardly knew I was there.

The Return

Up at dawn, driving up out of the morning fog into the sunshine hills behind Berkeley, I felt immediate relief to be out of Yoni's scene. Fighting back tears, I tried to make some sense of what had happened. I'd had a chance to make a home for both of my children and I'd failed. My money was nearly gone. I'd lost Rainbow. And now I had to return to Los Angeles.

The theft of "Prophet" and the rape had disoriented me. The strange encounter with the white-bearded man, followed by the vision of the three holy men, produced an altered state that precipitated my departure. I'd sacrificed everything to escape Taz, but I couldn't escape from myself. I'd pulled out of bad times before. I'd have to do it again.

Just as we were flowing into the rhythm of the journey, the engine heated up. I pulled off the freeway onto a country road, got out of the car and opened the hood. Delighted by the small community of log cabins and barns that looked like they'd been cast adrift in a sea of wild grasses, flowers, and sheltering trees, I wondered what it might be like to live in such a beautiful place. I let Choo and Love out of the car and taking their hands, I walked over to the nearest cabin. A handsome young man rocking on the porch waved a friendly greeting.

I waved back and asked, "Could you please give me some water? My radiator's boiled over."

"Sure, glad to," he said, as he got up from a bent-willow rocking chair and jumped lightly down the steps.

"Name's Noel," he said with a grin and a whiff of peppermint and he unrolled a long length of garden hose and turned on the water. Even though his buckskin pants, vest and moccasins made him look like a mountain man, his hair was neatly trimmed. I wondered if he lived up here and worked in Berkeley. Even though I was curious about him, I was too shy to ask.

"I've just been sitting out here on this beautiful morning enjoying the view. See how the sun brightens the fog from underneath, making it look like an ocean of light?" he rambled pleasantly as he pulled the garden hose over to the car and filled up the radiator in a slow, easy way.

Choo wanted to be in on the action, so Noel let him help hold the hose.

"Your children are beautiful," he complimented.

I looked at his log cabin, noticing the herbs and wildflowers along the path, the stacked wood, and the mustard-yellow curtains on the window. Everything about him felt clean and fresh and together, like his home was the most important thing in his life.

"Thank you. Your home is beautiful," I said, daring to look into his eyes.

Dazzled by the warmth of his friendliness, I looked away, at the trees, at the sky, anywhere but at his eyes. While he filled the radiator and chatted with Choo, I had one of those big thoughts that change the way you look at things. I wondered what would happen if I made my life a work of art? That made more sense than living like Taz who sacrificed everything that was good just to make a sculpture to sell to some rich person.

"Want to come in for coffee and rest a spell?" he invited with a smile and a flash of his eyes.

I contracted in fear and made an excuse, "No thanks. Have to get on my way. Have to be somewhere."

I gathered the children quickly, peeled out and left him standing there, scratching his head.

What was I afraid of? Maybe I could have made a new friend. I had to face the fact that I had become scared of men. Even though I hated my fear, I didn't know how to change. I had walls around me that felt as real as prison bars. I'm not that much different than Yoni, I realized with surprise.

In a few hours I'd be back at Taz's studio. I didn't want to think about what would happen when I got there, so I turned on the radio and sang along to the sixties songs, but I only mouthed the words. For months I'd been singing the "Going to San Francisco" song, believing in the dream. The difference between the song's promise and my ridiculous trip was painfully obvious. If I couldn't believe in the sixties dream, what could I believe in? There was no answer to that question.

We pulled into Santa Monica about midnight. In two weeks, I'd gone all the way from Berkeley Street to Berkeley and back again, all for nothing. Choo and Love were fast asleep, curled up together in the back of the station wagon. I looked at their dear, sweet faces. They were safe in their innocent deep sleep, while I was in deep desolation. Burned out, I covered myself with a blanket and fell asleep on the front seat.

I woke to a rapping on the car window. Reluctantly, I opened my eyes and there was Taz, making wild and silly faces at me, scratching and banging on the window like a crazed animal, trying to make me laugh. I rolled down the window.

"You're back," he said, stating the obvious. "What happened?"

"Couldn't find a place to live," I explained wearily.

"Where's Rainbow?"

"She stayed in San Fran. God, I'm so tired," I said as I rubbed my eyes.

"What are you going to do?"

"Don't know. Don't care." I stared straight ahead.

"Well, come on up. Have some breakfast," he offered. Without waiting for an answer, he opened the car door and picked up Choo.

Carrying a sleepy Love on my hip, I followed Taz upstairs, grateful that he was choosing to be kind.

When Taz served up oatmeal, toast and coffee, I cried between bites and sips, swallowing hot tears.

"What happened with Yoni?" Taz asked with unusual gentleness, holding Love on his lap.

"It didn't work out. Yoni's spaced. Nothing came together. I couldn't find a place to live," I muttered, staring at my empty bowl. I could barely talk. Hopeless fatigue had settled in my soul like an unbearable weight.

"Get some sleep. I'll take the kids out for a while," he ordered, flashing a smile that I couldn't help interpreting as "I told you so" and "you blew it again".

After he left, I looked sadly around his studio. It was messy and dusty. Smelly garbage bags filled the hallway. Taz worked night and day putting together amazing psychedelic environments, then he let them fall into dirty disorder. In Taz's scene, creativity alternated with destruction. What was the purpose of so much promise when it dissolved into waste a short time later? Where was the middle ground? Unable to sleep or answer my own questions, I soaked in the hot tub. When I closed my eyes, my silver heaven eluded me. A dark cloud blocked the light and the peace.

When Taz came back, I got ready to leave.

"You'd better stay the night," he said with an enigmatic smile. "Your room's still there. Saved it for you."

Without another word, I kissed Choo goodnight, picked up Love, went downstairs, and fell onto the bed. Love wasn't ready to sleep, so I sang to her for a while. Snuggled together, we fell asleep. When Love awoke before dawn, I got up and drove over to Nemo Street. Relieved to see the studio was still empty, I knocked on Winston's door.

Winston was surprised to see me.

"What happened? When I got back, you were gone. You just up and disappeared. What happened? We were all worried about you."

Tears welling in my eyes, heart aching, I told him about Holly, and offered a toned-down version of the fight with Taz that precipitated my departure.

He listened, showing sympathy for my predicament.

"Can I please have the studio back? Please?" I begged.

"It's already rented. The lease was signed yesterday," he said sadly.

"Oh, no," I moaned.

"They wanted papers this time. Clara and Arnie were upset that you left without notice."

"Please tell Clara I'm sorry. I can't face her now."

"What are you going to do?" he asked gently.

"Don't know. I don't have anywhere to go," I said, feeling the panic and fear expanding inside me like a storm cloud.

"Why didn't you call Clara instead of leaving like that?" Winston asked. "She would have helped you."

I didn't want to tell him that I hadn't even thought of her, so I turned to leave.

He called after me. "Holly's gone too. She left right after you."

"You mean I didn't have to go after all?" I blurted out, feeling more and more like the stupid person Taz always said I was.

The look on my face must have melted his heart, because Winston put his arm around me, invited me in, and put on a pot of coffee.

The comfort of his home made me feel more acutely the loss of mine. While he made toast and coffee, my mind went crazy. What was the matter with me? Why didn't I ask Clara for help? Clara had been like an angel in my life, but when she invited me to her home I felt shy and unworthy. I thought I'd be a nuisance, so I didn't go. Why did I keep myself away from people who cared about me? I could have learned so much from her. Now I was afraid to see her.

"I have a friend who works at the welfare office. Maybe she can help you," Winston offered. "I'll call her up and we'll go over and see her."

I barely knew what welfare was, but his offer seemed like the only open door, so I followed Winston to his friend's home in the Hollywood Hills above Sunset Boulevard. As we parked in front of a run-down Spanish hacienda submerged in an overgrown untended garden, Martina opened the door and her arms to us.

Martina was a classy Puerto Rican widow, whose financier husband had died, leaving her with two daughters to raise and educate. Winston had told me she'd had to go back to work and take in boarders to make ends meet. She was determined to keep the house until her daughters had grown. She'd had hard times too, but her laughing, positive strength revealed a strong fighting spirit.

Shame crept over me as I told my story to Martina. In the telling, I realized more than ever that I had created my own problems. Even though I longed for love, I couldn't forge intimate relationships. Instead, I clung to relationships that didn't work. However, one good thing came out of the San Francisco fiasco. Grounded in reality, I promised myself there would be no more illusions, no more pretending and no more denying.

Like a mother hen, Martina clucked over me.

"You poor dear. You can stay here until the welfare comes through."

Once Winston knew I was okay, he said goodbye and asked me to let him know how things turned out.

A refugee from my own life, taken in by a kind stranger, I felt awkward and embarrassed. Even when I was homeless, I felt ashamed to let someone help me. I lay awake for hours, crying, missing Rainbow, and longing for my silver studio.

The next morning, I followed Martina to her office and poured out my tale of woe to a sincere social worker with a crew cut and horn-rimmed glasses who was anxious to help me.

"You won't have any problem getting welfare," the kind young man said generously. "And you'll get food stamps and Medicare for yourself and your child," he added as he handed me forms to sign.

"We'll give you an advance and a letter to a landlord today, so you can get a place to live. You'll get the rest of the money in a day or two," he explained.

Trying my best to hide my surprise, embarrassment and relief that threatened a deluge of tears, I thanked him quickly and walked away with one hundred dollars.

When I got into my car, I sat for a long while, not knowing where to go next. Gradually, I became aware of the brisk sea breeze, and decided to go to Venice Beach. As I drove down Venice Boulevard, I saw a "For Rent" sign and turned off onto a side street. At the end of the block were four cute little furnished cottages in a poinsettia and palm tree garden. The landlord lived on the premises so I rented one and moved in right away. Glad to be settled after the storm of changes, I slept long hours, sunbathed in the garden, and walked on the beach.

My daughter did not seem to be affected by the difficulties of the last few days. She had adjusted to travel and change with full trust. Our relationship of love, affection, and caring remained the same, no matter what I was going through, and I guess that was what was important to her. Other than that, she seemed to live in a world of enchantment, excitement, and humor. I watched her grow, explore, taste, and touch her expanding world with focus and intense enthusiasm, wishing I could be like her.

Now that I had time to observe her more closely, it seemed as if every day she accomplished some new and amazing feat, like pointing elegantly to eyes, dots, or centers of flowers; or delicately shaping her first finger and thumb to pick up tiny crumbs. When I lifted her into my arms, she clung to me with every muscle, grasping me like a little baby monkey. Molecules of daughter love melting into molecules of mother love, she sought rest in union. I sighed and bathed in the living energy that poured through her tender skin into mine. Exuding the mist of divinity, she represented all that I longed to remember and become again.

But if I turned my attention to my own life, I sank into depression. Beached at low tide, I waited for change.

Roots In the Mud

Radio Free OZ advertised a Love-In, but I didn't go. I couldn't summon happiness, let alone ecstasy. Depressed, I dwelled on somber thoughts and unending, unanswerable questions. Why did I always need something or someone to make me happy? Why couldn't I be happy within myself? Why had I run away from a life I loved? Why couldn't I defend my studio? Why had I thought giving up my studio would be the answer to changing my life? I had sacrificed everything to get away from Taz and it hadn't worked.

Tired of failure and struggle, unable to bear the loss of my studio, I sunk deeper into negativity. I missed Choo with a great, raw hunger. Love missed him too. She kept asking for her brother in sweet child words, "Choo, Choo," but I was determined never to return to Taz's studio again.

I wrote him instead, begging him to let me have Choo. Three days later I got a letter via Venice General Delivery saying that I could never make a scene work and he wasn't going for any of my plans. Angry, I wrote back, saying that welfare said they were going to take Choo away from him because he was an unfit father. I was crazy to write that. You couldn't threaten Taz. A couple of days later, I woke up scared, thinking I'd better call him and tell him I wasn't going to make a scene, but when I went outside, my car was gone. I reported the theft to the police, and a couple of days later they told me my car had been found on the Pasadena Freeway. I couldn't pick it up. The towing and impound fees were more than I had.

After that shock, I bottomed out. I tuned out the Flower Power songs, and found new music on the black soul stations that resonated with my lonely suffering.

"...got to make the best of a bad situation..."

Without a car, I was grounded. I tried hitchhiking, but I was frightened on the road. The bus stop was too far from my cottage. Venice was scary. Strange, rough characters roamed the streets. Stuck inside and out, I stayed home, emptiness and longing weaving a familiar web of pain.

"...darkness all around, blocking out the sun..."

Late one night, three, loud knocks on the door startled me out of my dreamy dozing.

Frightened, I called out, "Who's there?"

"Taz and Choo," Taz's voice called impatiently. "Let us in."

I jumped up and opened the door. Choo flew into my arms. "Mom. Oh, Mom. I missed you so much."

I embraced him, feeling like I was drinking water after a long drought.

"How did you know I was here?" I asked Taz, blocking his entrance into my cottage.

"Your letter came from Venice, so I drove around till I saw your car," he explained.

"But my car isn't here," I said, confused.

"It was here. Oh, damn, I took it and left it in Pasadena. Your letter made me so angry. I'm sorry now. I came to see if you were okay," Taz said, pushing by me and shutting the door.

"You took my car?" I stammered, hardly able to take in what he was saying.

"Yeah, I took your car," he said clearly, with a short laugh.

Stunned wordless, I looked at Love and Choo. Laughing and hugging, they'd returned to play as though they'd never been separated. On another wavelength entirely, Taz and I had picked up where we'd left off.

"I want you to come home. I want to try again. I'll give up other women. I'll send Chanter away. What we're doing is crazy. We can't live together and we can't live apart. We must be meant to stay together, so let's do it right," he pleaded passionately.

I heard his words but couldn't respond. I didn't believe him. He tried to hold me, but I pushed him away.

"I don't have it in me to try again. I would have done anything for you, but I just don't love you any more."

"That's only because I've been so hard on you. If I can make you go away, I can make you want to stay," he promised, with a seductive smile that made me shiver when I remembered the hurtful things he had done to make me go away.

We sat on the bed, the children between us, quiet, listening, as Taz spun out promises and dreams. We must have drifted off because suddenly we were startled awake by loud knocking on the door.

"Open up! Open up!" a man's voice yelled angrily.

I stumbled sleepily to the door and opened it.

The landlord burst into the room, turning on lights, looking around.

"Who is this man?" he shouted. "He has no right to be here. Out! Get out!" he ordered furiously.

Taz jumped up and pushed the landlord back.

I stepped in between them.

"This is my husband. You've no right to burst into my home," I said, scared they were going to fight.

"I won't have men staying here," he shouted belligerently.

"He's not staying. He's visiting. He has his own home. We're talking. The children fell asleep. Why am I explaining this to you? I rent this cottage. I can have guests."

"No! You can't have men here at night. Out! I want you out!" he demanded.

"Get out yourself!" I shouted as I shut the door in his face.

He pounded on the door, so I screamed, "Don't worry, I'll go!" through the door.

"I guess you're coming home with me," Taz said with a grin.

We threw my stuff in his car and left. I didn't want to stay there another minute.

I returned to Berkeley Street, but I did not return to Taz. With stubbornness I didn't know I possessed, I retreated to my room and my children. I wouldn't go upstairs. I didn't believe he would change, and I wouldn't set myself up for pain again. Instead, I shut myself down, understanding how it was that women went mad. I reasoned that if I didn't open up, if I didn't feel, then I couldn't be hurt. I promised myself that I would never dream again. Trying to find a way out of my problems, I'd only fallen deeper. I didn't want to try any more.

One thing was different, though. This time I took responsibility for sending out the call that had pulled Taz to me. I knew I was helpless before my wild mind and my hunger for love. I understood that my mind was at the root of my problems. That was what I had to change, but how was I going to do that?

A few days later, Taz tried to pull me back into his scene.

"I'm having a party tonight," he invited. "TV crews are coming. Everyone who's happening is going to be here: Jim Morrison, Peter Fonda, Vito, Suzy Creamcheese, Frank

Zappa, and the Brotherhood of Man. Come and see what I've done to the studio. You've been hanging out downstairs too long," Taz coaxed. Decked out in silver, flashing a new bronze medallion, he was ready to party.

It was easy to get swept away by Taz's creative charisma, and get pulled in, only to be pushed away. I'd learned that lesson too many times. I wasn't going for it again.

"Maybe," I said casually. Playing it cool, I turned to leave.

"At least come on up and see what I've been doing," he insisted, laughing at me.

Giving in, I followed him upstairs, afraid one of his chicks might be there.

He had been busy. Silver paint gleamed on the floors. Large curved mylar screens mirrored distorted visions of black light sculptures and flashing strobes, while tapes throbbed the latest messianic messages from the Doors, the Stones, and the Beatles through banks of silver speakers.

Taz stood proudly in the center of his creation and boasted, "It's happening. The best so far. I want to create an environment that turns people on to the psychedelic reality."

Love was staring, wide-eyed, at the flashing lights and colors.

"Want a hot tub? Might be fun for Love," he invited.

I shook my head and said, "No thanks. We're going to sleep."

"You never stay up," he complained, making a face.

"There's nothing to stay up for," I said over my shoulder as I turned to leave.

He called after me. "Come to the party. Dress up. Meet all the happening people."

"Meet all your girlfriends, you mean? No thanks."

"They're not girlfriends. Everybody sleeps with everybody. It doesn't mean anything. It's a way of getting to know each other, getting rid of hang-ups. That's your problem. You're full of hang-ups. You can't let go. You're old fashioned, conservative, uptight. Whatever you want to call it, it's not cool," he yelled from the top of the stairs. "Free love, Baby. That's what's happening!"

"It's not free, and it's not happening. I'm glad I'm this way. I never want to be like you. It's not free love. You pay a price. I pay a price. Everyone pays a price. There's no such thing as free love," I yelled back as I slammed the door.

A little while later, music started pounding and all the far-out, happening people stomped up the stairs to the studio. I fell asleep nursing Love and would have missed the party, but Choo came bursting into my room.

"Mom, Mom," he called excitedly. "Come to the party!"

I couldn't refuse that wriggling, scriggling, bundle of goodness, so I lifted him high, throwing him in the air, singing the song that had given him his nickname.

"Choo-choo train, coming along, right side up, upside down. Chugga Chugga Choo-Choo…Whoooooo…"

Giggling, Choo wriggled free, calling "Come on, Mom, hurry up. I want you to come to the party," before he ran back upstairs.

I slipped a flower print shift over Love's head and combed her sun-bright curls. Then I put on the full-length, coral dress I'd worn to the Renaissance Faire and added a selection of my wildest earrings, necklaces, and bracelets.

When I went upstairs, the party was a full-on happening. The in-crowd, immersed in loud music, shouted to be heard. Pulsing strobe lights distorted the gathering of brightly decorated flower children, cool shaded hippies, far-out rock icons, and glitzy-glamorous movie stars. Suzy Creamcheese was dressed in a ruffled little girl's dress with her golden ringlets tied with bows. Carrying a naked child on her hip, she flitted and danced around the studio while Vito and the Brotherhood of Man watched her every move. Judith

Brewer made an appearance in a paper fur coat and stole followed by an entourage dressed in paper clothes. Frank Zappa wandered in and dug the scene from under a ragged top hat. The mylar panels and freshly painted silver floors reflected the lights, strobes, sculpture and guests, creating an unsettling, altered reality. Stoned party freaks wandered among the sculptures and stared at the art. Others huddled in mute groups, stunned by sensory overload while a TV crew filmed the party scene.

Love put her arms around me and rested her head on my shoulder as she checked out the scene.

Chanter walked over to me. He raised his eyebrows as usual, but he didn't say "Yes?" in his arrogant, insulting manner. He was on unsure ground himself.

"So this is your daughter; she's beautiful," he said reaching out to touch her, but I sidestepped him, poured a glass of punch, and settled on the aircraft-wing sofa.

Taz sauntered over, pleased I'd shown up, "You always pose," he said, smiling insolently.

"I'm not posing, This is just Love and me, being us."

"Don't drink too much acid punch. Might not be good for Love," he said with a short, sharp laugh.

I put the glass down immediately.

"Why is Chanter here?" I asked.

"It's a party," he countered as he turned and walked away.

Curled up with Love, I watched the cool characters in their extravagant costumes flickering like old-time movies under the strobes and gleaming like iridescent ghosts in the black light. Taz's studio was an incredible visionary environment, a holographic art experience that entranced everyone who entered into it, but for me it was too far away from all that was natural, from all that I loved. I closed my eyes, sinking into the pleasure of holding my daughter, the soft warmth of her body, and the sweet tickle of her breath on my neck. Sheltered within our comforting cocoon, in the midst of Taz's wild party, we fell asleep. Later, Choo curled up beside us, his first energetic snuggles dissolving into abandoned deep sleep. I awoke at dawn, Love whimpering and nuzzling at my breast. The studio looked like a ravaged beach after a storm.

Chanter moved back and the night trips resumed, but one thing had changed. When they brought young girls home, anger burned within me like a hungry flame. Amber, their latest hippie girlfriend, cultivated long, golden dreadlocks that hung around her pale face and hid her glazed eyes. A full-breasted, curvy young woman, she wrapped herself in a saffron gauze sari and hung a multitude of tiny bell-and-bead necklaces around her neck, arms, and feet. Tinkerbell gone mad, she jingle-jangled her presence, but I shut my heart against her.

"...reach out in the darkness...
and you will find a friend..."

One day, I remembered Yoni, and reached beyond my anger, my jealousy, and my fear. Amber was a sister too. We were both searching for a garden of love where we could feel at home. Amber moved on before I got up the courage to make her my friend, but my change of heart created a shift in consciousness that opened me to what was happening beyond Taz's mean scene.

"Flower children are blooming everywhere..."

Living the songs of the time, the flower children costumed themselves in their version of the psychedelic dream, but I knew they were colorful cover-ups for the fear and uncertainty that haunted their inner worlds. Even though they created personal styles that ranged from ancient times to the space age, from buckskin to black tatters, from

bell-bottoms to biblical robes, jump suits, and silver boots, beneath their disguises, they were the same. They wanted a new, loving world, but they didn't know how to make it happen, so they beat on the bars of their culture with their creativity, their courage and their charisma. Wearing their dreams, celebrating their longing for love, they were searching for their own unique soul song.

"...living in a world of love...love for all mankind."

The flower children wove strings of necklaces, bells, and ribbons into their long hair. Their bare feet, peace symbols, and painted T-shirts were more than decoration. They were messages revealing a powerful longing that couldn't be expressed in words.

Taz brought home a strange young girl called Meadow. Tall, bone-thin, angular, and awkward, she tore black dresses into tattered layers that fluttered around her as she flitted up and down the stairs. Long, straight black hair hung around her sad, pale face, framing dark, dull eyes. Taz and Chanter went for her like crazy. Her hopeless passivity was their endless opportunity. In her I recognized another reflection of myself. Lost, inarticulate, grateful for any scrap of affection, I welcomed her as a sister of sadness. Sometimes she watched me play with the children but she never joined in. She never said a word.

I set up a studio on the second floor, but I couldn't work. Taz picked up my car, but there was nowhere I wanted to go. Caught in Taz's domain, without the strength to escape, I lived like a shadow in the land of darkness. I only felt safe with my children. I only wanted to look into their innocent, loving, trusting eyes and feel the soft warmth of their loving embraces when I held them in my arms.

Imprisoned in Taz's harsh, alien world, I bided my time, waiting for an open door, the next wave, or the right time. I was ready for change.

BOOK THREE
Summer of Love

Love-In

When the Free Press announced a Love-In on the seventh of July, a thrill went through me, stirring the dormant seeds in the winter of my heart. I'd tried to forget Bodhi, preferring to live without hope rather than cling to a dream that couldn't come true. Now, I was ready for the Love-In. I was ready for love.

When I awoke on the morning of the Love-In, my heart was as light as a feather. I slipped on the dress I'd worn to the Renaissance Faire, and brushed my long black hair till it gleamed. Sure Bodhi would be there, I wanted to look my best. Choo wanted to wear his buckskins and moccasins and look like a little Indian. After I tied a headband with a feather around his head, he ran around making war whoops while Love chose a flowered shift. When she looked in the mirror, she pointed to Choo's headband, so I wrapped a scarf over her hair.

When we were about ready to go, sad, silent, and somber Meadow hesitantly approached our fun-filled, dressing-up scene. She must have heard the laughter rising up the stairs and wondered what was happening, but she did not laugh with us. Her face glistened like a white mask above the black tattered dress that fluttered in the Santa Ana wind blowing hot and strong from the desert, the wind known to drive people mad. Like a specter from the underworld, Meadow leaned against the door and watched our play.

"We're going to the Love-In. Wanna come?" I invited.

She silently nodded acceptance and followed us down the stairs like the shadow of our merry trio. She was already in costume. I wondered if she ever took her tatters off, if she slept in them, made love in them, even bathed in them. I couldn't imagine her without them. They wove the dress of her soul.

The powerful energy of the Love-In took my breath away. The Griffith Park meadow surged with costumed crowds, their constant movement stirring shimmering clouds of dust into the air. On the makeshift stage, the Fraternity of Man blasted good vibrations, pulling everyone into a mystical, magical, musical realm woven of our hopes and dreams. Colorful banners flew from tall flagpoles and balloons bobbed high in the summer sky. Rough, leather-clad Hell's Angels served free soup around roaring campfire kitchens.

Holding hands, my children joined the body-painted and costumed throng. Celebrating joy, ecstatic flower children exchanged restless glances as they passed each other, seeking connection, offering flowers, incense, fruit, and hugs as they shared their version of the kaleidoscopic, psychedelic dream. Even rednecks, squares, and critics could not resist beating time to the throbbing, infectious rhythms of the conga drums.

Flags flew high over teepees, tents, and tribal encampments gathered around flower-filled altars honoring Buddha, Shiva, Kwan Yin, and Christ. Candles and incense burned before woven woolen God's Eyes, Tibetan mandalas, Chinese black and white yin-yang circles and astrological symbols. Kindred spirits laughed in recognition as outer boundaries dissolved. Spirits flashing, we opened to each other and to love.

A clown took off his button-covered hat and offered it to me. I chose "God Is Watching, Give Him a Good Show" and pinned the button on my dress.

Meadow connected with friends and went off to get high. I took my children's hands and wandered through the Love-In. Suddenly a cloud passed over the sun and a cool, prickly sensation shivered through me. As I slowly turned, the crowd parted like the Red Sea, and there on a rise was Bodhi.

Without his biblical robes, wearing only blue jeans, he shone with quiet radiance as the magnetic power of his gaze fell upon me. An instant later, the crowds closed in and he disappeared. I stood still for a while, hoping he would come to me, but when he didn't, I wondered if he'd been a mirage. I felt excited, as if I had connected with the spirit of the day. Happiness welled up, and I welcomed it like gentle rain after a long drought.

The Iron Butterfly let loose with a set of intense songs. Surrendering to the music, I danced with my children, swinging, spinning, joining hands with others, laughing, and shouting, until we could dance no more. This was no dimly lit rock concert or alcoholic nightclub scene. We were dancing in the light of day, creating an enchanting intermingling of all our hopes and dreams.

"Joy to the world, all the boys and girls,
Joy to you and me..."

Faces radiated happiness. Eyes flashed brightly. Hearts merged in laughter. Finally, hot and out of breath from the dancing, I led my children toward the shelter of the trees.

At the top of the hill near the merry-go-round, I heard Bodhi's voice.

"I've been waiting for you," he said in his melodious voice.

I turned to him, heart flaming with joy, and said, "I've been waiting for you, too."

We looked at each other and melted into love. His eyes were so gentle, so welcoming, I could not look away.

"These are your children?" he asked.

"Yes. My daughter, Love, and my son, Choo."

As I said that, an image flashed in my mind's eye – a flame leaping and flowing with liquid light from a glowing fountain of fire. Surprised by the beauty and the intensity of the vision, I swayed. Bodhi reached out and steadied me, holding me.

My voice, solemnly oracular, spoke words that emerged from deep within me, "And if I ever have another child, her name will be Light."

"Light, that's beautiful, too," he said as his eyes spoke more than words could ever say.

"Light, for the flame of love and light that leaps toward the divine," I babbled, feeling faint with the intensity of the energy between us.

"I understand," he said softly, knowing me.

Waves of communion lapped against my soul.

His eyes shone into mine, seeking to know me.

"Let's head for the trees," he invited, as he led us to the shelter of the shade.

Wide-eyed and silent under Bodhi's spell, the children knew something important was happening. I sat down and leaned against a tree and they snuggled up against me, looking at Bodhi, then looking at me. The Love-In faded away. I was with Bodhi at last, and I wasn't going to leave him again.

"I've fallen into your love stream..."

I told him how I'd searched for him. "The Faire was cancelled, but I went to the grounds and waited by the bridge. Then I drove around the Valley looking for you."

"You went there? How wonderful," Bodhi said, openly showing his surprise. "I wish I'd thought of that. I looked for you at the last Love-In, but you didn't come," he said with a tinge of sadness.

"I couldn't come," I said, but I didn't tell him why.

Searching each other's eyes, exchanging waves of love, my shyness fell away. As the children fell asleep in my lap, Bodhi put his arm around me. I leaned against his chest, falling into his heartbeat sounds, our breath rising and falling together. At peace at last, I was with love.

"I'll follow your dream..."

Some time later, whispering voices and light laughter returned us to the day. When I opened my eyes, the women he'd been with at the Renaissance Faire surrounded us.

"We were wondering if you would ever come back to reality," a beautiful sprite giggled, her hands running through a mass of auburn curls.

Bodhi laughed wholeheartedly as he replied, "This is reality."

"They found each other," a golden Venus with tawny, waist-length hair teased as she sprang up dramatically, arms widespread to the sky as she danced in circles.

"The lovers meet," an exquisite white-blonde sister exulted, her ponytail bobbing with her energetic, playful movements.

"All he's been talking about is how he might find you again," another lovely young woman confided, her glowing face framed by shining, pitch-black hair.

Bodhi and I beamed shyly at each other, rejoicing at the miracle of our love. The four ladies hugged me in turn as Bodhi spoke each of their names.

"Lola. Deva. Starry. Magda."

I'd never met such beautiful women. Yet, for all their grace, laughter, and radiance, their blue jeans and T-shirts didn't do them justice.

"I'd like to give each of you a dress," I blurted out.

The ladies laughed, "Yes. Oh, yes!"

My dress designs had emerged out of my hopeful dreams that somehow, somewhere I would live the life

I longed for. Maybe now my life would match my dreams.

Bodhi leaned back against the tree. Overwhelmingly aware of him, I rested against his knees. Every movement, every word, every touch felt exquisite, biblical, profound. His presence drew forth my essence. I felt that I had become the woman I had always wanted to be. Shyness, hesitation melted into love.

"I'll be one with you..."

"Where's the father of your children?" Magda asked.

"Santa Monica," I said, unable to say more as sorrow surfaced in my heart. Fearing judgment, I turned to Bodhi but he radiated total acceptance.

"Tell us about yourself. Where do you live? What do you do?" he asked with enthusiasm. "We want to know you."

I told them about my studio on Nemo Street, Rainbow, and the Conspiracy. Bodhi's hand in mine made the telling of the trip to San Francisco easier, but I couldn't look at him.

"I love you," he whispered as he kissed me.

Accepted, welcomed, I rested in his arms, and the ladies formed a protective circle around us.

"I'll set you free..."

The afternoon drifted by as we hung out together. After a glowing golden sunset displayed a dramatic finale to the day, a night of stars slowly overtook the meadow heavens. Fireworks exploded into cascades of silver and gold sparkles. Drummers increased their rhythms to a fast, wild pulse. Dancers leapt like black silhouettes around brightly burning campfires. Spellbound watchers, we shared the Love-In ecstasy.

Suddenly, a cry of terror, then a multitude of screams pierced the rhythm of the drums. The music stopped. A fearful silence dropped like a dark net over the gathering. A line of patrol-car headlights flashed on above the hill, exposing a menacing line of policemen wearing hard hats and holding clubs.

"...battle lines being formed..."

A few seconds passed, as fear heightened the charge between the policemen and the Love-In merrymakers; then the police linked arms and moved slowly down the hill.

"What a field day for the heat..."

Hundreds of Love-In celebrants scattered, their screams rising in one great howl. Love was in my arms, but where was Choo?

"Choo!" I screamed, panic surging in me.

My son had disappeared into the crowds of frightened, scattering people.

"Stay here! I'll look for him," Bodhi shouted as he ran into the confusion.

The rest of us huddled under the trees and watched the malevolent gestures of the policemen against the flaming fires as they destroyed the Love-In. Long lines of cars packed with Love-In refugees moved slowly out of the parking lot. When Bodhi returned without my son, I called out to an officer, my fear for my son greater than my fear of the police.

"I've lost my son. Please help me find him," I pleaded.

"You shouldn't have brought him here," the policeman reprimanded, hostility hardening his voice as he fingered his club.

I resisted the impulse to say everything had been fine until they got there.

"Where would the police take him if they found him?" I pleaded.

"He'd be at the park headquarters, if they have him," he answered with reluctance, as if he was looking for a reason to arrest us.

"Thank you, sir. I'll see if he's there," I said politely.

We walked past toward the flickering fires, stepping

carefully over debris as we made our way toward the parking lot beyond the hill.

I trembled with fear for my son.

"Why didn't the police just ask us to go home? Why frighten everyone?" I asked Bodhi, on the edge of panic.

"They wanted to frighten us. Don't worry, we'll find Choo," Bodhi reassured me.

His four magic lady friends hugged me before taking off in their car. Bodhi took my car keys from me with a smile, and drove us over to the park headquarters. The scene there was shocking. The generous, free-food Hell's Angels were being roughly searched, ridiculed, and questioned. Dozens of dazed flower children had been arrested. The police had turned the Love-In into a nightmare.

"I'll find out if Choo is in there," Bodhi offered protectively.

"No. Let me go. They won't bother me," I insisted.

I put Love into his arms and, heart pounding, I feigned bravery as I walked through the crowd of flower children, hippies, and police into the office.

"Do you have a young boy here?" I asked the officer in charge. "He's nearly three and has blonde, curly hair."

The officer turned toward me and flashed a scornful, searchlight stare that violated my feminine essence.

"We have one young boy here," he stated reluctantly.

"Wearing buckskins and moccasins?" I asked, hope rising in my heart.

"Yes. What's his name?" he demanded roughly.

"We call him Choo. Can I see him please?" I asked impatiently.

The policeman opened a door and there was sweet, adorable Choo talking to three policemen.

As soon as he saw me, Choo's face lit up and he ran over and leapt into my arms.

"Hi, Mom," he said with open relief.

I caught him and held him tight, and whispered in his ear, "I was so worried about you."

Suddenly serious, he hurried to explain, "I got lost. The police brought me here. Wow! Did you see all the action?"

Silently disapproving, the policeman made me sign some papers and then he watched us walk away.

Bodhi opened the car door and helped me in. I sat for a moment, leaning against Bodhi, holding Choo and Love in my arms, so glad my son was safely with me again. Bodhi waited.

"Where are we going?" I questioned.

"Where do you want to go?" he asked in return.

"With you."

"I'll follow you wherever time will take me..."

"Then let's go home," Bodhi said.

Flowering Love

Bodhi drove out of the shambles of the Griffith Park Love-In and headed north on the Ventura Freeway.

Jim Morrison swept us along on waves of song.

"Come on baby, light my fire..."

Alight with joy, exquisitely aware of Bodhi's body touching mine, I felt the fire of desire tingle between us.

"Try to set the night on fire..."

The weeks of searching hunger were over.

The Love-In had brought us together.

"Girl, we couldn't get much higher..."

Leaning against Bodhi, looking up at his profile, feeling as though I were lost in a dream, I savored the beauty of his radiant, biblical, golden-brown hair and beard. Whenever he turned to look at me, his brilliant blue eyes shone like beacons lighting the path toward love. His body was manly yet graceful and his voice and movements were slow and smooth, unlike anyone I'd ever known. He grooved to a rhythm uniquely his own.

Deep in the San Fernando Valley, Bodhi pulled off the freeway, geared down and headed east, past a shopping mall, toward the hills. Turning onto a quiet suburban street, he pulled up in front of a brick bungalow. Light, voices, and laughter spilled out of the house into a lush garden. Suddenly nervous, I looked at Bodhi, silently questioning my welcome.

"It's okay. Don't worry. They want you to be here with me. Come on," he invited.

Bodhi gracefully lifted a fast-asleep Choo and carried him toward the front door. Holding Love, I followed him into a sunroom where we settled the children on a bed for the night.

When we came into the living room, Magda greeted us warmly. Simply dressed in a white cotton shift that set off her tanned shoulders and the shine of her pitch-black hair, she radiated friendly generosity. As I looked into the sea-green eyes illuminating her serene face, I saw a happy woman who was surrounded by love. Before I had a second to feel unworthy or afraid, she threw her arms around me.

"Welcome. Welcome. We've been waiting for you," she gushed.

Then she introduced me to her shy, bearded Hispanic husband, Pedro. He took my hand and welcomed me with a silent smile and a warm flash from his kind deep-brown eyes.

"Our boys are already asleep. You'll meet them in the morning," Magda said as she twirled away.

Deva, wearing a Pocahontas leather fringed tunic over soft, worn blue jeans, opened her arms wide to hold me to her heart. Immersed for a moment in a cascade of patchouli-scented tawny hair, I felt embraced by love.

Laughing in a most light-hearted, delightful way, she introduced the brother standing beside her, "This is my man, Tree, from the Hog Farm."

Tree was a magnificent, golden Apollo. With his curly blond hair captured by a braided headband, he was confidently casual in blue jean cut-offs and a psychedelic T-shirt. He flashed a friendly smile and pumped my right hand up and down. Deva's expansive, loving nature seemed like the perfect match for this radiant young man.

I couldn't imagine him coming from a hog farm or why he would want to tell me that, so when I questioned, "Hog Farm?" Tree laughed.

"The Hog Farm is a commune, out past Malibu. Good folks living free," he said proudly.

Lola waved at me from a rocking chair, her tight blue jeans and cropped T-shirt barely containing her voluptuous curves.

"Hi. Welcome to the Soul Clan," she said, running her hands through her curly auburn hair.

Starry was bending over a small boy about my son's age. Singing softly, she massaged her son's legs, easing him toward sleep.

"This is my son, Angel," she whispered. "He was hurt in a car accident."

Starry was dressed simply in a white shirt and shorts, with her fine, pale-blond hair pulled into a sleek ponytail. Blue-eyed and slender, her Nordic beauty shone like a diamond.

The introductions over, I looked around and admired the softly lit room with its abundant plants, comfortable pillowed sofas, wood floors, and oriental carpets. Glass doors opened onto a brick patio and a garden. Drawings of women were tacked all over the white walls. I moved closer to look at them more carefully.

"They are all you," Bodhi said softly.

A surge of warmth flowered into surprised pleasure on my cheeks. I looked at him in wonder.

"These past weeks, I've drawn only you," Bodhi whispered gently, his eyes glowing like stars.

Yes, there I was, but he had drawn me with halos and sparkling auras radiating around me.

"There's the dress I wore to the Renaissance Faire. There I am swinging Love. There's me by the bridge. How did you remember all this?" I asked, awestruck by the drawings.

"I searched for you as I remembered you, and now you are here," he said simply.

Joy expanded from my heart like the calligraphic auras in the drawings, and I leaned against him.

"The drawings are so beautiful," I murmured, aware that my iceberg-tip words revealed little of what I was experiencing.

"I draw when there's something I'm trying to capture," he teased with a laugh as he took me in his arms. "And now I've got you."

Holding each other, feeling our heartbeats melt into one, we shared sighs of peace.

"Come," Bodhi said, and he led me into the garden.

Surrounded by flowering bushes, their fragrance bursting sweet magic under a sky of stars, I felt as though we were walking on hallowed ground. We reclined on a swinging garden chair, facing each other, surrendering to the waves of bliss that flowed between us. Each moment emerged fresh and perfect as we shared the living light that flowed between our eyes. Just when I felt I had experienced the greatest possible love, a new wave burst on my shore, carrying me into even greater ecstasy. Completely satisfied by this universe of union, there was no urge to explore sexuality. The night passed in deep communion, eye to eye, spirit to spirit, heart to heart. Awake in love, we could not sleep.

The dawn chorus of singing birds heralded Magda's soft approach on the dew-fresh grass.

"Happy?" she asked.

We smiled our answer with full hearts.

Arms entwined, Deva and Tree entered the garden as if they were entering a court of love. Deva twirled free and lifted her hands to the heavens and cried, "The Lord be praised," to the awakening sky. "Never come down."

Starry carried little Angel out of the summerhouse and carefully put him in the pool. A moment later, Choo and

Magda's twin sons, Bruce and Brian, ran out of the house and jumped in with him. Lola and Deva brought Love to me, fresh from her morning bath. Magda served peppermint tea with such grace that I felt she was offering a blessing. Bodhi peeled oranges, offering sacramental segments to each one of us, while Pedro drank his morning coffee.

The morning activities flowed so naturally that I felt completely at home, as though we had always been a family. Each moment birthed spontaneously, like a spiritual ritual spun of slow, silent respect. Simple, natural actions were imbued with profound meaning. Whenever I turned to Bodhi, love burst forth like a nova, his glance bringing light to darkness, fullness to emptiness, and hope to despair.

"How does it feel to be one of the beautiful people...?"

As the morning passed, the women cherished me, each in her special way. Starry watched the children play in the pool. While Deva brushed my hair in long, sweeping strokes, Lola told me that Bodhi, Magda, and Pedro were inseparable friends who had grown up in the same neighborhood and gone to school together. After Magda married Pedro, Pedro supported Bodhi so he could focus on his spiritual work. The mother of all, Magda nurtured everyone, offering shelter, fun, and nourishment to the Soul Clan.

"Love is the grooviest thing up till now in the world..."

In the early afternoon, Bodhi reclined on the wicker garden chair. I leaned against his knees while his hand gently caressed my hair. Love played at our feet or crawled into my lap to cuddle and nap as visitors sat around us, drinking deeply of Bodhi's peace before they departed with shining faces. He nourished everyone, listening, talking through problems, offering solutions, and easing their burdened hearts. Nothing was more important than staying present in the love that transformed simple daily life into a sacred reality. I had found my garden of love.

"Come," Bodhi invited. "Let's make supper."

We followed him into the kitchen, where Magda was making refried beans. We put tacos together while we grooved to the radio waves.

"Sha la la la la, live for today
...don't worry 'bout tomorrow,
Hey, hey, hey..."

I had never seen anything like it – fun, happiness, and joy mixed together with cheese, tomatoes, salsa, lettuce, and beans. It was a feast for body and soul.

"I want to take you to my parent's house," Bodhi whispered.

My heart burst forth into an affirmative smile.

After I tucked Love and Choo in for the night, Bodhi and I took off with Tree and Deva in Lola's sunflower VW bug. Magda promised to watch after Love.

"Cherish is the word that I use to describe,
all the feelings that I have hiding here for you inside..."

We flew along on wings of song.

"...and I do, cherish you..."

Lola pulled up in an old San Fernando Valley neighborhood. Eucalyptus trees guarded the quiet street that led to Bodhi's parents' ranch-style house. Following him through lush greenery, we tiptoed along a stone path into the back garden. After circling around a rock fountain, bending under fuschia baskets and brushing by bougainvillea, Bodhi slid open the patio doors of a charming little summerhouse and we entered a wood-paneled room.

"This is my place. I don't live here anymore, but it makes my parents happy if I leave my stuff here," Bodhi explained, with a glint of humor.

Deva picked up a guitar and strummed it softly, while I explored, looking at everything, touching everything –

cushions, drawings, shells, books, and surfer gear – that belonged to Bodhi.

"You look so serious," Bodhi said as he watched me.

"I want to know everything that is you," I replied, skimming through his library of books on yoga, mysticism, theosophy, spirituality, and philosophy.

I walked over to him, knelt at his feet, and put my head on his knees, feeling content, marveling at the love that sheltered us.

After a while, he pulled me to my feet. "Come on. I want you to meet my folks," Bodhi invited.

As we passed through the garden, I picked two fuschia blossoms and hung them on my ears.

"Groovy," Bodhi laughed approvingly.

Bodhi led us through the kitchen door of his parents' house and into the den where his mom and dad were watching television. Respectfully and affectionately, he greeted his parents, leaned over and kissed them each on the cheek, then introduced us to his white-haired folks. They shook my hand, then talked for a few minutes about the latest news on television. They didn't ask Bodhi what he'd been doing, and he didn't tell them.

"Does your family know what you do?" I asked as we drove home.

"Nope. As long as I come home a couple of times a week and let them feed me, they don't worry. I give them what they need and we do fine."

We drove through the hot summer night, grooving with the freeway rhythm. The valley lights blurred into multi-colored ribbons. The Jefferson Airplane soared on the radio waves.

"Look into her eyes...just look at her smile..."

We returned to a party. Music blasted in the living room. Everyone was painting and singing and grooving together.

"...everybody get together,
try to love one another right now..."

I'd sung along to that song a hundred times. Now I was living it.

"Come on, join the fun," Magda invited. "Here's a paintbrush."

"Oh, no! I don't know how to paint," I said, feeling embarrassed.

A radiantly golden-tanned brother heard what I said and came over and introduced himself. "Hi, I'm Wheat. Let me help you," he said warmly.

I looked into bright green eyes surrounded by a halo of sun-bleached curls, and felt so pulled by the power of his gaze that the room dissolved for a moment. His look was so soft, so open, I felt as though I had almost melted into him. I stepped back and I had to shake myself back to reality.

"Listen to the music. What movements do your hands want to make?" he asked with a friendly smile, clearly aware of his effect on me.

"You hold the key to love and fear,
just one key unlocks them both..."

As I held the brush in my hand, I felt like I finally held the key that opened to love.

"Go for it!" Wheat cheered before he returned to his own painting.

More relaxed, swaying with the music, I playfully browsed the palette of colors, feeling myself move intuitively toward turquoise. Then I let the music guide my brush in waving lines. Enjoying myself, I added azure, aqua, and indigo.

Deep in concentration, unaware of Bodhi's approach, I heard him say, "Cool."

Startled, I looked up at him.

"Do these waving lines have a meaning?" he asked.

I paused, then filled the wave spaces with circles.

"What?" he asked, even more confused.

I darkened the pupils, making my waves into an ocean of eyes.

"The eyes of the world are the eyes of love," I said.

He took my hands and kissed them, and then he led me into the garden. Holding my face in his hands, he looked deeply into my eyes and said, "You're such a mystery. I've never known anyone like you."

"And I've never known anyone like you. Oh Bodhi, I'm so happy to be with you," I sighed and threw my arms around him.

Bathed in moonlight, breathing in the fragrance of the scented garden and each other, we embraced. Later, we went back inside. Happily weary, unable to keep vigil throughout our second night, we snuggled together on the sofa. Bodhi threw a blanket over us and we fell into a deep sleep.

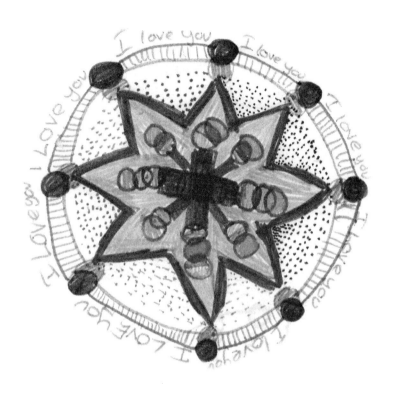

Love Sweet Love

arly next morning, Love called out to me. Leaving Bodhi sleeping on the sofa, I curled up with her and Choo, delighting in their pure child energy. Now that I was away from Bodhi's powerful presence, I had a chance to reflect on what had happened since the Love-In. As the events of the past forty-eight hours drifted through my mind, I felt that I'd been living in a dream.

Bodhi and his friends lived on a continuous high. With a natural confidence, they expected every day to be fully wonderful. They were kind to each other, always laughing and thinking of good and fun things to do. Until my entry into Magda's household, I'd never seen anyone enjoy life in such a playful way. Never Come Down was their motto.

The shadow lands I'd inhabited most of my life seemed absent in Magda's home. Where was their longing? Where was their pain? As wonderful as their life appeared on the surface, it didn't relieve the sorrow and the longing that flowed deep inside me like a powerful current. I determined to make the most of the happiness that Bodhi, Magda and their friends offered, and do my best to keep up with their free and happy-go-lucky ways.

Choo stirred, and I snuggled closer to him, humming in his ear. He smiled in his sleep and threw his arm over my face. What a dear soul, I mused. How strong he was, to endure and witness all that passed between Taz and me, and still remain his dear, wonderful self.

Just then Choo opened his eyes.

"I wanna go home. I wanna see my dad," he whimpered.

Talk about instant shadow lands, I moaned. It looked like I'd have to face Taz sooner than expected.

At that thought, my brain stirred from its drifting, dreamy, love state, and started thinking overtime. I needed to make decisions. I was working it out in my head when Bodhi walked in.

"What's happening?" he asked, hands on his hips, surveying our snuggled muddle.

"Choo wants to go back to his father, and Love and I need our things," I explained, embarrassed by the logistics of my life.

"I was wondering how long it would take you to get practical," he teased, then turning his head he called out,

"Hey, Wheat. How 'bout Santa Monica today?"

"Sure, let's go for it," Wheat answered from the living room. "We can take in Malibu on the way home."

As we dressed, showered, and breakfasted, our actions contained the same sweet flow as yesterday's repose. There was a rhythm, an understanding, as if everyone knew his place in the group dynamic. They were comfortable with each other. They belonged. It would take a while before I felt that ease, but I appreciated their friendly efforts to make me feel at home.

Deva and Tree wanted to come with us, and Lola promised to meet us later in Malibu.

Magda hugged me before we left, saying, "My home is your home. We're happy you're here. Bring some of your things. We'll make you comfortable."

Magda's words lit up my heart like a sunbeam.

"Thank you. Thank you," I whispered as I kissed her.

Magda waved at us as we piled into Wheat's chariot-of-love convertible, big kids and little kids going out for a treat. Flying along the freeway, singing to the radio, laughing and loving each other, we were the beautiful people making love real.

When Wheat pulled his maroon Mercury beside Taz's dune buggy in front of the Berkeley Street factory, fear did not coil in my stomach or overtake my heart. Love was all around and inside me too.

Choo pointed to the studio and shouted, "That's my dad's place."

As soon as the car stopped, Choo jumped out and ran upstairs.

"Do you want me to come in with you?" Bodhi asked respectfully.

I shook my head. "No thanks. I'll do this on my own."

"Just remember, Never Come Down," Bodhi whispered.

Glad I was on my way out of Taz's scene, I sang, "all you need is love", as I walked upstairs to my room. Humming happily, I collected my clothes and piled them on the bed.

A shadow fell on me. Taz was standing in the door, Choo at his side.

"Where have you been?" he burst out passionately. "I heard about the police scene at the Love-In. I thought something had happened to you."

"Something did happen. I went away with really cool new friends," I said clearly, looking him in the eyes.

"Why didn't you phone and let me know what was happening?" he demanded, trying hard not to get mad.

"I didn't think of phoning," I said, memories flashing of all the times he'd stayed away and never called. "I was having a wonderful time."

"You're leaving?" he asked incredulously.

Sitting quietly, his hands in his lap, Choo watched us, carefully listening to every word we were saying.

"Yes, I'm leaving. I want to live with my new friends."

"What friends?" he asked, trying to hide his feelings, but his hands trembled as he lit a cigarette.

I paused for a moment. How could I describe my new friends? They seemed like the only real friends I'd ever had. As each of them passed before my mind's eye, I smiled at the answer that came to me.

"They are my brothers and my sisters, my true family," I said softly.

His face registered shock and then, shaking, he asked, "Where're you going?"

"With them," I replied casually. "They live in the San Fernando Valley."

At that moment, I understood what the spiritual teachers meant when they said that the easiest way to leave something behind was to find something better.

Taz sat down on my bed and watched me put my most precious things in my red leather suitcase. Each one represented something special about my life. First, I put the shell stone I'd found on the beach in Oceano on the bottom of the suitcase. Then, I covered it with the full-length magenta and orange mohair sweater I'd knitted in the hospital in Vancouver when I was pregnant with Love. Next, I placed two hand woven mohair shawls alongside Love's brightly colored little outfits and several of my silken dresses. Finally, I wrapped my favorite pieces of jewelry from the Nemo Street studio in a striped, hand-woven Mexican blanket, placed it on top, and closed the suitcase.

Taz had a hard time getting the next question out.

"You're...are you...going with a man?" he asked, his voice quavering.

"Yes, I am. I'm in love with someone wonderful. He is..." I said, and stopped, unable and unwilling to describe him. "His name is Bodhi."

I picked up my red suitcase.

"Where's Love?" Taz asked, clearly at a loss.

"In the car," I said, turning toward the door.

"I'd like to see her and meet your friends, if that's okay."

"Sure. Come on," I said, wondering how he could act like he cared when I was leaving, but never when I was with him.

I looked around one more time, threw two more Mexican blankets over my arm, and walked down the dark stairwell into the sunshine-love of my new family, Taz and Choo following behind.

Bodhi opened the car door, got out slowly and took my suitcase.

"Bodhi, this is Taz. Taz, this is Bodhi," I said.

Light meeting dark, they measured each other.

"And this is Wheat, Tree, and Deva."

"Hi, man," from Wheat.

Tree called out, "Hey, bro."

Deva gestured a "Peace" greeting and flashed him a shining smile.

Love jumped out of the car and hugged her father's knees. Taz knelt beside both children, visibly shaken. I felt Taz's suffering, but there was nothing I could do. He'd played his part in the creation of this moment. Now that I was leaving, he had to face the consequences of his actions.

Taz's hands trembled when he put Love back in the car. Love's dear face was confused. Her little eyes opened wide with solemn concern as she tried to comprehend what was happening.

Choo climbed back in the car and hugged Love, then threw himself into my arms. He was doing his best not to cry.

Unlike Love, he knew that we were leaving, and he understood why.

"Take it easy," Taz whispered over an invisible, cold continent of pain.

We drove off, as simple as that, with no hassles. My shining, golden-haired son stood next to his father who was dressed in black from head to toe. Together they waved their farewell.

Heading north on PCH, singing along to the radio, hot summer breezes played through my hair. I rested my head on Bodhi's shoulder. I was home.

"It's a groovy day,
you're a groovy girl,
throw your cares away…"

"It's a fairy tale," I whispered to Bodhi.

"Which one?" he teased.

"The prince rescuing the maiden from the dragon. You're my knight in shining armor. No, no armor; you just shine."

Malibu was packed with Woodies, clusters of surfers checking out the waves, bikini-clad sun worshippers gleaming with oil, and children making sand castles. As we came out onto the beach, Lola ran up, all smiles and wild, waving auburn hair.

Free to play, we laughed and splashed in the waves, body surfing, diving deep, racing each other. Later, lying on the sand, soaking up the sun, I felt my heart bursting with happiness, a sensation I hadn't experienced for many years. I had friends. I was having fun. I was living love.

"I'm starved!" Wheat shouted. "Let's go home."

We raced down the beach, piled in the car and cruised through Topanga Canyon toward the San Fernando Valley.

Snuggled against Bodhi, Love asleep in my lap, my head rested against his shoulder.

"...we could float among the stars,
You and I...we can fly up, up and away..."

Dusk was settling as we pulled up at Magda's house. Glowing, vibrantly alive, we entered the cool quietness of her home. Bodhi and Wheat headed out to the garden for a smoke, while Lola, Love and I showered off the sea salt and sand.

When we emerged shiny clean with our hair gleaming, the living room had been transformed by dozens of ivory votive candles. Love's face lit up in wonderment at the beautiful sight. Hand-painted Mexican pottery bowls full of tacos, beans, cheese, guacamole and salad were spread in the center of the living room on a circular red tablecloth. My friends' smiles matched the joy in my heart.

After dinner, Wheat played his guitar and we sang songs, then we rocked out to the latest hits. I didn't want the day to end. I wanted to be awake forever, in love with love, living love.

"...life, I love you...all is groovy."

After everyone turned in, Bodhi and I walked into the starlit garden. Holding each other, our energies melted into a luminous, inner union.

As his hands caressed my breasts and hips, I sighed deeply, loving him loving me. I had been waiting for him to touch me like this, and I wanted more. Bodhi slipped my dress over my shoulders. I pulled off his T-shirt and pressed my breasts against his chest. Skin against skin, welcoming sweet softness, my arms circled his waist and shaped the curve of his back. He stepped out of his jeans. Naked, revealed, our bodies called to each other. Softly, tenderly, without urgency, we lay on the dewing grass. Slowly, gently, body to body, heart to heart, mind to mind, soul to soul, we merged, the universe of man and woman dissolving into a gently rocking sea of bliss.

In the morning, Magda smiled on us like the gentle morning sun as she announced with a smile, "I want you and Bodhi to have your own room."

"You're so kind," I thanked her shyly.

"Listen, sweet thing, we're happy you and Bodhi are together. Your love is beautiful for all of us," she assured me.

After breakfast, Magda put on the latest Jefferson Airplane's latest album, Surrealistic Pillow. Singing their latest songs, we moved Bruce's things into Brian's bedroom. When the room was clean, I made the bed and threw my Mexican blankets over the top. Then I draped bright woolen shawls over the armchair. Magda brought fresh flowers for an altar on a small wood table under the window. They added the final perfect touch to the candle, Clara's pin, the photo of Choo and Love in my arms, and the magic Pismo shell rock. I was home at last.

"...I'm so full of love,
I could burst apart and start to cry..."

"You brought all this with you?" Bodhi exclaimed as he looked around in amazement when he came in.

"Yes," I said proudly.

"...I realize how much I'm in love with you..."

"Beautiful. You are truly beautiful," he said lovingly.

"...it's taken so long to come true..."

I pulled him into my arms.

"I love you."

"I love you."

Ripening Love

"**M**agda, Deva, Lola, Starry! Come, choose a dress."
I pulled out several flowered dresses and threw them
on the bed. Happily talking and laughing, my beautiful sisters
paraded in front of the mirror. A sleek magenta Empire gown
enhanced Magda's black hair and deep tan. Delicate, blonde
Starry slipped into a pale-rose dress with silvery sage leaves.
A loose shift of golden sunflowers matched Deva's expansive
nature. Lola chose a duplicate of my favorite dress that I had
worn at the Renaissance Faire when I had first spoken with
Bodhi. I also had it on it when I met him again at the Love-
In. Spirals of soft aqua paisley fabric bordered by delicate
pink and lavender flowers flowed from tiny shoulder straps.
Wearing the same dress, arms around each other, we looked
at ourselves in the mirror – soul twins.

Ponytails and braids undone, we brushed each other's
hair. Deva led us in a jubilant procession into the garden
where we collected flowers and greenery and adorned our
heads with flower crowns and decorated the children. Then
we joined hands and danced in a circle. Draped with garlands
and leis, the children skipped and twirled in the middle of
our faerie ring while the guys watched our antics with
amazed delight.

Deva lifted her arms wide to the heavens and shouted to the sky, "Praise the Lord. It's all love."

Noble and abundant in her womanhood, Deva was also fearlessly loving. I longed to be like her.

"Let's go to the mall," Bodhi suggested, merriment twinkling in his eyes.

"Like this?" I asked, surprised.

"Yes, why not? You're perfect."

Our Soul Clan descended from our fantasy heaven into the hard, plastic, material mall. Bodhi strode beside me, a biblical noble draped in his brown and white striped robe. Wheat, luminous in his tie-dyes, strolled nonchalantly with Lola, voluptuously sinuous in her long dress. Tree and Deva skipped like golden children. Tree's sun-bleached hair glowed like a radiant aura around his head. We were vibrant and full of love. The shut-off, shutdown, hurried mall crowds seemed lifeless and dull by comparison.

Deva led us into a health food store.

"Praise the Lord. All you need is love," she chanted as she walked up to the counter.

Hair frozen by spray, heart locked against laughter, the waitress resisted our joy.

"What do you think you're doing going around dressed like that?" she said with bitter disapproval.

Deva met her hostile gaze with loving eyes. "It's all love," she sang as she danced up aisles, showering blessings. "Never Come Down. Never Come Down."

The woman blended our smoothies and banged them down on the table.

"She can't understand our playful freedom," Wheat explained. "She's shut herself off from love."

"We threaten her reality," Tree offered.

"My parents are like that. That's why I stay away," Lola shared, grimacing. It was hard to imagine a beautiful young woman like Lola being rejected by her parents, but I knew parents with a different mindset could hate everything about their children.

After we drank our smoothies, we waved goodbye to the waitress as Deva threw her kisses. Then we wandered the mall until we congregated at the waterfall garden under the skylight dome. After a few moments of repose, our next adventure began quite spontaneously.

"Let's have a picnic at the pond," Magda suggested, her eyes bright with anticipation.

The guys hooted their instant approval.

Starry clapped her hands.

I cheered, "Yes!" I would have followed them anywhere.

We drove home, packed up picnic baskets, and caravaned through Topanga. Just north of the Malibu pier, we turned toward Serra Retreat. There, we parked near a grove of eucalyptus trees. Carrying a sleeping Love, I walked barefoot on the hot sandy path, a luxurious profusion of wildflowers, herbs, and grasses bursting on both sides of the trail. Absorbing the beauty with all my senses, I inhaled the pungent aromas, realizing how long it had been since I had played in nature.

The path led to a swimming hole formed by a boulder dam that deepened the stream flowing toward the beach lagoon. Overhead, a canopy of palms and eucalyptus trees sheltered the grotto from the burning sun.

"Who owns this place?" I asked, awed by the beauty.

Magda smiled mysteriously, as she said, "It's God's place. See the monastery on the hill? The monks don't seem to mind our visits."

I lay Love on a blanket under a shady tree, hitched my dress above my knees and waded into the pebbly stream. As my feet felt their way over the smooth, round stones, I remembered the summers of my youth. You couldn't keep me out of the water then. How did I travel so far away from myself? Unable to understand the mystery of my life, I returned to the happiness of the present moment.

The warm, deep water and the natural beauty soothed my mind. Birds fluttered and chirped overhead. Bodhi's eyes, glowing like twin suns, energized me. I felt as though he was giving me all that I had been missing for a very long time. Suddenly unable to keep myself out of the water a moment longer, I dove into the pool. Turning like a seal released to freedom, I explored the cool, dark, slippery depths. Then, forced to reach for the luminous shafts of light above, I burst into the sun-bright air, gasping for breath. Every return to the depths offered the opportunity to rise toward the light and break free of the water's embrace.

Magda called us to supper. Exhilarated from swimming, I wrung out my thin silk dress and squeezed the moisture from my hair. As we gathered around the food, we fell spontaneously into silent grace. Simple? Yes, but if you've never had a happy family life, each moment of playful, loving sharing and fun feels precious.

The children ate quickly and ran off to play hide-and-seek, their shrill voices a lively backdrop for our contented leisure. Bodhi leaned against a palm tree. I lay beside him, Love in my lap. Wheat stretched out on the sand, watching palm fronds sway between him and the deepening sky. Tree played a wooden flute, and Deva danced to his melody with her arms stretched high to the first-star heavens. Starry perched on a rock, watching her son play with the pebbles. Pedro lounged on a blanket, smoking with quiet satisfaction while he looked at the emerging stars. This was a perfect moment, full, ripe, and complete. We were like fireflies radiating love as the darkening dusk settled quietly around us.

"It's time to go home," Magda reminded us.

Sleepy, we straggled along the still-warm, sandy path, carrying wet towels, picnic baskets, and bags of trash. As we drove home, we snuggled together in the car, warm, sun-toasted, each one of us full of all that was good.

Angels & Buddhas

One morning when I awoke, Bodhi was already up. Love was babbling happily in her little bed, so I picked her up and hugged her tight.

"Oh, Love," I whispered, "your mother is loved."

Snuggling with my beloved daughter, I quietly savored the happiness of my new life. It seemed like my dreams of family were finally coming true. At last I belonged to a circle of friends who took care of each other in a kind and friendly way.

A few minutes later, Bodhi came in, lit up with news. "Wheat scored some peyote. We're going over to Starry's and then to Malibu. It'll be great to trip with you."

Resistance surged within me. I thought I was through with chemical highs.

"I don't know," I answered reluctantly. "What about Love?"

"Magda's offered to take care of her," he announced, clearly proud of the support of his friends. "You don't have to worry about a thing."

"I've never taken peyote before," I said, still trying to find a way out.

"Hey, it'll be beautiful," he persuaded. "Come on. Let's get ready to go."

"Okay," I agreed, flowing with his excitement.

After a song-singing, taking-care-of-business morning, we piled in Wheat's car and took off. The energy of adventure captured us as we drove into Topanga Canyon and turned up into the hills. Sheltered in a meadow at the end of a long winding road, Starry's cabin was remote. When we turned into her driveway, Starry waved her welcome with a radiant smile. We tumbled out of the car and into her rustic little cabin, filling her one room with the laughter and love of friends.

Starry's handmade quilts covered the rough log walls. Firewood was piled neatly by a stone fireplace. Bricks and a sheet of plywood supported a mattress covered with multi-colored quilts and pillows and pictures of Christ, Kwan Yin, and Buddha hung above the bed. Starry and Angel's clothes were folded neatly in wooden orange crates. The kitchen shelf held a metal washing bowl, a crockery pitcher, assorted dishes and utensils, and metal canisters of food, all neatly stacked and pristinely clean. Without running water or electricity, Starry lived a simple life so she could be free to take care of her son full-time. Her car was her one necessity and her friends chipped in to keep it going. Even though her material life was basic, she was rich in friends who helped her and her son, and who included her in their adventures.

My friends settled on rocking chairs and benches on the porch to clean the peyote. Their chattering faded as I walked into the crackling, dry, golden summer grass. Crickets filled the air with their strident chirping as I breathed in the resinous scent of the towering eucalyptus trees. Birds flitted through the leaves, perching momentarily to twitter their songs before flying out their winged patterns. The sounds, the sun, and the smells were mesmerizing, full of the enchantment of nature moving toward ripe, harvest fullness. Sleepy, I lay down and put my arms under my head. Grasshoppers jumped on me and insects tickled my sun-warmed skin as I listened to seeds popping free of their pods.

I remained in my drowsy dreaming until footsteps rustled through the grass. Bodhi stood above me, a shadow against the sun.

"These are your buttons," he offered graciously, holding out his right hand.

Rising, I shaped my hands like a cup to receive the sacrament.

"Chew slowly. If you feel nauseous, stop chewing and concentrate your attention on the center of your forehead," he advised. Then he pulled me to my feet and we joined our Soul Clan circle on the ripe, bursting grass. Together we chewed the peyote buttons under the mid-day summer sun.

The bitter taste activated swells of saliva, but there was no nausea. Enjoying the sensations, I lay down on the grass, the buttons filling my mouth, feeling like a cow chewing her cud, giggling at the thought. Slowly, the trip came on. Relaxation deepened as time slowed. The good earth supported me. Eyes closed, I merged with the full, dry plants and the myriad lives they contained. Interconnectedness increased. Sounds sharpened, whispering grasses mingling with delicate insect rustlings, chirping birds, and fluttering leaves.

When I opened my eyes and looked around I saw the Soul Clan scattered around the meadow. Wheat and Bodhi hunkered on boulders, chewing, talking low. Starry lay face down, chewing, hugging a crumbling log as she watched Angel play in the grass. Tree and Deva sheltered under the eucalyptus tree, leaning against the patterned bark, absorbed in each other, chewing. Wearing the same dress as me, Lola stood transfixed in the grass near me. She chewed and sucked her peyote slowly, her eyes like torches, a wide smile spreading across her face as her glorious, auburn hair curled wild and free.

Each moment dropped like ripe fruit from a heavy bough. All the senses – sound, vision, taste, and touch – were palpable, visual. My happiness spread like butter toward Bodhi. Receiving it, he smiled shimmering iridescent ripples toward me. I had never seen living love before, but there it was, streaming, surging, singing. Bodhi walked slowly toward me, radiant as a god. Awed by his beauty, I couldn't contain myself.

"You're as bright as the sun," I said, admiring him.

"So are you," he complimented in return.

We laughed together and love burst like stars around us.

I would have loved to stay forever in Starry's golden grasshopper and eucalyptus heaven, but Bodhi took my hand and pulled me to my feet. It was time to go to Malibu. Starry decided to stay and trip with her son. The rest of us snuggled down in Wheat's car. As we curved slowly down the canyon, my senses worked overtime trying to take it all in. The invisible had become visible.

Suddenly, I sat up and leaned out the window. A magnificent man with long, waving honey-blonde hair stood on the side of the road. Dressed in a pure-white tunic trimmed with a purple and gold border and gathered by a silver cord, he held a shining, jeweled shepherd's staff.

"Who's that?" I yelled, pointing to the man.

"Who? Where?" my friends asked, looking around.

"Him!" I whispered in awe as we drew closer, overwhelmed by his shining, majestic beauty.

"I don't see anyone," Lola said, subtle annoyance in her voice.

"There!" I shouted, as if my shouting would make him more real.

For an instant, I looked directly into his beatific glowing face, into eyes of glorious, loving light. As we moved past him, he followed me with his radiant gaze. As I turned, I saw that he was floating above the ground. Then we curved around the next bend and he passed out of view.

"Didn't you see him?" I gasped, shaking, bursting with excitement.

"No," they answered, confused. I watched their expressions mirror my amazement as I described him.

"You saw an angel," Wheat announced as if seeing an angel was an everyday event.

"Wow. Far out! An angel!" Lola enthused.

I immediately accepted that as the only possible explanation for my vision of such a magnificent being.

"Primo nectar!" Bodhi praised. "A gift from God."

I still saw the angel shining in my mind, but I was too shy to say I wanted to go back and be with him.

Trembling, I snuggled up to Bodhi, whispering rapturously.

"He was so beautiful. He was so beautiful."

When we came out of Topanga Canyon and turned onto PCH, the ocean winds blasted me into the present. The angel dissolved into the past.

We parked south of Malibu Colony, where the Serra stream flows into the beach lagoon, and crawled through the fence into the brambly marsh. The tide was high. The path was under water.

I looked at the thorny brambles and then at my feet. I was barefoot.

"I must have left my sandals at Starry's place," I said.

Bodhi considered the situation.

"Take my shoes," he offered as he knelt down to take them off.

I shook my head, "No, thank you." The thought of the thorns on his feet was worse than the thought of them on mine.

"I'll carry you," Wheat offered.

Intensely involved internally, I shook my head again.

The problem wasn't personal. It was symbolic. The increased awareness, created by the peyote, accentuated my feelings to such a degree that the thought of putting my tender feet on the thorns seemed unbearable. Yet, as I paced back and forth, the obstacle became a conflict of universal dimensions cleaving through my consciousness. Suddenly my mind opened and reverence erased my resistance. The face of my angel appeared before me, transparently layered over an image of Christ. There was no doubt in my mind what I needed to do.

"I will walk across the thorns," I pronounced.

"Are you sure?" Bodhi asked, looking at me and then the thorns.

"Yes."

Without hesitation, I stepped my right foot onto the thorns as though I was going to walk on water. I felt something under my feet, but there was no pain. I looked down and saw a leather sandal underneath my right foot, and where I was about to place my left foot was its match. The universe seemed to explode with surprised synchronicity. I wavered and almost fell.

Bodhi caught me.

"Are you hurt?" he asked with concern.

Prickles moved up and down my body like electric currents.

"No. Look!" I said in amazement as I pointed to the soft, simple, brown leather sandals under my feet.

Silent shock waves expanded as my friends realized what had happened.

"They are a gift for you," Bodhi pronounced as he knelt down and took my right foot in his hands, kissed it gently and slipped on the sandal. Then he repeated the ritual with the other foot.

United in spirit, peyote singing in our cells, sisters and brothers of love, we walked over the thorns to the sea, moving beyond present time into primordial myth. The ocean waves rushed to meet us with sprays of mist, fine sand, and wild sound. Every grain of sand, every wave, and every cloud revealed messages, as if nature were writing the truth of the universe in ancient calligraphy, and I was reading the primal language of creation. The information overload was so vast, I almost fainted from the expansion. Sinking to my knees, I wanted to bury myself in the sand and be consumed by this living, divine energy. I stretched out on the ground, reveling in the power and the truth.

So much was happening on so many levels. I was living wisdom, with my heart, mind, and senses wide open to the cosmos, welcoming the universe with every pore of my being. Drifting, blowing, moving, changing, rearranging, I felt as though I was floating on a moving mist of particles, a pulsing continuation of the waves of the sea. I felt as though I could fall through the space between the sand granules, but there was no fear.

Bodhi, guardian of love, watched over me. Currents of love flashed like flames between our interior worlds. Ancient symbols of great meaning played within and around our auras. I read the messages with the thousands of eyes of my cells, but as quickly as I grasped them, they flew away and new ones took their place.

"Who are you?" I called to Bodhi through the interchanging dance of the sea, sun, sand, and wind energies.

"Your Self," he answered, laughing with love.

His words entered me with their truth, and then another truth flashed. If he was a mirror, then Taz must also be a mirror. The thought shuddered through me as realization bubbles swelled and burst within my mind. Too much was happening to hold on to anything, so I let my thoughts fly free and clung to the sand like filings to a magnet, held in the grip of an awesome presence, unable to move. Knowing was infinite. I was supremely aware that this pure, pranic, cellular recognition was the universe scripting itself moment by moment in my consciousness. I was part of the script. I belonged! My body felt as though it was undulating with a cellular pulse of primal, elemental being.

Messages of symbolic truth danced in love space-light fluidity. I felt the power of an inarticulate longing within me, a core of pure being that felt like a seed that wanted to know and be known.

Bodhi's eyes shone like an anchor of love, the center of a swirling vortex of energy spinning ultimate truth. My lighthouse of safety was the eternal love-truth recognition in his eyes.

Suddenly, Lola ran between us, wild and free, her long auburn hair curling in the wind. Mirror to myself, my soul sister wearing the same dress as me, she invited us to come play in the sea.

As soon as I left the earth behind, the wind captured me, and then the sea. As light as the sea mist and the twirling breezes, I entered the frothing, flying foam and plunged into the surging breakers. Skipping and splashing with my friends, we teased the waves to catch us, and then falling, rolling onto the sand, we scattered onto land. The sun burned into us as our gasping breaths slowed, filling us with light.

Wheat's voice rippled into my consciousness.

"Let's get something to drink," he said like a wise man recognizing truth.

I looked at the pier, the people, the cars, and Malibu. I'd forgotten they were there. Tasting the dry roughness of my tongue, wanting water, I felt like an aborigine on the edge of civilization.

"Having a good trip?" Bodhi asked.

I held his hand as we walked toward the pier.

"Oh, yes. I'm not afraid at all," I said, surprised at my response.

"You don't have to be afraid when you're with me," he reassured me.

His heart words reached my shore and blossoming gratitude opened in response. Feeling his protective, guiding male force, I wanted to cleave to him and surround him with the flowering of my love.

Lola and Deva took my hands and we skipped ahead, three suntanned, happy California girls. Golden goddess Deva led our beach dance and Lola cavorted like a wild nature spirit. Sun-kissed, water-kissed, and filled with love, I felt happy and proud to be with them. Then, as we neared the crowds on the beach, anxiety flowed around me like winter mists, and my mind pedaled backward into old, rough patterns as shyness and fear overwhelmed me.

"No. I can't go there," I said, digging my heels into the sand.

Deva and Lola stopped their dance.

"Hey, what's up?" Bodhi said, catching up with us.

"I can't walk by all those people," I explained, trembling.

"Why? What are you afraid of?" Bodhi said, putting his arms around me.

Wheat, Deva and Lola circled around me tenderly.

"I don't know. When people look at me, I feel self-conscious. I'm shy, afraid. I don't know what they're thinking about me. It's always been that way."

"They look at you and think you're beautiful and wish they were with you," Bodhi said with confidence.

Uncertain, I heard his words but couldn't believe them.

"We'll go back. We won't go to the pier," Bodhi decided. "Wheat can bring us something to drink."

Lola agreed. "Yeah. Go back. We'll go on our own. It's cool."

Lola ran off with Deva, both of them skipping, light and free.

Bodhi and I turned to walk back.

"Maybe its just another patch of thorns," I whispered to Bodhi. "It would be good if I went, wouldn't it?"

"You don't have to," he said gently.

"I want to," I said with determination.

I turned and faced the crowded beach. Even though I knew shyness, self-consciousness and fear weren't logical, I felt them just the same. My feelings and my body seemed to have an energetic life independent of common sense.

Bodhi took my hand and, as we walked toward the pier, I forced myself to look at the crowds. When we got closer, I saw that the crowd was made of individuals, most of them just doing their own thing. A few looked at us. Some smiled. A child waved. Instead of retreating before the minds of others, I found myself radiating. Suddenly, I was free.

"I'm all right now," I announced with pride.

"Of course you are," Bodhi assured me, and kissed my cheek.

As we walked out on the pier, I felt overwhelmed by the fragility of the man-made construction, as if the grimy, worn wood could barely resist the power of the pounding waves. Aware of my vulnerability, I realized that in the grand scheme of nature and time, our lives are insignificant. Then, I remembered that the movement of one grain of sand could change the shape of an entire dune. We are all important, I decided. Everything makes a difference.

"Coming to the ladies' room?" Lola's smiled, her invitation bringing me back from my soaring thoughts.

"I guess so," I responded reluctantly, not wanting to enter a public toilet. Feeling too shy to say no, I followed Deva and Lola inside.

Assaulted by the odor, stunned by the filth, I ran back outside.

"Hey, what's the matter now?" Bodhi asked like a gentle father.

"It's dirty...smelly...ugly. I can't stand it," I explained, feeling ashamed.

I wanted the world to be bright, light, clean and loving. The toilet exposed everything I didn't want to see.

"Public toilets are like that," Bodhi reassured me as if I was a child.

I closed my eyes and invited images into my mind – the face of the angel, clean sand, the pure wind, and the calligraphic messages of the divine, anything to wipe away the sensation of the smelly, dirty public toilet.

When Deva came out, she gave me a motherly hug. On one level, what was happening seemed silly and on another level, it felt cosmic. I must remember this when I'm with my children, I thought. Even small things reflect immense issues.

"Do you want to try again? Might be easier the second time," Bodhi suggested with a loving smile, his eyes shining into mine.

Embarrassed that I was freaking out on a peyote trip, I gathered my strength, thinking that I might as well face what I was always trying to run away from. Taking a deep breath, I opened the door and went in. Standing alone in the small, dank room, I felt the accumulation of the countless people that had been there before me. The room pulsed, overwhelming me with odors and filth.

At first, I felt the neglect was my fault, and it was my responsibility to clean it up. Realistically I couldn't do that, so I let the idea pass. Then, instead of reacting to the filth and odors, I let the vibrations of those sensations flow through me. Slowly, I relaxed into being there, until I was able to look at the room without resistance, and accept it as it was. I no longer identified with it or reacted against it.

A few minutes later, stronger and surer, smiling triumphantly, I walked outside into Bodhi's welcoming arms. By challenging my fear, I had discovered a way of moving beyond my resistance.

Back on the beach with my friends, we formed a circle and joined hands, love surging through our connected soul currents. Closing my eyes, I felt my spirit merge with the winds, the sun, and the moist sea air. Even the sand beneath us pulsed with the elemental dance of life. Spontaneously, we lifted our joined hands and created a circular love flower opening to the heavens.

When it was time to go home, I put on my blessed miracle sandals.

"Bodhi, where did these sandals come from? Did the angel bring them? What do you think?" I asked as we drove through Topanga Canyon. I still hoped my angel would be waiting for me by the side of the road.

"We'll never know for sure. Believe what you want, whatever feels right. The important thing is the choice you made," he explained.

"What choice?" I asked.

"When you chose to walk barefoot across the thorns, the universe gave you what you needed – the sandals," he stated. "It's as simple as that."

Back at the Soul Clan house, when the story of the sandals was told, Magda said quietly, "It's a miracle."

"Yes, I guess it is," I replied, awed by the wonder of the day.

Thankful that I was with people willing to accept the possibility of angels and miracles, I looked at my sandals and touched the soft leather straps, wondering who had worn them before they became mine.

Calmed by Magda's cool house, I wanted to be still. Sitting cross-legged on the living room carpet under one of Bodhi's drawings, my back against the wall, I closed my eyes. The peyote was still swirling inside me like a song.

Tuning in, feeling a vast space inside my head, an inner pull focused my attention in the center of my forehead. Unexpectedly, a tunnel appeared and expanded in a spiraling movement that opened into soft, translucent rainbows suffused with illuminated ringing sounds. Then, light exploded into a greater brightness that was followed by spinning. Entranced, my mind raced into this swirling tunnel as if it knew where it was going.

Spiraling, I saw myself birthing into life and dying into birth, being born into one body after another, alternating between male and female, revealing the continuum of birth, growth, maturity, aging, and death and the space between lives. There was a sensation of kaleidoscopic cultural costumes, body shapes, and personalities, but the speed gave me only a fractional glimpse of each incarnation before I traveled further inward. When the light expanded into soft diffusion, the spinning, spiraling lives dissolved.

As my body spontaneously shaped itself into a sacred posture, I became aware that I had merged into a Buddha reality. Centered in bliss, existing as compassion, I bathed in quiet ecstasy and infinite peace, the equilibrium uniting birth and death, inner and outer, high and low, male and female, dark and light. Like a magnetic anchor uniting duality, this endless loving peace contained everything, but it was also empty. Existing as mystery, I simply was my divine self.

An infinite time later, someone touched me on my arm. A familiar man's voice called to me.

"Where are you?" it said.

I didn't respond because I wanted to stay with the Buddha, but the voice and the touch tugged at me and I fell back into myself. As my head slowly turned toward the sound of the voice, a swell of annoyance accompanied my return to the world. I knew it was Bodhi calling me and touching me, but he seemed like a stranger. I looked at him from an indifferent distance.

"Where are you?" Bodhi repeated with concern.

Traces of my journey poured out of my eyes and burned into him.

"I was with God. I was the Buddha."

My voice felt deeply and strangely full, almost prophetic. Then, remembering the vague feeling of my body shaping itself into a posture, I noticed I was sitting in the full-lotus yoga meditation pose. The posture felt natural, comfortable. I didn't want to move. Weighted, complete, I turned from Bodhi to the darkening room. All my friends, even the children, were sitting in front of me. I looked from one to the other, aware of their curiosity and concern, aware of light torching from my eyes into theirs. Love reached out her arms, inspiring a mixture of laughter and relief as her cherub dimples pulled at my heart. Wheat was golden, radiating, floating above the rest, burning bright. He nodded his head, acknowledging where I had been.

Sadness overwhelmed me. Tears flowed down my cheeks. Before this inner journey, my children, Bodhi, this house, and these friends had been the greatest love I had ever known. Now they seemed like shadows compared with the light and the love of my interior world.

Trembling, weary, I leaned against Bodhi. A few minutes later, he led me to our room and I lay down on the bed. Bodhi held me in his arms and Love snuggled close, comforting me. When I looked into Love's eyes, Buddha recognition flared, soul-to-soul, as she smiled gently, knowingly, lovingly. Oh, if only babies could talk, they could help us remember where we have come from, I cried in my heart.

"I wanted to stay inside forever. I didn't want to come back," I wept, as I clung to Love and Bodhi, sadness seeping from my heart.

"I had to bring you back. I have to take care of you," Bodhi explained gently.

As the Buddha bliss faded, the outer world returned with a bittersweet mingling of loss and love that was indescribably beautiful. Blessings showered with shared tears, laughter, and comforting touch as my mind blossomed into visions of knowing. The light shining within me had promised that one day I'd be able to love truly, deeply, equally. It revealed that God was love in action, and the key to becoming love was to find the love in every moment, no matter what was happening.

Next morning, when I came into the living room, Wheat was packing his gear.

Grief surged through me, and I gasped with surprise at my reaction as I blurted out, "You're leaving?"

"Going to Newport Beach and Laguna to check in with the Brotherhood of Eternal Love. Wanna come?" he asked lightly.

Surprised by the invitation, but feeling awkward, I made excuses. "I can't. I mean, I'd like to, but I'm with Bodhi."

"Yeah, I understand," he smiled easily.

"The Brotherhood of Eternal Love? What's that?"

"The Brotherhood provides the highest sacrament. We turn people on to their high vibrations. Those were Brotherhood buttons that took you on your trip yesterday."

As Wheat stood before me, glowing, smiling, radiating, my heart expanded into his loving generosity.

"You were golden. You were the only one who knew where I'd been," I shared, tears welling up in my eyes.

Wheat pulled me into a bear hug.

"I know you, sister," he said softly in my ear.

Lola walked in carrying her bag. She was leaving too.

"I'll be back in a few days. Time for a change. Got friends to see," she said with a toss of her head and a quick smile.

They hugged me and then they were gone.

Never Come Down

Magda and Bodhi were deep in conversation in the garden. They looked seriously intense, so I hesitated at the patio door, too shy to interrupt. When they saw me, their faces lit up with a loving welcome.

Reassured, I walked over and knelt at Bodhi's feet, resting my head on his knees.

"That was some trip you had yesterday. How are you feeling?" he asked, stroking my hair.

"Whew. Spinning. So many changes. Wheat and Lola just left," I said, sadness clinging to my words.

"It's always changing around here," Magda said as she got up from the garden seat. "Everyone's always coming and going. You'll get used to it. Deva and Tree left early this morning, too."

After Magda left, I had a strange sense that she was mad at me. I didn't understand why, but my increased sensitivity was beginning to pick up peoples' thoughts and feelings. I knew that was a good thing, because in the past I'd gotten into a lot of trouble because I took people at face value. It troubled me, but I didn't want to talk to Bodhi about it. Perhaps there was more going on with Bodhi and Magda than I had realized, but what?

Resting in the garden, basking in the sun, I went over the multitudinous dimensions of my peyote journey.

Amazing as the trip had been, I was back in ordinary reality again. Why was I lifted to a place of peace on a peyote trip and then dropped back down? I vowed to find a way to return, but I didn't want to take peyote again. I knew drug highs weren't the answer. I didn't want to take something and get high, then have to come right back down again. I wanted to stay high. I'd always longed for something. Now I knew what it was. If I had peace, if I had love, I'd have everything. But how could I find peace and love here in ordinary everyday reality? And if I did, how could I keep them? Why was something that big so hard to find?

Later, when I went into the living room, the walls were bare.

"Where are the drawings?" I asked Bodhi, surprised and disappointed that they were gone.

"I put them in the closet. They're not good enough," he explained as he tacked fresh, white paper on the walls.

Magda seemed to have returned to her normal, friendly self. When Love and I sat on the sofa, she snuggled up with us and we watched Bodhi set up his art supplies.

"I love it when everyone goes. It's quiet. Then he draws," she said, her arms wrapped around her knees, happy as a child as she worshipped Bodhi.

In that moment, I glimpsed that her love for Bodhi was more than friendship. She worshipped him as everyone else did, but more than that, I saw that she harbored a desire for him. I saw that everything she did was calculated to keep him in her life and in her home. As the shock of that truth flashed through me, I flushed. Like a naïve idiot, I'd missed the subtle agendas playing out in the relationships around me. Fear constricted my heart as I realized how dependent Bodhi and I were on her hospitality. Without Magda, our scene wouldn't be happening.

"Look," Magda said quietly, her face radiant.

Bodhi stood still, poised before the blank paper, then quickly he moved into action, drawing simple graceful lines. Pausing, he lifted the pencil, turned and looked at me for a moment before returning to his drawing.

"You make me look like a Madonna," I said shyly.

"You are a Madonna," he affirmed matter-of-factly.

I couldn't accept the compliment. I couldn't respond. Instead, my shamed self repeated "I'm not a Madonna" inside my mind. As these words reverberated within me, I wondered who I really was. I seemed to be so many selves. What was my true self?

"A penny for your thoughts," Bodhi asked as he noticed my change of mood.

Taking a deep breath, I spoke my truth. "I'm not a Madonna. My life has been full of hurt, fear and pain – things you wouldn't believe if I told you."

Even though I knew I was breaking the Never Come Down rule, I felt Bodhi needed to know where I'd come from.

"None of that matters. Your true self has endured despite all that has happened to you. It's always been there, even when you were suffering," he said with conviction.

"Without you, without everyone here, I'm utterly alone, I said, starting to cry. "You don't know what that's like. You're always surrounded by friends who love you."

He sighed and said, "You can be lonely even among friends. Each one of us is alone. I know you've had a hard time. And yet, despite all that, you're beautiful. Your children are beautiful. Your spirit lives in your children. You're stronger than you realize. When you know that, you'll be free to be yourself."

Bodhi spoke intensely, sharing his strength, making me feel I could be free, that I could be happy, that I could find my way.

Magda shifted next to me and I turned. She had a frown on her face and she was picking her nails. She looked at me but she did not smile.

I wondered if Bodhi knew how she really felt about him. If she loved Bodhi and wanted him, why had she married Pedro? And if she loved and wanted Bodhi, how could she make her heart big enough to welcome his girlfriends to her home? Or was it all just play-acting? Or maybe he knew all this and gave her just enough love and attention to keep her in line. That thought scared me. Why did people use each other? Why was love so measured and calculated, so limited and disguised?

Magda got up and left the room. Bodhi returned to his drawing. Holding Love in my arms, I watched him create a portrait of a Flower Child Madonna. Was his portrait really of me, or was it his idea of who he wanted me to be? I was beginning to understand that everyone sees people according to their own ideas. How could I find a way to see beyond the personality and the projections? How could I see people as they really were in their deepest heart and soul?

Then Bodhi stood in front of me. As he pulled me to my feet and embraced me, my worrisome thoughts disappeared. He loved me. He wanted me. I was his. That was enough for now.

"Today I feel like pleasing you, more than before..."

I let go of my fear. I trusted. I was safe. I was loved. It was my time to blossom. Bodhi was my earth, my water, my sun, and my air. I was the flower gracing his garden of love. He was my holy man, my savior. He was my world. Bathed in the bliss of gratitude, enjoying a life woven of caring love and joyful play, I lived in the ecstasy of an open heart. Love also flowered under his care. Even though I longed for Choo to be with us, I didn't want to see Taz. At night, I dreamed of what life might be like if Bodhi was my husband and the father of my children.

"To be living for you, is all I want to do..."

One day when we were city-tripping, we drove by the Psychedelic Conspiracy. I wanted my friends to see my store but Bodhi didn't want to go in.

"You don't belong there. You belong in nature. You belong with me. I want to show you magic places. We'll live a life you never dreamed possible."

When Tree and Deva returned, Deva was high. Arms raised, she strode through the garden, shouting, "Never Come Down! Never Come Down!"

Watching her wild shouts and spontaneous dance, I envied her freedom. How I longed to be like her.

Tree joined in the shouting of "Never Come Down! Never Come Down!" and soon everyone in the household, even the kids, was running around the garden screaming, "Never Come Down! Never Come Down!"

That night at dinner Tree and Deva asked to be called the Never Come Down twins.

"How can you Never Come Down?" I asked Deva a few days later, when we were combing our hair in the bathroom.

"Whatever it takes," she said, shrugging her shoulders and laughing carelessly. "Sometimes it's making love, sometimes it's acid or STP, or my friends, or pot. Whatever it takes."

"But what if something happens that you don't like?" I insisted. "Surely you'd come down."

"Never, she said with total confidence. "I only go up, and that means love, my dear, no matter what's happening."

Later in the day, I discovered Tree and Deva making love in Magda's bedroom and drew back, embarrassed, but they laughed at my shyness. I loved their freedom. They were like gods, passing love back and forth like a flaming torch.

The phone rang. Bodhi answered it, and after talking for a while, he said, "We need to pick up Starry and Angel.

She's having car trouble. One of her neighbors just called. Wanna trip to Topanga?"

"Sure," I responded without hesitation. "Maybe I'll see my angel again."

"We'll go somewhere special first. Hey, Tree, Deva, want to come to a high waterfall?" Bodhi yelled.

A naked Tree peeked out from the bedroom door.

"Alllll right," he drawled. "Sounds primo. Be out in a sec."

Ever since I'd seen the elves and fairies painted on the exterior of Tree and Deva's Volkswagen bus, I'd wanted to take a ride with them. I climbed in and sat on the bed, noticing how they'd decked it out. The interior was draped with floral cloth and bells, subtly hiding the baskets and bags that contained their belongings. Handmade indigo velvet curtains hung at the windows and behind the front seat. Tree and Deva had a home on wheels that matched their free-tripping lifestyle. They made the rounds of their friends, camped at the Hog Farm, and sold their jewelry at fairs.

"Welcome to our home," Deva said with a bow, before she jumped into the front seat and slid over close to Tree.

"It's beautiful in here," I admired, feeling an impulse to own a Volkswagen van. "You guys really have your scene together."

"We live simply so we've got time to do the things we love," Tree said proudly as he pulled off the freeway at the Malibu Canyon exit and headed toward the coast.

Once we were up in the hills, Bodhi gave each of us a peyote button.

"Far out, man. Been holding out?" Tree teased as he placed the button in his mouth.

"Saving 'em for the right moment, man. Sacrament for the waterfall," Bodhi replied, in the same teasing way.

The view expanded as we grooved around the mountain curves. The bitter peyote cud released saliva, and the cellular churning heralded the familiar chemical dance. By the time we pulled over to park the car, I was high. The ocean was far below, but I could still feel the pull of the waves.

"This is a very special place. Plants that used to be here have disappeared and new ones have arrived to replace them. Nature is so mysterious," Bodhi mused as he led us upward through the scrub.

From the top of the hill we could see the ocean in one direction and the San Fernando Valley in the other. Hiking down a narrow trail, we neared a grove of trees and heard the sound of water. Excited, Deva ran ahead, Tree following close behind. Bodhi and I continued our slow pace until we pressed through lush ferns and emerged into the waterfall clearing. In the center of the pool, misted by a waterfall rainbow, Deva gracefully swayed and twirled a goddess dance, her hands curling expressively above her. Tree stood on the other side of the rainbow, under the waterfall, the water beating on his head and face as he lifted his arms upward to receive the force. Awed by Deva's exquisite movements and Tree's majestic devotion, I felt as though I was watching the flower children of God in the Garden of Eden.

Bodhi took my hand and led me into the pool. When I stood waist deep in the water, he scooped water into his hands and poured it over my head, saying solemnly, "I baptize thee in the name of pure love."

Then, obeying an urge for total immersion, I bent my knees and let myself sink deeper, my dress bubbling around me as I glided into the water. Sinking beneath the water, rising to the surface, then sinking again, I played in the radiating wave circles until I dared seek the waterfall. A few breaststrokes drew me under the strength of the falling water, and I gasped with the force of a natural baptism.

Floating, my long hair rippling into the water, I gazed at the delicate, misty rainbows shimmering above me.

The pouring water captivated me. Recognition startled my consciousness. Heart pounding, shaking, I felt as though the waterfall was seeing my womanhood. The mossy rocks glistened, exuding a power that moved me through shock waves of realization. Fear visited me again. I tried to hold on, but it was too painful, so I let go. I experienced a sensation of shattering into segments; waves of intense emotions – guilt, shame, fear, and sadness – burst into my mind, accompanied by an overwhelming sense of failure.

I sensed a mystical message emanating from my heart.

"The earth is dying. What are you going to do about it?" a primeval voice spoke from an ancient well of wisdom within me.

The moss on the waterfall rocks looked like a woman's vulva, the source of life, the entrance to the womb of creation. The identification was complete. I was the earth. I was dying. What was I going to do about it? Then the question faded as I heard another phrase.

"The earth is living. Enjoy it," the voice uttered.

Mesmerized by the appearance of the water falling over the top of the rocks, I was overcome by an intense desire to discover the source of the flow. Excited, I pulled myself out of the water and started to climb up the slippery rocks. Even though I heard Bodhi calling, I couldn't stop myself. The source of the water had me in its power. It wanted me to come home. Following the stream, I ran with extraordinary strength and agility, leaping from rock to rock, climbing mossy banks, sure-footed as a mountain goat, until, hot and breathless, I pulled off my dress and bathed in a pool. Refreshed, naked, I climbed further, the rhythmic babbling of the water changing its tune with every turn. The wind was hot and strong. The view expanded as I persisted with my ascent.

Striving to reach the top of the ridge, I pulled myself up, rock by rock, the stream diminishing as I climbed. Then

I stopped and closed my eyes. When I opened them again, there on the ridge stood three crosses where there had been none before.

Awestruck, I knelt down on the hot rock. As visions of Christ, bleeding bodies, skeletons, and churches flowed through my brain, I felt a chasm between my head and my body. I couldn't bear the surging visions, so I lay down and closed my eyes, trying to find the tunnel to peace, but it didn't open. Instead, nature's brightness expanded into a pattern of a vast, waving infinity. Released, unified, I bathed in the light of inner harmony, until the sound of falling rocks told me Bodhi was coming. I sat up and crouched like a mermaid on a rock, innocently happy in my nakedness as I watched him climb toward me. Slowly, he moved forward, step-by-step until he stood before me, a silent question in his loving eyes.

"Something pulled me here," I explained, unable to say more.

"And I was pulled to you," he said, smiling with quiet understanding.

Comrades, we sat on the rock, enjoying the powerful, peyote-pulsing, panoramic view. Nature was offering a screen of loving wisdom, but it was also secretly inviting and offering much more. I peered at the view, wishing I could penetrate it and see behind it, but the intense staring hurt my eyes. I gave up and tried to tell Bodhi what had happened to me, but the disjointed images that had meant so much were hard to explain.

"The earth is our mother. I am the earth, but I am also spirit. I saw three crosses on the ridge. I must do something to help the earth and its people," I whispered passionately.

Bodhi looked at me and then at the hill. The crosses were not there.

"What do these experiences mean?" I asked. "I can't make sense of what I saw and felt, but I know it was important."

"These visions are gifts, awakenings. You can't understand or explain them. They're only for you."

"What happens when you're high?" I asked, seeking to know him.

"Me?" he laughed. "I'm the visionary artist. I look at the light, the beauty, the patterns, what I call surges of love. What's in our head is the starting point. Our perceptions and journeys are different, but also the same. We find our own path to God. What I see, I draw. What I experience, I share. It's all love."

Sharing silence, we hiked down the stream. I found my cast-off dress halfway down and slipped it over my head.

Laughing, glistening wet from their play, Tree and Deva welcomed our return to the waterfall pool. When my eyes met Deva's, a flow of love surged between us and she embraced me, recognizing and honoring the essence of my awakening. I felt happy to be closer to her. I longed to be like her, simple, free, direct, and true. She wasn't afraid to be herself. She was pure and clear, like a bright light. I loved her with all my heart.

When the afternoon sun lowered toward the sea, we returned to our car. After cruising down PCH and through Malibu to Topanga, we picked up Starry and Angel, happy to add their company to the magic Never Come Down VW van. When we got back to the house, Lola had returned from Laguna.

"Hey, guys. Wow! Am I glad to see you," she said as she hugged us one by one, jumping up and down with joy. Soon everyone was yelling, "Never Come Down" and dancing around.

The Soul Clan had gathered to share our Summer of Love.

Heading North on 101

The Clan was talking up the Jefferson Airplane concert at the Fillmore in San Francisco.

"Let's make the scene, Bodhi," Lola pleaded excitedly.

Bodhi begged off, but Lola wouldn't give up. She was dead set on going and relentless with her pleading.

"What do you think?" Bodhi asked that night. "Should we go?"

Annoyed that Lola wouldn't leave us alone, I said plainly, "No. I don't want to go. Why doesn't she take some of her other friends?"

"She wants our company," Bodhi said, but I knew she wanted Bodhi to come so she'd be sure to have a high trip.

I tried to tell Lola how I felt. "Lola, I went to San Francisco twice this year and both trips were bummers. I'm happy here at Magda's house. I don't want to leave," I said.

"This time it'll be different, you'll see. You'll be with Bodhi and me," she said, ignoring my wishes. "Remember the toilet on the pier? Just face your fear. You'll have a great time."

Upset that Lola was talking like we were going with her, I went looking for Bodhi.

"Bodhi, I don't want to go. Please, let's stay here," I begged.

Unable to resist Lola's pleading, he decided to go. "I'd rather stay too, but Lola's restless. She wants us to make the San Fran scene with her. It'll be fun. You'll see."

I was bummed. I couldn't hide my disappointment.

"The concert will be cool," he enthused, trying to make me feel better. "We've never been on a road trip. Let's go for it!"

Lola was stoked that she was getting her way.

"Whoopie! Let's dig Kesey's Kool Aid acid test," she shouted, as she packed her bags.

I retreated to my room and packed my red suitcase with a reluctant heart. Even though I left my things in our room and my car in the drive, I was scared that everything would be different when we returned.

Magda watched with a silent smile that made me uneasy. A fearful thought surfaced. Maybe she wanted me to leave. The paranoia made me feel sick, so I tried to blot out my dark thoughts by saying, Never Come Down inside my head, but it didn't work.

When Magda hugged me and said, "Your room will be waiting for you when you return," I felt better.

Lola and Bodhi raved about the adventure ahead. All I could think about was what I was leaving behind.

Early the next morning, we squeezed into Lola's golden sunflower VW bug and headed north on Highway 101. The radio blasted the latest songs as we sped by hills torched brown from the summer sun. After a run on the Oceano beach, we soaked in Avila Hot Springs. It was nearly midnight when we pulled up at the Radiance Gallery in Big Sur.

Lola walked up the steps and rang the bell. When the door opened, a woman holding a candle peered out.

"Lola?"

"Yeah. Hi, Sophia. There's three of us here, and a baby."

"Come on in. Sorry I can't turn on the lights. Reggie's asleep. Quiet now."

Sophia led us into the living room.

"Make yourselves at home. See you in the morning."

We settled on the mattresses Sophia had prepared with sheets and blankets. When we awoke in the early morning, the house felt cold and damp, as if the thick sea fog had penetrated the house. We snuggled close to each other for warmth and were glad when we heard Sophia bustling around in the kitchen, stoking the wood stove.

A few minutes later, Sophia called to us, "Come on in, dears. Come on and get warm. The kettle's on."

Encouraged by the crackling flames, we huddled around the stove.

Sophia gave Love a piece of apple. Love chewed slowly, staring at Sophia with open curiosity, her eyes following her every move.

Wrapped in a woolen shawl she had wound around her flannel nightgown, Sophia's thick salt and pepper braid curved like a serpent between her shoulder blades as she shuffled around her homey kitchen in sheepskin slippers.

The aroma of fresh coffee blended with the fragrance of toasted homemade bread. Enriched with apples, currants and cinnamon, oatmeal bubbled on top of the roaring wood stove. Her old man stomped in just as Sophia's weaving of nourishment and comfort reached perfection.

Reggie was a huge man. Dressed in a red and black striped flannel shirt and well-worn blue jeans, he wore heavy workman's boots and a thick leather belt cinched tight across a bulging Buddha tummy. His massive shoulders curved like a bear's, making him look like he was prepared to drop on all fours at a moment's notice. He peered shyly at us from under dark, bushy eyebrows, his craggy face revealing quiet strength. Nodding his greeting, he sat at the large oak kitchen table, and took two sips of coffee and three mouthfuls of oatmeal.

"How long you staying?" he asked.

Lola spoke for us. "We're moving on to San Francisco this morning. We're on our way to see the Jefferson Airplane at the Fillmore tomorrow night. We sure appreciate you putting us up."

"Make sure they have a hot breakfast to see them on their way," Reggie instructed Sophia with calm formality, shyly hiding his pleasure at the opportunity to offer us generous hospitality.

Sophia winked at us as she poured oatmeal into wooden bowls and passed them to us. As we spooned down the warm oatmeal, Sophia passed around buttered toast and mugs of coffee until we were well comforted.

When Reggie got up to leave for work, Bodhi said, "Thanks again, man," and shook his hand.

Reggie nodded and waved at us before he shut the door.

After breakfast, Lola helped Sophia wash the dishes while I took care of Love.

Bodhi called from the window seat, "Look, the fog's lifting. Come on, I want to show you the garden."

Bodhi led me into the rising mist, where sun-streaming shafts of light danced in a mystical fairyland. Eyes wide, Love toddled beside me as we followed Bodhi along a stepping-stone path edged by aromatic herbs, up rough-hewn wooden steps, past violet-blue hollyhocks and delphiniums, and into a morning glory heaven. An antique white Victorian bathtub stood on black-clawed feet in the midst of a fragrant profusion of flowers. A wrought-iron framed mirror leaned against swaying bamboo. Strings of bells tinkled and crystals flashed rainbows from leafy branches. When I stared at myself in the mirror and saw the fairy dell all around me, I looked like I was standing in the Garden of Eden.

"Flower Child, you belong in a garden," Bodhi sighed with secret pleasure at my surprised delight.

Bodhi's words warmed my heart, and from somewhere deep within me a smile expanded until I had to throw my arms around him. My joy was complete when Love circled our legs with her dimpled arms, and loving laughter filled the flowering arbor.

Bodhi's eyes twinkled as he turned on the copper tap.

"Your bath, milady," he teased as he picked blossoms and fragrant herbal leaves and scattered them over the water.

"Flower Child will bathe in flowers," he pronounced, posturing with a make-believe wand before he threw us a kiss and returned down the path.

I slipped off my dress and shivered as I undressed Love. When I tested the water, it was perfect. Bodhi had got it right again. I turned off the tap and got in. After lifting Love above the water and letting her splash her feet, I sat down and settled her on my tummy. Love played with the flowers while I luxuriated in the most beautiful bath I had ever had.

Lola skipped into our bathing heaven.

"Can I come in too?" she asked.

Not waiting for an answer, she lifted her dress above her head and slid into our tangle of slippery, warm limbs.

Blissfully soaking in our steaming, scented bath, we watched the morning mist disappear under the strengthening sun.

"It's time to hit the road," Bodhi called from below.

Fragrance welcomed our feet as we stepped onto the chamomile lawn. Lola and I slipped our twin dresses over our moist bodies, and I wrapped Love in my shawl. Glowing with shining warmth, we stepped out of our fairy dell and greeted Bodhi with radiant smiles.

After saying farewell to Sophia, we drove north through the spectacular beauty of Big Sur, the roaring sea to our left and the summer-browned hills on our right. After a couple of hours, we hummed to a halt near a deep, shadowed cathedral forest. As we walked along the trail leading into the trees, even our footsteps felt too loud in the hushed, holy grove. Surrounded by lacy ferns, I knelt knee-deep in soft moss at the base of a great redwood. Placing my head on the earth, I gave homage to its powerful presence. Feeling kinship with the majestic trees, they reminded me of my own love-seeking spirit as they soared toward the sun, gathering energy to sustain their growth in the dim, verdant world below.

Love was awestruck by the sacred majesty of the gigantic trees. She turned her tender little head upward to the faraway light as her chubby hands grasped lush moss sparkling with tiny starflowers. I watched her child wonder alternate between the magic at her feet and the magic above her. See through a child's eyes, I thought, and the world would be a different place.

Bodhi guided us with playful, elfin gestures to a bubbling, drum-beating brook. Enchanted, we lay on deep, cushioned moss, listening to the playful water rhythms, breathing in fern freshness. Resting on roots and sheltered by branches, I felt the blessing of living grace.

"You've been through a lot, haven't you?" Bodhi asked gently.

I nodded, tears rushing to my eyes, sadness returning to my heart.

"You sink so deeply into a place and drink so fully of everything that is there," he said in a soft voice that respected the profound silent of the ancient forest.

"When I was a child, I always played on the beach or in the forest," I shared. "I'm just so happy to be in nature again."

After our rest, we wandered slowly back to Lola's car. Soon the forest was left behind and vistas of ocean waves, cliffs, and beaches opened before us.

We arrived at Bodhi's friends' house in Monterey before sunset. Voices low, we sat on the tiled patio of a Spanish hacienda courtyard, the star-filled night sky pulling our eyes toward the heavens. Crickets chirped a high-pitched chorus over the distant boom of the sea while Bodhi sketched.

When he finished the drawing, he presented it to me: a Madonna picture with words circling a halo around my head, "my mother the earth, my father the sun, my child, love."

Hate Ashbury

As we drove into San Francisco, I was overwhelmed by a sense of foreboding. The freeway quickly pulled us into crowds, noises, and smells that felt ominous and harsh. Lola dropped us off in Haight Ashbury and took off. Love was cranky. Bodhi had withdrawn. I wished we hadn't come.

The commune where Bodhi had arranged for us to stay turned out to be a dingy old Victorian hotel with four stories of rooms and shared kitchens and bathrooms. The brother in charge was a stoned, Rasta Jamaican wearing fringed buckskins. He assigned us our rooms with a brisk efficiency softened by Caribbean rap rhythms and undulating movements. In the hallway, we passed strange, stoned, shadowy hippies hiding behind sunglasses.

The kitchen down the hall from our rooms was filthy, but I did my best to keep my reaction down while I made sandwiches and tea. Submerged in a strange, dark house that vibrated with drug trips, the memory of the Big Sur forest still singing inside me, I felt the absence of nature like a heartache. Determined to make us comfortable, I unpacked my suitcase and cheered up the room with brightly colored shawls and blankets. Even though I snuggled close to Bodhi that night, my sleep was restless, and my thoughts were haunted by shadowy dreams.

"Bodhi, I don't know about this place," I said in the morning, uncertain as to how to express my fear and discomfort.

"Be cool. It's only for a few days," he reassured me.

We were getting ready to go out for a walk when three shaded hipsters knocked on the door.

"Hey, man, heard you were here. Far out, Bro. Long time no see."

They sat on the floor, lit a joint, and passed it around.

While Bodhi tripped with his friends, I took Love for a walk. I wanted to find the Digger house where I'd last seen Rainbow. A short time later, I stood in front of the derelict building. An angelic young girl with long blonde curls, and big, wide, brown eyes, who had tiny red hearts painted on her face, sat on the stoop in the sunshine, blowing bubbles.

"Rainbow moved on. We don't know where," was all she said before she returned to blowing bubbles.

I hung out in front of the drugstore on Masonic, digging the scene, watching everyone go by. I experienced the same reactions as the last time I was in the Haight, only more intensely.

The San Francisco scene felt fiercely intellectual, political, even revolutionary. Black Panther activists, civil rights protesters, Vietnam draft resisters, and the Peace and Freedom Party true believers mixed openly with the "everything is love" flower children. And now that the media had publicized the Summer of Love hype, thousands of kids had streamed from every part of the country into Haight Ashbury. The street scene was clearly on overload.

I walked past colorful hippies camped out in front of the painted, psychedelic-poster wall at the Print Mint. The scene was lively. Impromptu musicians played guitars, beat drums, and blew flutes while dancers shuffled and twirled. A preacher was raving apocalyptic, Christian warnings, threatening that Judgment Day was coming, while the dancing flower children blew him kisses and dropped flowers at his feet. At The Psychedelic Shop, locals wandered in and out, mingling with members of the Grateful Dead, rapping about Kesey's latest acid test, and discussing their latest plots to melt down the culture.

While munching doughnuts and sipping coffee at Tracy's Donut Shop, I was blown away by the intense conversations around me. Police had beaten up the "We are the People" Vietnam draft demonstrators who had resisted edicts telling them to disassemble. Playful, young, potheads were being sentenced to long prison terms for smoking a joint. Hippies were picked up and jailed for dancing naked in the park. San Francisco always showed me the dark side of Flower Power. The vibes scared me. I didn't want war. I wanted peace.

Later in the afternoon, Bodhi took us on a walk through Golden Gate Park. Even though the sun came out for a while, it didn't feel like summer. I shivered in the wind that blew from the sea, but Bodhi, seemingly impervious to the cold, carried Love easily as we walked briskly toward the zoo.

"I want to show you something," he said excitedly.

Then he led me to the reptile cages, right up to the rattlesnakes, and said, "Watch closely."

As he stared at the sleeping snakes, they slowly stirred, uncoiled and glided over to Bodhi. Then they pressed against the glass and looked at him. He repeated this with several snakes and then with other reptiles and animals.

"What is it? How do you do it?" I asked, amazed at his power.

"I call it love magnetism. I discovered it when I was a child. I concentrate my attention, send love, call them and they come."

"Is that what you did to me at the Renaissance Faire?"

Bodhi laughed but he didn't answer my question.

I didn't press him for an answer.

Later that night, when Lola and Bodhi were getting ready to go to the Fillmore rock concert, I realized I didn't want to go. Lola wanted to take acid and groove on the rock-star sound waves, and Bodhi was into being her friend, but I was scared to get high with thousands of trippers and melt down in Ken Kesey's Kool Aid acid test.

I knelt down in front of Bodhi, my hands on his knees, and looked into his eyes. "I want to stay here with Love."

"Sure; do whatever feels right," he said sadly.

Lola bounced around like she was glad I wasn't going, but I didn't care. I was more concerned about handling my first separation from Bodhi.

After they left, I locked the door and snuggled down with Love. She seemed uneasy too, so we looked at her picture books and I sang to her until she fell asleep.

Hours later, I opened the door to let Bodhi in.

"How was it?" I asked, relieved that he was back.

"Intense," was all he said as he lay down, fully clothed, on the bed and closed his eyes.

I put my arms around him, but he didn't respond. In the morning he seemed down, without energy. I'd never seen him like that before.

"Hey, Lola, when are we heading back?" I asked, impatient to be free of San Francisco.

"Bodhi didn't tell you?" she said in an offhand way, waving her arms impatiently, like I was stupid. "We're going to this cool place in Marin, you know, Bodhi's old buddies. Now that we're up here we want to hang out for a while."

Bodhi and Lola acted distant and strange. I felt out of sync, as though the magic had been stripped away and our connection had been broken.

Even though we were heading in the opposite direction from Magda's home in the San Fernando Valley, it was a relief to leave Haight Ashbury. I felt sad that I had never seen it when the

Love Generation was being birthed and the brothers and sisters were true and real. I only saw it in its death throes, when the innocent dreams had been eclipsed by the shadow.

Lola crossed the Golden Gate Bridge and drove up Mount Tamalpais to check out the view. I stayed close to Bodhi. He allowed affection, but he didn't respond or offer any himself. Usually his overflowing fullness nourished everyone. Now it seemed as if he had nothing to give.

"Just let him be," Lola reassured me. "Sometimes he has to work things out in his head. He'll be okay."

Always exuberant, she led me away to dance and play in the grassy meadow at the top of Mount Tam. With the spectacular view of the San Francisco Bay spread out at our feet, it seemed like we were angels dancing in the clouds. Bodhi leaned against a tree and held Love in his lap as he watched our graceful dance. After a while, a slow, sad smile dawned on his face.

After lunch in Mill Valley, we drove to their friends' house. Perched on a hillside, with a multitude of blooming potted plants and a redwood deck that circled a free-form swimming pool, the scene looked wonderful, but five minutes after we arrived, I wanted to leave. The owners, big time acid pushers, were hooked on sarcastic put-downs. When Bodhi started intense private conversations with them, I wondered if he was dealing drugs, then I shook the thought away and went into the garden.

Lola came out a few minutes later.

"Heavy," she grimaced as she rolled her eyes. "I have friends in Stinson Beach. We can split in the morning."

"Can't we just go home?" I pleaded.

"Can't you just have a good time?" she said, sarcasm rolling off her tongue.

"Yes, I can, but not here," I said, defending myself, feeling hurt. "I never wanted to come in the first place. I just want to go home."

"You want. You want. Why should Bodhi do what you want? I've known him longer than you," she said spitefully. "I was his fantasy lover once too, you know. We all were, and there are many more of his lovers who didn't stay in his Soul Clan. That's his way of never coming down; that, and a few good drugs," she said carelessly and dove into the pool. When she surfaced, she yelled at me, "You don't know him at all," and she swam quickly to the far end of the pool.

Without loving support, fear took over my heart and mind. It seemed like Lola was trying to break Bodhi and me apart.

"I want to go home," I shouted to her, but she ignored me.

I retreated to my room and curled up beside Love. Voices, footsteps, music, laughter, and arguments filtered into the room, keeping me awake. It was nearly dawn when Bodhi came in and fell on the bed. With him beside me, I finally fell asleep.

When Love woke in the early morning, I took her outside. Despite the beautiful garden, the sunshine and the swimming pool, I couldn't enjoy any of it. My mind and heart felt like they were stretched tight. Time passed far too slowly. I tried to contain the way fear was triggering my imagination, but I was clearly losing control.

Bodhi emerged hours later, stretching and yawning in the sunlight, his torso bare above his blue jeans. When he saw me sitting on the deck chair with Love, he came over and sat beside us, but he didn't kiss me or touch me. I felt myself wondering who he really was. The distance between us was real. It wasn't my imagination, but I still felt everything would be okay if we could just go back to Magda's.

Jefferson Airplane played through my mind.

"Everyday I try so hard to know your mind,
and find out what's inside you..."

"I want to go home. Please, let's go home," I begged. I figured if Lola could beg him into coming to San Francisco, I could beg him into returning home.

"Where's home?" he asked, without a smile.

"With you at Magda's house," I said, pain high in my heart.

"But not with me, here?" he said, scratching his chest.

"I don't like it here. I don't like these people," I said, but I was too afraid to tell him that he felt different and strange and that I did not know who he was anymore.

Then, Bodhi's laughter rang out and my heart was glad again. I had become aware of unspoken thoughts and feelings behind his eyes. Like undercurrents they pulled at me, but I pushed them away. I knew something was wrong. I didn't know what it was, and I was afraid to find out.

"Lola wants to hang out at Stinson Beach, but we could hitch back if you want," he said.

"I want," I said, and threw my arms around his neck.

His eyes brightened. He was back with me again.

"Let's go. Let's hitch. Now!" I commanded urgently.

He laughed his wonderful laugh again.

My kisses showered gratitude and I ran to pack.

Lola drove us south of San Francisco, but she refused to talk to either of us. Lola was bugged that Bodhi was pulling out of her adventure, and she was mad at me for convincing him to go. I wondered why I'd never seen how spoiled and selfish Lola was before. I kept looking at Bodhi, trying to figure what was going on inside him. The magic love field that had carried us along for weeks had dissolved. I just didn't know what was happening any more.

After Lola dropped us off, Bodhi, Love, and I stood alone on the road. For a moment it felt strange to be on our own, and then the energy switched. I took over the lead. Bodhi sat on my red suitcase holding Love, while I, as bright and confident as the colors of my magenta and mango knitted dress, stood on the road, hitching the rides to take us home. We met fine people, were treated to meals, and even were gifted with a hot spring soak in Esalen. It seemed like the magic was happening again. Bodhi was projecting his love-leader trip and everyone was falling for it. All our rides treated him like a king. Everyone thought he was the coolest dude going. How did he do it?

Our last ride took us right to Magda's house, and just like the first time I went there, lights and music overflowed into the garden, welcoming us back to her house of love.

Excited to be home, humming my favorite songs, I unpacked my red suitcase and spread out my blankets and shawls. Love helped me put away her little dresses, but she was rubbing her eyes, so I got her ready for bed and sang her to sleep.

Thorns of Love

When I slipped out of the room to look for Bodhi, I heard voices in the garden. Something about their whispering caused a strong reaction in me. Fear struck at my heart.

"What's up?" I asked, trembling as I walked toward them, afraid to hear the answer.

Silence. Bodhi looked at Magda. Magda looked at Bodhi.

Then Magda took a big breath and explained, "It's Taz. He placed ads in the Free Press offering a reward for information about you. Someone gave him our phone number and he called here. When I told him you were in San Francisco, he got angry. He yelled at me, saying crazy stuff, like we'd kidnapped you. Then he threatened to call the police."

The news hit me with a force that took my breath away.

"I've finished with Taz. I'm with Bodhi now."

I looked at Bodhi but he turned his eyes away.

"There's a lot of energy coming from him. Don't know what to make of it," he mumbled weakly.

"I won't go back to him," I argued.

"Magda had to hide the buttons and smoke. We've always been so free. We've never had trouble before," he explained with impatience.

"I won't let him come here. I have my own life now," I insisted, tears gathering in my eyes. I wanted things to go back to the way they were before we left for San Francisco.

"We want to go to the Griffith Park Love-In this weekend, but Bodhi isn't sure it's cool with Taz being so upset and all," Magda said with cold neutrality.

"He just wants to talk. He wants to see Love," I insisted, feeling like I was begging. "And I'd love to see my son," I added.

It was dark in the garden. There were no moon or stars to light the way. Intensely aware of the bonds between Bodhi and Magda, I felt like an outsider. In love with Bodhi, floating on clouds of bliss, I'd tripped on the surface of things. Now I was seeing another side.

I wanted to connect with him in our own space, in our own way. I wanted to feel his body, to look into his eyes. I held out my hand and led him to our room, but Bodhi wouldn't sit with me. He paced distractedly. I waited. Eventually he stood in front of me, looking down at me.

"There's something I need to know. We've been together for nearly two months. You haven't had a period. I need to know what's happening."

His words shocked me.

"I hadn't noticed," I said, color rising on my cheeks as I turned away from him.

Bodhi asked in a firm, almost parental voice, "When was your last period?"

I counted back and realized my last period was before the rape.

"Nearly three months ago," I said, closing my eyes and breathing deeply as I tried to calm the fear. I touched my breasts, recognizing the fullness.

"Yes, I'm pregnant," I confirmed, feeling as though my words rung a death knell between us. "I didn't know until now."

"Who's the father?" Bodhi demanded, pain in his voice.

I told him about the rain, and how I tried to find Taz to pick up our son, how Taz had come storming into the store and raped me.

"That explains it," he said with a sigh, falling back on the bed.

"That explains what?" I asked. Didn't he care that I'd been raped? Didn't he understand how terrible that was for me?

"This energy from Taz, the ad in the Free Press, the threats. He may not know you're pregnant, but the pull is there. He wants you back."

"He doesn't want me back, except on his terms. If he knew I was pregnant, he'd want me to have an abortion. He wouldn't want to be a father to this child. You don't know him, Bodhi. This doesn't change things between us, does it?"

"It's not up to us. Whatever's right will unfold."

I covered my ears as his words hit my body like a sword thrust. The present felt intolerable. Drowning in familiar patterns of fear, I searched inside, desperately seeking a way to make everything okay again. I hugged Bodhi, but he did not respond. His body was stiff and unyielding.

"Bodhi. You don't need to worry about expenses. I have money. I want to stay with you. We could make it work."

"It's not that. I have to be where the energy is high. I can't take care of you like Pedro takes care of Magda. I'm an artist, a high teacher."

Just like Taz, Bodhi divided love into compartments. It was okay as long as he was my teacher, turning me on to new experiences, but it wasn't okay if my ex-husband called me on the phone or if I was pregnant. He had lifted me into a dream, but he didn't want to make the dream real. No amount of wanting or stubborn determination could turn him into the man I wanted him to be. I learned that with Taz. He wasn't willing to stand by me, so I had to let him go.

In the morning Bodhi told me everything was going to be okay, but he did nothing to make it okay. Love watched us, eyes wide, and clung to me, her little arms holding on tight. I could tell she could feel my heartbreak, and she did her best to comfort me, leaning against me, hugging me, kissing me. Trying one more time to hold on to what was slipping away, I begged him to let me stay with him.

"It's not up to us. Let's see what happens at the Love-In," he sidestepped, letting me know he didn't want me anymore.

Magda knocked on the door and announced in a cool, formal voice, "Taz is on the phone. He wants to talk to you."

"I won't talk to him. I hate him," I cried out angrily.

"You have to talk to him. You can't avoid it," she insisted.

Bodhi led me to the phone.

"Hi," I said, bitterness tightening my throat.

"Hi. I've been trying to find you for weeks," Taz said, relief in his voice. "What's happening? How are you?"

The moment I heard his voice, I felt my heart shut down. "What do you want?" I said coldly.

"Are you and Love okay? Choo's been asking for you."

"We're fine. How's Choo?"

My heart ached at the thought of my son. The complexities of my heart overwhelmed me. Why must love be divided and measured? I kept myself away from Choo to be with Bodhi. Now Bodhi didn't want me anymore because of Taz.

"He's fine. We miss you. When are you coming back?"

"I'm never coming back."

"Can I come there and see you?" Taz asked.

"No, I don't want you to come here. I'll meet you and Choo at the Love-In, at the merry-go-round, about noon."

I hung up the phone and looked at Bodhi and Magda. Our shared dream had vanished. The ice-cold water of reality had doused my illusions. I had believed in Bodhi and Magda, in all of them. Now Bodhi and Magda had shut me out. A flame of jealousy leapt through my heart. Magda had a husband who took care of her and Bodhi was her best friend. I had nothing. Unable to bear their rejection, I turned away from them and went into my room to pack.

Starry and Deva skipped into my room to show off the costumes they'd put together for the Love-In, and asked me to help them tie ribbons and flowers in their hair. They didn't know about Taz. They didn't know I was pregnant. They didn't know I was leaving.

Then Bodhi stood at the door, Tree and Pedro beside him.

"We're heading out. See you at the Love-In," Bodhi said with a casual wave, but he didn't wait for an answer and he didn't say goodbye to me.

That was an omission no one could ignore. The girls looked at each other, eyebrows raised, and slipped quietly out of my room. Overcome by grief, I waited for a few minutes, then finished packing, When I couldn't delay any longer, I picked up my suitcase and walked into the living room.

Starry filled her arms with my blankets and shawls. Deva embraced me and held my hand as we walked outside. Magda took my suitcase and put it in the back of the car. Love toddled beside me, looking up at me, trying to understand.

As we rode to the Love-In, I knew this was the last time I would be with my beautiful sisters. They helped each other, but they wouldn't help me. My summer with the beautiful people was over. What would I do now? Where would I go? Pregnant, altered forever by the Summer of Love, I could not return to my old life.

Remembering the vision that appeared when I met Bodhi at the merry-go-round, the leaping flame that turned into a golden fountain, I realized that our beginning had always contained our ending. Even though I didn't know I was pregnant, my angel, or God, did, and it even knew her name, Light. This understanding helped me surrender to the change and the loss. I was determined to birth this surprise child even though I knew it would be difficult to raise her on my own.

Dressed in long, flowing dresses, and with ribbons and flowers woven into our hair, four sisters and one cherubic child walked into the Griffith Park Love-In. Bodhi and his brothers watched us from the shelter of the trees. I could still feel his power but it felt different. Instead of pulling me toward him he was sending me away.

My sisters ran to join Bodhi, Tree, and Pedro. I walked with Love toward the merry-go-round hill where I had promised to meet Taz. Sitting on the grass, holding my daughter in my arms, feeling abandoned as the Love-In swirled around me, I fell into pain, into loss, into darkness. I was alone again.

Caught between light and dark, between Bodhi and Taz, I sought understanding. Then it came, clearly and simply. I had worshipped men as if they were gods. No wonder I got into trouble. I had to stop looking to men for the answers and find the truth for myself. I had fooled myself that my Summer of Love Soul Clan was my true family of friends. I had learned the truth the hard way. Once I accepted this fully, a feeling like a fresh breeze swept thought me. A clear sense that something better was waiting for me in the future dawned in my heart.

A shadow fell on me. I looked up, hoping that is was Bodhi, but it was Taz, a new version of Taz that looked like Bodhi. Taz wore a full-length, striped, biblical robe but he had added wild, freeform, plastic rings and necklaces that wove strange patterns around his neck and arms. Even though he had grown a beard and was trying to change into someone like Bodhi, even though he was dressed as if he were my partner for the Love-In, he was not love. Ashamed and repulsed, I turned away.

Then dear, wonderful, wriggly, scriggly, energy-bursting Choo threw himself into my arms and I fell over onto the grass. As I held my beautiful son in my embrace, I saw my family of love watching my reunion with my family of pain.

Taz's voice shook as he asked, "Are you coming home?"

I didn't answer. Even though I knew he'd been worried about me, I did not want to speak to him. In my heart I blamed him for separating me from Bodhi.

"Things will be better now," he reassured me.

I heard the words but I didn't believe them.

A Beatles' song played like a river behind my pain.

"...a real nowhere man..."

"Why don't you say something?" he asked, already getting angry at my silence.

"...making all his nowhere plans..."

Then Taz yelled, "Can't you hear me?"

"I can hear you, but I don't believe you," I said simply.

"I want you to come home," he entreated. "Let's be a family."

"...he's as blind as he can be..."

"I will never come home with you. Take me to the store."

Bodhi and his family of friends watched us leave. A beam of love light passed between us, but there was no magnetism.

What began at one Love-In ended at another Love-In.

The wife of darkness and the mother of children of light, I walked out of a dream of love into the reality of my own life, knowing that it was up to me to turn my life into love.

BOOK FOUR
Garden of Love

Dream of Paradise

Like a refugee, I returned to the metallic, plastic wasteland of the Psychedelic Conspiracy, withdrawing into grief that felt like it would last forever.

"...when the truth is found to be lies
...all the joy within you dies..."

Even though swarms of summer tourists filled the store from morning till late at night, raving about the decorations and the fashions, I no longer believed in the dream. At night I curled up with Love on a mattress in the back of the store and wondered what I was going to do. Where did I belong? That was one question that didn't seem to have an answer.

I sensed that most of my problems came from an inability to understand other people. They said one thing and then they changed their minds. They acted one way, then a few days later they seemed like different people. Behind their words and smiles, their minds ran hidden agendas that suited their more selfish needs and desires. I had let strong people dominate me by their anger and selfish demands. They made sure they got their way, but I didn't want to be like them. I wondered how I could find my power without running over other people.

My lack of success with human relationships made me long even more deeply for a spiritual teacher. Now that I'd experienced the dissolution of the promise of love that had shone out of Bodhi's eyes, I wanted even more strongly a true love that would last. I wanted to be lifted out of my miserable human condition. I knew that wasn't going to happen until I mastered life, but how was I going to do that?

Taz noticed I was pregnant and flipped out.

"Get an abortion! The last thing we need is another child," he yelled, trying to intimidate me, his face glowering like a dark cloud.

Unmoved by his rage, I stood my ground.

"You made me pregnant. You're part of this, too," I yelled right back at him.

Taz's mood changed. With a sly smile he reminded me, "Ah, well, you forget it could have happened the next morning."

Surprised, I remembered the deep river of peace, the forgiveness that opened to love. Yes, she must have been conceived on that morning.

"I already know her name. It's Light, for the longing that leaps like fire toward love," I told him, feeling great love for this new child growing within me.

"What makes you so sure it's a girl?" he said, ignoring what I'd just said.

I gathered strength from my fear and pain and shame, and told it like it was.

"The same way I know everything. I just know! Light is my daughter. I'm going to birth her into my life, and there's nothing you can do about it," I said passionately, feeling like a flame of fire. If anger was a way to feel my power, I didn't know why I was so afraid of it.

Speaking my truth switched the energy. The paralysis that had overwhelmed me since I had left Bodhi shifted, and a sense of excitement came over me. I knew that something wonderful was going to happen. That night, I went to sleep thinking I needed a dream to help me out of my nightmare. Amazingly enough, the next morning I carried the memories of a beautiful dream into my waking consciousness. Visions of voluptuous, tropical flowers; cascading waterfalls; fern grottos; glistening grasses waving over rolling green hills; palm-circled beaches, and glorious sunsets melted the frozen wasteland of my heart. A seed of hope stirred in my soul as Hawaii blossomed in my mind.

Inspired, I worked long hours in the store, selling jewelry and fashions. In two weeks, I'd stockpiled enough cash for air tickets and money to live on for awhile.

Hope shone from my smile like dawn.

Taz noticed my happiness and grunted, "What's happening now, oh dumb one?"

"I'm going to Hawaii," I answered simply.

"And blow all you've got on another bad trip?" he snickered.

"No, this will be a very good trip," I insisted.

"You'll come running back," he warned.

His derision did not move me from my knowing.

"I will always try to get away from you," I said stubbornly, "and one day I'll make it."

In early September, I flew to Hawaii. High above the clouds, I read *The Tibetan Book of the Dead*, learning how souls experience the emptying of all dreams except the yearning to be born again in paradise. I'd bought the book because I felt like I was dead, only to find out I was about to be born again. Well, if that was what was happening, I was ready for a dose of paradise.

Hours later, after a long flight and a change of planes in Honolulu, we descended through streaming clouds. Maui appeared like a mystical magical emerald isle edged by white foam waves. As I stepped out of the plane, my hard core of endurance opened in joy. I inhaled the warm, moist, fragrant air like an inexperienced lover, uncertain before the wonder of pleasure. Carrying Love, I walked through the breezeways to the baggage claim area. After I picked up my bags, I looked around. Feeling fatigued, and not knowing where to go or what to do, I retreated to a wooden bench under a palm tree. Settled there, I listened to rustling branches and sighing breezes that mingled with the strains of recorded Hawaiian guitar music.

"Love, what will we do now?" I sighed.

She laughed and ran around the bench, picking up brilliant crimson and yellow hibiscus and staring wide-eyed at the sights of Kahului airport. Then she crawled into my lap and put her arms around me. Soothed by swaying plants and wafting fragrances, I felt I had returned to paradise.

"Oh, Love, it's so beautiful here," I whispered to her as she fell asleep.

Some time later, another plane landed and among the flowing mirage of neatly dressed tourists necklaced in flower leis, I glimpsed four flower children, three brothers and one sister. The glowing, buoyant longhaired guys were wearing tie-dyed rainbow T-shirts and the island sister with them was wearing a sarong. They smiled their hellos, instantly recognizing me as one of their own.

"Hi. What's happening? Are you our aloha welcome?" a friendly brother asked as he flashed a mischievous grin. His sun-streaked ponytail, love beads, and bell-bottoms revealed his L.A. hipster groove.

"Just got here myself. I'm looking for a place to crash," I said. "I'm Flower Child, and this is Love, my daughter."

Love woke gently, smiling shyly at our new friends as she clung to me.

"We're hitching to a farm in Haiku. Come along. Name's Anchovy," he said, with a warm, friendly smile.

"And I'm Honu," a sun-kissed surfer with a mane of thick golden hair said gallantly as he bowed and kissed my hand.

Honu gestured toward a shapely Hawaiian girl wrapped in a white and crimson hibiscus print sarong. Her smile burst like a ripe fruit beneath her luminous eyes as he said, "And this is my lady, Ono."

With a graceful gesture that sent her lustrous, waist-length coal-black hair swaying, Ono hugged me to her abundant breasts.

Then Honu pointed to a dreadlocked hippie with wild eyes. "And this is Bro."

Immediately, Love and I were engulfed in a tumultuous embrace. "God bless you and keep you with us," Bro exclaimed dramatically before he set off, staff in hand, like a biblical wanderer, hawk-like nose sniffing the air, his sun-bleached hair glowing like a golden aura around his bare torso, arms, and legs.

"Love, love, love; all you need is love..."

Like a long-lost tribe, we followed Bro and his friends out of the airport and down the road toward Kahului. With cosmic synchronicity, destiny had provided Love and I with a guide. The door to Maui had opened.

"We'll hang out here," Bro decided as he dropped his pack and set his staff against a tree.

While we waited for a ride, Bro said they'd been camping on the Big Island of Hawaii, swimming with dolphins in Kealakakua Bay near the City of Refuge, and they were heading home to the Zendo in Haiku. I told them about my studio, the store on Sunset Strip and my dream of Hawaii. It turned out both Anchovy and Bro had been in the Conspiracy. We all agreed it was a happening.

"Where are you from?" I asked Bro shyly, wondering why he looked like a fasting Essene hermit wandering the biblical deserts in search of God.

"Idaho-ho-ho," he laughed wildly. "Who would believe I came from potato-ho-ho-land."

"How did it happen?" I giggled.

"Didn't fit in. I was the youngest son of a third-generation farming family; you know, all-American pitchforks and apple pie and the fourth of July. My parents were Swedish, and they were very into the land. My dad was a tyrant, setting me and my brothers against each other, promising one of us his inheritance one day, then another the next.

"One day my eyes opened. I'd been singing the flower power songs with my high school buddies. I'd been turned on and felt my mind open, and was starting to look at things in a different way. One day my dad was yelling at me. I just looked at him, and you wanna know what I said? I said, 'I don't want a piece of your pie,' and walked out."

"I stayed with friends in Boise for a while, then rode the rails west to Haight Ashbury. I hung around with the Diggers in the early days, dropping acid and growing my hair, and creating some of the happenings, but the San Francisco scene was getting out of hand with the Summer of Love propaganda, so I came to the islands."

"Wow," was all I could say.

"Yeah, wow," he repeated.

"What are you looking for?" I asked a minute later.

"Not looking for anything. This is it. I'm a wanderer. It's all about whatever comes down the road."

Every time a car drove by, Bro stood up, raised his hand, and commanded the drivers to pick us up. Within a short time, a farm truck stopped and we piled in the back. Hair flying, breathing in the perfumed air, we sped toward Hana. The hulking volcano, Haleakala, loomed on our right, with gentler, greener hills bowing at its feet. To our left, glistening sugarcane fields rippled vibrational continuations of the rolling ocean waves. We passed an old sugarcane factory, black smoke steaming from its stack. Then we entered the little town of Paia, a cluster of ramshackle old wood buildings barely resisting the twining, vining tropical vegetation. Our first ride dropped us at Baldwin Road in the center of Paia.

Cooled by the breeze blowing up from the beach, we crouched under the scant shade of a plumeria tree. I threw down a shawl and lay on the thick grass, glad to rest for awhile. Love picked the flowers lying on the grass and dropped them all over me. Soon I was covered with exquisite golden-white blossoms. With every breath I inhaled their delicate sweet fragrance.

Ono took Love for a walk on the beach, and the guys wandered away to talk to the gas station attendant.

Weariness drew me into a dreamy slumber as my body relaxed into the lush grass. I became aware of a deep exhaustion, and then I felt it slowly flow out of me into the earth. As my tension released, I felt a connection with the energies of the foaming sea, the tropical vegetation, and the swirling breezes. There was no need to dream anymore. My dream was all around me.

"Hawaii is so beautiful," I whispered to Ono when she returned with Love.

"Beautiful and savage," she said, laughing. "Wait till you meet your first centipede or greedy real estate agent."

"Darkness is everywhere – even in paradise," I said.

"Paradise isn't enough anymore. People want mansions and beach houses and fine hotels and restaurants. I'd like to go back to the old ways, but even the ancient Hawaiians had their problems. We just have to put up with being a tropical vacation spot for hard working taxpayers," Ono said bitterly.

"This could be paradise," Honu said, putting his arm protectively around Ono, "but it isn't, so we make our dreams come true as best we can."

As Ono leaned into his embrace, they looked like the union of Hawaii's past and present, the very reality they resisted.

Resting in silence, we watched the ripening reds, oranges, and pinks of the sunset sky. As stars began to emerge from the spreading darkness, a battered pickup truck pulled up to the gas station. Bro walked over and talked to the driver.

"We've got a ride," he yelled triumphantly.

We grabbed our things and ran over to the truck. An old Hawaiian lady squeezed close to her husband to make room for Love and me up front. Their deeply tanned and wrinkled faces lit up with joy and their eyes glowed as bright as embers when they saw Love. Fascinated by the aged grandmother, Love reached for her with her chubby, dimpled hands.

"Your baby, huh? Beautiful baby," she crooned. "You want give baby away? We take her anytime. Raise up, adopt?" the old lady said hopefully, smiling widely as she took Love into her arms.

Not sure if she was playing or serious, I just laughed.

"No. Oh, no. I'm happy to raise her myself," I said.

The grandmother grinned knowingly, her broken and missing teeth adding a unique touch to her wise, wrinkled beauty. As we sped through the pineapple-scented darkness, she amused Love with ancient Hawaiian chants. Their mingled laughter brought tears to my eyes. This is the way life should be, I thought, the young children and the elders playing together. I'd love to have grandparents like these. Why was I so far away from what was human, natural, and good?

Turning inland on Holokai Road, we drove past lush hedges and tall trees that stood like shadowed sentinels against the indigo sky. When the truck stopped, the headlights revealed a rickety gate draped with morning glory vines.

"Careful," Bro cautioned as he helped me out of the truck.

"Looks like everyone's asleep," Anchovy whispered as he picked up my pack and slung it over his shoulder.

Carrying Love with one arm, I held on to Bro with the other as he led us up the garden path to the steps of the front porch.

"Anyone home? It's Bro, come from Big Island, with friends," he called out as he opened the screen door and led me up the steps.

"Hey man," a sleepy male voice answered.

"Find a space. Sack out," another guy called out.

"See you in the morning, man," a third bro mumbled.

Disoriented, feeling my way in the darkness, I slipped along the wall to my right until I discovered a wide, empty bench. Feeling more balanced with my eyes closed, relying totally on feeling, I pulled my shawls out of my pack to make a makeshift bed for Love and me. It was completely disorienting to be in total blackness, not knowing where I was or what I would see when I woke up. Then, remembering the descriptions in the *Tibetan Book of the Dead,* I realized destiny was giving me the experience of the "bardo", the place between death and rebirth. Feeling entombed, I struggled against the darkness, searching for the light of dawn, waiting for release.

Holokai Zendo

My eyes were open when the first rays of light glowed in the east. Love was still asleep, papoosed in colorful shawls, arms thrown back above her head, her soft, sweet face relaxed and calm. Dawn slowly filtered into the room, illuminating several blanketed bodies stretched out on the floor. Tatami mats, pictures of the Buddha and Christ, candles, and flowers suggested an ashram rather than a home. The living room had four doors, all closed.

As light filled the room, Love whimpered and sat up sleepily, looking around in confusion. Her irresistible arms reached out to me. I picked her up, holding her close to me. Her gentle murmuring and nuzzle-nursing slowly woke the drowsy sleepers sacked out on the floor.

"Hey, look who's sleeping on the coffin," a bearded, redheaded guy commented with surprise, then sat up to take a better look.

"Sister, you've been in the grave," a young crew-cut kid joked. "That's a coffin."

Smiling shyly at the guys staring at Love and me, I wasn't surprised to learn I'd been sleeping on a coffin. That would tie right in with the perfect *Tibetan Book of the Dead* scenario.

Anchovy, Honu, and Bro greeted everyone with big hand slaps, hugs, and the latest slang.

"How de do, dude?"

"Far out."

"Cool, man."

"How goes it, Bro?"

"Righteous!"

Anchovy introduced me.

"Hey, guys, Flower Child and her daughter, Love, need a home. You got space?"

"Yeah, that room's free," the blonde, teenage surfer pointed to the west door. "Nothing in it, though."

Holding Love, I stood up, swathed in shawls, my long black hair falling free to my waist.

Bro gasped and cried, "Holy mother and child."

Anchovy chanted, "Om," dropped to his knees, and bowed his head.

Unused to such chivalrous attention, I laughed awkwardly.

"She's a high lady from the City of Angels. Treat her sweetly and she'll add magic to the place," Anchovy promised his friends with merry humor.

Anchovy and Bro introduced the Zendo Family, offering bio tidbits with each name. The awkward, freckled surfer kid shook his sun-bleached white-blonde shoulder-length hair proudly, then waved his hand as he said his name, "Wave," smiling as he dug his own joke. He had graduated from a Huntington Beach high school, then hit it to Hawaii to be near the waves. The quiet, red-haired bearded guy, Warrior, was a civil rights activist taking a break from the race-riot horrors of Tennessee. He shook my hand seriously as he peered deeply into my eyes. Hiding behind small, round, rose-colored glasses and a bushy brown beard, the last brother leaned against the wall like a tall, thin shadow passively tripping on us all.

Bro nodded toward him, saying simply, "Totido," then turned to Anchovy, raising his eyebrows.

Anchovy whispered in my ear, "Totido is short for Turn On, Tune In, and Drop Out. He's the living LSD dream. Watch him and you'll learn what happens to someone who thinks acid is everyday food. He's in his own world."

Honu whispered in my other ear, "He's a New York trust-fund baby, a cool, harmless stoner. After awhile, he kind of disappears into the background, but his vibe is groovy, man. He keeps us in tune, and the Zendo in the dough."

What I saw was a hiding-out, head-tripping hippie who kept his distance and dug the happenings around him, but was committed to silent cool.

Warrior took charge as he turned on the radio.

"Hey! Let's bring on this day. Oatmeal, brown rice, and coffee coming up," he chanted as he headed for the kitchen. Everyone followed him to help out. I was about to do the same when Anchovy took my hand, swept his arms like a cavalier and bowed.

"Your room awaits you," he said like a gracious courtier.

Joining his game, I put my hand on his arm, and walked like a queen going to her chambers.

Anchovy opened the door and stood aside while I walked slowly into a small, pleasant room. The west-facing window overlooked an overgrown orchard where gentle morning light streamed through rustling, pale green banana leaves onto the white walls and worn wood floors.

"It's perfect!" I exclaimed, grateful for the Zendo generosity and my good fortune.

"You can pick up a mattress and get whatever else you need in Paia later on today," Anchovy suggested. "It's a nice room. You'll be happy here."

"Why do they keep a coffin inside?" I asked when we returned to the living room.

"No other furniture, I guess. Maybe they dug it up outside," he suggested with a grimace.

"What a thought. Do you think there is a skeleton inside?" I wondered, grimacing back at him.

Anchovy laughed. "Take a look if you want."

I shook my head and changed the subject.

"Who owns the Zendo?"

"The farm belongs to a university professor in Honolulu. He's retiring soon and wants to turn this place into a Zen monastery. He's asked a Japanese monk to come and live here next year. Old Prof is letting these guys stay here in exchange for clearing the land and cleaning up the house. It's cool; he won't mind you being here. He'll be glad to have another helper."

Back in the kitchen, everyone was moving to the radio tunes, drinking coffee, and getting breakfast together. The table was filling up with toast, honey, yogurt, papaya, and pineapple. Ono sprinkled raisins and cinnamon on top of the oatmeal with beautiful swaying movements while Honu stirred.

Warrior was turned on. He sang as he cooked with a lilting tenor.

"Oh, what a beautiful morning,
Oh, what a beautiful day..."

Warrior handed me a cup of coffee with a smile.

"We have bananas, papayas, and avocados growing on the land, and there's a guava orchard on the hill behind the house," he explained with pride.

"We're putting in a vegetable garden. We're into macrobiotic brown-rice-and-veggie meals," Wave said proudly in a one-word singsong rush.

I stepped into the garden and walked past a shiny-leafed noni tree heavy with pale, eye-patterned fruit. Sitting on the steps of the front porch, I sipped my coffee and looked down the path that led toward the arched front gate that was draped in morning glories. Airy ironwood trees dominated the land across the road. On either side of the path, the untamed, overgrown garden took over. Flowering trees and bushes swayed in the breeze, displaying brilliant red, orange, and yellow blossoms. Laughing, Love ran like a fickle honeybee from one exotic flower to another. As I tucked a scarlet hibiscus behind my ear, I noticed a gigantic spider hanging in a glistening web on the porch roof above me. Frightened, I picked up Love and ran back to the kitchen. After filling my bowl with oatmeal, I followed my new friends back into the garden.

"There's a huge spider up there," I said, afraid to sit on the porch steps.

Anchovy laughed at my fear.

"That's just a cane spider. He's harmless, quite beautiful really. They don't bother people. The Hawaiians consider them good luck."

I sat down cautiously, keeping the spider in view, not quite trusting it.

"Chew slowly. Contemplate the beauty of this day," Warrior said as he opened his arms to the glory surrounding us.

I looked at him for a moment, wondering what brought him from his civil rights battleground to this run-down farm. He was clearly a leader. Though I wondered, I felt too shy to ask him. The present moment was too beautiful to delve into the past.

Later in the morning, Wave took me shopping in Paia. As he cruised over the bumps and potholes on the Holokai dirt road in the Zendo's rusty old Cadillac, I glimpsed the neighborhood farms and fields we'd passed in the dark the night before. As we turned onto the highway and headed toward Paia, the rich natural surroundings glistened, reflecting the sun's radiance. Shining, swaying sugarcane tossed in the wind and the white-capped sea crashed its endless breakers onto the cliffs beyond the prickly pineapple fields.

"How did you find your way to the Zendo?" I asked Wave, curious to hear his story.

"I had this dream that I had to make it to Hawaii, so I worked at the local drug store during the school year and every summer. My friends were saving for cars, but I put all I had toward coming here. Right after I graduated, I flew to Honolulu, but I didn't like the big city vibe, so I came to Maui. When I landed in Kahului, I stayed in a youth hostel so I could get the feel of the island and make friends. One day, I go into a store to look at surfboards, and this really cool guy was in there. Like, I couldn't take my eyes off him, his vibes were so mellow. He was like everything I wanted to be, so I asked him if he knew of a commune or family where I could stay, and he brought me here. His name's Jeremy. You have to meet this guy. He's so cool."

"Are you planning to stay on Maui?"

"Yeah, man. This is it. Jeremy gives me work whenever he can. He's teaching me construction, and I take odd jobs on this side of the island. I'm moving over to Lahaina side in a month to help him build a house. Yeah, this is the life for me."

Wave's story was so unlike my own. He was no refugee from a bad trip or a "bardo" soul seeking paradise. He was a young man who trusted his heart and followed his impulses. He'd already found someone he wanted to be like, someone who'd taken him under his wing. Sadness coursed through my heart. Why couldn't I have had a destiny like that? Why did my life have to be so complicated? Tired of feeling sorry for myself, I turned once more to the beauty around me.

Wave parked the car in front of the Paia post office. We ambled down the boardwalk toward a clapboard warehouse. Impassive, elderly Japanese men watched our every move as we looked at bamboo furniture and household goods. I bought two single futons, two pillows, a tatami mat, towels, candles, incense, a vase, and a wicker basket. After we loaded up the car with my purchases, I mailed a letter to Choo at the local post office. Our last stop was the food store to pick up supplies for the Zendo.

342

Eyes closed, gently fatigued, I held Love on the soft leather seat of the old luxury car as Wave drove us back to the farm. Warm, fragrant air breezed softly onto my face as gentle happiness blossomed in my heart. My dream had come true. I was in paradise.

Refreshed by the rhythm of cool, soothing afternoon showers tapping on the banana leaves, I scrubbed the wooden floors and windows of my new room. When all was clean and dry, I unrolled the futons on either side of the window and spread the tatami mat between them. Next, I cut the roll of paisley silk I'd brought with me into sheets and curtains. Then I stitched the leftover silk into pillow covers. After hanging our clothes and packs in the closet, I placed Love's toys in the wicker basket. Under the window, I created an altar with candles, fresh flowers, and incense, then carefully placed my favorite photograph of Choo and Love next to Clara's silver pin. Pleased with my homemaking efforts, lulled by the rustling banana leaves and caressed by soft, fragrant breezes, I snuggled down with Love for a nap.

Awakened by footsteps on the roof, I picked up Love and went outside. An evening sky was blending spectacular rose, magenta, and gold to celebrate the end of the day. My new friends were sitting on the roof watching the sunset show.

"Come on up," Warrior invited with a playful wave.

Ono took Love for a walk down the path and Warrior pulled me up the ladder. I perched on the roof, taking in the view all the way to the white-capped sea. To my right, a pyramid-shaped hill emerged from a grove of heavily laden guava trees. Behind us, noble eucalypti stood like proud sentinels against the violet-rose sky. As the sunset played out its glorious light show, the guys hooted and hollered their "far-out's" and "cool, man's." Then, before darkness eclipsed our view, we climbed down the ladder.

Ono put her arm around me, smiling her recognition of my enchantment. "The evening performance here sure beats TV, doesn't it?" she said warmly, the lilt of her Hawaiian accent charming my ears.

I nodded, deeply moved by the glorious sunset.

"Do you come here often?" I asked Ono.

"Whenever I can. My family's in Honolulu. It's a big family with endless aunties and uncles and cousins. The old folks are always getting luaus together so the young kids have something fun to do; you know, picnics on the beach, hula, music and song, and lots of food. Both my mom and my gran are kuma hulas. They teach the traditional style hula. I was raised dancing, and they want me to be a kuma hula."

"How wonderful," I said. "You are so lucky to have a family like that."

"Yeah, its great, but sometimes I feel like I just have to take off and feel who I am for myself. So I trip around with friends and visit the sacred sites and all the beautiful places, and I dance with the waves and the wind and the trees. The performance thing gets to me, with all the competition for who's the best and all that."

Amazed that someone who was gifted with a rich and warm family life felt an urgency to escape from love, I remembered my own dancing childhood.

"I trained as a dancer when I was a child, but I haven't danced in a long time," I said sadly.

"Then you must dance again. Look, it's all around you. Everything is dancing – the trees, the flowers, the waves, the clouds, and the breezes. You just have to dance with it all. That's what the hula is all about."

I looked with new eyes at the dance of life around me, and felt myself sway softly. Yes, it was time to dance again.

"Come on, let's make a salad and cook some veggies," Ono said warmly, and I followed her into the house.

After helping out in the kitchen, I spread one of my colorful cloths on the living room floor and decorated it with banana leaves and flowers. I lit candles and incense, then surveyed the beautifully decorated table with satisfaction. It was hard to believe that this was my first day in a Hawaiian paradise, but I guess in paradise, anything is possible. Laughing to myself, I struck the gong. My new family gathered for supper, each person lighting up as they saw the efforts I had made to create a special feast.

Bro strummed his guitar while everyone gathered in a circle. While we held hands, he led us in prayerful song,

"Bless this food, bless this life,
bless this day, bless this night..."

Then, eyes closed, silent for a moment, we offered our gratitude for the bounty of the Zendo.

Anchovy broke the silence.

"I told you she'd bring magic to this place," he said, looking around at his friends.

"The magic was already here," I said in return.

After dinner, when the guys brought out smoke, I turned in instead of on. Wrapped in beautiful fabric, I fell into happy dreams.

I woke calm and rested. The dark, grief-filled wasteland had vanished. I promised myself that when hard times came again, I'd remember that nothing lasts forever.

Now that I was free from my all-consuming obsessions with Taz and Bodhi, new feelings and instincts awakened within me. Instead of feeling shy and afraid with my new brothers and sisters, I found myself interested in them. Natural affection and curiosity slowly overcame the fearful shyness that had been with me most of my life. I wanted to know what my friends thought and how they felt about life. I figured if I learned about other people, maybe that would help me understand myself.

One day after lunch, when Warrior and I were doing the dishes together, I asked him what I had wanted to know the first morning at the Zendo. It had taken me a few days to figure out how to ask him what had brought him from his civil rights war in the South to this run-down tropical commune in Hawaii.

"I really admire you for fighting for civil rights. I've always been afraid to fight," I said shyly, waiting to see if I'd captured his interest.

"Why so?" he asked in return, obviously checking me out, waiting to see what I had in mind.

"Well, I guess I'm afraid that if I start fighting, I'll lose who I am and start hating. I don't want to hate people, even if they hate me or want to hurt me," I said, surprising myself with my own answer.

"Ah, that's the real issue, isn't it? Do we create change by fighting or do we create it by loving? Or perhaps more accurately, what kind of change do we create by fighting, and what kind of change do we create by loving?"

"But you were motivated by love, weren't you? You wanted to help the black people, didn't you?" I asked, surprised at Warrior's intense response.

"Yes, we wanted to help them, but we were also mad as hell at the bigots and the KKK and all the scruffy young, holier-than-thou white males who killed and raped and hurt the blacks. It was war, all right, and talking about it still makes me angry," he said bitterly.

"Is that why you're here?" I asked gently, feeling his pain.

"I was losing it. I was becoming like them. I wanted to kill them all, and I think I would have if I hadn't jumped on a bus one day. It wasn't a freedom fighter bus; I'd had enough of those. It was just a Greyhound heading west. When I got off in Los Angeles, I wanted to go further. When a friend said he was sailing to Hawaii, I signed on, and I'm not leaving till this anger leaves me."

"Well, you're in the right place, aren't you? This is the home of aloha," I suggested.

"Yeah, there's aloha here all right, but the warriors fought some pretty intense battles here, too. I know war is a part of life, but I don't want to hate anymore. I want to find the way to compassion. That's why I'm here at the Zendo. The master is coming from Japan in a few months, and I want to study with him. I go to the Buddhist temple in Paia, and I've got a ton of books. I have to find the way to peace," he said with determination. "The real peace," he added, "peace in my own heart."

The dishes done, we looked at each other. All I did was ask a question, with sincere interest to know him, and he had revealed his world to me.

"Thank you," I said humbly. "Thank you for letting me know you. Please let me know if there is anything I can do to help you."

"Thank you, sister, thank you for your love," he replied, and started to reach out to hug me, but, struggling with his pain, he turned instead and slipped into the garden. Something in my heart told me he was going to cry, and I was glad. Tears softened anger and opened the way to gentler feelings. I knew that because I had cried so many tears.

Zendo days were woven of an easygoing balance of work and play. The orchard and the garden provided almost everything we needed, and everyone pitched in to buy supplies and gas. When it was time to play, we drove to the Hoolawa twin waterfalls, where guavas fell into flower-filled pools, releasing their ripe aroma. As happy as innocent primitives, we lay in the flowing stream above the falls, jumped into the pool and swam until we were ready to stretch out on sun-warmed, water-smoothed stones. Worry and tension faded into simple happiness. Every night we climbed the ladder to the roof to celebrate the sunset before gathering for our evening feast.

Anchovy was always up to something: going to Lahaina, island-hopping, making connections, bringing friends by, all the while singing his favorite song. He had a momentum that nothing seemed to change. Nothing could keep him in one place for long.

"Leaving on a jet plane,
don't know when I'll be back again..."

Every time I heard him humming that song as he bounced up the path to the farm door, I ran to greet him, happy my champion had returned. He had taken on the role of my protector. He always made sure we were having a good time and that we had everything we needed. It was interesting to observe my growing feelings for Anchovy. They reminded me of the way I used to feel about playmates when I was a child. I felt very affectionate toward him. I wanted to put my arms around him and hug him and be close to him, but there was no sexual attraction, no desire. He was a true brother, and I know he felt the same way. He always wanted to do fun things with us, like take us to the waterfall, or to the beach. Yet, there was always respect, an almost formal distance. We'd set natural boundaries without even talking about it.

Going deeper with Anchovy was more difficult. He had a slippery way of evading personal questions. Whenever I tried to tell him about Taz, or my longing for love, or how I missed my son, he'd laugh and tickle me, teasing me back into the present. He loved to say, "It's all happening now, baby." That seemed to be his version of Never Come Down.

Every day I walked around the farm, holding my ripening abdomen, feeling a kinship with the abundant nature around me, aware of the power of my fertility. My favorite sanctuary was the pungent shade of the somber, stately eucalyptus grove at the base of the pyramid hill. I'd hang out there for hours, walking with Love, napping, staring at the sky, inhaling the purifying aroma, and collecting eucalyptus seeds and pods.

Sometimes I'd look up and see Totido watching me, peeking out like a shadowed gnome from behind a tree. I knew I existed like a phantom in his psychedelic projections, so I played the part. Sending him beams of love, I did all I could to make his trip a good one.

Acutely aware of the primeval, purifying power of the eucalyptus, I collected the seeds and pods and soaked them until they were soft enough to make into beads. During the evenings, or on rainy days, I strung them into necklaces and sewed them around the collar of my brown and white striped robe, sometimes adding seashells I'd collected on the beach into the designs.

I loved the stormy days, when clouds swept in, dropping rain in great bursts and cooling the air. It thundered on the tin roof and pattered on the banana leaves, the two rhythms blending in harmony. When the elemental forces forced us to stay inside, we played music, sang, and worked on creative projects. Love toddled from person to person, receiving loving attention from everyone.

Totido remained silent, distant, and separate, immersed in his own world, hidden from the rest of us by his ever-present rose-colored glasses. One day, Love scrambled into his lap, and sat there looking up at him. For a moment he acted as if she wasn't there, but slowly a smile twitched his beard, like he was barely controlling mad laughter. When she reached out her arms, asking to be lifted up, he rose in a graceful motion and swung her around, his great, wonderful laugh mingling with her happy shrieks. When Love ran off to some other game, he faded back inside himself, turning into a passive observer again.

I wanted to ask Totido what it was like to take that much acid. One day, after he had been playing with Love, I decided that if Love could propel him into action, maybe I could give it a go.

"Hey, Totido, I took a few acid trips, but I can't imagine wanting to trip all the time. How do you do it?" I asked, trying my best to sound casual.

The room turned silent. Everyone got very busy with what they were doing. Ono and Honu left the room. Warrior made a face at me, like, Sister, you blew it, but I just waited, looking at Totido, wanting to know what made him tick.

It took a long time for him to lift his head up and turn in my direction, and even longer for him to open his mouth. I'd never heard him talk before.

"I don't do it. It does me," he said in a thick New York accent translated into an acid drawl.

His words made me think about the bad trip in the dunes and how I'd held on instead of letting go, and I figured what he'd just said must have had something to do with letting yourself go into that fluid love energy that feels like all-powerful God.

"I was afraid to let it do me. I held on," I said.

I could feel my words float across to him. Like a contact high, talking to him was taking on another dimension, as if we were both in slow molecular motion. As he received my words, I felt them swirl around inside him, and his reply come rolling out like waves on the Oceano seashore.

"It's both holding on and letting go," he stated simply, and then he stood up and turned toward the door.

"But why do you want to stay there? It's so unreal. Don't you want to know who you are and what life is beyond an acid trip?" I called after him.

He didn't answer that question. He walked out of the door and into the rain. He stood in the deluge for a moment, clearly digging the rain plastering his hair and wetting his clothes. Then, I watched him lope down the path, open the gate, and head off down the road toward the eucalyptus grove.

"Sister," Wave said, "that's more words than any of us have ever heard from him. That's our agreement. He contributes to the food and the car expenses. He's loaded, but he doesn't want to be out there in the world of wealth and pleasure. He had a real rough time when he was a kid. He never saw his parents. They're big-time shark-city socialites from New York, always dressing up and running around the world like life is a continual party. He has his own world and he doesn't want to come out of it. We give him space to trip and make sure he eats real good food because he doesn't think about things like that. He loves to walk in the hills and swim in the ocean, but he doesn't want to talk anymore. If he has to communicate anything, he writes a note. He says he's gone beyond words."

"Wow, you should have told me. I hope he's okay," I said, feeling like I'd blown it.

"Yeah, he's okay. He likes to walk in the rain," Warrior reassured me.

That night when I turned in, I thought about what Totido had said. I remembered the acid trip space, but I never had any desire to stay in that place. Each trip made me want to find the real truth even more strongly. Maybe he had found the place beyond words but it was dependent on a little white pill. What would happen to him if there were no more acid tabs? One way or another, sooner or later, I felt sure the universe would find a way to release him from his addiction and return him to raw reality. In my experience, everyday reality was a hungry place that forced me to search for something that was true and good and lasting.

There was only one explanation for the longing that filled me and made me want something I couldn't get on a drug high. Something or someone had to be pulling me. Was it faith that made me feel that somewhere, somehow, sometime, I'd get where I wanted to go? Even though I didn't know what it was that was pulling me, I believed I'd recognize it when I got there.

My motto was definitely not, Never Come Down. The words I'd raved on that bad acid trip summed it up for me, "I'm going to get there if it's the last thing I ever do." Where that place was, however, still remained a mystery.

As the weeks went by, I remained passive, like a leaf blowing along with whatever was happening. My friends were my magic and I was theirs. Together, we formed a naturally harmonious community built on unspoken boundaries. We each enjoyed our private world within the group. The guys worked in the garden, picked fruit, harvested vegetables, repaired the old house, and kept the car running. Ono was the gracious Hawaiian princess who danced as she gardened and cooked, her soft aloha spirit warming our hearts and opening us to the beauty around us. I played out the role of the mother, taking care of Love, preparing food, creating flower arrangements, and decorating our supper table. We all took turns cleaning the house and washing the dishes, including the guys. I played out my fantasy and my sister and brothers played out theirs, and we looked out for each other along the way.

House of the Sun

"Anchovy, I want to go to the House of the Sun," I stated passionately as I stared out the window at the distant volcano. Captivated by its immense, magnetic energy, I could feel it pulling me.

"You haven't been up Haleakala yet?" he asked, surprised.

"No. I want to walk up the mountain like a true pilgrim," I continued, feeling deeply connected to primal myth. "I want to spend the night waiting for the sun."

"Cool. We'll gather a group to go with you," Anchovy offered, digging my intensity, "and I'll look after Love so you can trip on your own," he added.

The magic of the Haleakala pilgrimage captured everyone's imagination at the Zendo. Bro, Honu, Wave, and his friend Jeremy from Lahaina wanted to come. Impatient for the ascent, the guys examined the sky and listened to the weather reports on the radio while I completed the eucalyptus-pod and shell decoration around the neck of my pilgrimage robe.

Finally, the perfect day arrived. Before dawn, under a clear, star-filled sky, Anchovy chauffeured four far-out pilgrims in the pink Cadillac to the entrance of Haleakala National Park. As sunrise revealed the brooding cone of the volcano, Jeremy pulled up in his truck. After a quick discussion, we decided Anchovy would drop us off further up the mountain. We'd hitchhike back down to Jeremy's truck in the morning, and he could take us to Lahaina. The Zendo kids would catch a ride back to the farm with Warrior at the end of the day.

As Anchovy drove us further up the massive volcano, I checked out Jeremy, admiring his long, chestnut-brown hair tied in a ti-leaf braid, and the sunrise shell necklace that revealed his ultimate, local cool. Older and island-seasoned, he seemed peacefully together, not like the soul-searching seekers of my generation. He'd found his place under the sun, or rather, under the House of the Sun. Appreciating his quiet presence in our light-hearted group, I was glad he was coming along.

Curving up the mountain, we passed magnificent eucalyptus groves standing in luxuriant grasses, violet morning glories twining at their feet. Slowly, the climate changed, and when we reached the edge of a pine forest, Anchovy dropped us off. Leaving the lush meadows and eucalyptus groves behind, we hiked through the pines into aeolean, windblown shrublands. Determined to get to the top by dark, we hiked vigorously all morning. True pilgrims honoring our sacred quest, we wore magic clothes for our magic journey. Occasional cars whizzed by as we walked upward at a steady pace, the drivers and passengers turning to stare at us.

The vegetation changed gradually with the rise in elevation, altered by the varying elemental influences of moisture, soil, sun, and wind. Ready for a rest by noon, we basked in the sun as we ate our lunch and took in the splendid view. The island spread out before us, a verdant emerald tapestry ringed by white waves dancing around its shores. At our feet, tiny blue lobelia flowers and yellow evening primroses grew profusely, mingling with dark-leafed bushes that were richly studded with red berries. Bronzed ferns carpeted the earth on both sides of the road.

By late afternoon, we were surrounded by a barren moonscape. Only dry, grassy tufts, low bushes, and tiny ferns grew close to the ground at this altitude. Occasionally, a noble silversword rosette opened, silver-green and luminously otherworldly, out of the coarse red-black lava. Even more rarely, I glimpsed the mystical silhouette of a lone silversword projecting its tall flower stalk into the sky.

Weary, tensing against the increasing cold, legs shaking from many hours of walking, I resolutely followed my brothers upward. As a glorious magenta-and-gold sunset gentled into an indigo, star-bright night, we trudged toward the summit.

"We're pilgrims to the House of the Sun, the House of the Sun, the House of the Sun. Haleakala. Haleakala," we chanted as we hiked the last mile.

Finally, our tired, cold cluster of pilgrims stood under a canopy of diamond stars at the Puu Ula Ula summit. The observation shelter offered protection from the wind, but the cold was even more intense inside the concrete building. As we emptied our packs, put on all our clothes, and wrapped blankets around our shoulders, our breath misted white in the freezing air. We stomped, danced, and rubbed each other's backs and arms during the long night, but we couldn't get warm. Exhausted and shivering, our spirits lagged in the ice-cold hours before dawn.

The moon was absent. Only brilliant, icy star patterns illuminated the infinity of darkness. Passive and weak, we huddled together, waiting to be delivered, everything gone from our minds except the desire for the sun's warmth.

"Let me tell you a story," Jeremy whispered.

We turned to him, surprised. He'd been silent most of the day.

"Let me tell you about the legend of Haleakala, the House of the Sun. Long ago, Hina, mother of the demigod Maui, complained that the day was too short for her to dry her bark cloth. So, good son that he was, Maui went to the great mountain volcano, and when the sun's spidery rays crept over the edge of the crater's rim, Maui lassoed the rays and secured them, one by one, to a williwilli tree.

"The sun pleaded, 'Give me my life,' but Maui held the rays fast, and bargained, 'I will give you your life if you promise to go more slowly across the sky.'

"The sun agreed, and that is how the volcano was named Haleakala, the House of the Sun."

"What a wonderful son," Bro said. "He made his mother happy."

Warrior chuckled, "Maui was a good negotiator. The sun didn't have a choice."

"Can you tell us anything about Pele?" I asked.

Jeremy smiled at me, and said, "Pele is the primeval goddess of volcanic fire that erupts and creates new land, the feminine heat of creation. Her molten white, gold, and red lava-veins flow down the volcano into the sea. After her burning blood cools into a crust, the raw lava breaks open, then chips and flakes into new land that receives the bountiful greening power of nature. Some say that her body is the Hawaiian Islands stretching over the ocean."

Jeremy's tale was interrupted as Bro leapt up wildly, shouting, "And then there was light."

Sunrise had arrived. Jumping up and down, celebrating every increase of light, we waited for the rays to touch us with their blessed warmth. Like the myth, the sun's rays peeked brightly on the horizon, then spread over the edge of the volcano. Our vigil was accomplished. The frigid air retreated as we triumphantly danced our joyful gratitude. Each of us worshipped the sun in our own way.

Bro stood tall, his arms wide in reverence.

Honu jumped up and down like a madman.

Wave knelt, bowed to the earth, and raised his head to the sun.

Jeremy spun a laughing, whirling-dervish salutation.

Stretching my arms toward the sun, I danced a sacred blessing.

"Haleakala," Jeremy cried, spinning.

"Ha-le-a-ka-la!" I answered.

Seeking more of the sun's warmth, I walked out of the concrete shelter. A trail wound between the red-and-black streaked cinder cones down into the crater. I knew I couldn't take that steep path. As I turned away from the sun, I found myself staring into a full moon. Surprised by its unexpected presence, I stood transfixed between the sun and the moon, the universe swirling around me like the wind and water currents around Maui. Profoundly aware of my presence at the top of Haleakala, in the middle of the Pacific Ocean, I felt as though I was connected to an immense, mystical ceremony occurring in cosmic space.

A silversword rosette beckoned at my feet, and I knelt in homage to its beauty. Peering into its silver-green iridescence, I admired the minute hairs glowing with captured radiance as it opened to and received the energy of the sun. Storing light within itself, it gathered strength for years until its time came to thrust its tall, golden-flowered spike toward the sun. Rising out of the jagged, crumbled lava, the silversword was like the sun and moon, both male and female. Even though it received the sun, it still searched for union. It longed to become one with the sun.

Purposefully, I walked up the small hill opposite the observation house. Feeling fatigued when I reached the top, I lay down on tumbled lava rocks that looked as though they had once formed an ancient shelter, the sun on my right and the moon on my left. Experiencing a mysterious equilibrium, I awakened to the powerful energy of the celestial bodies in the sky above me. My spirit soared in humble gratitude as my body absorbed the warmth of the sun. I closed my eyes to light-filled visions as smiling ancient Hawaiians chanted me into their spirit world. Wearing flower and fern leis and brilliant red-and-yellow feather capes, they swayed before me, gesturing elegant aloha welcomes. Then, like a bird, I flew over stone temples and thatch huts, glimpsing fishermen in their canoes, and women weaving, cooking and pounding poi. Hawaiians of all ages and rank streamed over paths to and from the mountains, villages, fields, and the sea.

The sun and the moon fused into one brilliant, blinding brightness within me as my mind expanded in a harmony of song. No longer aware of my body on the stones, I rose into a free, timeless light.

Some time later, I heard steps on the crumbling lava path and familiar voices.

"There you are," Bro called out with relief.

I opened my eyes. The sun was high and the moon had disappeared.

Wave smiled at me, "Come on, sister. We have a ride."

Lost for a time to my company of pilgrims, yet found within myself, I followed my brothers to the parking lot. I barely saw the driver who took us down the mountain, and hardly knew when we transferred to Jeremy's truck. My interior world was so full that I did not want to open my eyes. I felt Jeremy's strong presence next to me as I leaned on the leather seat. I was tuned to him and felt him tuned to me. Bro, Honu and Wave stretched out in the back of the truck among our packs and Jeremy's surfboards. No one talked. We had all traveled beyond words.

Lahaina was bustling. I didn't want to go to the restaurant with the guys, so I asked Jeremy to let me out at the banyan tree. I needed to be alone for a while. After resting for a while under the tree's vast, cool, leafy shelter, I strolled down Front Street, past the Pioneer Inn. Casually picking up a few of the waxy, pinkish-white plumeria flowers scattered on the grass, I walked onto the green by the harbor sea wall and took in the view of the island of Lanai across the channel. Waves rolled in. Yachts bobbed at their moorings. Picture-perfect, puffy white clouds drifted across the sky.

Sitting under a palm tree, I closed my eyes to savor the memory of the mystery and beauty of Haleakala, still seeing the sun and the moon within me. Awakened to an interior universe, I had become the house of the sun and the moon. Delighted with the magical, mysticism unfolding in my life, I played with the plumeria flowers, inhaling their exquisite fragrance, placing two of them behind my ears and scattering the rest around me.

For some time, I drowsily watched a small sailboat tacking toward the harbor. When it pulled up at the pier, two scrawny barefoot sun-bronzed and bearded guys dressed in ragged shorts jumped off the boat. Howling wildly, they ran over to me and threw themselves down on the ground and rolled around on the grass.

"We made it! Hawaii!" they raved like madmen.

"We bring you homage, dear Queen," the blonde one chanted and bowed as he picked up some of the flowers and showered them over me.

"Aloha," I spoke from my heart, bowing as I tilted my head regally and placed fragrant blossoms behind their ears.

"We've sailed many moons to come to your beauteous land!" the other shouted, flashing his sea green eyes and tearing at his curly black hair.

They lay on the grass, joyful madness in their eyes.

"You're the first person and the first land we've seen for weeks," the first sailor cried as he brushed away the windswept sun-bleached hair that hung around his thin cheekbones and nearly covered his brown eyes.

Howling with happiness, his friend yelled, "Sunburn, seasickness, storms – all over at last. Wowie!"

That inspired the other sailor to scream, "We saw nothing but sun, seaweed, and surf all the way from San Fran."

Their playful madness inspired me to join in their fun, so I stood up tall and opened my arms to the sky.

"This is a time of heavy magic. I was sent here to welcome you. Let me tell you about Haleakala, The House of the Sun," I chanted.

They rolled around, waving their legs in the air, laughing until hiccups took over and they gasped for breath. I joined in their laughter and forgot about telling them the story.

Just then my Haleakala brothers arrived and surveyed the scene with amazement.

"They've just landed after weeks at sea," I giggled.

"The Queen of Hawaii," the sailors shouted, throwing themselves around on the thick, tropical grass.

Jeremy held out both his hands in welcome and said, "Aloha. This is where the royal house used to be, where King Kamehameha's favorite wife, Queen Kaahumanu, welcomed guests to the island."

Shivers ran up and down my spine. Goose bumps rose on my arms and legs. For an instant, past and present realities merged into a glowing, liquid that seemed to be flowing all around us. Suddenly fatigued, having had enough of mystical realities, I lay on the grass and listened to the adventurers talk about their journey at sea. Their mad joy was the perfect completion to our Haleakala pilgrimage.

Warrior arrived to take us back to the farm. We said our farewells to the sailors and surrounded Jeremy with a group hug. Weary from the hike up the volcano and our sleepless night, Bro, Wave, Honu, and I leaned against each other and slept all the way back to Holokai Road. When we arrived, Warrior had to shake us awake.

Even though I was sleepy and tired, I was glad to cross the threshold of the Zendo gate, walk along the garden path, up the worn wooden steps past the good luck spider, through the screened porch, and over the tatami mats to the cool, shaded interior of the house. When I opened the door and entered the quiet, restful beauty of my room, Anchovy was reading to Love. When he looked up and saw Haleakala happiness shining out of my face, he reflected it with his own great smile.

Love ran into my arms, laughing and pointing her little finger at me and then at Anchovy, telling her story as we told ours.

The day after the Haleakala pilgrimage, Anchovy left for the mainland. I was sad to see him go. He'd been a true friend. I would miss him dearly.

Quiet days followed Anchovy's departure. The volcanic pilgrimage had changed my inner landscape. Now, whenever I closed my eyes, the darkness was gone. I had not only captured the sun like the demigod, Maui, but also the moon. They were both within me now.

Kwan Yin for a Day

few days later, Honu knocked on my door.

"Flower Child, someone's here to see you."

My heart leapt. For one wild moment, I thought it might be Bodhi, but when I opened the door and saw Wheat, I wasn't disappointed. He was the one who had glowed golden bright when I returned from the Buddha peyote trip at Magda's house.

"I'm so glad to see you!" I said after throwing myself into his arms. "How did you find me?"

"I went into the Conspiracy a few days ago and Taz told me you were at the Holokai Zendo," he said, clearly pleased he'd found me.

I gestured for him to sit down, and he knelt on the tatami mat.

"How's Bodhi and everyone?" I asked nervously, my voice shaky as the memories of my departure from the Soul Clan surfaced. Wheat wasn't there when I left, but if he had been, I knew he would have been kind.

"He's well. He sends his love," Wheat said.

"And the Soul Clan?"

"Everyone's fine. You know, the usual playful scene, except for Deva and Tree. They got pulled over and some dumb cop didn't buy their love trip. Bastard searched their van and found their stash. The judge sent them up for five years," he said bitterly. "We're gathering funds for lawyers. We're going to do everything we can to get them out. God, they even cut Deva's hair," Wheat moaned. "What's prison going to do to the Never Come Down love angels?"

Stunned, feeling my heart explode with pain as I imagined Tree and Deva in prison, I could only murmur, "No, oh no."

Wheat took my hand in his. Slowly my shock turned to tears, and I wept in his arms. Why was their ecstatic dance of life ending in a prison cell? What lesson was God giving them? How would Deva Never Come Down in prison? Where was the love in that?

When I was still sniffing in his arms, Wheat whispered tenderly in my ear, "When I went back to Magda's, you were gone. No one was willing to talk about anything real. So, what happened?"

Before I had time to answer, Wheat spoke again, "Bodhi and Magda are together now."

The news hit me like cold water, washed over me, and left me clean. More quickly than I could have imagined, I shook off the ghosts from the past.

"That makes sense. They were so close. It's cool," I said, wondering why I didn't feel angry or jealous. "And Pedro? How's he taking it?"

"They worked it out. Pedro's been with Magda for ten years, and I guess they decided it was Bodhi's turn. Pedro's still going to live with them and, I guess they're going to try to be one big happy drug dealing family."

When he saw the look on my face, he added, "You never knew about that, did you? You came in like an angel, like one of Christ's true disciples, believing the mirage. You never had a chance, but let me tell you, they're acid and peyote pushers and dope dealers. Sure they're fun, but you need to know what's really happening in Magda's home."

"Do I?" I said. "I believed my own reality. I was so in love. I thought Bodhi was a god. I thought they were together because they loved each other, but there were so many undercurrents, so much going on that I never knew about. I thought they wanted me to be with Bodhi, but after the first few high weeks that kept them grooving in their drug fantasy, they were just waiting to get me out of the way so they could get back to normal. They were bugged I stayed so long. They got tired of hiding what they were doing. I don't know why they didn't tell me. I probably could have accepted it, but on second thought, I think I would have been too afraid to stay."

"I'm not like Tree and Deva, I continued. "They acted like they were invincible. They believed that love would open all the doors, and look what happened to them. I could never take a chance that I'd be separated from my children. Nothing would be worth that," I said.

I took a breath and kept talking. "When we were in San Francisco for the Fillmore Concert, Lola let me know that she had prior claims on Bodhi. She turned from a twin sister into competition. She told me that they were all his old girlfriends. Seems like he had a regular influx of enchanted ladies, so he could keep himself up. Never Come Down had more meaning than I had imagined in my blissed-out state."

"And you're probably wondering why I hang out with them, knowing how they pull people in and take them on their trip," he said defensively. "The truth is, I bring them high acid and the best peyote going. I work with their heads and occasionally rescue some innocent from their clutches. You were too far gone to take off with me, though," he joked.

"Yeah, I was, wasn't I?" I laughed, wondering how it was that I could have been so blind. Considering the depth of my infatuation with Bodhi, it seemed incredible to be talking about him this way.

More relaxed now that Wheat knew I'd cut loose from the Bodhi fantasy, he chatted about what was happening in the Summer of Love on the mainland. Suddenly he stopped talking and his eyes opened wide with surprise. He'd just noticed my swelling abdomen.

"Yes, I'm pregnant with my ex's child. That's why Bodhi and I split up, or at least that was his excuse," I explained.

"How could he drop you like that? I wouldn't have," he said fiercely. "Having kids with you would be totally cool."

Heat flamed on my cheeks. I turned away from the intensity of his gaze.

"How long will you stay on Maui?" I asked, changing the subject.

"A few days. I brought some high medicine for the island people from the Laguna Brotherhood of Eternal Love. It's the best, the highest sacrament. I'll pass it around, then head back to Laguna," he said, watching Love play happily with her shells and stones. "It looks as if Hawaii agrees with you."

"We're happy here. My brothers and sister are loving and kind, and they're real. I can talk to them, and they tell me who they are. As far as I know, there are no secrets here. Seems like the Zendo attracts a different kind of traveler."

Wheat switched to a more intense energy as he leaned forward and looked deeply in my eyes before saying, "I dug what happened to you on your peyote trip, so I brought some orange sunshine acid for you. Let's trip tomorrow."

"Wow," I said, taking a minute to get used to the idea. Orange sunshine was the best acid going. I wanted to trip with Wheat and see how high I could go, so I said, "Yes, let's go for it."

"How early can you be ready?" Wheat asked.

"Let's go at dawn. It's so beautiful then. Ono can take care of Love. There's a glorious place on the Hana Highway that's perfect for a high trip."

Early next morning, as nature's dawn symphony wove its magic around us, we walked down Holokai Road. Soft, warm breezes tossed the grasses, leaves, and blossoms in a whispering, fragrant dance. Birds trilled their morning songs above us, and dogs barked their territorial warnings from the farmhouses as we passed by. Turning right at the highway, we hiked toward Hana for a short distance, then hopped over a fence into a pasture.

Wheat touched my arm and said solemnly, "Let's take the sacrament now."

With slow, gentle respect, he unfolded the white paper, promising, "It's going to be a beautiful trip."

With a graceful gesture he put the acid tab on my tongue.

"Here's to a beautiful trip!" I said, raising my arms to the sky and circling in a joyous dance.

A few minutes later, saliva surged in my mouth. Undulating, cellular sensations pulsed through my mind and body as we walked through an ancient kukui grove onto a cliff-top meadow. Rings of foaming white waves broke on the shore below, releasing swirling sea mist into the air. Enchanted by the view, I let my feet sink comfortably into the warm moist earth. As the magic of the place wove its spell around me, I instinctively reached outward with my right hand to touch the transparent breezes. A moment later, I cupped my left hand at waist height as if to receive them. As my body formed this divine *mudra* hand position, an incredible thrill shivered through me. There was no reason to move from this exquisite state of balance. Giving and receiving had become equal. This was perfection.

Listening, feeling, seeing, I absorbed the living energies with all of my being. Each buffeting gust bore visionary messages. Nature played through me as though I were an instrument. Each fresh cloud formation offered delightful variations of graceful ecstasy. With imperceptible slowness, my sunflower face followed the sun's passage across the sky. As my interior stillness opened into receptivity, the universe melted on my shore. The eternal present expanded into infinity.

As the sun lowered in the west, I became aware of the rough, red earth and the coarse grasses holding my feet in their moist grasp. Like the silversword, I had become both heaven and earth. Wheat whistled from the branch of a kukui tree. As I slowly turned toward him, our eyes flew into each other with total knowing. Ecstasy lingered as chords of loss played through my heart. As my hands fell from the *mudra* position, I took my first reluctant steps. As one foot slipped out of the earth's grasp, and then the other, I remembered words.

"Let's go to the waterfall on the way home," I called to Wheat, as he jumped down from the tree and strode toward me.

Attuned, vibrating with each other and everything around us, we walked through waist-high grass until we stood on a ledge of mossy rocks that overlooked a waterfall grotto. Unable to resist the water's invitation, I dove into the cool depths, remaining immersed for a moment in its liquid embrace before surfacing. Then, suspended like a bubble between the elements of air and water, I swam through floating guavas and damp blossoms. Wheat jumped in with a great splash. Soon we were throwing guavas at each other. Some of them squished in our hands or burst on the rocks, freeing the ripe scent into the air.

Finally, breathless and weary, I pulled myself out of the water and lay down on the sun-warmed stones around the pool. Seeking rest, I adjusted my body to the shape of the stones, gasping as the captured heat radiated through my bones. As my body absorbed the heat, I moved onto fresh hot stones, luxuriating in the burst of fire on my flesh and the deep inner baking. Wheat sunned naked, silent and still, draped on a large, round boulder, facing the sky as it moved toward sunset glory.

Resisting drowsiness, aware of the oncoming dusk, we climbed out of the waterfall grotto and walked along the luxuriant grassy path beside the stream.

Back on the road, rusty trucks and flashy tourist convertibles painted in bright colors floated by like foreign, dead-metal spaceships. Neighbors picked us up and dropped us at the farm. When Love came running toward me, her face as bright as the sun, I lifted her into my arms and swung her around. Her squeals of delight and the sweetness of her chubby perfection felt like honey. I couldn't get enough of her.

The cane spider's cobweb glistened an intricate, indecipherable calligraphy over the entrance. When I stepped inside the old wooden house, it seemed dim, worn, and shabby. Every flaw, odor and rusty nail intruded on my heightened sensitivity, so I returned to the garden with Khalil Gibran's book, *The Prophet*.

The goddess of the day still resonating within me, I turned the pages with elegant gestures. As I read aloud, my voice rippled divinity into the cosmos. Wheat and my Zendo brothers and sisters gathered around in a tableau of sacred devotion, and even after I ceased to read, we lingered silently in the scented darkness, absorbing the patterns of the constellations and the radiations of the planets and stars.

"Wheat, the house is so worn, so dead. I don't want to go inside," I whispered. Then I opened my arms to the bountiful, ever-replenishing, nurturing nature around us. "I want to stay outside, where nature is clean and pure and filled with life."

"We'll create our own energy in the room. You'll see," Wheat said.

He took my hand and led me to my room. "You'll be okay."

When I passed the mirror in the hall, I caught a glimpse of my sunburned face, burning eyes, and wild wind-tangled hair. I couldn't bear the sight of myself.

Wheat laughed at my shocked expression and said, "Let's put some aloe on that burn." And then he teased me, chanting, "Bliss into blisters," as we laughed together.

After tending to my sun burned face, we sat opposite each other on the futons while Love played between us with her shells and stones. Gradually, the candles, flowers, and fabrics comforted me and I closed my eyes. Instantly, my attention gathered in my forehead. I shifted into the full-lotus yoga position and my internal world opened into a clear vision.

Repeating the experience of the Buddha journey I'd had with the Soul Clan in Magda's home, I tumbled from one life into another, only this time I knew where I was going. The spiraling went faster, as though surprise had been a weight that had slowed me down during the first journey. I was also less interested in the various personalities of male and female and their cultural expressions that had so captured me last time. There was no resistance. I opened more fully into the experience and when I reached the Buddha peace, the contentment was so deep, weighted, and complete, that I never wanted to move again. As when I had been in the *mudra* position in the meadow earlier in the day, I did not want to relinquish the truthful beauty of the perfect form in which I was resting. The form itself seemed to create a container for something much bigger than myself.

Resting in the center of the peace, past and future mirrored each other in the infinity of the present. I was awake, but my body had dissolved into a transparent envelope that opened inwardly and outwardly to many different dimensions. My consciousness grew from a tiny point deep within my forehead into the wholeness of my being, into the moment, into my body, and into my soul. From the Buddha perspective, everything was perfect, yet I also felt my human imperfections. I was seeing from two viewpoints simultaneously.

Just as I wondered if I was going to stay there forever, a pain pierced my left arm. I resisted for as long as I could, but the pain became unbearable. I slowly turned my head and saw a mosquito sucking my blood. As I shook my arm I descended from the Buddha place. I watched the mosquito fly away, sadly accepting that it was the messenger sent to bring me back into my so-called normal self. This time, my return was natural and easy; I did not suffer the grief, loss, and strangeness that I had the last time.

When I looked around my room, I saw that it was beautiful. Candles glowed, radiating golden circles of light throughout, softening what had seemed worn and shabby before. Fresh flowers brightened the altar at the foot of the window, where paisley silk curtains fluttered in the breeze. Love was curled up on her futon, fast asleep in sweet, innocent bliss, her dimpled, plump arms and legs softly open in relaxed comfort and total trust.

Wheat waited, respectfully tuned to my process, until I turned to him. Still radiant from our internal journey, we smiled our soul connection, waves of understanding and appreciation flowing between us.

Suddenly aware of deep fatigue, I said, "I must sleep, Wheat. You're welcome to stay on the other bed."

I lay down next to Love and closed my eyes. Imprisoned again within my body, I felt the aches and fatigue from my long day in the meadow. But then my inner eye opened to vibrating, exquisitely colored, luminous mandala patterns that seemed to be floating through the entire universe, connecting everything and everyone.

"Sweet dreams," Wheat said, as if he was blessing me.

I pulled Love close to my ripening belly, sheltering my unborn infant between us. I felt the presence of my new daughter and communicated heart-spirit welcomings to her infant soul. Snuggled with Love and Light, I dreamed the night away. Together their names shaped the dream of my soul.

Things happened too fast the next morning. Wheat switched into his "I have to get going" mode and split for Lahaina, calling over his shoulder, "Here's my number. Come. Call me. Got people to see. Got things to do."

I didn't want him to leave. When I threw my arms around him and hugged him, I felt myself holding on to him. He was all I had left of the Soul Clan.

"I'll never forget our trip. It was so mystical," I whispered, unable to describe my vast continent of visionary feelings.

He held my face in his hands and said, "You were the goddess Kwan Yin."

Surprised, I remembered my mother's statue of Kwan Yin. Even though I had looked at it every day during the years I was growing up, I hadn't been aware that I had embodied her spirit. Yes, I had stood like my mother's statue for one full day, my long, draped dress caressing me, my right hand opened to give and my left hand to receive. I had been Kwan Yin for a day. She had filled me with her grace and her peace. She would be a part of me forever.

Resting in bliss-filled dreams all day, absorbing the beauty of the trip, I savored each twinkle that my cells released, in awe at the mystery of it all.

Wheat's Fields

The next day, I caught a ride to Lahaina with Warrior. Wheat would only be on Maui for another day, and I wanted to see him again. When Warrior dropped me off, Wheat was sitting on the porch of his friend's house, ripe and ready to share another magic day.

"Right on. Let's go," Wheat said, opening his rental car door and settling Love and I on the front seat.

Wheat pulled out of the driveway and headed up the Kaanapali coast as he sang, "Are we ready? Yeah! We are ready, ready, ready, to have a cool, groovy, high day. Ladies, we are on our way."

I'd never been past Lahaina before so I grooved on the scenery for a while before turning my attention back to Wheat.

"Do you have a place of your own anywhere?" I asked, curious to learn more about him.

"Nope. Don't need one. I'm a connection man."

"You travel light," I said. All he ever carried was an old duffel bag that he slung over his shoulder, a small leather toiletries bag, and a Mexican blanket that he threw over himself when he slept. I'd only seen him wear a pair of tropical print shorts that doubled as a bathing suit or a pair of faded denim jeans with the same two rainbow-colored psychedelic T-shirts. Once or twice, he'd put on a worn blue wool sweater that was the same color as his eyes. It was the same story with his feet. He wore either a pair of hand-made leather sandals or some funky old sneakers. He seemed as comfortable on the floor as he was on a sofa or a bed, and never made any demands.

"Yeah. Keep life simple and focus on the important things. That's my scene," he explained.

"Why do you turn people on? Surely that's risky?" I asked, concerned for him now that Deva and Tree had been busted.

"There's always a risk when you try to make the world a better place," he explained. "The Brotherhood of Eternal Love offers high trips for high people," he said with conviction.

"Why is the government turning the acid scene into a bad trip, when it's clear that with the right setting and the right guide, acid can help us?" I wondered out loud.

"That, my dear, is the question. The CIA's been in on it from the beginning, hoping to use acid to get information out of people. They even take it themselves, but their paranoia seems to be that people might actually get happy and not want to work or pay taxes or commit crimes or go to war, and then what would they do? They'd be out of a job," Wheat said with a laugh, before he sang a line of the Graham Nash favorite.

"...change the world, rearrange the world..."

"My trip was amazing. Thank you," I said, beaming affectionately at him.

"It's all love. I enjoyed watching you go so high," he said warmly.

"I reached the same beautiful Buddha place that I did at Magda's house, but I still couldn't stay there," I shared sadly. "Would you believe a mosquito bite brought me back? What would I have to do to stay there?"

"Catch the glimpse, then use it to change your life. Seek and ye shall find. You're on your way, sister, but there are dead people out there who haven't even started on their path. We've got to wake them up, get them to 'turn on, tune in, drop out' and change the world," he said passionately.

I heard the words of Leary's acid mantra, and something happened to them in my head.

"It makes more sense to me if it's 'turn off, tune out, and drop in'," I said, giggling at the thought.

Wheat gasped, "What?" and pulled the car off the road. Turning off the ignition, he looked at me. "What did you say?"

Hoping I could remember, I pronounced it slowly, "Turn off, tune out, and drop in."

"And what does that mean?" he exclaimed.

Amused at his reaction, I described my truth. "First, I'd rather turn off from this world and the senses and desires that bind me to it than turn on to it, and that's not what happens with acid. The world becomes more beautiful and captivating when you're high. Then, I'd love to tune out of my mind instead of travelling into it with acid or peyote. Best of all, I want to drop into myself, my true self, my highest self, my God Self."

"Well, who would have thought that little Flower Child could outdo mega-thousand-trips Leary! Far out!" and then he burst into outrageous laughter. "Wait till the Brotherhood hears this one."

A short time later, Wheat stopped on a blustery, gusty bluff, and we got out of the car. Standing high above the surf, we watched the wild waves pounding the cliffs below, and spraying the boiling white froth into the air.

While Wheat set Love on his shoulders and walked along the bluff, I stepped inside the branches of an airy ironwood tree that seemed to be inviting me to enjoy its auric embrace. Enclosed within its long-needled, wind-dancing shelter, I wrapped my arms around its trunk. Appreciating its patient strength, I wondered if it felt the perfection of each moment like Kwan Yin, and if it connected with other trees where their roots mingled in the earth.

For a moment, I imagined the tree's existence. I sent my mind down into its anchoring roots, and felt them absorbing the minerals from earth that had been enlivened by billions of insects and bacteria so that the yearning sprout could thrust itself above the imprisoning earth toward light and warmth. I felt the roots soaking up the water and lifting it back up through its trunk and out to every tiny branch so that the leaves could breathe. I understood for the first time how the elements give to each other so that the miracle of nature could take place. I visualized how the earth-bound roots mirrored the unfolding branches, leaves, and flowers in the realms of sun and air. In that instant, a vision of the elemental womb of nature filled my mind, and I understood with an instinctual body-centered feeling, how our bodies are born of and nourished by nature's elements and returned to her at death. But where does the spirit come from that enlivens the elements and enables them to become form, and where does it go after the body is gone? That's what I wanted to know.

"Hey, wake up," Wheat called. "You asleep on a tree?"

He peered into my ironwood hideaway.

Startled, I released my arms.

"You moving in there?" he asked, laughing at my confusion.

Love peeked inside the tree, discovering me as she touched the prickly-needled ironwood branches with careful curiosity.

"Mama," she called sweetly.

I pulled my darling daughter within the tree's embrace and held her in my arms. She gazed in wonder at the magic of the tree, while I told Wheat about my elemental nature vision.

"Yes! You're seeing and feeling the energy behind

the surface of life. This is great," he said, excited by what I had said.

"There's so much more happening than we can imagine. We only see as much as we are willing to open ourselves up to," he explained as we continued up Kaanapali to Fleming Beach.

After Wheat parked the car, we walked on the black sand beach, catching glimpses of surfers rising and falling on the white-capped waves beyond the breakers. Small specks on an undulating horizon, they waited for their perfect ride, just as I waited for the right person, urge, dream, idea or invitation to take me on to my next change.

The strange, wild beauty of the beach awakened another profound communion. As bubbling foam melted into the black sand, smooth stones clicked in sighing, wave-dissolving rhythms. As I walked along the beach, I could see the elemental energies dancing and exchanging energies with each other, earth-lava, water-waves, fire-sun and wind-air. And, beyond the dance of the elements, I sensed an even more primordial nature pulsing an infinitely varied, yet harmonious chord of sound and light throughout all creation.

I realized I usually tuned all of this out by being up in my head and out of my body. For a moment, I wondered why I indulged in worries and illusory dreams when I could be present with natural divinity. Then I surrendered to the moment. On that sacred Hawaiian beach, I was the dance of nature yearning to share love, a flowering soul awakening to the love behind the apparently cruel cycles of birth and death.

"It's all love," I said. "Nature speaks with her whole being."

Wheat smiled, his silence the perfect answer.

Back in Lahaina, at his friend's house, I walked into the bedroom to comb my hair. There I saw a Japanese scroll ensconced in an elaborately carved lacquered altar. Enchanted, I knelt on the cushion and admired the beautiful arrangement of bells, candles, fruit, and evergreen offerings on the table. Then I picked up a little book and tried to recite some of the Sanskrit words.

Wheat looked in the door. "Do you know anything about these people who chant that Sanskrit mantra, *Nam Myoho Renge Kyo*?" he asked.

"One of my friends, a Los Angeles fashion designer, is into it in a big way. She claims she gets everything she chants for. I think it's crazy to chant for material things. I'd chant for enlightenment."

"Enlightenment, huh? Come on, lighten up, let's eat," he laughed, pulling me to my feet.

Wheat had set lunch out on the lanai. We dove hungrily into salad, brown rice, and veggies, chewing up a storm.

"I have to go to Honolulu tomorrow. Want to come?" he asked quickly, casually.

"No, thanks," I said, surprised by his invitation. "I don't want to go to Honolulu."

He paused, put down his fork and looked right at me.

"What I really mean is, come with me to Honolulu for a couple of days, and then let's hit it back to Laguna and the Brotherhood of Eternal Love. You'd dig the cool people there. You'll have everything you want. I'll take good care of you and your daughter."

I looked into his open loving face and felt his kindness, but I didn't want to tag along in his restless, acid-dropping life. I'd finally found a scene I loved and didn't want to leave. Besides, I was too afraid of getting busted.

"I can't go on the road. I need to be settled," I said, making excuses.

He sighed, "I'm a Brotherhood connection man. Have to keep moving."

"I'd go with you if things were different. I want you to know that."

We walked back along the sea wall, through the town, to the shade of the giant banyan tree. It was nearly time to catch my ride back to the Zendo with Warrior.

I hugged Wheat, feeling sad that he had to go.

"I'll try to get back to Maui before I hit it for the mainland. Love, Sister."

"Love, Brother."

Local Offerings

October came in with heavy rains and changes. Wave moved to Lahaina to work with Jeremy. Ono returned to her hula teaching on the Big Island. Honu went back to college in Honolulu. Bro got a job in Kahului and was gone all day, Monday through Friday. Warrior and Totido still hung out at the Zendo most of the time, but I felt lonely. My family was breaking up, and the changing vibes of the Haiku farm made me uneasy. I was six months pregnant. Feeling alone and vulnerable again, I called out in my heart to the universe. I knew I needed something, but I didn't know what.

Soon after, Warrior and I returned from shopping in Paia one day and found a box of pineapples sitting on the steps. We looked at each other in wonderment. Where had it come from? Who would give us such a gift? We baked the pineapples with sweet potatoes seasoned with lime and ginger, and served them with saffron rice. It was a special dinner made even more delicious by its mystery.

A couple of days later, we got home from the waterfall and found a box of vegetables by the kitchen door: carrots, pumpkins, zucchini, and lettuce. The generous offering was a week's supply for the Zendo family. The produce offerings continued, but we never saw who brought them.

Some time later, early one Sunday morning, a truck pulled up in front of the Zendo gate. Five young Hawaiian guys got out, and after messing around in the back of the truck for a while, they walked down the path carrying something heavy that was wrapped in sacks.

Warrior greeted them in the local slang.

"Aloha, Bras."

"Aloha, we bring a wild pig for a luau," one of the brothers said proudly.

The young men put down their load and showed off their prize.

"It's fresh from the hunt, for the woman with the child."

We hung out on the grass and talked story. After describing and acting out the hunt in great detail, they gave instructions for cooking the pig in a fire pit. We'd never had a visit from the locals before. It was a milestone in community relations, and we made the most of it. When the young men got up to leave, they bowed formally. Five handsome young men were making sure I had enough to eat. They were watching over me and it touched my heart. They didn't know I was vegetarian and I wasn't going to tell them.

A few days later they returned. Carrying flowers, sporting brightly-patterned aloha shirts, and looking bashful, they shuffled up the steps into the Zendo. Mystified, the Zendo family sat in a circle on the tatami mats with our visitors and made small talk until the young men finally pushed one of their own to his feet.

He cleared his throat a few times, bowed, and then spoke formally. "We want to marry this lady here who's waiting for her child."

He coughed, looked around at his friends, wiped his brow and started again. "Not all of us, I mean; only Kimo here. He's been watching over her since she's been on the island. He wants to marry. He'd like to take care of her and her children and give them a home."

Relieved his task was over, he shuffled back and sat down again.

Surprised and touched, I looked shyly at the young man. He seemed a fine, handsome Hawaiian man, but I couldn't marry someone I didn't know.

Bro looked at me, eyebrows raised in a silent question.

I whispered in his ear, "I can't say yes, Bro. I don't know him. Help."

Bro acted the older brother.

"We thank you for the gifts and this offer of marriage. As you fine young men know, this lady already has a child. She also has a husband. He's not with her and he's not taking care of her either, which is most unfortunate. She really appreciates your offer, but she isn't free to marry. We hope you understand."

They nodded, looked at each other and then looked away. A moment later, they all started talking at once, commenting about the weather and asked about our luau.

I glanced shyly into Kimo's deep dark eyes as the others talked, regret washing over me. I wished Bro hadn't closed the door so firmly, but Bro didn't know I was divorced.

The young men shuffled and teased and backslapped their way down the path and into their truck. I shared one more glance with the man who wanted to marry me, and then they drove away.

Later that night, quiet and alone in my silken bed, I thought about Kimo's proposal. Hawaii had sent me a husband. I couldn't help wondering what might have happened if I'd said yes. We could have invited him to come and visit. We could have gotten to know each other. Maybe the formality was only a sign of respectful courtship, of serious intent. I wondered where he lived and what his family was like. His eyes were so clear and warm. Perhaps he was a kind man. I was free. I could marry. Perhaps I should tell him I was free, but the moment I thought of trusting my life to another man, sheer terror coursed through me. The memories of my years with Taz and my recent experience with Bodhi held me in bonds of fear.

I saw Kimo the next time I went to Baldwin Beach in Paia. I felt his eyes on me and turned to meet his gaze and smiled at him. I wished he'd come closer, but I never thought to beckon him. His eyes burned into mine, but he didn't return my smile. I was afraid to go to him and he didn't come to me.

Paradise wasn't perfect. Even though I lived in a happy hippie commune, I was still chained to fearful reactions that shaped my destiny. How could I break free? I longed to understand life, but veils of ignorance kept me in submission to unconscious patterns.

Introspection, fueled by imaginative inward searching, helped me approach truth. I loved the beautiful garden around me and wanted to create the same harmony within myself. I imagined God as the sun and myself as a flower, blooming in response to divine, nurturing power. Wondering what my blossom might look like, I figured it must be either a rose that grows out of a ladder of thorns, or a lotus that cannot hide its humble beginnings. But flowering was not enough. I must complete the cycle of life and offer seeds to the garden. What could I do that would enable me to leave something of value? I consoled myself by thinking that if it was my nature to bloom, then it must also be my nature to offer seeds.

Hawaii provided the opportunity to look within myself. My friends thought I was resting when I lay around with my eyes closed. Shut off from the outer world, I was awake within. Searching for understanding, following powerful, inarticulate surges of yearning, my heart and soul sought love. I couldn't rest until I achieved a vision or a gift of grace. My inner longing created an insatiable restlessness. This mystic hunger would have to lead me to the light – it was all I had.

Local Offerings

I hadn't been born into a culture, community, or family that provided a spiritual example. When I was a child in Sunday School, I longed to be a disciple, sitting adoringly at the feet of the Son of God and worshipping with the devotion depicted in the Christian paintings. When my Sunday School teachers said I couldn't be with Christ because he was dead, I never returned to church. Instead, I began my search for a living Son of God.

All my questions led to one question. How could I turn darkness into light?

Morning Glory
Makena High

I'd heard the locals say that morning glory seeds were a subtle high that lifted you into the spirit of a place, and I was curious to give them a try. The next time Jeremy came by the Zendo, I asked him to take me to Makena Beach. Pleased that I had asked him to show me around, he stayed overnight at the farm so we could get an early start. We set off the next morning in his off-road vintage Jeep, the engine roaring so loud we could barely hear the radio, let alone talk. Holding Love in my lap as we breezed along, I took in the beauty of the day, admiring the glistening, tossing sugarcane fields and the marshmallow clouds scudding across the sky. When we turned left along the gently lapping leeward beaches, Molokini reef curved like a crescent moon offshore.

Surprised at myself for taking the initiative, I dared a few admiring glances at Jeremy, taking in the red and brown seed lei around his neck and the braid tied with fresh ti leaves taming his long sun-bleached ponytail. Nearly forty, fifteen years older than I, he grooved to the slow, island rhythm. Attuned to nature, he sensed subtle changes, paying attention to everything around him and responding intuitively and respectfully.

As we neared Makena, desert lands opened before us – hot, dry, and dusty. Giant cacti dominated the scrub where we turned down a dirt road toward Makena Beach, a smooth round hill, like a pregnant belly, on our right. Driving under a kiave tree tunnel, we stopped at a ramshackle old plantation house. Jeremy's friends weren't home, but an immense cane spider greeted us from its glistening web on the porch. When I'd first moved to the farm, I had feared the Zendo spider, but as time passed, I learned to understand its weaving wisdom. Respecting the spider's place in the web of life helped me accept the power of nature or *mana* of Hawaii instead of fearing it.

Scattered seedpods patterned the sandy trail that wound its way through the lichen-softened tangle of broken twigs and fallen trees. Red-feathered birds flitted and chirped their joyful pathways through the overhead branches and trembling pale-green leaves.

Love pointed her little finger at the bright red birds and cried, "Aah, aah."

After a few minutes, we broke through the alternating light and shadow of the kiave grove into scrub bushes and the brightness of the sun-drenched beach. Breakers crashed against a steep wall of sand. To the right, black lava cliffs jutted into the ocean, and to the left, a curve of low bushes and rocks completed the half-moon bay.

Just past the scrub, a profusion of morning glories twined over the sand. Pale, white-rose petals unfolded their violet fragile trumpets to greet the morning sun. While we knelt on the sand, gathering tiny seedpods from the sturdy, leafing vines, Jeremy told me that he'd lived near Lahaina for nearly twenty years, enjoying a slow-paced life that gave him plenty of time for sailing, surfing, and deep-sea diving. A carpenter by trade, he spoke with quiet satisfaction about how he'd built his own house. A gentle, kind man, he emanated a peaceful power. Comfortable with silence, easy to be with, he had never married. I found that hard to believe. There must be something the matter with this perfect guy, but what?

The heat burned more intensely as morning drifted into afternoon. Strong, hot winds blew sand against our skin, and giant rollers pounded the shore.

Once we had collected a few of the tiny morning glory seeds, we sat down and started chewing. Wondering if the morning glory legend was hype, I lay back on the sand, closed my eyes, and tuned into the sounds of the waves. In a rush, my spirit soared into spiraling colors. I was on. When I opened my eyes, everything around me seemed pure, radiant, infused with light.

I turned to Jeremy. "Will you watch Love for a little while?"

He nodded, his twinkling eyes telling me he was on too.

Love looked up, her tiny fingers holding seashells. "Shell," she said with quiet satisfaction. She was exploring the universe, and like me, she was trying to figure things out.

I kissed her and said, "I'm going for a walk, cherub."

She smiled and returned to her intense examination of the high-tide line.

I was magnetically drawn toward the rough black lava cliffs on my right. They seemed charged with energy. As I approached, a precipitous path revealed itself, and I pulled myself up the wall. The gritty raw lava pumiced the soles of my bare feet and my hands as I climbed. When I stood on top, surf surged on three sides of the promontory, two sandy bays gleaming like twin scimitars on either side. Jeremy and Love seemed small and vulnerable next to the pounding breakers.

Walking toward the rocky point of the promontory, I entered a perfect circle of trees where the enclosed earth descended into a smooth, grassy cone. There, within the grove, all was peace and balance, a sanctuary. Awed by the sacred, natural temple, I fell to my knees on nature's altar. Dizzy, I lay down and looked into the blue sky beyond the leafy canopy and felt my spirit soar into its infinity.

Transported, I reached a sacred place within myself where the elements of life revealed their mystery. Feeling myself breaking free of the gravity of earth, my consciousness opened in pulsating waves. Leaping free of boundaries, my spirit flamed into heart-beating light. Vibrations hummed inside my throat and ears, harmonizing all the sounds of the universe into one. A beam of light pierced the darkness inside my forehead, which opened like a flower to receive the cool, sweet blessing of divine grace. Rejoicing, my awareness awakened into knowing, dancing wisdom.

Some time later, I opened my eyes and stepped out of the circle of trees. The sun was lower in the west. The cliff cast a long black shadow on the sand. Then I saw my daughter walking on the beach. Each crashing wave seemed hungry, immense, as if it wanted to devour her. Fear coursed through me, constricting my heart. Screaming her name, I scrambled down the cliff. The booming breakers powered my panic as I ran down the beach. Catching her in my arms, lifting her high, I carried her away from the waves. Then I noticed Jeremy lying on the sand.

"You look like you just saw a ghost," he said, surprised.

Embarrassed at my panic, I tried to explain.

"From up there it looked like the waves were going to swallow her."

The contrast between the expansion of my spiritual high and the contraction of this fear caused a great grief to swell in my heart. Uncomfortable with being lifted up to heaven in one moment and dropped into the hell of fear in the next, I wondered how I could find my way beyond these highs and lows.

"I was watching her. She was okay," he reassured me with a slow smile.

I sat down beside him, clinging to Love as my breath calmed down and the panic dissipated.

"Still on?" he asked as he lay back on the sand with ease.

"Yeah, full on. You?"

"Yeah. It's a smooth high. It makes what's already high even better."

"I don't want to get high any more," I announced. "This is my last trip."

"Why so?" He said as he turned to look at me fully.

"I have these great experiences and then I'm right back again, feeling fear or grief or anger. I don't want to get hooked on highs or have to keep trying to escape lows. I want to find a way to get truly high and be able to stay there."

"I know what you mean. I just dig making life easy and good. That's high enough for me," he sighed laconically.

"You're lucky. My life has never been easy or good. It's always been something I wanted to escape from. It's like there's something within that's calling me, and yet no matter how high I go, I still come back to my fears and my problems. I want to find a way to go beyond them."

Saying those words out loud made me feel their reality at a deep level, and I sat stunned as if in a trance. Jeremy looked at me curiously, but he didn't say anything.

Silently sitting together, we watched the great foamy waves curling upon the shore. Slowly, a sensation came over me, an experience of fullness, as if I was a ripe fruit falling from a harvest bough. My body sank into the sand. My attention dissolved into my heartbeat and I welcomed the pulsing waves onto my inner shore.

"Ready to go?" Jeremy's voice whispered softly.

Slowly returning, I opened my eyes.

Jeremy leaned over me. "Let's go to Lahaina. Let's go to my house."

Turning from the force of the wind and sea, we made our way through the morning glory ramblings and the crouched, windswept bushes into the shadowed shelter of the tangled kiave grove. The good-luck spider welcomed our return to the old wooden house, but Jeremy's friends were still not there. Ravenously hungry and thirsty, we peeled hot red mangos and devoured their sweet flesh. Sticky juice dripped over our faces and hands. Laughing, we sprayed water from the garden hose to cool and cleanse ourselves.

Leaving the cactus lands, we drove toward Lahaina. Jeremy's all-seeing eyes noticed something on one of the gentle, lapping beaches. He stopped the Jeep, picked up a branch of black coral, and offered it to me. For the rest of the drive, I held the coral treasure like a scepter. We were the Love Generation, living the dream of the Summer of Love, taking care of each other, sharing whatever we had, getting high, and helping each other along the way.

A few miles beyond Lahaina, Jeremy turned down a dirt road toward the sea. After passing through a grove of banana and papaya trees, we parked in front of his plantation house.

A spacious lava rock waterfall entry offered a generous welcome. I entered shyly into Jeremy's handcrafted home, sensitive to the understated elegance and refined comfort. Hand carved wooden pillars reached toward the vaulted ceiling. Warm breezes played gently through the louvered windows. Indonesian rattan sofas and chairs blended with wood floors, raw-silk pillows, and Oriental carpets. The living room window offered a spectacular view of a grassy bluff, where a scattering of red-black lava rocks defined a path to the beach. Jeremy opened the sliding doors in the kitchen and we stepped onto the lanai, the lovely Hawaiian name for a veranda. Plumeria, spider lily, and ginger flowers blossomed fragrantly around the outdoor dining deck. Beyond the abundant herb and vegetable garden, lemon, avocado and noni trees danced in the wind.

Then he opened another door with respectful grace.

"This room is for you," he said.

A simple wooden bed, covered with a quilt stitched in a pineapple design, faced a picture window that opened to the sea. Brass lamps and white wicker tables stood on both sides of the bed, a carved teak chest at its foot. A bamboo floor gleamed around the edges of a hand-woven oval carpet.

Jeremy opened the louvers to freshen the room.

"Would you like a shower?" he asked.

Awed by the beauty of his home, I smiled and took the bath towels he offered into my arms.

Jeremy picked up Love and I followed him to the outdoor shower. Sheltered within a circle of breadfruit, papaya, and banana trees, we rinsed off the sea, sand, and lava, and washed our morning glory high down the drain.

After a simple supper of avocado sandwiches and ginger tea, I tucked Love into bed and curled up beside her while Jeremy strummed his guitar to the sunset sea. As I listened to his gentle music, my mind went back to the circular grove at Makena. I wished I could have stayed in the beautiful heaven that opened within me, but I had to care for my children. I had to live the mystery of my life.

After Love fell asleep, I joined Jeremy in the living room. My shy reserve melted into the music and I closed my eyes, feeling deep peace.

When the music stopped, I opened my eyes into his.

"What do you want?" he asked with sudden strength, his words hitting me like a north-shore wave.

Confusion foamed on my shore. Color bloomed on my cheeks.

"I don't know," I mumbled as I turned away, afraid, ashamed, and too shy to speak my deepest longing and my truth.

"I can't figure you out. What are you waiting for? What do you want?" he persisted, his eyes focusing intensely on me.

I wanted to escape. Restless, uncomfortable, I got up and paced the room. What do I want? What am I waiting for? His questions contracted my amorphous longing into harsh reality, but I was afraid to say what I wanted.

"I'm waiting for my baby to be born," I said, side-stepping his question with something he already knew.

"But what will you do? You need someone to take care of you," he insisted, his strong gaze fixed on me.

I longed to shout, "I want a true husband! I want a beautiful home like this. I want a father to love and protect my children. I want them to grow up in a family of love," but I could not, would not, say those words.

In answer to my inarticulate secret, he gave voice to my dream.

"Come and live with me," he said intensely, his eyes burning into mine as he sat forward in his chair. "I'll take care of you and give you and your children a home."

"Me, here with you?" I asked.

I looked at the sunset and the glorious sea, anywhere but at his eyes that had uncovered my truth.

"I'd like you to be my woman. You're a fine lady. I've always wanted children. I'd love to take care of you."

"You want me even when I'm pregnant?" I asked, surprised, remembering Taz and Bodhi.

I thought I'd tripped on Makena Beach, but this was something else. The memory of Bodhi's rejection still fresh in my heart, I found it hard to trust. Jeremy might mean what he was saying at this moment, but what if I gave him my heart and then he changed his mind? I didn't want to go through that again.

Jeremy must have felt my fear because he backed off.

"Don't rush. Think about it. I look at you and your daughter and I think that you're the most beautiful girls I've ever seen. I see your love for your daughter, the farm, and the Zendo Family, and I want you in my life. I don't think you realize how you affect people. You must have had a hell of an old man not to appreciate who you are. I'm on my own because I've never met a gal that could settle into my quiet life. You're different. I can see you living here with me."

Fear surged in me. I resisted what I'd always longed for. "I need time to get to know you. I need time to think about it," I said, making excuses.

"Take all the time you need. I'm not going anywhere," he said softly. He picked up his guitar and strummed his gentle tunes, then he sang softly and sweetly,

"I've been waiting so long, to be where I belong,
in the sunshine of your love."

Sitting silently in the darkening room, aware of the change between us, I imagined what it would be like to live with him in his beautiful house.

"I'm with you my love,
the light's shining through on you…"

Tears welling in my eyes, but too shy to cry in front of him, I got up to go to bed. He put down the guitar, walked quickly over, and took me in his arms, pressing his cheek softly against mine. Then he led me to my bed and tucked me in. Holding my hand, he stayed with me until I fell asleep.

I awoke in a state of wonderment, gazing at the tossing grasses, the billowing, cloud-dancing sky, and the lapping waves tenderized by the reef. I longed to stay in Jeremy's house, to never go back to the farm, to never think of Taz and pain and hurt again. I longed to melt into Jeremy's strength and become one with all that was there. I never knew why I didn't. Perhaps I didn't believe he would really love me and take care of me. Perhaps it was my fear. Perhaps it was his friends who came over in the morning and filled the house with surf talk. If only he'd invited me to stay, instead of giving me space, I would never have left. Instead, when my friends came to pick me up, I said goodbye and returned to the farm.

"I'll come over to the farm on the weekend. We'll spend some time together," he promised.

I nodded shyly, but I didn't know that change was coming and that I would never see him again.

Gold Smuggler

When I got back to the Zendo, a yellow convertible was parked outside the gate. Instantly excited and curious to discover who was visiting, I ran down the path, greeted the good-luck spider, opened the screen door, and found myself looking at the most elegant and attractive man I had ever seen in my life.

"How do you do," he greeted me with a formal bow.

Trying hard to stay cool behind my smile, I replied just as formally, "Very well, thank you," as my eyes took in his impeccable white linen shirt and trousers, fine leather sandals, and gold watch.

He lifted my hand to his lips for a lingering kiss.

"Leander," he said, introducing himself with a refined British accent, humor curling his mouth into a flirtatious smile, "but everyone calls me Leo."

Captured by the warmth of his amber eyes, I left my hand in his. I couldn't resist asking, "Where did you come from?"

He laughed and said playfully, "Honolulu now; Japan last week; England originally. And where do you come from, lovely lady? You look like the Hawaiian dream."

I kept the fun going. "From Sunset Strip in Los Angeles; from Vancouver, Canada originally; and the other side of the island right now."

He laughed a rich, resonant laugh that vibrated through me and started to pull me toward him as if he were going to kiss me. My heart beat wildly with a mixture of fascination and fear and I pulled my hand free and ran into the kitchen. He followed me, asking questions about our life on the farm as I made the salad. Then he helped me gather leaves, fruit, and flowers to decorate the dining room. His presence made me want to give my best, so when everything was ready, I ran into my room to change and freshen up before I beat the dinner gong.

After the Zendo family gathered around, Leo took command of our gathering with abundant leonine ease. Like the sun, he emanated power, warmth, and confidence, the luster of his charm falling equally on everyone.

"I'm a gold smuggler," he announced with outrageous pride as soon as we had finished saying grace.

Silent, breathless, we waited for him to continue.

"I deliver gold, jewels, coins; all things rare, wonderful, and expensive. I make a fortune, and in between jobs I travel, look around, have adventures, and play," he said with the charisma of an ancient storyteller.

Sure of his power over us, he told us of his noble birth, the ruin of his family through indulgence and bad investments, his expensive tastes, and the smuggling career that rescued him from boredom and genteel poverty.

"I won't go on like this forever. I save. I invest. In a few years, I'll retire and live off the interest. Meanwhile I am, as you say, having a ball."

"But why are you here, in this old farm house, with us?" I asked.

"I want to experience the real Hawaii. When I travel, I'm as likely to take a camel caravan into the Sahara as I am to stay in a luxury hotel. Both are utterly entertaining and necessary for me."

He took my hand and pressed it to his lips.

"Come with me tomorrow. I want to swim in a waterfall with you."

The invitation thrilled through me.

"I'd love to."

"Good, we'll start early. Where shall we go?"

Without hesitating I said, "The Seven Sacred Pools near Hana. I've wanted to go there ever since I arrived on Maui."

"Sounds bloody marvelous," he said as if he were the king of the world.

After dinner, the Zendo family shared what we knew about the island, its myths and legends, and its sacred places. When I told him about the morning glory Makena high, Leo's laughter exploded through our Zendo. His spontaneous joy transformed the energy at the farm to a high tide, and I was flowing with it.

Restless, unable to sleep that night, I thought of Jeremy, his beautiful home, and all that he offered. I remembered the wonderful feeling of safety in his house. Then the thought of Leo sent shivers through me. Caught in a spell of enchantment, I put on one of my Conspiracy creations and danced around the room, delighting in the layers of transparent pink and orange chiffon that fluttered delicate color variations over a lime silk shift. When I put on my biblical angel sandals, I would be dressed for a day with a prince.

I took off the dress, wrapped myself in a towel, and slipped quietly out of the house. If I couldn't sleep, I might as well have a starlight plumeria flower bath. After soaking for a long while, I washed my hair. After toweling dry, I oiled my body, pumiced my feet and filed my nails. I crept back into my room and put on the chiffon dress. I was dressed for my day with a prince, but day had not yet come so I returned to the garden. Trying to calm the excitement that was charging through me, I sat in the garden chair and let myself become part of the velvet breathing darkness. Impatient for the night to end, I watched the moon's too timid journey across the sky. Hurry, please hurry, I whispered to the moon. I can't wait to discover the mystery of today.

At last the glowing dawn relieved my waiting. Dressed in flowing layers of chiffon, feeling like a softly opening flower in a garden of light, I was ready to receive the sun. As light streamed into the garden, tiny water prisms on the leaves and flower petals created miniature rainbows all around me. Glistening dewdrops glowed like magic necklaces on thousands of fine spider webs spun throughout the garden. Birds trilled their rapturous response to the morning's birth. I felt acutely alive, as though this was the first morning of creation and I was the only woman.

At that moment, Leo walked onto the porch. When he opened his arms, I ran into his embrace as if I were going home.

Leo took my hand and swung me around.

"Absolutely bloody marvelous. You could be at a London ball," he complimented graciously.

Admiring his East Indian silk kurta, linen trousers, and Moroccan sandals, I complimented him in return.

"And you could be at a Ravi Shankar concert."

Laughing as easily as old friends, we went inside the house and gathered our things. Following Leo down the path, I carried Love, pressing my face against her curls, adoring her angelic face, flushed and drowsy from sleep, and feeling her tender skin warm against my arms, as though she had melted into me.

Leo lowered the convertible top and we took off, flying down Holokai Road and along the road to Hana, the landscape rushing by in a blur.

"Leo, if you want to see Hawaii, you'd better slow down," I warned nervously.

Immediately, he switched to a slower pace, guiding the rental car like a chariot, allowing us to catch breathtaking views of hills, bays, waterfalls, and horses leaping through long grasses. Love, her cherubic face alight with joy, stood on the seat between us, clapping and reaching her chubby hands toward the profusion of flowers and draping vines.

"What a beautiful child," he said as he looked at Love's happy delight.

Instantly, memories of the lack of love and support during my pregnancies and births wafted through the perfect moment. No matter what I was going through, I always knew my children would be perfect. If I'd known how to create perfection with a husband, I might have had the family I longed for. With a toss of my head, I let the painful memories fly into the wind.

As we came around a curve in the road, an exquisite waterfall came into view. In a heartbeat, Leo parked the car, leapt out, stripped off his clothes, and dove into the pool. After hitching up my dress, I led Love slowly over round, smooth pebbles into the cool water.

"I didn't know proper Englishmen played like this," I teased.

"Why do you think we colonized half the world? So we could play in places like this," he shouted as he jumped off a rock into the pool.

Leo pulled Love through the water until she shrieked with joy. Then he shook the branches of a tree until the pool overflowed with golden-yellow blossoms. He streaked to the car, rummaged in the trunk, pulled out a camera, and took pictures of us covered with flowers, lying on the rocks, and under the waterfall.

"Enough! Enough!" I cried, the morning already halfway to noon.

Fresh-water cooled, hair drying in the sun, we continued our journey. An hour later, we pulled into Waianapanapa Park. Awed by the raw beauty, we stood on the ledge, admiring the black-sand beaches and the rugged lava formations that anchored the pure white clouds spiraling across a clear cerulean sky. Attuned to each other and this sacred place, our senses absorbed the profound primordial energy.

Exploring further, we followed an eerie, root-stepped hau-root tunnel down an incline. Love clung to me, eyes wide, as she experienced the strangeness of the tangled passage. The tunnel opened into a clearing that enclosed a picturesque pool and the dripping entrance to a cave. Entering the rock cave, earthy dampness sheltered us from the heat and the sea winds. Safe inside the cave, lulled by gently lapping water and the rhythmic dripping from the moisture-laden ceiling, we leaned against the cool stone walls and stared into the shallow, sandy pool.

Leo pulled a small tourist guidebook out of his pocket and read aloud, "A legend says that a beautiful Hawaiian princess came here to escape her cruel husband. She was hiding on this ledge when he saw her reflection in the water and murdered her. Once a year, the water turns red in her memory."

The thought of the murder made me uneasy. I didn't want to stay there anymore, so I ran out of the cave and back up the hau-root tunnel. Leo followed more leisurely, carrying Love on his shoulder.

Back on the green, free of the brooding presence of the cave, we picked ferns and wove a head-lei to crown Love's golden curls. After decorating each other in ferns and flowers, Leo and I spread our picnic under a mango tree.

"Where do you travel?" I asked.

"Anywhere, everywhere. North Africa is a favorite. I love the desert."

"Me too. I love deserts as much as tropical paradises."

Laughing, we turned on our sides to face each other.

Usually, when I was attracted to someone, I was afraid or shy, but I felt completely comfortable with Leo.

"What brought you to Hawaii?" he asked more seriously.

I looked into his amber eyes for a moment, hesitating, feeling the fear, then plunged ahead with my story. "I had a terrible marriage. I tried to free myself for years. Then dreams of Hawaii captured my heart, and I flew over in early September. The islands are healing me. I'm beginning to find out who I am."

"You lived his life, didn't you?" he said compassionately, stroking my arm, sending shivers through me.

"Yes, but I'm learning to live my own life now," I said proudly.

Just then, Love clambered over Leo, and he sat up and pulled her into his lap.

"What was he like?" he asked in a casual manner that combined a perfect mixture of curiosity with an "I don't want to intrude" respect.

As I watched Leo with Love, strong chords of pleasure mixed with pain as my dream for a good husband and father awakened in my heart.

"Taz is handsome, talented, a charismatic and wildly creative artist, but he is completely awful to live with. Women love him, even though he is – how do you say? – a rotter?"

"How do you say? – a bad trip?" Leo joked in return, understanding flowing easily between us.

Ukulele chords startled us out of our absorption with each other. We looked up and saw a Hawaiian family tumbling out of an old pickup truck onto the park green. Dressed in a traditional white muumuu and wearing a plumeria flower head-lei on her silvering hair, the abundantly plump mother radiated wisdom and cheerful good humor as she directed her husband and children to set up their picnic.

Leo watched them, openly fascinated by their family harmonics. He held out his hand and pulled me up as he said, "I want to meet them. Come with me."

Leo greeted them with respectful grace, and asked if we could join them. When the mother gestured for us to sit down, her husband and children gathered around her like a court.

She patted Love's golden curls and smiled at me as she said, "Your daughter is very beautiful. You make good children."

A strong feeling burst from deep within me as I looked into her eyes. She reminded me of Clara, even though they looked very different. The laughter sparkling in her eyes, her happy face, and above all her warm, motherly wisdom touched my heart. I wanted to put my head in her lap and become her child.

"So do you," I replied, admiring her beautiful children as tears welled up in my eyes.

"I wish I was one of your children," I said, surprising myself for expressing my longing for a mother like her. "I wish I could stay here forever."

"Not for you. You go soon," she said softly, as though she understood all the unspoken inner words and feelings coursing through me.

"But Hana isn't so far from Haiku," I replied, not wanting to hear what she'd really said. "I'll come back again."

"No. You leave Hawaii. Not come back for very long time," she insisted, with gentle certainty.

Her words shocked me to the core.

Leo looked at me and raised his eyebrows.

She didn't explain.

I didn't ask.

Instead, I turned away and closed my eyes. Leaving Hawaii? What did that mean? Where would I go? Back to Los Angeles? When I thought about L.A., my whole being contracted. No, I would not go back there. Then I thought of Clara. I loved her as a mother, but somehow I always felt unworthy around her because she was so wealthy. This

Hawaiian woman was like a magnet. I could feel her power even though I had turned away from her. I wanted to throw myself into her arms, but I resisted. Feeling such strong fear and longing at the same time paralyzed me. I could hear Leo asking questions and talking casually to the family, giving me space to calm down.

Then he pulled me to my feet and gave me a big hug.

"It's time to go, dear one," Leo said gently.

I took a big breath, and when I turned around to say goodbye, she held out her arms to me. Without hesitation, I flew into a divine motherly hug that lasted a very long time. When she released me, she gave me a great kiss and then laughed. Her loving embrace had given me something far beyond words. I felt totally blessed.

They watched us drive away, smiling and waving at us as if we were best friends. Even though meeting this *kapuna*, this wise elder, gave me a glimpse of the motherly love I had been seeking all my life, my happiness was mingled with melancholy because I sensed the truth in her words. The tide was running out. Changes were coming. My time in Hawaii was coming to an end.

The Seven Sacred Pools

When we left the park, we turned toward Hana, driving by lush, waving grasses that receded into emerald-green, temple-shaped hills. As we drove through the small country town, we passed a few wooden cottages, a church, and a store, then returned to the rainforest. Curving around the winding roads, over narrow stone bridges, and by beautifully handcrafted lava walls, we caught glimpses of plantation bungalows, tropical gardens, waterfalls, and wave-washed coves. By mid-afternoon, we arrived at the Seven Sacred Pools.

The information posted on the bulletin board said that the pools and the surrounding area had once supported a large Hawaiian village. Their favorite trees – mango, golden papaya, medicinal noni and sacred kukui – still grew in profusion.

"Should we walk up or down?" I asked as we stood on the bridge, the midway point between the upper and lower pools.

"Let's start at the bottom and work our way up to the source," Leo said with confidence as he lifted Love on his shoulders and carefully headed down the path. I followed, stepping cautiously over muddy, slippery leaves.

A short time later, we reached the bottom pool, immersed ourselves in the flowing water, then lay on the hot rocks to rest and dry in the sun.

"My friends on the island like to believe that the seven pools represent the seven chakras, our spiritual centers," I said. "When I was a child I used to stare at the drawings of chakras in my mother's yoga books and try to figure out what they meant."

"I know what you mean. Books can only take you so far, but since I've talked with yogis in India, I have a better idea of what the books are talking about."

"You've been to India? Oh, how wonderful! I'd love to go there one day," I enthused. "When I was very young, my mother was always reading yoga and Buddhist and mystical books. I'd pick them up whenever I had a chance and look at the pictures, trying to understand what they were saying. She also took me along whenever she went to lectures and meetings. She made a point to meet every spiritual teacher who came to town. I guess it's in my blood."

Turned on, I let it all pour out.

"My husband separated me from all the things I loved by ridiculing them, and I let it happen. I loved him. I wanted to please him, so I let everything I loved pass out of my life."

I shook myself, splashed my face with water, and continued. "Thankfully, that's in the past. The amazing thing is that ever since I left him, and especially this summer in Los Angeles and on Maui, I've been experiencing blissful states of grace and mystical visions. Each experience was like a direct communion. Sometimes I get the feeling that God is all around me, teaching me, showing me, guiding me. Some of the experiences happened naturally in nature; others were on LSD or peyote, but drug highs are not my thing. I've always wanted to be a disciple of a living teacher, someone I can love with all my heart, someone who will guide me and teach me the mysteries of life. Someone who can show me how to live and how to die."

"You're looking for a teacher?" he asked intensely.

"Yes, and no. I don't know how or where to look, and I'm not free because of the children. They say that the teacher appears when you're ready, so I try to prepare, but I don't know what to do and my life is such a mess. Sometimes I doubt that a holy man would want to have someone like me for a disciple. Then again, I don't seem to have a choice. I have this longing that just won't go away."

Leo walked over to the edge of the pool and stood on a rock, looking down at the surging waves that met the water as it fell into the sea.

"Don't jump in," I warned. "Sharks feed where a stream enters the ocean."

"That's good to know, isn't it?" he said as he turned and smiled. "I was just thinking that if the Seven Sacred Pools represented the seven chakras, this pool would be the root chakra, the earth chakra, wouldn't it? The yogis say the earth chakra represents the safety and health of the physical body and all the things in the world that support health, good fortune and abundance, but more essentially, it comes down to our primary needs. What do you need to keep alive – water, air, food, shelter, clothing. Earth is about the basic necessities, the physical needs of life."

I pulled my hair away from my face and hunched down to escape the force of the wind sweeping up from the sea. "Most of the world never gets beyond the struggle for basic necessities," I mused.

"I saw that in India. Even though they have all that spiritual wisdom, you see people enduring the most appalling conditions. Then you see a sadhu, yogi, or saint living in enlightened poverty and you realize consciousness is everything."

As I listened and tried to connect my problematic, personal life to my soul life, I felt very small and very large at the same time. My limited human self was expanding to contain infinite truths and my soul self was emanating the longing to build a bridge between these vastly different points of view.

"I don't really understand what 'chakra' means," I said. "When I was growing up, I used to look through my mother's books and stare at the drawings of the flower-petal chakras along the spine of a yogi's body, and wonder what they felt like. The yogis write about them in such a detached, intellectual way that I could never understand what they were talking about."

"I know what you mean. You have to experience something to really understand it," Leo said as he leapt off his rock and came over and sat down beside me. After I met and talked with the yogis, I have a better idea what the authors of those books are trying to tell us."

"What would a chakra feel like? That's what I want to know," I mused.

Leo thought for a moment, then replied. "It helps me to get a sense of the living energy of the chakras if I relate them to the evolution of human life. Think about how people struggle for their basic necessities and how they fear not having enough. Ironically, even when they have enough, they fear losing it. We fear whatever threatens our existence, whether it's hunger, thirst, illness, old age, loss, or death. So it's obvious, isn't it? Fear is the emotion or passion of the earth chakra. And the earth chakra even has a color. It's red, not dirt-brown or grass-green but red, the color of blood. From there, the colors rise upward in rainbow order – red for earth, orange for water, yellow for fire, green for air, blue for ether, indigo for the third eye in the middle of the brow, and violet for the crown chakra on top of the head."

"A rainbow path. How beautiful! And how practical, too. What you said helps me to understand what the chakras mean in terms of daily life. I know I live on the edge of fear all the time," I admitted. "And not just when I'm threatened. So my earth element must be way out of balance."

"Most of us live on the edge of fear. That's the earth chakra, plain and simple. We try to make ourselves feel safe by surrounding ourselves with material things, but that kind of security only goes so far. True freedom from fear is a spiritual state."

Sitting on a rock, hugging my knees with nervous excitement, momentarily immune to the beauty around me, I remembered how fear had ruled my life.

"Not having fear must feel like a spiritual state," I said, trying to imagine what that would be like.

"It would be wonderful," Leo agreed. "We're so used to feeling fear, we can't even imagine life without it."

"I think we should learn from children. Look at Love. She is helpless, innocent, and totally trusting. Even though we pretend to be grownup, aren't we just as helpless? She's always so happy, so interested in exploring everything. She doesn't seem to know fear."

"Not yet, anyway." Leo looked at Love and said, "There are not many people who keep that child-like quality throughout their lives."

My thoughts kept running. Fear kept me silent when I should have spoken. It made me unable to give and receive love, to let go or to change. When I tried to imagine what it would be like to live without anxiety, an image of joy leapt in my mind like a dolphin.

"If I didn't have fear, I could be myself!" I shouted, wanting more than anything to be free of the fear that held me in bondage.

"That's it! It's either fear or creativity, and the greatest creativity is to be yourself," he agreed with a jump into the sky that landed him on the rough lava and nearly tipped him off the edge and into the water.

"Being your true self would be so cool," I commented, enjoying the flow of ideas. "You feel all kinds of wonderful things inside you, but you just don't know how to let them out. Didn't someone say that self realization leads to God realization?"

"Yes, I think we've got it," Leo sang like a *Pygmalion* actor as he set Love on his shoulders. "I think we've got it! Yes, we've got it!"

Looking down at me, Leo added, "The Hindus believe that each chakra has a positive state. For the earth chakra that happens to be good health, abundance, security and money, or we could say, just plain good luck. The Hindus wrapped up all that into an elephant deity called Ganesh. You see his picture and statues all over India."

"An elephant. Wow! That's earthy, all right. An elephant is huge and heavy. Gravity – that's earth for sure!" I said excitedly, amazed at the commonsense wisdom emerging from our playful, exploring conversation.

"Yes, earth is all things heavy, contracted, and structural," Leo agreed. "It's the energy that organizes everything."

"Like bones, teeth and hair, and nails," I said, and then we laughed as if a cosmic joke had birthed between us.

"Come on," he invited as he headed up the path. "Let's follow the orange ray of the rainbow to the water chakra pool and see where that leads us."

We ascended through the damp, thick vegetation and eased carefully over slippery rocks to the edge of the second pool that became the water chakra pool in our eyes.

"Let's play a game. I'm not going to say anything. Just close your eyes and feel and hear and think about water and see what you come up with," Leo suggested with a merry look.

He lifted Love off his shoulders and carried her into the middle of the pool. She shrieked with happiness as he dipped her toes in and out of the water, then pulled her back and forth while she kicked and splashed.

I lay carefully down on a rock near the edge of the pool and relaxed. When I closed my eyes I heard more clearly the bubbling, rippling, flowing stream sounds mingling with the more distant roar of the sea. I dangled my feet in the cool, rushing current and welcomed the waterfall spray misting my face. As I harmonized different experiences of water within myself, images of water took over my mind-stream – baths, ocean waves, boiling kettles, washing machines, hot springs, rain, clouds, frozen ponds, thinly iced puddles, frost patterns on winter windows, sea foam, glasses of water, snow, icicles, mud, tea, lakes, and tears.

Excited, I burst out, "Water is always changing, just like feelings. It has so many moods. It flows like this stream or rages during oceanic storms. It forms crystals like ice, snow, hail, or frost. It wears down rocks over centuries and carries sand and silt to the sea. Ocean waves crush shells and coral into sand. Ice even breaks boulders open."

Delighted with my discoveries, Leo joined in.

"Water is steam and mist. It rises into clouds, then rains down again. It follows gravity and sinks down into the earth. It's deep, silent, and dark on the bottom of the ocean, but it moves in powerful waves on the surface."

"Emotions are like that, aren't they, Leo? You can feel empty like a desert one day, then fall in love the next, and be lost in a jungle of feeling."

"That's it. When emotions depend on outer things they're changeable. But when you rise to the heart center in the air chakra, you live love, regardless of what's happening, because love becomes your state of being."

"I can imagine that, but I still can't imagine living from my brow or crown chakra. How can I get there if I don't have any sense of what they are?"

Leo smiled mysteriously. "Let's see if we can figure that out by the time we get to the highest pools."

Staring into the subtle patterns of the rushing water, soothed by the rhythmic sounds, I imagined love flowing like a fountain from the center of my being.

Leo rambled on, his voice merging with the sounds of the water. "If the earth is about survival of the physical body and its needs, then the water is about the exchange that happens between people through attraction, all the way from sex to birthing to family and friends. And everyone is born through the water element. Sexual fluids create life within the watery womb and after we're born, we suckle breast milk in our mother's arms."

As he spoke, I could feel the complex blend of watery desires, sexuality, and emotions, and how those energies drive us from desire and courtship into marriage, parenting, family, and community. What a dance!

Leo continued, "The yogis said that the prominent passion of the water element was lust, and that all desire was intertwined with attachment. I'm still trying to figure out what that means. I can understand it with my head, but I have no experience of what it would be like to live without desire or a sense of possessiveness for what you love."

"I know what you mean," I answered. "We're hopelessly, imperfectly human and the information is coming from saintly people who have transcended human weakness and desire. I just wish they could explain it better," I complained, frustrated at my inability to believe I could ever be like that.

"Explaining isn't necessarily the answer," Leo consoled me. "The yogis and saints have experienced these truths, and they try to inspire us to do the same. We'll find the real answers when we're ready to travel the path within ourselves, but we have to be interested enough to do it, and we have to be willing to leave all this behind," he said as he gestured at the beauty all around us.

"Why would we have to leave all this?" I asked, confused. "I've just found this Garden of Love. Why would I have to leave it?"

"The inner path takes time, energy, devotion, and sacrifice. If I were a yogi I wouldn't be here today," he explained, "And I wouldn't be smuggling."

"Why does truth have to be so black and white? Why can't we have both?" I wondered, "or at least have spirituality and a normal life?"

"That's what I'm trying to do," he sighed as he stared into the moving water, "but I'm not sure it's working. And," he grimaced, "To quickly change the subject, will you look at all this water hurrying downward into the ocean. We're made of mostly water, you know. Look at us, we look solid, we feel solid, but we're mostly water."

I laughed, "I've just learned to feel the earth and now you're telling me I'm all water?"

"I know, it's strange isn't it? Think of all the fluids in the body and how they affect our lives. Men and women come together through the most primal need for love, touch and companionship, but at the same time as they are home and baby making, most people are also dealing with the difficulties of human relationships."

"Most people? Don't you mean all people?" I teased. "Do you know anyone who isn't struggling with relationships? I know there are a lot of people out there who have more stable lives than I do and happier families, but they're not really happy and they're not free of suffering."

"We all have our share of suffering. We're trying to be comfortable in a world that was never meant to be comfortable. We're just passing through, pretending the door of death doesn't exist," Leo mused.

Captivated by the patterns of light and the musical pulse of the water's passage, feeling mesmerized, I tried to understand what he was saying and relate it to my own life experience.

"So you're saying the water chakra caused the problems in my marriage?"

"In part. Your husband's lust for free sex made him chase after many women, but fire-chakra power struggles had a lot to do with your marriage problems, too. He was selfish. He did what he wanted, regardless of the effect it had on you and the children, and worst of all, he tried to force his ideas on you."

"I couldn't create a life with Taz," I said, feeling the sadness well up inside me, "because he was always destroying everything."

"But you didn't give in to him. You had your own beliefs and you resisted the temptations he put in front of you. You were able to break away and live from your own truth."

Intensely aware of the earth energy of the rock I was sitting on and the water flowing by, I lifted my eyes to the sun and the sky. As Leo talked, I visualized how the chakras, the elements of life, and their corresponding emotions were dancing within me as well as outside in the world.

"I'm getting a sense of how my feelings change, but they're all mixed up. I never feel just one thing at a time," I said as I lounged on my rock, my hands playing in the powerful current.

Leo put his arms around me. "Yeah, we move from passion to desire to emotion to reaction, toward pleasure and away from pain, trying to find a comfort zone," he teased, "unless you're really mixed up and you think pain is pleasure. Seriously though, once the elemental emotions are in balance, it's supposed to be easier to live love in daily life."

Once again, I glimpsed how the elemental emotions affected me. For sure, fear took over every time I got near Taz. I could never be myself around him, but I couldn't escape him either because the attachment to my son and my dreams of a happy family life kept pulling me back. Even my wish to have my dreams come true imprisoned me in a power struggle with Taz. I denied the resentment and frustration that had not been expressed for years. And then a volcanic blast of anger set me free. After my blissful fantasy love affair with Bodhi, I returned to grief. Clearly, passions fueled the tangles of my life.

"Leo, I can see how emotions make me do things, but how can I rise above them? How can I be stronger than my passions?"

"That is the question, my dear. Can we feel our feelings but not be ruled by them? All the psychiatrists and psychologists say that if we repress or project our feelings onto others, they act out unconsciously in our life dramas and tragedies. Then we're really in trouble."

Looking into the rippling dark water, imagining Taz's face emerging as a mirror to my own, I shuddered at the raw truth of Leo's words.

"So Taz was a reflection of my own unconsciousness?" I said with some resistance.

"Like the Jung shadow theory – if we don't bring our unconscious shadow into the light, we see it reflected in front of us. I go for that. I just have to work out the greed aspect and then I'll be fine," he joked. A moment later, more serious, he added. "I have to admit that I want the world more than I want the spirit, and yet, I also want it all."

"You can't go in two directions at once," I whispered, as though I were speaking to myself. "You have to choose one or the other."

"You have to go with what's strongest," he countered. "You have to be yourself."

"We can't be our passions. They're too changeable. Our true self must be beyond them," I said.

"That's true. My problem is that I enjoy the passions and I love change. I'm not ready to leave either of them behind. They say that when you still your mind you experience peace," Leo said quietly, his voice melting like water into my stream of consciousness. "But I enjoy the movement."

417

"I want peace," I said with certainty.

"I want it too. I can see the path beckoning, but I still find the rest of life juicier. I keep putting off the spiritual life."

Just then, Love slipped out of my lap and toddled over to Leo. He wrapped his arms around her and held her close to him.

"It's wonderful to see how softly and sweetly you hold Love. Taz never cuddled our children in that way. He was always fighting us off, except for my son. He's so afraid I'll do what his mother did to him that he won't let me raise my son."

"Mothers," Leo replied, sidestepping my personal issues, "are a big deal in the water element. First of all, women have more of the water element naturally because they need to be more sensitive and loving. But men can express their feminine sides as well, you know," he added with a smile.

"We're more emotional because our feelings are closer to the surface," I contributed, aware that Leo and I were painting a mind picture, one stroke at a time. Even though I couldn't visualize the whole image, each step of the truth brought me toward a change in perception that I felt would alter my life.

"Yes," he agreed. "Men definitely have more fire, but I remember the yogis saying that we all have both masculine and feminine energies within us and that part of the spiritual journey is to learn to balance those energies within. Have you seen the drawings of the ancient symbol, the caduceus? You often see it in doctors' offices, you know, the two serpents twining up the spine? One serpent is the feminine and one is the masculine, and they meet in each chakra, where the challenge to balance the energies is more pronounced, because of the challenge of the emotional passion."

"So, you're saying I have masculine energy inside me?" I questioned in disbelief. "But I've always been the most feminine person." I put my feet into the cool, rushing water as I tried to digest the concept. Then it started to make sense. "Maybe I had to have a dominating husband so I could develop my masculinity until I could become strong enough to stand up to him."

"Listen to you," Leo said. "Once you start thinking and talking about things, it's amazing how much you already know."

I received his praise with an open heart. "Yes," I agreed. "It's true. I can let my mind follow its own path to the answer."

"Forget about following the mind," Leo laughed. "Let's follow the yellow brick road," he sang for a moment as we set off up the path. "Maybe the answer lies in the fire chakra."

"Can't we change it to the golden flower path?" I teased. "I'm into flowers, and the path of the golden flowers seems like a pretty beautiful path."

"That's what we'll call it – the path of the golden chakra flowers. I like that," he said, leaning over to kiss my cheek.

As I followed Leo, painful memories of my power struggles with Taz surfaced, and I was glad when he continued his explanations.

"When man discovered fire, it brought people together. It kept them warm. It protected them. It helped create homes, families, and communities. Unfortunately, whenever people come together, power struggles also ignite sparks that burst into roaring flames of war and destruction. There's always someone who wants to win, lead, dominate, or control everyone else, someone who wants to be right. Most of us have had someone like that in our life. As hard as their lessons are, they represent a reality we have to learn to deal with. Once we've learned how to be strong without running over people, there's a whole world of unconditional love. In that world, no one needs to dominate. Each person respects the other, even when they work together toward a common goal."

"Where would that be?" I asked with a wry grimace. "I've never found it. I had to fight to defend myself from my parents, my siblings, and Taz, and even with neighbors and so-called friends. The only time I experience 'free love' is with my children."

"In the fire chakra level, someone always wants to be right, someone always wants to win. My dad was like that."

"So were Taz's parents. He never got respect or love when he was growing up, so how could he give it to anyone else?" I contributed.

"He couldn't. Some people can experience the worst of life and still find it in them to give love to others, and some can't.

"What makes the difference in people?" I asked.

"Therein lies the mystery, my dear, the mystery of where love comes from," Leo said enigmatically.

"Why does love have to be a mystery," I complained.

"Can't answer that, my dear, so I'll just ramble on here. I was afraid of my father. I couldn't do what I wanted until he went broke. Now I get to be my outrageous self, and he can't threaten to disown me. There's nothing left to inherit."

Leo's laugh of freedom rang over the rushing water. He was making the most of the loss of his family fortune. I wanted to turn my family disaster into a victory, too, but how was I going to do that?

"What's positive fire? Let's get specific," I asked, excited by the opportunity to learn more.

"You have to get beyond the power struggles to experience the joy and laughter that comes along with cosmic humor. That's about as positive as you can get. Just look around. So many people are using up their lives fighting and struggling, and yet they take nothing with them when they die. When you catch a glimpse of the potential of your own life, you'll see it makes sense to withdraw from conflict, put all you've got into your own life, and see if you can help anyone else along the way. You know the phrase, 'a change of heart'? It's like that. One day you see that conflict is a waste of time and you're genuinely not interested in participating. You have better things to do than trying to prove you're right."

"Wow," I said, standing up and jumping onto another rock, needing movement to express the excitement aroused by our conversation. "It's that simple and yet we get caught up in the struggles like they're the only thing going."

It was Leo's turn to laugh at me.

"But how do you let go when someone you love is trying to push you around or take advantage of you or hurt you?" I asked, remembering how I had clung to Taz.

"You use the energy and power of fire for transformation so that you can enter the realm of the heart, where compassion reigns. I'm sure you know what that's like. 'I'm fed up. I can't take it anymore. I'm going to let go, break free, and change things no matter what the cost'."

"Yeah, I know that place only too well," I agreed, the image of the sewing machine floating through my mind. "Let's walk the green ray of the rainbow path into the heart chakra," I invited, enjoying our game. "Since we've moved from earth to water to fire, I guess it must be air's turn."

"Yes, it is," he affirmed. "Air element, here we come."

He held his hand out to me and said, "Shall we?" with full-on British manners.

We scrambled up to the next pool, sat down on the rocks, and immersed our feet into the cooling water. When I closed my eyes, I heard heartbeat rhythms pulsing in the stream, ba-boom, ba-boom. Entering into the rhythm, my mind calmed down. Everything slowed until, heartbeat by heartbeat, I felt that I was living love. More than anything, I wanted to stay in the love and never be separated from it again.

"Okay. What do you think is the secret of the heart center?" Leo asked, tickling me out of my trance.

"Is there a secret?" I giggled, pushing him away.

"There must be, because so few of us know how to live from the heart," he said wistfully.

"Maybe we all have to find out for ourselves," I offered as I drew heart-shaped patterns on the water with my feet. "What do you think the secret is?"

Surprising me once again, Leo sang a nursery-school song and Love clapped along with him.

"Love is like a magic penny,
Hold it tight and you won't have any,
Learn to spend it and you'll have so many,
They will roll all over the floor."

I teased him by repeating what he'd said to me a few minutes before, "Maybe you know more than you think. Can't you apply that to your fortune hunting?"

"I wish I could. Seriously though, what takes us away from love is greed and speed. That's the Alice in Wonderland syndrome. You know the 'I'm late, I'm late for a very important date', song of the white rabbit. The faster people go and the more they try to get all the things they think they want and need, the more they feel they don't have enough, and the faster they go."

Laughing, I chanted, "There isn't enough time. There isn't enough money. There isn't enough love."

"You have to focus on what you have instead of what you don't have," Leo confirmed. "I can say that easily, but doing it is another matter."

"Yes. If we could stop the selfishness and the fear long enough to stay in the present moment. If only our love were stronger than our desire, we'd have a good chance to stay in the love that shines like the sun – the love that shines equally on everything."

"If I felt all those things, then maybe I wouldn't be looking and searching for something," Leo said as he put his arms around me.

Nestling against his chest, I heard his heart beating.

"Let's stay in this love forever," I said.

Heartbeat by heartbeat, I let myself feel the love without the fear.

After a while, Leo got up and as we walked up the path from the heartbeat love pool toward the mystery of the ether pool.

I couldn't keep back the question that had been bugging me for years, "What about this longing I feel all the time? What does it mean? What do I want?"

"Hah! That's great. The right question at the right time. I asked the yogis the same question, and they said that longing was the emotion associated with the ether element in the throat chakra. Like all the other chakras, ether contains so-called positive and negative aspects. When longing flows into daily life, it gets wound up with fear, attachment, anger, and greed. It becomes desire for temporary, worldly, material things, or it turns into grief whenever something is taken away. True longing wants only to return to union with what is eternal and divine."

"So this hunger is there because I want to return to where I came from?" I asked.

"Ahhh, so many questions. You've got me working hard to answer them. Let me see what I can do with this one," Leo said, putting his head in his hands as if he was about to enter deep thought.

Impatient for his answer, I wriggled inside like an excited child. Leo was the first person I'd been able to talk to about the questions that haunted me.

"Okay, the yogis said that ether was emptiness that was full of potential," he stated seriously.

"If ether is empty, how can it be full?" I asked, confused by the paradox.

"The answer can only be that it's not really empty, and its not really full, my dear child," he responded, play-acting like a sanctimonious priest. "The elements flow out of ether into the world and to ether they return."

"How does emptiness contain earth, water, fire, and air?" I asked with disbelief, giggling at his expression and his accent. That concept seemed impossible to comprehend.

Leo looked at me with wry amusement. "You seem to be able to contain opposites, so why shouldn't ether be able to do the same?"

"Hmmm," I mused. "I see what you mean. Please go on."

"Think of ether as an ocean of sound and light containing endless wave frequencies or patterns that manifest in the physical realm," he said with the gestures and mannerisms of a yogi with an Indian accent.

"Okay, okay, I'm beginning to get the idea. Empty, yet full of possibilities," I relented, trying to get used to the idea.

Meanwhile Leo continued his academic pontifications. "Myths refer to ether as the goddess of the rainbow. Her name is Iris, like the iris of the eye, because that's where primary colors flow into prismatic physical reality."

"When I was a child, I used to dance to the *Somewhere Over The Rainbow* song," I interjected spontaneously, remembering how happy I used to be when I was dancing. "I'm used to skipping along a rainbow."

"Ah, a budding rainbow goddess? Cool. Very cool," he praised humorously, then returned to his academic tone. "*Over the rainbow* means back to the mystery of ether. Ether has other qualities also, such as beauty and grace. Because it contains the energies of all the elements, it gives you discrimination, the knowing that helps you become aware of the effect that choices might make upon you and your life before you make them. When we live from a compassionate heart, we achieve a natural spirituality. We want to make the world a better place and fulfill our life purpose."

"So many people want that, but so few accomplish it. How do we do it? I am always asking that question."

We both sighed at the same time as we looked down toward the ocean and the lowering sun.

"Shouldn't we ascend to the third eye?" I asked. "It's getting late."

We scrambled up the path, then sat on a rock that overlooked the water falling into the ether pool below us. Gently fatigued, we listened to the bubbling tabla rhythms of the flowing stream, and continued our conversation.

"I've felt the third eye on peyote and acid, but I don't understand how I can have an eye in my forehead," I said.

"I only know that the yogis say that the third eye is a place of concentration, the threshold that opens into the inner life after you have developed the strength to withstand the five passions of the lower chakras."

"But how do we do that? If I knew how to tame the passions, I'd do it," I said with an edge of desperation in my voice. "Why does God make it so hard for us?"

Suddenly I felt tired and grumpy. As if Love was mirroring my despair, she started wailing.

"Come here, honeybee," I said as I took her in my arms mirroring her cry, "Waaa, waaa, waaa."

Love started giggling at my poor imitation of her, and Leo laughed uproariously. That made me even madder.

"Waaaaa. Waaaaa. I'm fed up. I want out or maybe I should say, I want in," I cried, laughing at my own humor.

"Well, my dear, if I were God, I'd welcome you with open arms," Leo said with such charm that I snuggled into his embrace.

"I can't think anymore. I just want to be," I whimpered like a baby. "I don't understand anything."

"That's a good sign. Come on, let's go to the last pool."

I held onto his belt as he hiked upward, letting him pull me up to the seventh pool.

"The drawings of the crown chakra make it look as if we have flowers growing on the top of our heads," I grinned, enjoying the humor that passed between us. "I loved to touch the soft spot on the top of my babies' heads and feel it pulse. I used to wonder whether it had something to do with the crown chakra. What's a flower on the top of your head supposed to mean, anyway?"

"I think the artists are trying to say that it would be great if we had a mind that was like a garden of perfumed flowers," Leo teased.

"I know you're making fun of me, but the truth is, that is what I want. I want to get rid of all these sad, fearful thoughts and restless desires and fill my mind with beautiful flowers, but what would flower thoughts be like?" I asked.

"My first flower would be 'Thank you'," Leo said as he picked up a hibiscus and threw it in the pool."

I picked another flower and threw it in the stream, "And mine would be 'All you need is love'."

"What about, 'What can I do to help someone today?'"

"Or, 'What can I do to help myself today?'"

Leo threw another flower as he said, "Contentment."

I screamed, "Courage!"

"That's the idea," Leo laughed as we threw flower after flower into the crown chakra pool. Love helped us, tottering from flower to flower, throwing them, then clapping her hands and laughing with glee. The flowers collected by the rocks at the edge of the pool and then, with one rush, they flew over the waterfall.

"And down the flower thoughts go, through all the chakras and throughout the body," I cried. "Soon everything will be a perfumed garden."

Exhilarated by our imaginative play, we lay back on the rocks, Love between us, savoring the perfection.

After a while, my curiosity surfaced and I murmured, "What else did the yogis say about the crown chakra?"

"Mmm. Back to questions, are we?" he teased. "Happy to oblige, my dear. Let's see. The crown chakra is like a seed that is waiting to flower on the top of your head where your mind and soul meet. The journey of life offers us the opportunity to flower into the divine. But, in order to connect with our souls, we have to still our minds and empty ourselves of everything that makes us feel separated from the Lord. We have to long only for God and be willing to receive whatever He gives as love. To top it off, when we leave our body, we have to have given more than we have taken from this world."

What he said seemed so impossible that I lifted my arms in helplessness. "Oh, is that all? How can I achieve any of these things when I already have so many problems?"

"They say problems automatically go away when we focus on the Lord," he consoled me with a gentle smile.

"I do focus on the Lord. I'm always thinking about Him. Maybe He is solving my problems and I just don't know it. I need a daily spiritual practice, something that will help me clean out my mind. I need a teacher who will help me."

Frustration was growing, so I closed my eyes and imagined the chakras directing my destiny. I felt the longing pulling the elements upward to dissolve into the etheric throat chakra. The third eye in my forehead beamed like a lighthouse of concentration, and my crown chakra gathered to open and flower. Then it all seemed too much. Sure, I wanted spiritual truth, but I also wanted to live a simple, happy daily life.

"I'm so tired of my mind. I want to stop my desires. I want to meditate. I want all this, but I also need human love," I complained.

"We all need love. Even the spiritual journey is about love," he reassured me, stroking my hair as if I were his child. "You will find your spiritual path. You're probably on it right now. With such strong longing, you will find your way."

Seeking relief, I stood near the waterfall spray, appreciating the cooling angel-mist that felt like minute droplets of moist light caressing me.

Leo bowed formally and took my hand in his. Together we watched shafts of golden light underline a procession of billowing clouds as the vermilion sun settled into the sea.

"Every cloud has a golden lining," I said with a smile as we headed down the path to the parking lot.

When we got to the bridge, I reached for Leo's hand and pulled him to a halt. "We mustn't forget what we're here for, Leo. Let's make a promise."

Standing there, under the darkening tropical sky, we vowed to remember our spiritual journey. We placed our right hands on each other's hearts and spoke our promises out loud, weaving an alchemy of joyful laughter and profound intent.

Leo drove through the warm, scented, star-filled night, maneuvering the hundreds of curves like a race driver. Love slept in my lap, satisfied and sweetly tired. I leaned my head on Leo's shoulder, savoring the love and the bittersweet desire that wanted this fullness to go on forever.

"Let's go to Lahaina tomorrow," Leo invited as we pulled up to the Zendo.

"Oh, yes," I agreed, thankful we would spend another day together.

That night I dreamed that the energies of my chakras had awakened. Exquisite petaling wheels of light spun and radiated within me. Each element offered a difficult challenge and a special gift to help me on my journey. Even though I still didn't understand the mystery of life, I had gathered a few more clues.

There Is Only Love

Early the next morning, we set off for another day of adventure. Leo drove down the Holokai Road eucalyptus tunnel past the Banana Patch hippie commune to the Hana Highway. Then we sped south through sunrise-shiny, prickly pineapple fields toward Kahului. After cutting across the valley on a tree-lined road that led to the western shore, we turned toward Lahaina. Passing through the bustling town, we continued up the Kaanapali coast until Leo pulled off at a public beach. Enjoying the ease of being together, we walked on the sand, content to let Love lead us along. When we saw three stones leading into the sea, we stepped onto them, Leo on the outer one, me next, and Love on the smallest one closest to the beach. As each wave swirled into foaming surf, Love shrieked, both afraid and thrilled by the water surging around her. Leaving the stones behind, we swam in a gentle lagoon protected by coral reefs before stretching out to dry on the hot sand.

"Let's have lunch," Leo said, pointing to a luxury hotel.

Although I was ravenously hungry, I eyed the hotel with suspicion. I'd never been in one of the island hotels before.

"But that's the Sheraton," I said anxiously.

"I know. They have a great restaurant. You'll love it."

"Like this?" I questioned, looking at myself.

"You're beautiful. Don't worry," he reassured me as he picked up Love and took my hand.

Acutely aware of my damp dress and the tangles in my long black hair, I followed Leo into the spacious, cool, marbled lobby. Escaping immediately to the ladies' room, I laughed at the image of the wild, tanned woman in the mirror, her hair full of sand and seaweed. Determined to make us presentable, I took off Love's dress, put her in the sink and let her splash around while I combed my hair. When we walked into the dining room, we were glowing with happiness and full of the blessings of Hawaii.

After Leo settled Love into a high chair in a leafy alcove decorated with orchid sprays, we ordered lunch. Crystal glasses, silver cutlery, white linen, and fine china enhanced the delicious fresh fruit, salad, and juices. The luxurious comfort pleased me almost as much as the wild immersion in Hawaii's sea, sand, and wind. I wouldn't mind the best of both worlds, I decided, as long as I didn't get separated from the nature that nourished me.

"I'm leaving tomorrow. Come with me," Leo announced abruptly.

My heart pounded in my chest as I asked, "What do you mean?"

He sat tall, beaming good will, like a golden Apollo as he explained, "Why let this happiness end? Good companions are rare."

"Where? To do what?" I stammered.

"Well, after Honolulu, I return to London to see family and friends. Then, who knows where the next job will take me. The whole world will be our playground."

Although Leo presented an irresistible picture, I knew it wouldn't work, so I made excuses.

"I'm having my baby soon. I need to be settled."

"We'll get a flat in London," he promised.

"You're mad!" I said, laughter disguising my terror.

He tried to persuade me. "It's a wonderful idea. Look how we get on."

"I don't have money. I don't have clothes."

"I've got scads of money. I'll take you two shopping on Bond Street," he said enthusiastically. Then, his voice took on an urgency I hadn't heard before. "I want you to share my life. Come with me," he said as he kissed my hand.

"Leo, don't you think the timing is off? Look at me. I'm six months pregnant. You've been on your own. You've no idea what it's like to take care of children."

"Don't let my lifestyle confuse you. I'm perfectly prepared to take care of you and your children. In fact, I'd enjoy it."

For a moment, I imagined sharing my life with him. It was true that I enjoyed his company more than anyone I'd ever known. He awakened a passion that never flowered in Taz's dark world or in the ungrounded bliss with Bodhi. Even though I felt drawn toward his elegant confidence, I felt as though I would be stepping off a cliff into a world where I would never belong, and I panicked.

"I need to go outside. I need to think," I said abruptly, standing up.

He responded immediately by signaling the waiter and paying the bill. Carrying Love as tenderly as if he were her father, he escorted us gracefully out of the dining room. I watched them together, wondering what kind of life she would have with him. I couldn't imagine living in London. If I went with him, I'd lose Hawaii, and what about my son? A hurricane of conflicting thoughts was tearing apart my heart.

We walked through the hotel gardens to the beach where sea, sand, and wind waved their eternal dance of changes, rising and falling, ebbing and flowing.

"You're used to getting what you want, aren't you?" I teased.

"Yes," he answered simply.

"What if you get caught or don't come back? What would I do then?"

"My luck is too good for that, but I'll put a thousand pounds in a bank account for you, if that will make you feel better. Then, you can go home whenever you want."

Even though Leo said and did everything he could to reassure me, I was still afraid. I used to trust everyone, even when I shouldn't have. Now it seemed I couldn't trust anyone. My mind was in a torment of confusion, so I asked Leo to drive me back to the farm. I wanted to return to familiar ground.

Soon, we were flying along in the fragrant air. Shining sugar cane rippled like waves in the wind. White surf edged the pure, blue water. Rich green grasses and blossoming trees swayed against a cloud spiraling sky. My heart ached with the beauty of it all. I had become part of Hawaii's elemental dance and I didn't want to leave.

Back at the Zendo, Leo sensed my need to be alone, so after holding me for a moment, he bowed out of the room. As much as I enjoyed being with him, I was relieved to be away from his powerful energy. Did I want to be with another man? If I let him go, I might never see him again. A gold smuggler! I must be mad to even think of it. He was an international criminal. No, he was an adventurer. I had never met anyone so full of life, so elegant, so easy to be with. Tired of thinking, I searched inside for peace and light, and unexpectedly received a showering of bliss that quieted my mind and enabled me to sleep. My last thought was that this must be what they call divine grace. Whatever it was, it was beautiful.

In the dark of night, I awoke in confusion. Love, how wonderful when you come, but how painful. I thought of the men who had come into my life during this Summer of Love. Bodhi, my stoned savior had rescued me, then rejected me. The shy Hawaiian brother, Kimo, proposed marriage, even though he didn't know me. Golden Wheat from the Brotherhood of Eternal Love had invited me to go on his acid-dropping, turn-on trips. Gentle, wise Jeremy had offered me his home and his protection. The elegant Leo wanted to take me on his globetrotting smuggling journeys. Each one stirred my heart in different ways. Each one offered a different world, but none of them mine. Of them all, Jeremy and the life he offered attracted me the most, but why then did the company of the elegant and magical Leo give me so much happiness?

I wondered why so many different men had come into my life one right after the other. Perhaps they were attracted to my vulnerability. Perhaps Hawaii had blessed me and made me seem more than I was. I know I thrived in the elemental nature on Maui. I know I was happier than I had ever been before. Perhaps that was it, or maybe they wanted to help me. I wished I had had these opportunities at another time of my life when I was not so wounded and afraid of men. Even though my heart was touched by their offers, I couldn't trust myself to love again. I wanted to give my heart to God but I didn't know how to do that yet. My tangled human heart sought to make sense of what was happening and then it let go and I slept like a child, certain that somehow everything would work out.

A rooster crowed before first light.

Birdsong awakened the dawn.

Leo slipped into my room and whispered in my ear, "Come to Honolulu with me. You'll see what it's like for us to be in the world together. I have to be there for a few days. Come, come."

I felt my energy surge toward him, resist and then let go. I didn't want to leave. I wanted to go with him.

"Yes, I'll come," I agreed, almost sadly.

Love helped me pack. While she placed her collection of shells and seedpods in her basket, I folded her little dresses in the flower-print backpack I'd made for her. My Holokai brothers thought I was coming back, but I wasn't so sure, so I took everything with me. I was leaving the farm almost against my will, yet there was a relief at leaving that I didn't understand. Currents of confusion and uncertainty blended with surrender.

I took one last look at the room that had been my haven these past autumn months. The futons were bare. The fruit bowl was empty. Incense ashes dusted the altar. A half-burned candle and a vase of dry flowers were all that remained of my beautiful room. Holding back tears, I glanced out of the window into the banana orchard, appreciating how much the Zendo had given me and how much I'd changed since the first night I slept on the coffin.

Love tugged at my dress.

Leo was waiting to lead me on my next journey.

We flew out of my Maui dream paradise into Honolulu. The big city rhythms soon erased the natural ones. Within an hour, Leo had collected our baggage, rented a car, and checked us into the Halekulani Hotel. Leo's fine luggage and our hand-made backpacks made an incongruous pile in the elevator that swept us into the sky. Even though our room overlooked the sea, I felt as though Hawaii was slipping away from me. Immersed in luxury, I already missed my simple garden room and my close contact with nature. Seeking comfort, I draped my colorful cloths over the furniture and spread Love's stones, shells, and seedpods on the carpet.

Leo switched into business mode, making appointments, calling England and Hong Kong, speaking foreign languages.

Then he strode over, lifted me up and swung me around.

"I'm so happy you're here. Enjoy yourself. I have to go out. Order anything you want," he offered generously. "I'll be back in a couple of hours."

Leo flashed his irresistible smile and left.

Without his powerful presence in the suite, I felt suddenly out of place, uprooted from myself, like a wild thing captured in a cage. Restless, I glanced at Leo's open luggage. A prince of style, he folded his exquisite silk, linen and cashmere clothes immaculately. Gold and silver toiletries, monogrammed handkerchiefs, and custom made shoes were tucked neatly into special compartments. Happy in my own unique, carefree designs, I couldn't imagine dressing in fashionable clothes or being as perfect as he was.

Rain dashed against the glass, blurring the colored lights of the city below. As Love made patterns with her shells and stones on the carpet, I wove patterns with my mind, imagining sharing Leo's life: the gold smuggling, the wealth, the wheeling and dealing, and the traveling to London, Tokyo, Venice, and Hong Kong.

When the rain stopped, I slid open the glass doors and stepped onto the balcony. Honolulu's brightly-lit windows and neon lights almost eclipsed the stars. Even though I was glad to feel the soft, moist tropical air against my skin, the fragrance of flowers and roar of the sea seemed too far away.

When I stepped back inside, Love had fallen asleep, so I curled up beside her. Relentless questions troubled me. I'd never asked questions when I met Bodhi. Now I was asking them. That was progress. If I went with Leo, I might lose myself again. What did I really want? I was afraid to answer that question when Jeremy asked me. Now it was time to know the answer. What was my truth? How could I find it? What did I really want?

First, what I didn't want emerged. I felt fear when I thought about trusting my life to another man. I didn't want to be hurt again. I felt the pull of attachment when I thought about living far away from my son. I wanted to be part of his life. I didn't want to move to another country and feel out of place in a class-and-wealth-conscious culture. I didn't want to live in a cold climate, with strangers whose values were different from mine. I couldn't live off Leo's smuggling. I'd be anxious, always afraid something might go wrong. If he were caught, I'd be an accessory. I'd go to jail. Then what would happen to my children?

I started to panic before I remembered the heartbeat rhythm of the heart chakra pool. When I breathed deeply, my fears and anxieties eased. Slowly my mind quieted and emptied and a question emerged. What does your heart want? After a time the only impulse I felt was that I wanted myself, my own life, my own world. Yes, I wanted to follow my own life currents of spiritual longing and creativity. Well then, if that was what I truly wanted, that was what I should go for, I decided.

A short time later Leo returned with guests. He was speaking Japanese. What could Leo not do? He came into the bedroom and put on his smuggling jacket. Tailored from the finest cashmere, fitted inside with secret pockets, it was padded and exquisitely shaped to conceal contraband gold and jewels. Transformed from tropical white linens to Bond Street elegance, a walking treasure chest, he looked at himself in the mirror, winked at me, then walked out and shut the door.

After he left, I walked over to the full-length mirror. Even though I saw the image of a sun-browned, pregnant island woman, it was something else that caught my interest. I looked stronger, more confident. My eyes were brighter. They weren't afraid to look clearly at what was in front of me. My interior world was beginning to reveal itself. I didn't have to ask who I was anymore. I simply was myself.

Later that night, Leo eased his warm beautiful body next to mine. I sighed and pressed against him, wanting to dissolve into his strength, but my instincts, tuned to a deeper truth, warned me.

"Leo, I can't go with you," I said abruptly, because I didn't know any way to make it easier.

His body stiffened, but he did not answer.

"I can't be part of your smuggling thing," I continued.

He turned on the light and looked at me.

"It's what I am. It's all I know," he explained with desperation.

My heart melted when I saw his face but my resolve was strong.

"I've fought hard to find out who I am. I have to be true to myself," I said. "In many ways it will be harder to face the choice I am making right now, but I know it is the right way, the only way for me."

"What are you going to do?" he asked.

"I'm going back to Los Angeles. I have to face the life I've been running away from. That's how I'll find out who I am. Please understand."

"I do understand," he said sadly. "I smuggle so I can I live like a king. I also want to do what you're doing and live a spiritual life, but it seems I must make myself rich first."

He laughed harshly, mocking himself.

"Why don't you go back to the farm? To Maui?" he asked.

I sat up and hugged my knees, and said simply, "I can't explain, other than to say that I need to be near my son."

Leo put his hands on my shoulders and looked deeply into my eyes before he said, "I can't believe you want to go back to Los Angeles and your husband."

"I'm not going back to him. I want to face my problems and be near my son. Leaving Hawaii is very hard for me. I love it here. It's the only place I've ever felt at home, but I'm leaving because I have to find a way to create harmony and beauty inside myself and in my life. That's what Hawaii taught me. You see, you helped me find the courage to be myself."

"Then stay with me," he said, pulling me into his arms.

His embrace stirred my heart but didn't change my mind.

"You say that because we have such a good time together. Realistically, I don't belong in your world. I'd be out-of-place, shy, uncertain, an alien. A few months down the line, you'd see it wouldn't work. If I were free, I might come with you for a while, and maybe we'd stay together or maybe we wouldn't. But I'm not free. I have to build a life for myself and my children."

"I could help you, protect you, take care of you," he offered again.

I sighed. His offer was tempting, but it wasn't right.

"You've helped me more than you know," I said.

"Then why won't you come with me?" he insisted grumpily.

"I can't go away with anyone. I have to find my own life," I said simply, wishing I didn't have to reject him. "It's too late for me to just enjoy life. I have to think of the consequences of everything I do. I have to be conscious of where my choices will take me. I have to be more like a warrior, even if that means giving up things I'd love to do."

As I tried to share my feelings, Leo pulled away.

"Do you need tickets?" he asked formally after a moment.

"No thanks, I've got return tickets."

Once more the English gentleman, he made a generous offer, "Stay. Let's explore Oahu, have some fun."

"Leo, I can't. I'm taking the first flight tomorrow."

Silenced, he stared at me like he couldn't figure me out. I wanted to comfort him.

"Leo, I adore you. As hard as it is to say goodbye, I'm excited about transforming the mess I've made of my life. I'm ready to do it. I know I can do it."

He turned out the light and turned away from me.

In the darkness of the hotel room, I glowed with happiness that felt as light as clouds.

There Is Only Love

In the morning, I put on my striped Haleakala robe. The collar of eucalyptus buds and shells wove a circle of beautiful memories around my shoulders. After I pinned Clara's silver pin on my robe, I was ready to go home.

Open grief mingled with our morning breakfast chatter, but as strong as the attraction was, I did not change my mind. Leo was particularly attentive to Love, and thankfully, he did not try to convince me to stay. After we checked in, he draped a fragrant *meile* lei around my neck.

I knew I was leaving a true friend and a unique opportunity, but I didn't waver from the decision that was best for my soul journey. My roots were planted in my internal world now. I didn't need to cling to outward things. I knew what I had to do, and I wasn't going to let anything stand in my way, no matter how tempting.

I hugged Leo, blessed him with all of my heart, and shed a few tears. Then, holding Love, the flower-print backpacks slung over my shoulder, I climbed the steps into the airplane. This was one flower child that was going all the way home.

The long flight gave me a chance to feel the changes within myself. Alive and awake, my life purpose stirred like a bud within me, revealing the promise of a flower waiting to bloom. I didn't have to look for love. I didn't have to fear the world. I didn't have to seek paradise or run from hell. My garden of love was within.

I knew my spiritual teacher was waiting for me in the future. Every day that passed would be one day closer to meeting him. In the meantime, I'd live as if I were already with him. What was that fairy story about that mean old man? What was his name? Rumpelstiltskin! Maybe it should be Taz! At that thought, I laughed out loud in the sky. If I could still laugh on the ground, I'd be on my way.

I'd turn my weaknesses into strengths. I'd take the straw of my life and turn it into gold. I had searched for love, thinking it was something I had to find. I didn't understand I only had to overcome my fear of giving and receiving love. Now my fountain of love could begin to flow into every moment of my life. Instead of seeking the sun, I would become the sun.

I promised myself I'd do my best in every moment. I'd have to turn whatever came to me into love. I wasn't perfect. I knew it would be hard. I'd make mistakes, but in the middle of all the confusion and mystery, I'd devote my life to one goal. I would look for a spiritual teacher, a living Son of God. That was what I wanted when I was a child. That was what I wanted now. I no longer needed to ask the question. I was the answer.

Waiting for Taz outside the airport, basking in the warm autumn haze, Love and I watched the California dreamers. Showing off their far-out fashions, grooving to their favorite tunes, or just plain rushing along, there were hippies, rock-n-rollers, mini-skirted show-biz hopefuls, business drones, old ladies with heavy makeup, teeny boppers, soldiers on leave, and kids with their moms wandering by. In the midst of it all, a dozen saffron-robed Hare Krishna devotees trance-danced, chanting their mantra, selling their books, trying to get people to join their cult.

I looked at my Haleakala robe and laughed with delight. I'd come a long way from the jump suit and silver boot days of the spring of the Summer of Love.

Autumn is the time when leaves flame red, gold, yellow and orange, offering their glory before they fly free. Shedding my fantasies like leaves, I felt ready to face the reality of my dysfunctional life and my wild mind. I wanted to deal with the difficulties of my life and find a way to turn them around. I was willing to raise my children on my own and continue the preparation and the search for my spiritual teacher. I was ready to face the winter of my soul.

There Is Only Love

Taz and Choo drove up in the yellow Lincoln convertible. Choo stood up on the seat, waving. Taz, cocksure and indifferent, smoked a cigarette.

"Get in. You blew it again. Back on my case," he blurted, pretending not to be glad to see us.

Immune to Taz's forced hardness, I kept within my own happiness.

"Hi, Choo."

My son's eyes glowed with merry joy. When I lifted him in my arms his strong, golden body clung to me.

"Mmm. I'm so happy to see you," I whispered in his ear.

Love threw herself at Taz's knees and hugged them. He lifted her up, trying his hardest not to melt down.

After Taz pulled out into the traffic, he looked at me.

"You look different," he said, appearing confused.

"Different? Guess I've got a tan," I laughed, "and a bigger belly."

"No, it's not that. It's something else."

I couldn't explain it if I tried, so I didn't say anything. Let him figure it out.

"So, you had a good trip?" he asked.

"Yeah, a really good trip," I said, feeling like a sunrise and a sunset as I held my two beloved children on either side of my pregnant belly.

"I'm glad you'll be running the Conspiracy again. That piss-ant manager rips me off. I'll throw that stupid bastard out. You can take over right away."

"Having troubles?" I asked gently.

"Nothing but troubles, and I don't need more. Don't want be involved in this baby stuff. Dig?"

"I'm cool. What's new with you?"

"God, what isn't new? Everything's falling apart. Yoni OD'd on heroin. Her mom called me. Was she pissed! She has to raise the kids now. Yoni just checked out. Damn, so stupid!"

Yoni gone! My mind and heart raced overtime. Images and memories flashed of the places where we had spent time: Oceano, Santa Monica, Berkeley, and Haight Ashbury. I had hardly processed that shock when Taz made another announcement.

"I'm getting married next month," he gushed with peacock pride.

"To who?" I blurted, unable to contain my surprise.

"Her name's Trinity. She's cute, small, and slender, and has long black hair. You'll see; she looks just like you."

"Like me?" I stammered, unseated from my cool. Just when I thought I had it all together, here I was, surprised again.

"Yeah, she's hot, a total sex kitten. Doesn't want kids. She promises to keep me so well-loved, I won't feel like tripping the Strip," he said, beaming with satisfaction.

I had to laugh. L.A. was the same. Taz was the same. As I tuned to my inner being, Taz's ranting faded out. Without resistance, I opened to the freeway traffic, the heat, the smog, and the city vibe. It was the same scene, the same actors, but a different script. I was seeing everything in a different way, seeing behind the surface of things, seeing the bigger picture. L.A. was definitely not the City of Angels. It was more like a smoggy Babylon. Taz was not the good husband I longed for, or the ideal father for our children, but if I looked at him from my new perspective, he had been the worthy adversary, the perfect goad to nudge me along my spiritual path. It had been his job to wake me up, to help me reach deeper, higher and wider concepts of love.

After all, I had put enlightenment at the top of my life list. Maybe I'd got what I'd asked for, even if it hadn't happened in a way that I could understand. Now that I could see the purpose of suffering, I didn't need to run away anymore. Besides, there was nowhere to go to except deeper into my heart and soul, and I could do that anywhere.

There Is Only Love

The Summer of Love was over. The mild California autumn was balmy, but I knew winter storms were on their way. Hard times would come, but it didn't seem to matter. I felt sure I could handle whatever came my way.

I'd lived the magic of the Summer of Love and there was one thing I knew for sure – the Summer of Love would always bloom in the garden of my heart, and in that garden there was only love.

Empty Husk, Potent Seed

I shivered as I stepped onto the stainless steel floor of the Psychedelic Conspiracy. Entering the plastic, mirrored womb of an old dream, I felt like I was being enclosed in an empty husk.

After experiencing the living, breathing, powerful nature of Hawaii, I saw our attempts to create an alternate reality with black lights, strobes, mylar, plastic, and stainless steel with new eyes. Even though the lights and reflections gave the illusion of a simulated acid trip at night, the clear morning light revealed only grimy, writhing plastic and wrinkled silver mylar.

The store had gone downhill since I'd pulled out. Except for the creation of the interior, Taz had never been interested in running the store. His thing was hanging out on Friday and Saturday nights, checking out the action, talking to the famous and happening folks who wandered in, and hitting on the cool chicks. Maybe Taz's neglect and the nonchalance of his string of managers had killed the living energy, but it was more than that. I had outgrown the Psychedelic Conspiracy.

When we created the environment from our visionary dreams, it seemed to have energy and power beyond the physical materials. It seemed as if the psychedelic reality scripted itself in synch with the customers who flowed into our happening store. Was it our imagination and desire that had transformed the space-age materials into something transcendental? Or was it simply that we had included everyone in our temporary, psychedelic head-trip? In place of a living dream, all that was left was a lifeless shell.

My time in Hawaii had reconnected me to the love of nature that I had felt so strongly when I was a child, and now it seemed that nature itself was my teacher. I experienced the seasons of hibernation, growth, flowering, and seeding in my own life.

1967 began with the spring of the Summer of Love; the excitement and the power of the new energy expanded into the ripeness and fullness of summer, only to be stripped clean in the autumn. Now I faced the reality of the coming winter. Even though I felt the challenges ahead, I was also aware that the potent essence of the seed gathered energy during hibernation to create the beginning of its next cycle of growth. When I returned to Los Angeles, I had thought I might start a new creative phase at the Conspiracy, but now I knew I could not stay for long. My energy felt poised on the cusp of a new cycle, but my direction was still a mystery.

Taz was yelling at the manager, accusing him of theft, demanding the key, and refusing to pay him any salary. I watched, holding on to Love and Choo, feeling like a displaced person inside one of Taz's sculptures. When the scene was over, Taz couldn't wait to get back to Trinity, and he left Choo with me. That was an unexpected grace. There were clearly benefits coming from his marriage to a second, younger me.

After Taz left, I took the children and my backpacks into the workroom and considered what I could do to turn it into a living space. Within a short time, I had transformed half of the space into a colorful fabric tent. Choo and Love thought the tent was a great adventure and we snuggled up inside. While Love drifted off, I told Choo about my adventures in Hawaii and felt the power of my memories strongly within me. Closing my eyes and inhaling the scent of my eucalyptus beads, I could easily imagine lying on the roots of a tree in the grove next to the Zendo, or on the rocks by a waterfall. I had let go of Paradise to face reality, but somehow Paradise lingered within me.

After the children fell asleep, my thoughts drifted to my present situation. If I lived in the back of the store, I could save money. There was a grocery store a half block away and plenty of restaurants in the neighborhood. I'd buy a bucket and towels to take Japanese-style baths in the washroom and bring in a hot plate and an electric kettle. I didn't know what I wanted to do, so I figured I might as well hang out and make some money till the right thing came along. Meanwhile, I would do my best to raise the vibes in the store. As uncertain as my future was, I went to sleep with a happy heart.

Maria

The next morning, as I walked up the Strip to the grocery store with Love and Choo, I noticed a new boutique. After looking in the window, I wanted to see more, so I opened the door. When the bell rang, Maria walked out; not the Maria I once knew, but a happy, pretty Maria wearing a lovely silk dress.

Standing gracefully, clearly proud of her flattering hairstyle and beautiful teeth, she proudly announced, "This is my store."

"Your store! Wow!" I said, looking around. "How did all this happen so quickly?" I asked.

As if I'd turned on a switch, she started talking excitedly, "After you left, I thought that if Flower Child can leave, so can I. This store came up for rent, so I took it. I had the mover come on Sunday. You remember, Carlos sleeps all day Sunday after his big Saturday night on the town. I would have loved to see his face when he came into the shop and saw that everything was gone."

"You walked out on Carlos?" I said, stunned, wondering why I hadn't thought of opening my own store instead of blowing everything on my San Francisco fiasco.

"Yes, just like you."

Maria turned and waved her arms at her creation. "This is such a good location, I have too much business, too much. I slept in the back for a while, but now I have my own apartment nearby. I walk to work. And look, I have my hair and my nails done every week, and I'm seeing a dentist. I don't have to be afraid anymore. Best of all," she smiled coyly, "I have a boyfriend who is helping me with the divorce. We're going to get married and have children."

"What will you do with the shop?" I asked, impressed by the positive changes in her life.

"I have a manager starting soon. I have seamstresses working at home. I will be boss, but a good boss, even when I'm pregnant, even when I have baby, like you," she announced with satisfaction. "Now, come sit beside me and tell me how you are."

"Well, we're neighbors again. I'm staying in the store for a while. I just got back from Hawaii."

"You want to make designs?" she offered brightly. "You helped me. I want to help you."

"I'll think about it," I said. "I haven't decided what I want to do yet. I'll let you know."

"You are happy for me, yes?" she asked like a child.

"I am happy for you, Maria. You deserve to be happy. You'll make a great mother."

"Come by and meet my fiancé," she said, flashing her diamond ring. "He is from my country, but he is not like Carlos. He is good and kind."

Empty Husk, Potent Seed

After I returned to the Conspiracy, sadness overcame me, but instead of crying like I usually did, I dropped into guilt. First, I raged at myself for blowing everything on the San Francisco trip. Then jealousy overpowered my heart. Maria had a store. Maria had a fiancée. I had nothing. After all my success, I didn't even have the resources to open my own store. After crying and wallowing in self-pity for a while, I pulled myself out and returned to truth.

I was glad Maria had found a kind man who wanted to make her happy. She was a good person, and she'd served hard time with Carlos. She'd earned her good fortune. Even if looking at her success made me feel my own lack, the deeper reality was that I had a lot to be thankful for. I felt instinctively that whatever was due to me would come naturally. I had my chances. I made my choices. Even when opportunities came my way to be with good, kind men like Jeremy, I always found a way to say no.

I was beginning to realize that, beyond my desire for a loving life partner, there was a deeper desire to be on my own. Just thinking that made me feel better. I was on my path. That was all that mattered.

Anchovy

A few days after I settled into my rainbow-tented, psychedelic campout at the back of the Conspiracy, Anchovy came bursting in the door. Wow, was I glad to see that brother! I rushed forward to give him a big hug.

Without the Zendo camaraderie and the gentle warmth of Hawaii around him, Anchovy seemed thinner and smaller, and his ever-present restlessness felt more like city tension vibes.

"Wow, Flower Child! What a treat! Didn't expect to find you here. What happened?" he gabbled, prancing like an elf, acting like he was on speed.

Without giving me a chance to answer, he lifted Love in the air, making her laugh with delight.

"Things are changing, Flower Child. The dark side is moving in on Flower Power. Be careful, that's all I can say. There are people out there that look like us, but they're playing some other game that's not cool and it's not fun. They're out to get us," he whispered, looking over his shoulder at a guy who had wandered in after him.

"Where are you staying? Do you have a phone? How can I reach you?" I asked, feeling him poised for a quick departure.

"Staying nowhere. Got to go. I'll stop by again," he whispered as he edged toward the door.

"Come back soon. I want to talk to you," I called to his retreating back, but he had gone on his hurried way.

After he left, I sold some mirrored sunglasses to the guy who had set off Anchovy's paranoia. I checked him out good, and there *was* something strange about him. He acted cool, but he wasn't open. His eyes were hard, like they were hiding secrets.

What had Anchovy said? "The dark side is moving in." Maybe that's what I was feeling. The magic of the Summer of Love was gone. The autumn of '67 had an entirely different flavor.

 Bodhi

Seven months pregnant, with my belly popping out, I sewed a maternity dress of pure-white raw silk. Thinking the Hawaiian muumuu needed decoration, I cut out ripe, purple-crimson grapes from a bolt of printed silk and appliqued them on the shoulders and bodice. When I wore it with my crimson clogs, and let my long waving black hair flow down my back, I felt like a mother goddess from some ancient, Mediterranean culture.

One morning I woke up, put on my new dress, looked in the mirror, picked up the phone, and called Bodhi. Until that moment, I hadn't even considered the possibility of doing that, so there was no time to even think about what might happen if I did.

"Hi, Bodhi. This is Flower Child. How are you?" I said easily, a happy lilt in my voice.

"Oh, wow. Flower Child. You're back from Hawaii?" he asked, surprised.

"Yeah, got back a few days ago. A great trip. I loved it there, but I wanted to be near my son, so I'm camping out in the back of the Conspiracy, waiting to see what the next move is; you know how it is," I rambled, feeling cool that I was talking to him in this light-hearted way. "What's up with you guys there?"

"Man, changes, always changes. Wheat said he told you about Deva and Tree. We're still trying to get them out of prison. Lola had a major bummer in San Francisco. Some guys passed her some bad stuff in Golden Gate Park. She was raped and beaten. Hasn't been the same since. Just lies around here stoned, hardly says anything, then disappears, we don't know where, for days on end. Then comes back and does it all over again. Mostly I'm here with Magda and Pedro and the kids. The Clan scene just isn't happening. It's everyone for themselves these days. Since the media went crazy with the Summer of Love scene, every cool hangout has been flooded with runaways and hitchhikers and escapees. It's overloaded, man, and its over. We're going into hiding. We're all waiting for the next thing, and for sure, we're not going to tell anyone about it."

"Yeah, me too. I was thinking of driving out and saying hello. Thought it might be good to see you now that I've cleared the adoring disciple-of-Christ illusion out of my head."

I had the rare pleasure of hearing Bodhi fall into a full-on laugh that ended up making me feel great about myself.

"That'd be cool. No hard feelings, huh?"

"No hard feelings. Be there in an hour."

After leaving Love with Maria, I drove into the San Fernando Valley. As I pulled off the freeway, I wondered how my imagination could have turned the heat and smog of dusty, crowded suburbia and the drug-dealing, happy-go-lucky Soul Clan in Magda's ranch-style house into a world of magic and visions. A couple of months later, I had to face the fact that most of it had happened in my own mind. What was reality, then? Certainly it was not my imagination. Something as unpredictable and changeable as my own mind could not be reality. So what was?

I'd learned that my beliefs could make the outside world take on the energy of my imagination. That was why Magda's clan had worked for so long. Fueled by a group belief in the sixties dream, and shaken loose from the culture by mystical drug experiences, we tried to make the dream real. Why had we failed? That was a question I didn't know how to answer, so I let it go as I pulled into Magda's driveway.

As soon as I turned off the car, Bodhi came out of the door. Handsome and biblical-bearded, he still looked like Christ, but there was no shimmering energy around him. He was just a cool, sixties hippie artist, living by his wits and warmth, trying his best not to get sucked into the American materialistic scene. My heart went out to him, and I got out of the car to give him a big hug.

"Wanna go for a drive?" he said, rolling his eyes back at the house, as if to say, let's not get involved there.

"Sure," I agreed. "Let's go."

We got into my station wagon and took off into the wasteland of suburbia.

"Let's get out of here. Let's go to Topanga and sit by the river," Bodhi said. "It's quiet there. I love the sound of the water."

Empty Husk, Potent Seed

Amazingly comfortable and present with Bodhi, considering our history, I drove along the winding Topanga road, sensing and feeling who he was with my new perceptions, giving him lots of space. This might be my only opportunity to find out who he really was, so I wanted to make the most of it.

The wait was worth it because after a while, he looked at me and said softly, "You look beautiful pregnant."

I turned, smiled at him and said, "Thank you. I love being pregnant."

After another pause, he said even more softly, "Your dress is amazing. Did you make it?"

"Yes," I laughed. "I feel like a ripe fruit, so I thought I might as well have a dress of ripe, luscious grapes."

"So, you're happy?" he said more easily.

"Yes, as happy as I've ever been. I mean, I still have a lot to work out, but I feel like it is easier to be myself; a lot of the fear is gone. Hawaii was wonderful for me. I wanted to stay, but I have to be near my son."

"What are you going to do?"

"Hang around the Conspiracy. Work. Wait. Give birth. I'm on the lookout for a teacher. I've always wanted a spiritual path. I'll wait till the right thing comes along. What about you?"

"Much the same. The scene with Magda is coming to an end. She wanted me all these years, and I finally went for it after you left. I thought it would work with you because you already had your children, but when I found out you were pregnant, I freaked."

"What were you afraid of?" I asked gently.

"I didn't want to come down," he said reluctantly, making a face. "I didn't want a family. I wanted you to worship me so we could keep everyone high and live the dream. I couldn't see that happening if we got sucked into babies and money and cars and places to live. I was afraid if

I committed to being with you on that level that Magda would tell us to go. I didn't want to get real."

"Thanks for telling me this, Bodhi. I like you real."

"I'm glad someone does. I tried my best to make it with Magda, but when we changed roles, it didn't work. It blew the whole scene apart. I want out, but I don't know where to go. Guess I'll move back home for a while."

We pulled up at the creek. The autumn air was cold, so I took a few of my blankets from the car and spread one on the ground. I draped one over Bodhi's shoulders, and wrapped the other around myself. Looking like displaced Mexicans on the dry, dead grass, we continued our conversation.

"Well, Bodhi, if you could do anything you wanted, what would you do?" I asked, glancing at the bare branches of the trees above us, thinking that when the leaves and the flowers are gone, the structure is revealed.

"I'd go to India. I hate the American scene. I want a spiritual life, but I know now I can't weave it out of drug dreams and love fantasies and expect it to be real, or expect it to last. I don't want to work or own a car. I don't even want a place to live. The only thing I want is out," he said with a stronger voice, as if vocalizing his truth had brought him back to life.

"Well, then, why don't you go for it? Do what you have to do to get the money together and split. Do it and see what happens. That's what I did with my Hawaiian trip," I encouraged him. "And you don't have anything to make you come back like I did."

"You think I should go?" he asked, surprised. "Everyone else wants me to stay and ride the next wave of change."

"Do what you need to do for you," I said passionately, amazed that things had switched so much between us that I was now encouraging Bodhi to follow his dream.

He lay back on the blanket and as we listened to the sound of the flowing water, I remembered Leo and our day at the Seven Sacred Pools. Quietly, slowly and softly, I told Bodhi what I had learned of the wisdom of the chakras, the elements, and the emotions.

Bodhi listened without interrupting. When I had finished, he said, "That's what I need to do, find a way to understand myself, to understand life."

"Seems like the only thing worth doing," I said. "Doesn't mean you can't live and love and work and play, but it does mean that finding the truth has to be at the top of the list."

"Did you hate me when I made you go away?" he asked, his lips trembling as he turned to face me.

"I was deeply hurt, but I don't remember hating you. It was more like you blew apart all my illusions. I think I saw that you and Taz were the same."

"Yeah, we are. When I watched you leave the Love-In with Taz, I remember thinking, I am just like your old man. I'm surprised you didn't hate me. You should have, but I guess hating myself was enough. You made me see how I pulled in girlfriends, one after the other, just like Taz, and lived off their worship. I saw how I rejected them when they wanted to get real. I saw how I used women and I hated myself. That's why I tried to get real with Magda. I figured if it was going to work, it would have to be with her, but that turned sour. I don't know how to live without fantasy. I wanted to be Christ, but only like a dream, my dream, my way. That sucks. I suck."

"Hey, don't be so hard on yourself. It was beautiful. I had a wonderful summer with you and the Clan. I will always be happy you were in my life," I enthused, wanting to help him out of his downer.

"You will? Except for Starry and Lola and Deva who stayed on as sisters of the Soul Clan, all the others got angry and hated me and left."

"Your vision was beautiful, but it wasn't real. Just remember that God is moving us along," I said. "That's why everything is temporary. Just think if we had to live this permanently. Yuck!"

Too chilled to sit outside any longer, we got in the car and took off. We didn't say much on the way back. We felt the peace between us and that was enough.

When we pulled up to Magda's house, we smiled at each other, fully, person to person, as real as we could be.

"Thank you, sister," he said simply, before he took me in his arms.

"Thank you, brother. Happy travels," I said, pressing my cheek against his for a moment.

Winston

One day I was winging down Santa Monica Boulevard toward Beverly Hills. When I came to Nemo Street, I couldn't resist stopping to take a look at my old studio. New tenants had moved in. Although their pottery studio looked crafty-cool, the vibe of the courtyard had changed. They'd painted the store bright yellow and trimmed the plants and put little white stones along the drive. A pang of loss throbbed in my heart and I couldn't help wishing the studio were still mine.

Holding Love, I stepped carefully along the stone path that led through aromatic herbs and colorful flowers, under the overhanging bushes, past the birdbath and the elf sculpture to Winston's door. I got happy as soon as I heard his footsteps and even happier when he opened the door and smiled at me.

"Flower Child, Love! Boy, am I glad to see you two beautiful girls. Come on in. Things are okay? Sit here. Let's have a coffee and, look what I have here, fresh doughnuts! I must have known you were coming." He stopped and took a good look at me and said, "You look like a Hawaiian."

456

"I've just come back from the islands," I said, delighted at his warm welcome.

As we sipped coffee and munched doughnuts, I told him about my life on Maui and the reason for my return.

"Your adventures are as good as a book," he said, pointing to his piles and shelves of books. "You must write this story one day."

As I got ready to leave, he said, "Go and see Clara. She wants to see you. She was worried about you. She was hurt you didn't ask her for help. She loves you and wants to see you. And if I were you, I'd go soon. She hasn't been well."

"I will go and see her soon. I promise," I said, as I gave him a hug. "Thank you for your kindness. Thank you."

Clara

I kept putting off going to see Clara until I realized what I was doing. Even though Winston had reassured me that she wanted to see me, I was still scared to go. It seemed weird that I was just as scared to visit Clara as I was to see Taz. As much as I longed for love, there always seemed to be pain associated with it. Receiving love seemed to be as difficult as being denied it. I was doing my best to change myself, but it wasn't easy.

Finally, I couldn't put it off any longer. I woke up one Sunday morning and said out loud, like a command, "Go and see Clara today."

Once I'd made up my mind to go, I got excited, and that made the going easier.

As much as I loved and admired Clara, the distance from my dysfunctional struggle to her heaven-on-earth seemed too far. Even though the first time I went to her house changed my life, I never had the courage to go back, even when she invited me. Although I aspired to be like her, I never felt good enough to be her friend.

She had been an important witness to the creativity at the studio and the Conspiracy, but I hadn't seen her since I left Nemo Street. Now, nearly seven months pregnant, I was homeless again. It took a lot of courage to go to her house the first time, and it took a different kind of courage to return.

Arnie and Clara's gravel drive offered a magic tapestry of autumn beauty. Although it was not the spring flowering of my first visit, it was just as welcoming. The furry tufts of golden pampas grasses glowed like radiant halos. Red-berried bushes, crimson-and-golden-leafed trees, and solemn evergreens that had retreated behind the garden's buoyant spring blossoms celebrated their opportunity to show off.

I pulled into the brick courtyard, turned off the engine and took a few deep breaths, working up the courage to take the last few steps to the door. Clara spared me the journey by stepping sprightly onto the porch and waving at us. As beautiful and elegant as ever, she wore a gray silk tunic. Her amazing hair wisped and curled around her head like a silver aura. As soon as I helped Love out of the car, she swept me into her arms.

"Oh, my dear. I'm so glad to see you, so glad to hear you are doing fine," she bubbled happily. "Winston told me he had seen you. I've been waiting for you to come and visit with me."

My relief melted into tears and I clung to her, crying my heart out. "I'm so sorry I left without telling you. Please forgive me for not asking for your help."

"Oh, my. Oh, my dear," she whispered, holding me and rubbing my back until the deluge slowed down. Love hugged my knees, looking up at me, trying to understand why her mama was crying.

As I stood before her, softly open, unafraid, and humbled by my tears, I noticed a fragility I'd never seen before. She seemed nearly transparent. Her silvery quality had increased, as though she was being filled with light. I felt a wrench in my heart, accompanied by an intuition that she would not be alive much longer. I was glad I had overcome my fear of visiting her.

"I always wanted to visit you, but I felt unworthy. You are so beautiful and everything here is so perfect, I felt ashamed," I confessed.

"My dear, you must understand that the house and the garden, the wealth, and even Arnie, none of that matters. It may seem important to you because you don't have a home like this or a wonderful husband. Because you don't have them, you're intimidated. I know that. I understand. I was like that before I met Arnie. But truly, when you have them, you realize that what's important is something else entirely. The longing for what's true and lasting you have already. You must forget about wanting all of this. Don't waste time like I did," she said earnestly, looking deeply into my eyes while she held both my hands in hers. "Life is so precious, my dear. Don't wait until you're finished with life before you try to find out what is waiting for you on the other side."

"I was so worried about you. And look at you, so beautifully pregnant, and such a lovely dress you have made. Still populating your world, are you?" she teased. "Come in. Arnie is waiting to see you," she said, leading me by the hand. I followed her, grateful for her forgiveness and her love.

Over tea, I told Clara and Arnie the story of how I met Bodhi at the Love-In, the difficulties at the Conspiracy and the reason for my sudden departure. Then I described, in more detail, my time with the Soul Clan in the valley and my trip to Hawaii. When the story was finished, I realized Love had fallen asleep on the couch, and that Arnie and Clara had been completely engrossed in my series of adventures for nearly two hours.

"My dear, you're becoming a storyteller. Such adventures you have had. Such wonderful experiences and realizations you've been given. Forget the studio and the store. You are on your spiritual path now. What are your plans?"

"I don't know yet. I'm working at the Conspiracy, waiting to see what unfolds. The only real desire I have is to find my spiritual teacher, but I don't know how to do that. I have to work and live somewhere and take care of my children, but other than that, I just don't know. I feel the next step is coming, but I don't know what it is or when it will happen."

"Let it come to you," Arnie said quietly. "It's the best way."

"That's all I can do," I confirmed.

Clara got up and left the room. While she was gone, Arnie chatted about his work in the garden. Finally I asked the question that had hovered at the back of my mind since I had heard that Clara wasn't well.

"Is Clara all right?" I asked. "She looks so fragile."

A great pain washed across Arnie's face; his voice trembled and caught in his throat as he said, "She is fading away. She's hardly in this world, and there's nothing I can do to keep her here."

"Is she in pain?" I asked, finding it hard to imagine their home and garden without her.

"No, thankfully. She spends her time in prayer or walking in the garden. She knows she's going soon, and she's put everything in order. She doesn't want to talk about it and she doesn't want to see her children. I don't know what I'm going to do without her," he whispered, his voice cracking with grief.

When Clara walked back into the room, she startled me with her ethereal beauty. She glowed with an incandescent light, as if she already was a radiant being from the spirit world.

Coming up to me, she placed a little silk pouch in my hand as she said, "I want you to have this."

"What is it?" I asked, surprised and a little embarrassed.

"Open it. Open it," she urged excitedly, like a little girl.

I pulled the string on the pouch and pulled out an antique gold cameo brooch. The carving depicted a young woman embracing a swan.

"The woman is from the Greek myths. She is Leda, the mother of Helen of Troy. See this swan? This is Zeus, the ancients' supreme god, in disguise because he wanted to be her lover. I know it's only a myth, but I wanted you to remember that your true beloved is God."

Overwhelmed by the beautiful gift, I found it hard to understand what she was trying to tell me.

"Put it on. Put it on," she said, taking the brooch and pinning it on the bunch of grapes on the bodice of my white silk dress.

Then, as if she had used up all her energy, her luminous light-filled beauty faded. She leaned back on the sofa, suddenly looking like a frail, old white-haired woman. I'd never seen her look like that before.

I glanced at Arnie, and silent grief flared between us. Then I got up and kissed her velvet-soft cheek, feeling anguish roar through my heart.

"I love you," I said, and the relief of saying it made my heart ache.

Clara patted my hand, gave me one last beautiful, loving look, and closed her eyes.

Feeling a great sadness, I lifted Love into my arms.

As Arnie led me to the door, he said kindly, "She so much wanted to see you. You lifted her up for a little while, but she's like that nearly all the time now," he said sadly.

"Thank you for letting me come," I said as I got into the car, and then I added, "Clara is the most beautiful woman I have ever known. I can't begin to tell you what knowing her has meant to me."

"She has loved you like her own daughter; even more, I sometimes think, because you were like her. She watched over you and it made her happy to see all the wonderful things you did. Your visit today has given her peace. She knows you're going to be fine."

"I always wished I could have been her daughter," I said wistfully, pleased she'd thought of me that way.

"No you don't," Arnie stated emphatically. "She spoiled her kids. They never had to struggle. They had the best the world has to offer, and we love them, but they're complainers. They never had to work for anything. Be glad you're who you are. Even though you struggle and suffer and you are alone in the world with your children, your good fortune will come one day. You have a great heart and you want the good and true things. Goodbye my dear. Bless. Bless."

When I pulled out of the driveway, I was filled with an extraordinary feeling, as if great joy and unbelievable grief had woven together in my heart. Even though I would never see Clara again, she would be a part of me forever.

Wheat

A few days after my visit with Bodhi, Wheat breezed into the Conspiracy.

"Bodhi told me you were back. Couldn't wait to see you," he said as he picked me up and twirled me around. Love wanted her turn, and after a whirlwind of playful laughter and fun, he switched to a more serious tone.

"Bad things are going down," he announced. "The Brotherhood is changing." Wheat turned his head away, but not before I saw the look of pain that passed over his face.

"We had such a dream. We were going to change the world, but it seems like the government and their agents were controlling the game all the time. The Psychedelic Conspiracy," he said with a grim laugh. "Ain't that the truth.

Empty Husk, Potent Seed

Money-hungry, coldhearted creeps have infiltrated the Brotherhood, and God knows who's behind them. I have to get out. I can't work with these new guys. God, I'm paranoid. I was never paranoid. They don't dig that I know so much. Sometimes I think they're planning to get rid of me, I mean, really get rid of me, so I'm splitting."

"What are you going to do?" I asked nervously, feeling myself getting pulled into his panic. "Where can you go?"

"I'm on my way now, leaving southern Cal for good. I'm going to hang out in the boondocks with some folks I know, play it real cool till it all blows over. Hopefully, these guys will forget about me. None of my friends can know where I'm going. Some of my brothers got busted. I don't want to do time. I was only trying to help people. Look at me. I've got nothing, and all the time my so-called brothers were salting away big bucks."

"We've all had our illusions blown apart, it seems," I said quietly as I placed my hands on his heart. "What we thought was real wasn't real at all, so we need to move on. Look at this store; it's an empty husk. Kind of fitting, don't you think? The Psychedelic Conspiracy store and the whole big-time psychedelic conspiracy disappearing into its own shadow."

"Flower Child, what are you going to do?" Wheat asked. Without waiting for an answer, he entreated passionately, "Come with me. We could make a real cool scene in the country."

"Oh, Wheat, I can't go. I always end up saying no to you, and I'm sorry. In another time or place, it might have been real fine. I came back from Hawaii to be near my son and this is where I'm staying. I can't run any more."

"Yeah, I figured as much, but I couldn't leave till I asked you," he grinned, looking more like his former self.

"Thank you for coming to see me."

"I'm changing my name and the way I look. I'm going to live a whole new way of life. Bodhi's going to India, you know.

That's cool. I could hide out there, but I never had the urge to do that trip. Don't even know what I want to do. Sometimes I think I could be a minister if I could find a free and loving church. How 'bout that? I really dug turning people on and watching them go so high. I keep wondering if I can find a way to make that happen without the sacrament."

"That's what I'm looking for," I confided, relieved I could talk to him about the way I really felt. "I'm looking for a true teacher and a spiritual path. It's what I've wanted ever since I was a child."

"How come you never told me?" he asked, surprised.

"Well, you were always so sure acid was the only door that I didn't want to bring you down."

"Well I got brought down, didn't I? Got brought down right to the bottom. There's no further down to go, except prison, and I'm moving on before that happens. There's no one-more-time for me. I'm outta here."

Wheat stood up and once again he was the golden Apollo, the loving, generous emissary of the sacrament of higher consciousness. To me, he would always embody the ideal of the Brotherhood of Eternal Love.

For a moment he held me in his warm embrace, and then he was out the door, moving on to his next high, his next name, and his next cycle. I felt as though he'd shed the husk of his past life in my store, and the potent essence of his seed was already on its way to its new flowering.

"I love you," I whispered, blowing him a kiss.

Then I picked up Love and held her close to my heart.

Rainbow

With all my old friends appearing one after the other, I wondered who was next. I didn't have to wait long, because the day after Wheat's visit, Rainbow came into the Conspiracy.

"Rainbow," I cried, opening my arms to enclose her in a welcoming embrace. "I'm so glad to see you."

We held each other closely, and then I stepped back to take a good look at her. She looked different, older. She had turned into a ripe young woman who knew who she was and where she was going. Without the frizzy Afro styling, her coppery-red hair flowed luxuriantly down her back, and instead of hiding her body, she wore a form-fitting dress that enhanced her lithesome curves.

"I dropped in to see Choo and Taz and he told me you were back," she said sweetly. Turning to the young man behind her, she added, "This is my love brother, Manna."

The young man bowed respectfully and shone his clear-light eyes into mine. He had Bodhi's grace, but his simplicity offered a clear view into a pure heart. There was no charisma shrouding him, no fantasy control vibes. He was what he was – a loving, kind young man who was glad he had found a beautiful young woman who wanted to share life with him.

Manna had tied his long, tawny hair into a thick braid that fell heavily to his waist. Loose white cotton shorts and a T-shirt with the Sanskrit seed syllable *Om* drawn in black calligraphy revealed his spiritual inclinations and his worn leather sandals reminded me of my peyote gift. Manna and Rainbow were beautiful together. Their happiness made my heart ache.

"Oh, Rainbow. You've found a true love," I gushed. "A true friend."

"Yes," she said, putting her arm affectionately around Manna's waist. "We found each other in Golden Gate Park and we've been together ever since, living out of his cool VW van. I needed to come back to Los Angeles and clear things with my parents. We're moving to a farm near Ashland, Oregon to live in a yoga community. We're going to build a house, have a garden, and make babies."

"You're going to live the dream," I said wistfully, feeling like a proud mother.

"Right on!" Rainbow said happily. "I always knew I wanted to live in the country and weave and make pots and grow herbs. If I hadn't run away from my parents and met you and learned to make it on my own, this would never have happened."

"Have your seen your parents?" I asked.

"Yeah, that part was easier than I thought. Turns out they were glad I was gone. At first they thought I wanted to come back and live with them, and were they were relieved to find out I was just passing through. Once things were cool, I brought Manna in so they could meet him. They liked him, but how could anyone not like Manna? They thought it was cool that we were going to live the good life and they gave us some money. We're set, aren't we?" Rainbow asked Manna, and he smiled the smile of the early wise.

"We're heading north tomorrow," he said with authority, and Rainbow rested her head on his chest.

"Oh, Flower Child, I love you. Thank you for everything. I'll never forget you," Rainbow said as she reached out her arms for a good-bye hug.

After Rainbow left, I cried as a mixture of feelings coursed through my heart. Even though I was happy that Rainbow had found her heart's desire, I also felt sad. I would have loved to raise my children in a yoga community with a man like Manna. My future was still uncertain. Everyone was moving on. What was going to happen to me?

I started to drop into the "everyone is happy but me" state of mind, then I shook myself free. I didn't have the time or the energy to feel sorry for myself. I had my own dream.

I touched the new brooch Clara had given me, feeling the carving of Leda and the swan beneath my fingers as I remembered what she had said.

Empty Husk, Potent Seed

I wished I'd had more time to talk to Clara. The last time I saw her, I could feel that she was looking forward to her passing, as though she would be relieved to shed her body. Most people would do anything to live longer, but Clara was different. My beloved *is* the Lord, she had told me. It was hard to imagine someone as your beloved when you couldn't see him or talk to him, but I felt that what she said would make more sense as time went on. If I were going to live my life in preparation for a spiritual teacher, I'd have to trust that the teacher would come at the right time. The desire for a teacher was the strongest and most consistent desire of my life, so I was ready to go for it and see where it led me. There was no where else I wanted to go, so this had to be it.

 ### Judith

A few days later, I looked out the window of the Conspiracy and saw Judith Brewer, the paper clothes fashion designer who had featured my jewelry in her Beverly Hills shop, driving her Porsche down Sunset Strip. I rushed outside to call her, but she turned up Hilldale and stopped in front of a house. I closed up the store and, holding Love's dear little hand, walked slowly up the hill. When we reached the house, the front door was open, and Judith waved us to come on in.

The first thing I noticed in her living room was a *Gohonzon*, the scroll that the founder of the Nichirin Shoshu sect, Nichirin Daishonin, had inscribed after his enlightenment on Sado Island in Japan. The dramatic black calligraphy was mounted on silk fabric and hung inside a lavishly carved, black-lacquered altar. Candles, incense, a bell set on a tiny silk cushion, and vases of greenery were carefully arranged in front of the *Gohonzon*.

Over tea and cookies, Judith raved about what was happening to her.

"I get everything I chant for. That's how I found this cute little apartment, and my new store. You must come to the meeting tonight. Sogohonbucho, our leader, is coming. You have to see him."

Still sad that my friends were moving on, I felt open to something new, and I was curious to find out about the chanting. If I could chant for anything, maybe I could chant for enlightenment and a spiritual teacher.

That evening, Judith picked us up at the store and drove high into the Hollywood Hills. Her friend's luxurious home was filled with paintings, sculptures, lush pillowed sofas, antique Buddha statues, plants, and thick, soft rugs. Holding Love, I retreated to an armchair near a massive fern in the back of the room. As dozens of older, conservative, obviously well-to-do couples and energetic young men and women filled the room, I felt out of place. I wanted to hide my wild hair, the white silk dress covered with grapes, and my full belly. I wanted to leave, but there was no escape.

The host, a charming older man with silvering hair, brought the meeting to order by ringing the bell. At that signal, everyone knelt and chanted *Nam Myoho Renge Kyo.* Judith had explained on the way over that the translation of this chant meant devotion to the mystic law of cause and effect, so I tried saying the words. Then a much longer prayer, the Sanskrit Lotus Sutra they called *Gongyo* rolled off their tongues. I couldn't follow, so I closed my eyes and let the soothing sounds wash over me. Love fell asleep in my lap and I began to drift off too.

Unexpectedly, the front door opened and a Japanese man, followed by a retinue of other Japanese men and women, entered the room. I figured this must be the leader they called Sogohonbucho. The group gave him their immediate full attention and bowed to him with respect. The host moved aside and Sogohonbucho began to speak with such force that I felt stunned by the energy that radiated from him. He talked intensely about *kosen rufu*, which meant world peace, but mostly I found myself overcome by his positive, energetic confidence. He had a mission. He knew where he wanted to go. I wanted to be like that.

When Judith drove me home, she asked if I would like to accept the *Gohonzon* and chant. I said yes. Even though I knew it wasn't the path I was looking for, I was grateful for what was being offered. On Sunday, she took me to the temple and I received the *Gohonzon* scroll. When I got home, I walked up Sunset to the grocery store and picked up a wooden orange crate. That night I made a makeshift altar for my *Gohonzon* and draped it in beautiful fabric.

The Sanskrit words were difficult to pronounce, but Judith kept taking me to meetings, so it didn't take long before I was able to do the *Gongyo* chanting practice. I loved the chanting. It made me feel good and it gave me peace.

As the birth time neared, Judith offered me her guest space. I was glad to move out of the Conspiracy. As the pregnancy ripened, Love and I enjoyed the autumn days before the birth of her baby sister.

Bella

When I called my mother to tell her I was going to have another child, my sister, Bella answered. It was not the Bella I knew, but an enthusiastic, talkative Bella who told me how she had left home and hitchhiked across Canada. She'd had many adventures since her visit just before Love was born. When she heard I was pregnant and facing an uncertain future, she offered to fly down to Los Angeles and help out.

A couple of days later when I picked Bella up at the airport, I barely recognized her. She had broken through her introvert shell and emerged as an outrageously wild hippie. Wearing rich jewel-colored velvet clothes and soft leather moccasins that were decorated with intricate beading and shell buttons, she flashed a rich assortment of engraved silver British Columbia Indian bracelets, and Hopi silver and turquoise jewelry. Her long auburn hair waved and curled down her back as she laughed and moved with natural grace. It seemed hard to believe that her unique creativity had emerged from such a fearful child.

I watched my sister with amazement. Bella was tender, loving and trustworthy whenever she took care of Love. She exuded an instinctive common sense that felt like authentic natural wisdom. Like an Indian or a gypsy, she carried a sewing bag and she was always making something beautiful. Perhaps not going to school was turning out to be a blessing.

During the last few days before the birth, we had an opportunity to talk about our family and our lives. Our sharing proved healing for both of us. At night when I settled into sleep, I marveled at how the people I had known and loved were coming back and showing me the positive changes that were happening in their lives. There is more love in the world, I told myself. I can see it. I can feel it.

Light

I was at a Shakabuku meeting when the birth cramps came on strong. Bella stayed with Love and Judith drove me over to the UCLA hospital. Judith stayed with me throughout the night. Even though we chanted *Nam Myoho Renge Kyo* and *Gongyo* for hours, my baby was not yet born. The contractions were powerful, but the cervix was not dilating. Several times, the nurses and doctors tried to convince me to let them interfere with the process.

Each time I insisted, "No. This baby knows how it wants to be born."

Judith left for work at six o'clock. Shortly afterward, my body doubled up in one immense contraction, and when it opened, my baby's head had crowned. I had dilated all at once.

Feeling immense joy and excitement, I rang the bell. The nurse took one look and wheeled me into the delivery room.

When the doctor tried to take over and control my birthing process by strapping me down, I pushed him away.

"I know what I'm doing. Please, leave me alone," I said confidently.

Feeling an immense power, as if the spirit of thousands of women were inside me, I closed my eyes and connected with powerful waves that seemed to originate in my forehead. I tuned into those waves and followed them, undulating with them, pushing my daughter down, releasing powerful sounds that eased the process of opening. As the contraction crescendo reached its apex and the perineum opened like a blossom, there was a sensation of stretching heat, but no pain. Wild, wonderful, beautiful sounds came out of me, as if my daughter's birth was the greatest orgasm of all time.

When my newborn infant was laid on my breast, I felt immense elation mingled with awe at the miracle of her birth. I had ridden the waves of the ocean of creation with my daughter to the shores of this world. I had brought her forth from my own creative essence, without fear and without outside control. Although I'd experienced natural births with Choo and Love, with Light I let go and gave birth fully and freely. Who I was felt wonderful.

An image of a ripe fruit came into my mind, accompanied by the words; "The freedom to be your Self is the fruit of the Summer of Love."

Later, the doctor told me Light's powerful, fast birth was the only way she could have survived. Because the umbilical cord was wrapped around her neck twice, a normal slow dilation would have strangled her. I was right! She knew how she wanted to be born.

One and a half years before, Love's birth had marked the beginning of my freedom from Taz. Light's birth celebrated my commitment to a life dedicated to spiritual practice. As I held my newborn Sagittarian daughter in my arms, I knew nothing was going to stop me from reaching my goal. It was the first moment of my life that I knew the meaning of triumph with every cell of my body and every particle of my being.

Jim & Pam

When Judith needed her guest space for her Christmas guests, Bella returned to British Columbia to be with her friends. I didn't want to move back into the Conspiracy so I decided to put the *Gohonzon* to the test.

I sat in front of the *Gohonzon*, and said to myself, I want a place to live. I chanted all night, my fear for my vulnerable situation stronger than my fatigue.

The next morning, as I was I driving down La Cienega past the art galleries, I noticed Pam Courson, Jim Morrison's girlfriend, getting out of her Porsche. I pulled over and called out to her. Pam was turned on like I'd never seen her before.

Pointing to a nearby shop, she said, "This is my new store. Remember I told you I wanted to do what you were doing? Well, here it is. What do you think?"

She unlocked the door and as I admired the decorations and chic, pricey fashions, she raved on, "It cost a lot, and Jim's mad about that, but I know it will be a big success. He'll see that I can be creative too."

When Pam found out that I was looking for a place to live, she offered me a spare room in her new apartment in Westwood.

"That'll be cool," she said. "We can work together. I'd like to create a happening line of clothes."

I had got what I chanted for, and fast.

The next day, I moved into Pam's apartment. When I called Taz and told him I wouldn't be running the Conspiracy any more, he was relieved. He told me that someone had offered to buy the store. I agreed to the sale, glad that the Psychedelic Conspiracy would still be happening on the Strip.

Jim Morrison returned from a tour and hung out at Pam's place for a while. Being around him on a day to day basis shifted the dynamics of our relationship. I found it hard to take his drunken binges, so I figured out ways to nurture him. If I cooked Hawaii style feasts and laid a colorful table on the living room floor, Jim would talk and laugh and enjoy the evening, instead of zoning out with a bottle in front of the television.

"You're the only one who cooks for me," he said. "Everyone else is out to get whatever they can." When he said that, Pam got mad.

I stayed out of their fights. After witnessing the screaming accusations and a few passionate makeup scenes, I left them on their own. I'd retreat with my children into my room and play with them or chant. Jim loved my kids, but he was more into watching them closely than interacting with them.

Often when he heard me chanting, he'd open the door and stand there, listening.

"What do you get out of this?" he said.

"Think of it as a song," I replied.

"But it's not your own song," he said.

"I've had enough of my own song," I answered. "I want to sing a holy song that will lift me *out* of my own song. The chanting takes me to a place of peace. Unless every one of us achieves inner peace, there will never be world peace."

"Peace," he snorted. "That's just a word."

"It's a word I want to make real," I said.

Jim asked so many questions about the chanting that I invited them to a Shakabuku meeting at the Nichirin Shoshu headquarters in downtown Los Angeles. I introduced him to Sogohonbucho after the meeting but even the Sokagakkai leader's energetic, positive power made no impression on either Jim or Pam.

Other chanters stood around Jim, waiting to shake his hand and ask him if he was going to get a *Gohonzon*. "Jim Morrison," they whispered to each other, like he was some kind of god.

I know that many people idolized him, but they hadn't seen him stoned or dead drunk in front of the television, guzzling hard liquor. They didn't see him vomiting and passing out or screaming and fighting with Pam. They didn't see that he was killing himself trying to be free.

A few days later, Jim left on tour and Pam went away for the holidays. Love stayed at her Dad's studio for a few days and I had a chance to be alone with my newborn daughter.

 ### Become the Garden

During this blissful, gently fatigued private time, I rested, savoring the enchantment of getting to know the child I had carried within me for nine months. The soul energy of my infant daughter seemed to magnify during nursing dreams, and understanding came to me in visions.

One afternoon, as the strong suck of my daughter on my breast contracted my womb, I focused internally on an image of myself as a flower reaching toward my spiritual sun. Even though I loved the innocent spirit of the flower that longed to offer only love and joy and beauty to the world, I knew that I also had to embrace the harsher realities of the shadow side of life. Accepting that each part of the journey of life had its richness, I determined to let all the non-essential thoughts and desires fall away like leaves and petals, until only my deepest desire for a spiritual teacher remained. With that realization, I felt the concentration of seed power within me for the first time. It seemed so simple. If I let go of everything except my true desire, everything else would revolve around that choice. At that moment I connected with the true purpose of my life. There was a sense of great relief combined with the belief that now it was only a matter of time before I would realize my goal.

Later that night, I experienced a realization that appeared within me like a vision. I found myself entering into the life of a imaginary tree that seemed also to be the tree of my life. I was able to experience how the tree expanded out of its seed, growing both downward and upward until it, too, offered flowers, fruit, and seeds to the garden. The vision showed me how the deepening of the roots supported the striving tree as it grew upward. I glimpsed a joy that seemed to say that someday I would be able to offer shelter and nourishment to the world.

This experience taught me that every life carries the unique unfolding of its destiny in seed form. I realized that my soul was like a seed that the Lord had planted within me and that it already knew how it needed to grow to fulfill its destiny. This understanding helped me to trust the choices I had made, even though so many of them seemed like mistakes.

It seemed miraculous that nature was teaching the deepest principles of spirituality. I resolved to become as observant as a baby lion cub and watch everything around me for clues. Then I giggled at the thought that I had to become a detective to be a good disciple.

A day or two later, the vision opened in another way. First I felt myself grow sprout leaf wings out of a seed in the dark cold earth and grow toward flowering, but when my flower opened my consciousness expanded until it included the entire garden.

Amazed and delighted by the freedom of the concept, I spontaneously imagined what it would feel like to be the sun shining on every part of the garden, offering warmth that brought forth life and beauty. Then I felt what it would be like to be the soft, forgiving grass that kept growing even when it was cut or walked upon. When I looked up, I experienced becoming a tree that offered shelter and nourishment to all who lived in and around the tree. From there, I discovered the magic of drinking the nectar of flowers like the bee or the hummingbird or travelling with migratory birds and butterflies over oceanic distances.

I sensed that every part of the garden was a reflection of spiritual qualities. Even the seasons and elements offered challenges that resulted in the strengthening of the plants in the garden. The sun represented unconditional love; the grass, acceptance and forgiveness; the tree, generosity; the hummingbird, the ability to find and choose the nectar, the best nourishment from all that was offered.

During this reverie, I received a strong belief that I could develop these same qualities within me. Enchanted by the visions, I dreamed the hours away. The image of the flower had carried me through many difficult times. Now it was time to let go of only being a flower and open to a garden of opportunities. In my mind and heart, the flower had become one with the garden.

I knew I had struggles ahead. I knew I had to work. When I chanted, I felt as if I were drilling through a wall. Like the heroine of the childhood fairy story who had to transform straw into gold, I needed to transform the dysfunctional raw material of my life into love. I instinctively believed that if I consciously made good choices every day, I could change the direction of my life.

Even though I longed for all that was beautiful and good, I knew I couldn't get it by reaching for heaven. Escape didn't work. I had learned that paradise was an ephemeral dream-cloud floating over the darkness. I wanted to go beyond heaven and hell, somewhere where I didn't have to long for what I didn't have, try to escape what was uncomfortable, or fear losing what I loved.

The way up seemed to begin with the way down. Knowing this increased my determination to face all the things I was afraid of. I was beginning to understand that embracing my darkness had profound value on the spiritual path. If I thought of darkness as the mud that a lotus needed to nourish its growth, I could accept the hard lessons that life offered and appreciate the resistance instead of resenting it and wishing it would go away.

When I remembered Taz and the rape that had precipitated my departure from the Conspiracy and my disastrous trip to San Francisco, I felt thankful, instead of angry. I would probably still be running the scene there if Taz hadn't flipped out. I wanted to learn to live more consciously so that the need for such dramatic and seemingly hurtful changes was minimized. I was glad I could recognize the good that had come from that painful experience.

I wondered how many times I'd have to face myself before I'd find my true Self, the one the mystics write about, the Self that is not the mind, but the Soul.

Meanwhile I had to admit that I was totally, imperfectly human. Helplessly driven by a mind woven of fear and longing, my heart called out for rescue, but who could rescue me from myself? I knew the answer was God, but who was God? Where was God? How could I find God? That was as far as I could go with my questions and answers, so I gave up trying to figure it out. After that turning point, everything was a leap of faith, lit by a touch of cosmic humor and an optimistic hope for the best, which left me with one wild thought-card.

Maybe I am a letter to God, and only He can open my envelope of mystery.

Epilogue

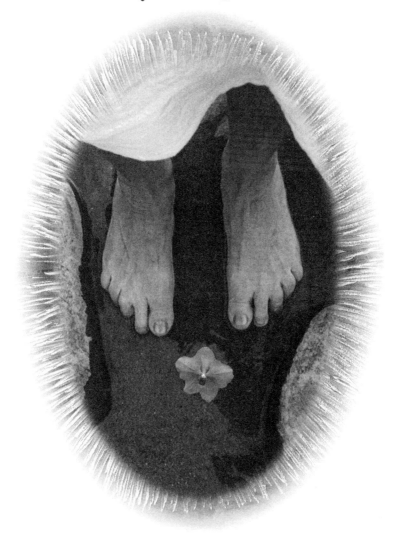

You told me "There is only love,"
and I believed you.

The Path

At the tender age of nine, after reading Yogananda's *Autobiography of a Yogi*, I put enlightenment at the top my first list of life goals. When I read the chapter where the young man meets his spiritual teacher I knew with all my heart that was what I wanted. This marked the beginning of my search for true spirituality. Soon after that I left Sunday School because my teacher said I could not meet Jesus because he was dead. When I looked at the pictures of disciples adoring Christ, I knew that I wanted a living son of God for my teacher. No matter how difficult my life was, I never lost sight of this goal.

Nine years after the Summer of Love, when 1967 had become 1976, I found what I had been seeking: a spiritual teacher who embodied the nature of true love. My teacher was everything I had longed for and more than I had imagined. Through his compassion and guidance, I now realize that there was always only love.

Along the way, I have learned that enlightenment is not something you attain but rather a journey that unfolds daily as a gift of grace. Enlightenment is the growth of wisdom, the ever-increasing capacity for living the essence of love. It is not intellectual knowledge or miracles of the ego. It is a deep, mysterious and living connection with your soul.

Epilogue

As I approach my sixtieth year, I am moving into the seeding time of my life. It is time to offer myself to the garden. Sharing my story in *Flower Child* is my gift to the young people who will inherit the future. It is also an opportunity to share my experience of the sixties with other flower children who remember that magic time.

Although I have worked as a practitioner, author and teacher of natural medicine for nearly thirty years, my creative and professional life has progressed naturally to writing and transformational seminars. I enjoy watching participants awaken the joyful enthusiasm of their creative essence as they explore their inner worlds.

My three children are now grown. They lead successful lives, each in their unique way. My two daughters are happily married and each have a daughter of their own, while my son is engaged to be married in 2001. It is a great joy to be a grandmother. I have learned much by observing my granddaughters' naturally happy learning and growing explorations during their infancy.

I have always believed in sharing the truth of my life experiences with those for whom my story may have some meaning or value. Although names and situations have been altered in *Flower Child* to protect the privacy of others, I have presented the truth in regards to myself. I have never felt that there is a positive purpose to pretending that all is well when it is not. I believe that the depths and the heights of life are equally valuable in creating an authentic, fully integrated human being. If you know someone that you think has a perfect existence, think again. We all experience challenges, anguish, longing, laughter and joy. I sincerely hope that by sharing my full reality, others may realize that we are not so different after all and take comfort in companionship. I have received many telephone calls and letters over the years from people who have read my books and told me how the reading of my life story helped them with their life journey. It was that appreciation that encouraged me to continue to the completion of *Flower Child*.

I offer this story to all those who seek love. No matter how much pain and sorrow we experience in life, I believe if we long for true love with all our heart, that longing must eventually lead us to our goal. One day, we will be able to look back and see and know that all of those seemingly difficult experiences were love. This will enable us to participate more consciously in this process called "life", that seems to me more like a continuously interweaving cycle of life, death and rebirth.

During the writing of this book, I asked myself if I would have liked to meet the person that I am today when I was the young woman portrayed in *Flower Child*. I am very fortunate to be able to say "yes". This knowledge alone makes the life that I have lived seem worthwhile. I bow to the divine and with all my heart say, "thank you."

Voices of My Children

 Choo

I have a flower child mother, a mother of nature, love, and adoration. As the decades pass, I treasure her reassurance and regard. She is an icon of the freedom and love from which we emerged into this world of fire and ice. Our visits are like reality checks where I have the opportunity to explore the question, "How far have I wandered from the source?" The more my life unfolds, the more I truly appreciate my mother's spirit.

When I first read *Flower Child*, it was like reading fiction, a story of someone else's life. However, the pages gradually sparked the memories, and dormant thoughts began to surface. Our family history has been both bright and dark. We have grown strong and we have all found our own ways to deal with the past.

Life really is so short. It seems like yesterday I was running around in the Psychedelic Conspiracy and the flower children were running with me. I remember my mother's love and my father's love. I remember missing my mom and wondering where she was. I remember missing my father and wondering where he was. Through the eyes of a child, the world is full of magic and mystery and around every corner lies another surprise.

There were many magical moments in the sixties. The sixties were a time where one's personable qualities eclipsed the importance of one's accumulated wealth and career. I remember people reaching out, making friends, sharing, and taking pleasure in simple things. Perhaps I am romanticizing the past because the sixties had a dark side as well. However, I believe people are happier when they participate in group collaboration without fear and rivalry. Fear has consumed our freedom by restricting our lives and our minds. I feel our culture has wandered far from innocence in its insatiable quest for materialism and wealth. Today, the result is isolation, competitiveness, and provincial lifestyles that create a pang for the days when freedom reigned.

As I read *Flower Child*, I was able to renew perspectives on personal relationships and reassess our current cultural predicament. I was able to release resentment and truly love my parents.

For me, *Flower Child* is a labor of love that reflects a magical time in a joyous and tumultuous era. I was thrilled to support her with the project and enjoyed editing the manuscript. I consider the birth of *Flower Child* akin to a new addition to the family. I hope you enjoy its candid authenticity and savor its tales as much as I do.

 Love

Even though many of the sixties flower children lost touch with the ideals of their youth, it is very meaningful for me that my mother chose to keep those ideals and continue the search she began as a young woman. My mother wasn't very sophisticated as to the ways of the world or to put it another way, street wise, and I think that many of her generation, and mine, will relate to how lost she was at that time.

There are advantages to being lost. For one, you may just find a new way of getting where you want to go. Does the seed know that it will some day become a tree? We all start somewhere. Leaving behind the conditioning of her childhood, my mother faced the world, met her longings face to face and embraced her spirituality in a world that often places little value on the inner landscape of an individual.

I am happy that this book is going out into the world because it so clearly communicates the fears, insecurities, dreams, and ultimate triumph of youth. The story of *Flower Child* is as true for young people now as it was then.

Also, as I was a wee infant at the time when this story takes place, it is a pleasure for me to have insight into the beginning of a life path that my memories join at a later stage of the journey.

Light

Participating in the birth of *Flower Child* proved a valuable, integrative learning experience for me. It reinforced my appreciation of my mother's uniqueness, strength and spirituality and inspired me to face the inherent challenges of the journey of life and young motherhood, secure in the knowledge that every step brings us closer to the destination that is right for us.

It was particularly interesting to learn more about the 'shadow' of the sixties, an era that is frequently idealized as a time of freedom and innocence. The impact of free love, drugs and the chronic lack of structure that lay beneath the idealism took its toll on the health and longevity of marital relationships and families and often thwarted the maturation of young adults by legitimizing extended adolescence.

Flower Child explores both the dark and the light side of the sixties, offering a more holistic and realistic representation that contributes significantly to our understanding of the sixties and the impact it made on our culture.

Continuing the Journey

Farida Sharan's transformational dance workshops and seminars are offered in the U.S.A. and in other countries.

Workshop processes include: The Love-In is Within, Rainbow Metamorphosis, Primal Impulse, and Chakras, Elements & Emotions.

School of Natural Medicine training seminars, home study, summer school, healing journeys and transformational healing are offered in naturopathy, herbal medicine, and iridology.

Please check the website for details and dates.

Web: www.purehealth.com
Email: farida@purehealth.com
Tel: 888-593-6173
Fax: 888-593-6733

Index of Illustrations

*(541-942-9057) www.newmoonvisions.com

P.O.Box 23, Lorane, OR, 97451

Index of Lyrics

SUMMER OF LOVE

245. Iron Butterfly, *Joy to the World*

246-48. Jefferson Airplane, *My Best Friend*

249. Buffalo Springfield, *For What It's Worth*

251. Jefferson Airplane, *My Best Friend*

253. The Doors, *Light My Fire*

257. The Beatles, *Beautiful People*

257. Peanut Butter Conspiracy, *It's A Happening Thing*

258. Grass Roots, *Let's Live for Today*

258. The Association, *Cherish*

259. Jefferson Airplane, *Today*

260. Youngbloods, *Get Together Now*

268. Love Generation, *Groovy Summertime*

269. Fifth Dimension, *Up, Up and Away*

269. Harper's Bizarre, *Feelin' Groovy*

270. Jefferson Airplane, *Today*

294. Jefferson Airplane, *Today*

314. Jefferson Airplane, *She Has Funny Cars*

324. The Beatles, *Nowhere Man*

GARDEN OF LOVE

327. Jefferson Airplane, *Somebody to Love*

331. The Beatles, *All You Need Is Love*

340. Rogers & Hammerstein, *Oh, What a Beautiful Morning*

345. (Anonymous) *Grace*

348. Peter, Paul & Mary, *Leaving on a Jet Plane*

374. Graham Nash, *Change the World*

395. Cream, *Sunshine of Your Love*

422. (Anonymous) *Nursery Rhyme*

Music to Read Flower Child By

Turn! Turn! Turn! . . . . .The Byrds

Fifth Dimension . . . . .The Byrds

The Grateful Dead . . . . .Grateful Dead

In-A-Gadda-Da-Vida . . . . .Iron Butterfly

Crown of Creation . . . . .Jefferson Airplane

Surrealistic Pillow . . . . .Jefferson Airplane

This Time Around You Can Be Anyone . . .Timothy Leary

Freak Out! . . . . .The Mothers of Invention

Best of Bob Dylan – Vol 1 & 2 . . . . .Bob Dylan

Donovan's Greatest Hits . . . . .Donovan

Donovan Super Hits . . . . .Donovan

Knock Yourself Out . . . . .Jimi Hendrix

The Big Hits . . . . .Rolling Stones

Still Life . . . . .Rolling Stones

Rock 'n Roll Circus . . . . .Rolling Stones

The Doors – Greatest Hits . . . . .The Doors

L.A. Woman . . . . .The Doors

The Best of the Doors . . . . .The Doors

Yellow Submarine . . . . .The Beatles

Magical Mystery Tour . . . . .The Beatles

Sergeant Pepper's Lonely Heart's Club Band . .The Beatles

Forrest Gump – the Soundtrack . . . . .Epic

Summer of Love . . . . .Vol 1: Tune In

Summer of Love . . . . .Vol 2: Turn On

Billboard Top pop Hits – 1966 . . . . .Rhino Records

Psychedelia – The Long Strange Trip . . . . .Sony

20 Original Chart Hits: 1967 (UK) . . . . .EMI

The 60's – NBC Soundtrack . . . . .Mercury NBC

Positively '60 . . . . .Capitol Records